Sol Plaatje

Selected Writings

Sol Plaatje

Selected Writings

Edited by
Brian Willan

 WITWATERSRAND UNIVERSITY PRESS

OHIO UNIVERSITY PRESS, ATHENS

Witwatersrand University Press
1 Jan Smuts Avenue
Johannesburg
2001 South Africa

ISBN 1 86814 303 1

First published in the United States of America in 1997 by
Ohio University Press
Scott Quadrangle
Athens, OH 45701

ISBN 0 8214 1186 1

Library of Congress Cataloging-in-Publication data available

Typeset by Photo-Prints, Cape Town
Cover design by Thea Soggot
Cover illustration by Thea Soggot
Printed by Creda Press, Cape Town

*For Jenny, Julia
and Richard*

Contents

List of documents and extracts

Part Two 1910-1923
'Champion for the cause of our peoples'

Part Three 1924-1932
'A pioneer in literature'

List of illustrations

Acknowledgements

I have incurred many debts of gratitude in the process of compiling this selection of Sol Plaatje's writings, and many people have helped in seeking out information of one sort or another for me.

I should like particularly to thank to thank Mrs Lesley Brits, Africana Librarian, Kimberley Public Library, for seeking out information for me on some of Kimberley's lesser known personalities; Terry Barringer, Royal Commonwealth Society librarian, now based far more conveniently from my point of view in the Cambridge University Library; Mrs Anna Cunningham and Ms Michele Pickover, Historical Papers, University of the Witwatersrand; Ms A. Fanarof, of the South African Library, Cape Town, for help in tracking down a variety of references and in seeking out a great deal of obscure information on my behalf; the late Michael Crowder, for passing on to me copies of letters from Plaatje to Tshekedi Khama, one of which is reproduced in this collection; Stephen Gill and the Reverend Albert Brutsch, Morija Museum and Archives, for providing invaluable information relating to Plaatje's visit to Basutoland in 1927; Dr Robert Edgar for generously pursuing for me some elusive references to Robert Moton and Plaatje's American contacts, and much else besides; and Dr Neil Parsons, Jeff Ramsay and Barry Morton for sharing with me their immense combined knowledge of Tswana history: the information they have provided on the background to the Sekgoma case has added much to an understanding of the context of Plaatje's own account of this sorry episode in British imperial history.

Others have very kindly translated material for me, compensating for my meagre linguistic skills. I should particularly like to thank Dr Bill Nasson (Afrikaans), Dr Peter Seboni (Tswana, Xhosa), Mr B.O. Segopolo, Mr Simon Lekhela and Dr Joe Tsonope (Tswana). All have helped in a variety of other ways as well.

I carried out an important part of the research for this book during a particularly fruitful visit to South Africa in October 1992. I am indebted to the British Academy for the award of a research grant which made this possible, and also to the African Studies Institute (now the Institute for Advanced Social Research), University of the Witwatersrand, for their hospitality and for the facilities they placed at my disposal during this visit. I should particularly like to thank, in this connection, Professors Charles van Onselen and Tim Couzens.

To both Tim Couzens and Andrew Reed, long-time fellow Plaatje enthusiasts, I am indebted for many kindnesses in passing on references, photocopies and a variety of other oddments which pass for research, and which have all helped, over the years, to build up a fuller picture of Sol Plaatje's life and work, and to enhance this published collection. Professor John Comaroff, whose splendid edition of Sol Plaatje's *Boer War Diary* first drew my attention to Plaatje over twenty years ago, has provided encouragement, support and advice throughout.

I have continued to receive a warm reception from Sol Plaatje's family and descendants: in particular from Mr Solomon Molema (grandson), Mr Johannes Plaatje (nephew), and Mrs Mary Plaatje (daughter-in-law). For them in particular I hope this book will go some way to repaying the encouragement, the warmth and hospitality they so willingly and generously provided.

Hermann and Anna Knothe, descendants of Ernst Westphal, Sol Plaatje's missionary mentor, have also extended to me many kindnesses and their warm hospitality, as well as giving me access to their family papers.

My thanks, too, to Stella Batt, for her patient and highly accurate typing of the documents reproduced in this book – scanning technology still has a long way to go before it can come close to the proficiency displayed here; and to Jo Sandrock who has copy-edited this book for the Witwatersrand University Press: her professionalism and high level of editorial skills have improved this book immensely and saved me from many a *faux pas*.

Finally, my grateful thanks to jenny, my wife, whose tolerance of my enthusiasms, and the time they have taken up, together with her support in so many other ways, has enabled this book to be both contemplated and completed. To her, and to our children, Julia and Richard, who will be glad to see the back of it, this book is dedicated.

Brian Willan
Cambridge
June 1995

Acknowledgements for Permission to Reproduce Documents and Published Extracts

The author and publishers are indebted to the following individuals, organisations and institutions for permission to reproduce both published and unpublished documents and extracts in this collection: Botswana National

Archives and Record Services, Gaborone: 101; Birmingham University Library, Chamberlain Papers: 69; Bristol Unversity Library: 57,58; Central Archives Depot, Pretoria: 38, 43, 79, 97; John Comaroff: 7; John Comaroff c and Meridor Books, Cambridge: 1; Cory Library for Historical Research, Rhodes University, Grahamstown: 2, 4, 5; De Beers Consolidated Mines Limited, Kimberley: 46, 60, 61, 62; Free State Archives Depot, Bloemfontein: 19, 24; Historical and Literary Papers, University of the Witwatersrand: 3, 10, 11, 37, 51, 61, 80, 73, 175, 414; Howard University, Moorland-Spingarn Research Centre: 330; Kimberley Public Library: 63; Library of Parliament, Cape Town: 83; Natal Archives Depot, Pietermaritzburg: 72; Public Records Office, London: 68; School of Oriental and African Studies, University of London: 47; School of Oriental and African Studies, University of London, MS 375495: 301; South African Library, Cape Town: 39; Transvaal Archives Depot, Pretoria: 28; Trustees of the South African Institute of Race Relations and Historical and Literary Papers, University of the Witwatersrand, Johannesburg: 78, 90, 94; University of Massachusetts, Amherst: 69; Tuskegee University Library, Alabama: 77, 85, 100.

Introduction

Sol Plaatje has a claim to be one of South Africa's most important political and literary figures. A pioneer in the history of the black press, he was one of the founders of the South African Native National Congress (SANNC, later the African National Congress), a leading spokesman for black opinion, and the author of three well-known books: *Mafeking Diary* (his eyewitness account of the siege of Mafeking, during the Anglo-Boer War), *Native Life in South Africa* (the classic black political statement, published in 1916), and his historical novel, *Mhudi*, published in 1930. Plaatje devoted much of his life to fighting for the rights of his people, and articulated perhaps more clearly than any of his contemporaries a wider vision of a common society in South Africa, warning of the inevitable consequences of injustice and discrimination. At the same time he played a key role in the preservation of the Tswana language and the furtherance of its literature.

Yet Plaatje's published books, important as they are, represent only a small part of his prolific output as a writer and as a political spokesman. As a newspaper editor himself, as a journalist who contributed extensively to many other newspapers and journals throughout his adult life; and as a very active political leader, the articles he wrote, the speeches he made, the interviews he gave, the evidence he submitted to government commissions of enquiry, all provided further vehicles, further mediums for the expression both of his own views and those of the people he sought to represent. Collectively it amounts to a perceptive and very readable commentary on South African social and political affairs during the era of segregation .

Plaatje was, moreover, a prolific and articulate letter-writer: in his letters, and indeed in many of his other writings, published and unpublished, a forceful personality shines through, reflecting upon his own experiences to provide a personal and often a very passionate view of what he saw going on around him.

The main aim of this book is to bring together, from disparate sources, a representative selection of Plaatje's writings, published and unpublished, and to make these accessible to a wider audience. In view of their importance, and the story they tell, it includes selections from both his *Native Life in South Africa* and his *Mafeking Diary* as well as from his rather less well-known

1

Sechuana Reader and *Sechuana Proverbs*. Most of the pieces reproduced in this collection, however, have either not been published before (letters, manuscripts), or have not been published since their original appearance in a newspaper, journal, pamphlet or other contemporary source. In view of its interest from both a literary and a historical point of view, Plaatje's journalism is particularly well represented.

Overall I hope this collection conveys a flavour of the richness and diversity of Plaatje's writing, and that it will help to fill some of the gaps, as it were, between the better known milestones of Plaatje's career as a writer: his diary at the turn of the century, *Native Life in South Africa* in 1916, *Mhudi* in 1930. In this way I hope the collection will make possible a better understanding and appreciation of the books themselves, and of the political, social and personal contexts in which they were written; and also to map out something of the terrain their author travelled, as it were, between these three dates.

The collection has been organised chronologically so that Plaatje's writings may be read in the context, and in the order, in which they were written. Set out in this way the effect is also to provide a broader picture of Plaatje's life as he lived it, and as it unfolded; and to balance the public persona of the political spokesman or literary theorist with the more private concerns of the diary or personal letter, the one often shedding light on the other. To undermine these connections by a more thematic form of organisation did not seem to me any more condusive to an appreciation of Plaatje's writings than an understanding of his life as a whole. I have sought, rather, to draw out a number of these themes in the introduction and commentary which accompanies the selection; and I have provided a listing of all the items reproduced in it according to category (newspaper articles, letters, extracts from books) as well as in the order in which they appear.

Editorial Notes

This collection is divided into three parts (1899-1910, 1910-1923, 1923-1932), corresponding to identifiable phases in Plaatje's adult life. Between 1899 and 1910 Plaatje lived in the small town of Mafeking in the northern Cape, employed first of all as an interpreter in the local magistrate's court, and then earning a somewhat more precarious living as editor of the *Bechuana Gazette*. In 1910 he moved to Kimberley, became involved in national political affairs in the newly created Union of South Africa, was instrumental in founding the SANNC, and travelled overseas on two occasions to seek outside intervention in South Africa's affairs. And from 1923 to his death in 1932 he earned his living as a journalist, continued to occupy a prominent, albeit increasingly lonely, role in public affairs, and became heavily involved in his pioneering work in Tswana language and literature.

Each of these three sections containing Plaatje's writings is preceded by a biographical outline of the relevant period in his life, providing some further information about the themes with which he was concerned, and setting this within the context of the wider social and political developments of the time. Where necessary additional information is provided with the documents and extracts themselves in order to explain the circumstances in which they were written, to indicate the nature of replies received to letters written, or the impact of an article or speech.

Further explanatory notes, collected at the end of the book, have been provided for the letters, documents, articles or other extracts reproduced – clarifying allusions or references which may not be wholly self-evident to today's reader, or adding brief biographical details about individuals referred to. Included in these notes are references to other books, articles and other sources which I have drawn upon, and where further information can be found.

I have sought here to strike an appropriate balance: to be informative without being intrusive. Annotation tends to be more extensive in relation to correspondence rather than newspaper articles, pamphlets or extracts from books, since the the latter were written for a wider public consumption in the first place and are largely self-explanatory. In general I have sought to explain references to contemporary events or individuals only where this facilitates or enhances an understanding of what Plaatje had to say. Where Plaatje wrote of historical episodes I have provided very little annotation.

In the biographical commentary, my aim has been to provide sufficient information to draw together the threads of Plaatje's own writings, and to convey a sense of the broader social and political context. Fuller biographical information is to be found in my *Sol Plaatje: A Biography* (Ravan Press, Johannesburg, 1984). Where appropriate, however, I have also referred in the end-notes to particular sections or chapters of this book in order to point those who may be interested to fuller information about particular episodes or themes in Plaatje's life.

The documents and extracts in this collection are arranged in chronological order, according to the date they were written or published. In only a few cases is there any ambiguity or uncertainty on this, and where this is the case the issue is addressed in the notes accompanying the particular document or extract. In one significant case I have departed from this general rule. Plaatje's unpublished manuscript which combines 'The Essential Interpreter' and 'Sekgoma – The Black Dreyfus' has been separated into two, the former being included in the section concerned with Plaatje's career as a court interpreter, the latter being located in the context of the period in which Plaatje came to be particularly concerned with the Sekgoma issue, some three years before he wrote about it in this manuscript.

Plaatje wrote extensively in English and Setswana, and on occasion in Afrikaans, Xhosa and in several other African languages as well. This book, however, consists almost entirely of material written originally in English. Where Plaatje interspersed his English with words, phrases and on a few occasions sentences in Setswana or Afrikaans, these have been retained in the text, and English translations added at the foot of the page on which they appear.

The only piece of Plaatje's to be included in this collection in translation is his Introduction to *Diphosho-phosho*, his Tswana version of Shakespeare's *The Comedy of Errors*. Difficulties of translation notwithstanding, it seemed to me sufficiently important in terms of content to justify inclusion and hence to be an exception to this general principle of selection. A published collection of Plaatje's writings in Setswana must remain a high priority for the future.

The question of authorship is worthy of some comment. In the majority of instances this is straightforward. Plaatje's name was clearly attached to an article, book, letter or pamphlet, and there is no doubt that he was the author (though he may not always have been responsible for titles or sub-titles under which newspaper articles of his appear). In some instances, however, things are not quite so straightforward, in particular the articles and editorials, reproduced in this selection, which originally appeared in the *Bechuana Gazette* between 1902 and 1907. Plaatje was, for most of this period, editor of the newspaper, and on one occasion he did say quite specifically that he generally wrote most of the original matter in it. Certainly all the pieces included do appear to bear the imprint of Plaatje's style, his thinking and his concerns. Having said that, there can be no absolute certainty, only a very strong probability, that Plaatje did indeed write all these articles himself.

In the case of the letter written in Plaatje's hand to the Civil Commissioner in Mafeking in January 1900 (Doc. 3, pp.40-42), on behalf of the Barolong chief and headmen, the issue of authorship becomes more complex; and the same would be true of the letter written to Sir H.J. Goold-Adams, the Lieutenant-Governor of the Orange River Colony, in April 1903

(Doc. 19, pp.73-75), purportedly by Silas Molema, but carrying a signature in Plaatje's hand. Together these two examples provide an important reminder of the inter-relationship of the public and private persona in Plaatje's activities, and – I would also suggest – of the need to avoid being over concerned with the issue of individual authorship. Uncertainly on this point does not appear to me a good reason for exclusion.

Finally, a word about orthography. Orthographic conventions for African languages were notoriously fluid during the period covered by this book. I have sought to achieve consistency of spelling (in Sechuana/Setswana, for example) within individual documents or extracts, but I have not attempted to achieve consistency across the collection as a whole, nor to impose modern standardised conventions. Linguistic experts will, I hope, be sympathetic to this approach.

Prelude ~ Sol Plaatje's Early Life 1876-1899

Sol Plaatje was born on 9 October 1876 at Doornfontein, a farm in the Boshof district of the Orange Free State. In the family circumstances into which he was born two characteristics were to be of defining importance in his identity: his family's awareness of their Barolong ancestry, and their commitment to the Christian religion and the outlook and way of life which went with it.

Plaatje and his family traced their origins to Modiboa, believed by the Barolong to have been their eighth chief. Disposssessed on Modiboa's death from the main line of succession, the Barolong *ba ga Modiboa* nevertheless remained intensely conscious of their royal origins as well as a wider Tswana identity, and were never fully incorporated into the four main Barolong chiefdoms which later emerged. Many of the Barolong *ba ga Modiboa*, the Plaatje family among them, found refuge and protection with the missionaries who appeared on the scene in the early nineteenth century, and by the 1850s or 1860s they had become particularly associated with missionaries of the German Berlin Missionary Society in the Orange Free State.

At the time of Sol Plaatje's birth his family were were living on an outstation of the Berlin mission at Bethanie in the Orange Free State, but within a few years had moved to another mission station at Pniel, near Kimberley in the British colony of Griqualand West. Both his father and his eldest brother, Simon, were elders of the church, and they played a very important role in the religious and social life of the mission.

Plaatje spent most of his early years at Pniel, attending the mission school run by the Reverend Ernst Westphal, who had joined the mission in 1881. Plaatje proved to be a particularly able pupil – Westphal considered him the most talented child he had had in the school in eleven years at the mission –

and he was given additional tuition by both Westphal and his wife, Elizabeth. He demonstrated a particular talent for music and languages: living on a polyglot mission community he learnt English, Dutch and German, and several African languages in addition to his native tongue, Setswana.

Plaatje remained at Pniel until early in 1894, by this time employed as a pupil-teacher at the mission. Although the Westphals had been seeking ways and means of enabling Plaatje to continue his education elsewhere – the school at Pniel could only take the pupils up to Standard III – he applied for a post as a messenger with the Post Office in Kimberley, an institution well known locally for the opportunities it afforded mission-educated Africans. He was offered the job, and commenced work there on 1 March 1894, at a salary of £72 per annum. He was seventeen years old.

The four and half years Plaatje spent at the diamond fields were crucial in shaping a humorous, self-confident personality, and in developing the precocious talent which stands out so clearly in the diary he kept a couple of years later during the siege of Mafeking. In Kimberley Plaatje found himself part of a well established mission-educated African community, attracted to the town because of the jobs it offered.

Most members of this community were of Xhosa or Mfengu descent; they came originally from the eastern Cape, the earliest and most successful field of missionary endeavour in southern Africa, and they shared a readily identifiable set of values. Generally speaking they were committed Christians and church-goers and believed in the ideals of 'progress', 'improvement' and individual advancement through education and hard work. They also tended to be strong supporters of the institutions of the Cape Colony: in particular the non-racial Cape franchise (the vote was open to any male citizen who possessed property worth £75 or received an income of £50 a year, and who could fill in a registration form); and a judicial system which claimed to uphold the principle of equality before the law, regardless of racial or other distinctions. They generally identified themselves, moreover, with the cause of the British Imperial Government, to whom they looked for the protection of both the rights and liberties they enjoyed.

Plaatje was soon participating in the busy social and intellectual life of this African community in Kimberley, keen to explore to the full the opportunities that lay before him. One local association provided an especially significant forum for him: the South Africans Improvement Association, formed in Kimberley in 1895, 'firstly, to cultivate the use of the English language, which is foreign to Africans; secondly, to help each other by fair and reasonable criticism in readings, English composition, etc, etc'. The Society met fortnightly, and Plaatje seems to have been among its most active members.

He made his debut at its second gathering, reading a chapter from *John Bull and Co*, by Max O'Rell. The presentation was not an unqualified success: 'his style of reading and pronunciation', it was reported, 'were fairly criticized'. But his contribution to another meeting a month later, when he read a paper entitled 'The History of the Bechuana', was rather better received: 'Being a Bechuana,' it was reported on this occasion, 'he showed great mastery over his subject' – an early indication of a topic to which he was to return later in life.

Plaatje was also a diligent reader in private, and developed a particular fascination for Shakespeare, whose plays he went to see performed at the Kimberley Theatre (Doc. 53, pp.210-12). At the same time he studied a number of languages with a view to securing a position as a court interpreter, undoubtedly encouraged by the example and friendship of Isaiah Bud-M'belle, a very talented man of Mfengu origin who was at that time employed as clerk and interpreter to the Griqualand West High Court in Kimberley. Through this friendship he met Bud-M'belle's sister Elizabeth, whom he married in January 1898 – a controversial inter-tribal marriage in the eyes of many at the time, but for Plaatje and his bride the beginning of a happy life together.

Later that same year, 1898, Plaatje found the career opportunity he had been looking for. The post of clerk and court interpreter in Mafeking, some two hundred miles to the north of Kimberley, fell vacant. He applied for the job, did well at the interview and accepted the job that was offered to him, commencing his duties on 14 October 1898.

In fact Plaatje was no stranger to Mafeking. He had visited the town on several occasions in the late 1880s and early 1890s, and his father – after leaving the Pniel mission – had moved to a farm in the district several years previously. Indeed Plaatje himself was already sufficiently well known to the leading Molema family to have secured from Silas Molema a recommendation for his new job. Molema, for his part, had every reason to believe that a young man of Plaatje's education (albeit much of it self-acquired) and ability could be useful both to his own family and to the chiefdom as a whole – a hope more than vindicated, as it turned out, by Plaatje's involvement in the affairs of the Barolong of Mafeking over the next twelve years. Undoubtedly Molema's recommendation helped convince Charles Bell, the local magistrate and civil commissioner, of Plaatje's suitability for the post.

Plaatje's duties at work required him to interpret in the local magistrate's court when it was in session, and to act as clerk and translator (predominantly

Dutch and African languages) when it was not. As he makes clear in 'The Essential Interpreter' (Doc. 10, pp.50-61), he enjoyed the work, took his duties very seriously, and soon became highly proficient. Certainly Bell was pleased: in April 1899 he noted that Plaatje was 'a steady, diligent person', to be trusted in every respect, and a great improvement upon his predessessor, Andries Jan Moloke.

Plaatje himself was keen to make the most of his new opportunities. During the first half of 1899 he studied for a number of Cape Civil Service examinations, hoping thereby to qualify for promotion and an increased salary. Although he was sent the necessary registration certificates some weeks later, they never arrived. For southern Africa was about to be engulfed in war, the culmination of years of growing tension and hostility between the British Imperial Government and the Boer republics.

PART ONE
1899-1910

'All we claim is our just dues'

Previous page:
Sol Plaatje, around the turn of the century

'All we claim is our just dues' – Plaatje, in an editorial entitled 'Equal rights',
Bechuana Gazette, 13 September 1902.

Introduction and Commentary

On 9 October 1899 (Plaatje's birthday) Paul Kruger, President of the South African Republic, issued an ultimatum to the British Imperial Government, demanding the immediate removal of all imperial troops from southern Africa – the culmination of years of deteriorating relations between Boer and British in their struggle for control over South Africa's new source of wealth, gold. Mafeking, close to the western Transvaal border (now Mafikeng in the North West Province), was always a likely target in the event of the outbreak of hostilities, and within hours of the expiry of President Kruger's ultimatum the people of Mafeking – Barolong and European – found themselves surrounded by a force of several thousand men under the command of General Piet Cronje.

Thus was the scene set for one of the most famous, and certainly one of the best documented, episodes in both British imperial and South African history. For Sol Plaatje, just 23 years old, it was to provide a wonderful opportunity to practise and develop his many skills and talents. Indeed his linguistic talents in particular were in short supply in the besieged town, and he soon became the crucial intermediary between the British forces led by Colonel Robert Baden-Powell, and the Barolong population of some five thousand people who lived in the town, relaying vital military intelligence, collected from Barolong raiders who crossed the Boer lines, to Charles Bell, the magistrate and civil commissioner, and thence to the military authorities. With the imposition of martial law Plaatje's services were also required as both Dutch and African language interpreter. Later on in the siege he was given the task of carrying out a census amongst the African population of the Barolong village, and in writing regular reports about 'the native situation'.

There were other opportunities as well. In anticipation of a good story a number of war correspondents had made their way to Mafeking. At least three of them employed Plaatje at various times as secretary, typist or interpreter; and Vere Stent, one of these war correspondents who was to remain a friend of Plaatje's for the rest of his life, took him on as a 'liaison officer', so he described it, ' between me and my little corps of native dispatch runners'. For an aspiring journalist and writer contact with such men provided invaluable.

Many such experiences are related in the diary Plaatje kept during the siege, extracts of which are reproduced in this collection (Doc. 1, pp.21-47). Plaatje's first diary entry was for 29 October 1899, and he persevered with it until 30 March 1900, some six weeks before Mafeking was relieved. Plaatje was undoubtedly inspired to keep a diary by the knowledge that so many other people in the besieged town were doing the same, including his boss Charles Bell: amongst Plaatje's many duties, in fact, was typing out Bell's diary for him.

In many ways Plaatje's siege diary, the first of its kind to have been written by any black South African, has a unique importance. In shedding light on the part played in the siege it explodes the myth, maintained by belligerents, and long perpetuated by both historians and the popular imagination, that this was a white man's affair: from Plaatje we hear not only of the experiences of the African population during the siege, the hardships they suffered and the difficulties they faced, but of their contribution to the defence of the town – and the exploits, for example, of the famous Mathakgong in his many expeditions across Boer lines.

And for Plaatje himself the Diary provided an ideal medium in which to practise and to develop his facility with the English language. For in it Plaatje reveals a remarkable capacity to describe what he saw going around him, to convey his moods and feelings, to reveal an intriguing sense of humour, and an ability to describe not only the hardships of life under siege, but also its moments of humour, the incongruities of a daily life that fluctuated between the banal and the tragic.

Several other documents are reproduced in addition to this selection of Diary entries. Plaatje's handwritten report on 7 November 1899 (Doc. 2, p.25) was one of many reports he wrote for Charles Bell about the military activities of the Barolong contingent, barely mentioned in Baden-Powell's General Orders during the course of the siege; in January 1900 there was a revealing exchange of correspondence between Plaatje, Charles Bell and Lord Edward Cecil, Baden-Powell's Chief Staff Officer, in which Plaatje requested additional financial remuneration for services rendered by him (Docs 4 and 5, pp.42-43); and in the same month Plaatje wrote a letter to Bell, on behalf of the Barolong chief and headman, complaining about the way in which arrangements relating to the provision of a grain store for Africans in the Barolong village were being implemented – a revealing example of Plaatje's role as spokesman for the Barolong co-existing with that of government employee. On occasions like these, these two loyalties could come into conflict (Doc. 3, pp.40-41).

The following month, February 1900, one of Plaatje's reports to Charles Bell was in fact published (evidently with the permission of the military censor) in the *Mafeking Mail Special Siege Slip* – the first known piece of Plaatje's writing to have been published; and in a letter to an unknown recipient, in Kimberley, in the same month, Plaatje wrote to convey news to his friends, telling them that he had 'never felt better in my life' (Doc. 7, pp.45-46).

Plaatje remained in his job as clerk and court interpreter in Mafeking for some two years after the relief of Mafeking (17 May 1900). On several occasions he wrote to his employers to seek an increase in salary or an increase in the local allowance. In both letters reproduced here Plaatje reveals not only an ability to present a very strong case for consideration of his request, but also a clear sense of the seriousness and application he brought to his work. Such attributes come through even more clearly in 'The Essential Interpreter' (Doc. 10, pp.50-61), a more detailed and extended account by Plaatje of his experiences as a court interpreter, and of the views he formed about the crucial importance of efficient and conscientious court interpreting – an issue to which he was to return on numerous occasions in his subsequent public career. 'The Essential Interpreter' has a unique importance as an inside view, from a knowledgeable and experienced practitioner, of the part a court interpreter could play in the administration of justice in South African courts, and of the unfortunate consequences which could so often result from the use of unqualified or inexperienced interpreters – 'amateur interpreters' as Plaatje had referred to them in derogatory terms both in his siege diary and elsewhere.

In 'The Essential Interpreter', as well as in his siege diary, Plaatje's remarkable linguistic abilities are quite evident. By this time he spoke eight different languages, African and European, and it is clear that his experience as a court interpreter in Mafeking was to provide an ideal foundation – as he himself was to acknowledge – for his subsequent linguistic work, and in particular his translations of Shakespeare's plays into Setswana.

By the end of 1901, however, it was clear that Plaatje was becoming increasingly frustrated with his position as a civil servant, and keen to find a means not only of realising his personal ambitions but also of using his talents and abilities in the service of the people amongst whom he lived. Increasingly they looked to educated Africans like himself to protect, to represent and to act as their spokesman in the political, social and economic circumstances in which they now found themselves.

Plaatje's opportunity came with the establishment of a Tswana-language newspaper, *Koranta ea Becoana* (or *Bechuana Gazette*), which first appeared in April 1901. Plaatje had probably been associated with this venture from the beginning, along with the two other principal figures involved – Silas Molema, whom Plaatje by this time knew very well, and G.N.H. Whales, editor of the *Mafeking Mail*, the local 'white' newspaper. As a civil servant, however, Plaatje was explicitly prohibited from 'becoming editor of a newspaper, or taking any part in the management thereof', and he had to be extremely careful of any public involvement in the venture.

In September 1901 Molema took full control of *Koranta ea Becoana* from George Whales, and it expanded from one to two pages (both in Setswana). But then more ambitious plans began to take shape: with Silas Molema's support, *Koranta* was to expand further, to include some matter in English as well as Setswana, and to acquire not only its own printing press but a full-time editor, Plaatje, following his resignation from the Cape Civil Service in March 1902. After a delay of several months the first issue of the new, expanded *Bechuana Gazette*, with Plaatje installed as its editor, was published on 16 August 1902, launched with the good wishes of the magistrate and civil commissioner, and of prominent representatives of Mafeking's white and black communities, at an impressive ceremony outside the *Bechuana Gazette*'s office in Main Street, Mafeking. It was widely regarded as a pioneering venture, and it was the first English/Tswana newspaper to have been started and run by Africans themselves.

As editor of the *Bechuana Gazette* Plaatje joined the ranks of a select band of black pressmen in South Africa. In 1902 only two other African newspapers appeared with any degree of regularity, but within the next few years several more were started. They shared a common perception of their purpose in life: they were the 'mouthpiece' of the community they served and represented, and their editors regarded it as their duty to provide in the columns of these newspapers a forum for the expression and formulation of 'native opinion', and the means of conveying both aspirations and grievances to the authorities. At the same time these newspapers had a powerful educational role, and were committed to conveying and extending to a wider audience the values and beliefs of the educated elite who ran them.

Once Plaatje was installed as editor it was not long before the *Bechuana Gazette* was proclaiming its dedication to 'the amelioration of the Native', and its commitment to the four principles of 'Labour, Sobriety, Thrift and Education'. Soon it built up a weekly circulation of between one and two thousand copies per issue, predominantly in the Tswana-speaking areas of the Bechuanaland Protectorate, the Cape Colony, Transvaal and the Orange Free State. On the editorial masthead each issue also carried an assertive biblical motto, appropriately enough from the Song of Solomon (Doc. 11, p.61), which Plaatje was to use on all the newspapers he edited subsequently.

As editor of the *Bechuana Gazette* Plaatje was responsible for writing editorial matter (and much else besides), and it was in these that he made the greatest impact on the world around him. Mostly Plaatje's editorials were concerned with the political and social issues of the day, and his aim always was to provide an African – and on occasions a specifically Barolong – perspective on events as they unfolded. On occasions, though, Plaatje set out some of the principles that underlay his views of the world around him, most notably in an editorial entitled 'Equal Rights' in the third issue of the *Bechuana Gazette* on 13 September 1902 and repeated several times thereafter (Docs 11, p.61; 17, p.71). In this Plaatje links his claim for equal political status for the African population, subject to certain restrictions which should apply to all races, with a disavowal of claims to social equality – to the extent of advising 'every black man to avoid social contact with the whites, and the other race to keep strictly within their boundaries'.

In the aftermath of the Anglo-Boer war, with the political future of the South African colonies yet to be decided, this spectre of black domination exercised a powerful effect on the popular white imagination. In adopting a path of caution and pragmatism, Plaatje thus sought to defuse white anxieties. Similar sentiments are expressed in a letter sent to Sir H.J. Goold-Adams, Lieutenant-Governor of the Orange River Colony in April 1903 (Doc. 19, pp.73-75); and a year later – in an editorial entitled 'What are equal rights?' – where Plaatje addressed the question of the extent to which 'equal rights' was actually practised in different parts of the country (Doc. 27, pp.86-87).

Implicit in Plaatje's notion of 'equal rights for all civilised men' was a belief in the essential interdependence of black and white in a future South Africa: 'The white race can no more do without the black, and the black without the white, than the right hand can do without the left', states an editorial advising on which political candidate to support in an election in the Cape Colony in

1903 (Doc. 22, pp.77-78). A small number of Africans in the Cape Colony (but not the Transvaal or Orange River Colony) exercised the franchise, and for them the kind of electoral politics on which Plaatje expressed his views were very real matters of concern.

In general Plaatje's primary concern was to address the social and political issues of the day and to formulate a distinctively African response to them. On a number of occasions he drew attention to what he perceived to be obvious injustices – the treatment of Africans on railways in the Orange River Colony, or the operation of the pass laws in the Transvaal (Docs 26, pp.85-86; 30, pp.90-91), or discrimination against African Christians (Doc. 16, pp.70-71)). This was campaigning journalism of a high order, and Plaatje often followed up what he wrote in the *Bechuana Gazette* with letters or petitions to the authorities, or in advising Africans on recourse to the law courts – in the case of Paulus Malaji, for example, on the matter of African land purchase in the Transvaal (Doc. 36, pp.102-104).

Plaatje was also concerned with the particular interests of the Barolong of Mafeking, and in protecting their rights and status. One such campaign developed around the time of the visit of Joseph Chamberlain, the British Colonial Secretary, to South Africa in 1903. Plaatje's editorial in the *Bechuana Gazette* helped head off a plan to secure African support for the annexation of both the Bechuanaland Protectorate and the Mafeking district of the Cape to the British colony of the Transvaal (Docs 12, pp.64-65; 14, pp.67-68).

Plaatje himself was well pleased with Chamberlain's visit to Mafeking (Doc. 15, pp.68-70), bearing out as he believed it did the views he had expressed earlier, contrasting communal relations in Mafeking in particular and the Cape more generally with the rather less hopeful situation in the Transvaal (Doc. 13, pp.65-67). And the unambiguous public utterances the Barolong drew forth from both the Colonial Secretary and the Prime Minister of the Cape on the subject of the future rights and status of the Barolong was an undoubted triumph at the time, even if in the long term their words were to count for little. Certainly in the view of the influential *Diamond Fields Advertiser* they had secured a considerable political victory.

A second major theme in Plaatje's editorials in the *Bechuana Gazette* during these early years of the twentieth century was the advice he proffered to his African readers on how they should behave. Underlying this was his belief that if Africans were to be justified in their claim to 'equal rights for all civilised men' then they needed to demonstrate their adherence to 'civilised' norms of behaviour. On occasions, indeed, Plaatje was very critical of his own people when he perceived this not to be the case (Doc. 18, pp.71-73). Similar sentiments underlay Plaatje's views on liquor (Doc. 29, pp.89-90): he favoured total abstinence, in line with the *Bechuana Gazette*'s commitment to sobriety. Other issues on which he took a strong stand in criticising the African people included the failure of an African clergyman to take the trouble to give evidence of his views to a government commission of enquiry (Doc. 21, pp.76-77); and his strong criticism – expressed to the South African Native Affairs Commission in 1904 as well as in the columns of his paper – of the behaviour of some African clergymen in the African Methodist Episcopal Church.

In addition to editorials written by Plaatje for the *Bechuana Gazette* several other items are also included in this selection. Of particular interest is Plaatje's letter of complaint to the Transvaal Attorney-General (Doc. 28, pp.87-89) following the abusive treatment he received at the hands of the South African Police in the small town of Lichtenburg in the western Transvaal – a vivid reminder of the personal abuse and humiliation to which Plaatje, and others like him, were on occasion subjected, but an example also of the measured response Plaatje believed it appropriate to adopt; and his evidence to the South African Native Affairs Commission (Doc. 31, pp.91-96), charged with the task of finding a common 'native policy' for a future federation of South African colonies, which provides an interesting insight into Plaatje's views on key issues of the day, in particular the question of the African franchise: throughout his life Plaatje was to be one of its most fervent and consistent defenders.

The *Bechuana Gazette* appeared with reasonable regularity at least until the end of 1904, but thereafter it ran into increasing financial difficulty. Despite Plaatje's hard work and commitment, and Silas Molema's willingness to subsidise the venture to the best of his means and ability, the *Bechuana Gazette*'s proprietors could do little to overcome the basic difficulty it faced: the very low level of literacy among its potential readership. As time went on the *Bechuana Gazette* fell more and more into debt, there were several changes of ownership, and few issues seem to have been produced between 1905 and 1908. For Plaatje himself it was a difficult time, and without regular employment as a newspaper editor he was forced to look elsewhere for a means of income, and 'for a short while in 1909 acted as the 'Bechuanaland Representative' of the Mines Labour Supply Company Limited, recruiting labour for work on the Rand.

There was one political issue which did particularly concern Plaatje during these years, however, and which he very probably wrote about in the issues of the *Bechuana Gazette* which were published: the treatment of Sekgoma Letsholathebe, a Batawana chief from the north-western part of the Bechuana-land Protectorate. Plaatje's account of the chief's treatment by the Protectorate authorities was written in late 1908 or early 1909, and sought to draw attention not only to the injustice suffered by Sekgoma, but also to the wider legal and constitutional issues raised by the episode (Doc. 37, pp.104-19). It amounts to a damning indictment of the way in which the Protectorate was administered and governed, and it was to be one of the main reasons why – unlike many of his colleagues – Plaatje favoured incorporating the Bechuanaland Protectorate into the Union of South Africa rather than allowing it to remain under the direct control of the British Imperial Government.

Plaatje left Mafeking with his family in May or June 1910 to return to Kimberley where he had begun his career as a messenger in the Post Office in the 1890s. He had found backers for a new newspaper. With the new Union of South Africa now in existence it was the beginning of a new era for South Africa. It also opened a new phase in Plaatje's life.

Selected Writings

1

Mafeking Diary 1899-1900 [*selected extracts*]

This section (pp.21-47) consists mostly of extracts from the diary Plaatje kept for much of the siege of Mafeking, first published in 1973.[1] Interspersed with these diary entries, however, are a number of letters and several examples of the reports Plaatje wrote for the military authorities. In the interests of flow and readability details of their provenance have been included in the notes, rather than in the text prior to each document.

Plaatje's diary was handwritten, mostly in English, but with Tswana, Xhosa, Zulu and Dutch words and phrases interspersed. It came to light only in the late 1960s, and was subsequently edited and prepared for publication by John Comaroff, an anthropologist who had been carrying out fieldwork in the Mafeking district. The extracts which follow constitute approximately a quarter of the whole, and contain abbreviated notes. Fuller notes are to be found in the published Mafeking Diary.

Plaatje's first diary entry (reproduced below) is for Sunday 29 October, over two weeks after the commencement of the siege. The title page of his manuscript, however, describes its contents as 'Continuation of my notes on the Siege of Mafeking', so it is likely that he had in fact started his diary, or something close to it, before this. No trace of this document, however, has been found.

1899

Sunday, 29th October

Divine Services. No thunder. Haikonna* terror; and I have therefore got ample opportunity to sit down and think before I jot down anything about my experiences of the past week. I have discovered nearly everything about war and find that artillery in war is of no use. The Boers seem to have started hostilities, the whole of their reliance leaning on the strength and number of their cannons – and they are now surely discovering their mistake. I do not

---

* Originally a Nguni term meaning (literally) 'not there'; now a popular South African colloquialism, it simply means 'no' when used in this way.

think that they will have more pluck to do anything better than what they did on Wednesday and we can therefore expect that they will either go away or settle round us until the troops arrive

To give a short account of what I found war to be, I can say: no music is as thrilling and as immensely captivating as to listen to the firing of the guns on our own side. It is like enjoying supernatural melodies in a paradise to hear one or two shots fired off the armoured train; but no words can suitably depict the fascination of the music produced by the action of a Maxim, which to Boer ears, I am sure, is an exasperation which not only disturbs the ear but also disorganizes the free circulation of the listener's blood. At the city of Kanya[2] they have been entertained (I learn from one just arrived) with the melodious tones of big guns, sounding the 'Grand Jeu'* of war, like a gentle subterranean instrument, some thirty fathoms beneath our feet and not as remote as Mafeking; they have listened to it, I am told, with cheerful hearts, for they just mistook it for what it is not. Undoubtedly the enrapturing charm of this delectable music will give place to a most irritating discord when they have discovered that, so far from it being the action of the modern Britisher's workmanship going for the Dutch, it is the 'boom' of the State artillerist,[3] giving us thunder and lightning with his guns.

I was roaming along the river at 12 o'clock with David[4] yesterday when we were disgusted by the incessant sounds and clappering of Mausers to the north of the town: and all of a sudden four or five 'booms' from the armoured train quenched their metal. It was like a member of the Payne family[5] silencing a boisterous crowd with the prelude of a selection she is going to give on the violin. When their beastly fire shut up the Maxim began to play: it was like listening to the Kimberley R.C.† choir with their organ, rendering one of their mellifluous carols on Christmas Eve; and its charm could justly be compared with that of the Jubilee Singers[6] performing one of their many quaint and classical oratories. But like everything desirable it ceased almost immediately.

The Maxim is everybody's favourite here. Whenever there is an almost sickening rattle of Mausers you can hear them enquiring amongst themselves when 'makasono' is going to 'kgalema'.‡ Boers are fond of shooting. They do not wait until they see anything but let go at the rate of 100 rounds per minute

---

*   French, 'the great sound', or 'great performance'.
†   Roman Catholic.
‡   *Makasono* is the Tswana rendering of 'Maxim'; *kgalema* is a Tswana word meaning 'scold' or 'speak angrily'.

at the least provocation. I am afraid if they could somehow or other lay their hands on a Maxim they would simply shake it until there is not a single round left to mourn the loss of the others. One can almost fancy that prior to their leaving the State their weapons were imprecated by empyrean authority – and the following are my reasons for believing that the State ammunition has been cursed: when I passed the gaol yesterday afternoon Phil[7] told me that while some prisoners were working in front of the gaol one of them was hit by a Mauser bullet (from the Boer lines) on the ribs. They expected the man to drop down dead, but the bullet dropped down (dead) instead. Immediately after, another hit a European's thigh. It penetrated the clothes but failed to pierce his skin; and just as if to verify this statement, another came round and struck the shoulder of a white man, who was shocked but stood as firm as though nothing had happened, when the bullet dropped down in front of him.

I have already mentioned that on Wednesday (the day of the all-round attack) I was surprised to find that on getting to town not one person was killed – while the Dutch ambulances were busy all the afternoon.

On Friday morning Teacher Samson[8] and 15 others crept along the river until they were very close to a party of Boers, who were busy sniping the location[*] from an ambush. They killed eight of them and wounded several; they were all going to return without a hitch – but they advanced to disarm the dead men, and Samson received a slight wound on the shoulder.

Yesterday 22 Fingoes[9] went out to the brickfields, which may be said to be exactly on 'disputed territory': they took shelter among the bricks and killed several of them, which vexed the latter to such an extent that they fetched one of their 7-pounders and cocked it right into the kilns. Our men lay flat against the bricks, 7-pounder shells crashing amongst them with the liberty of the elements. They went for the bricks, knocked spots out of the ground they lay on, and shattered the woodworks of their rifles between and alongside them; in fact they wrecked everything except the flesh of human beings. It affused several of its mortal discharges over them and when convinced that every one of them was dead, cleared away leaving 22 men quite sound, but so badly armed that if the Boers had the courage to come near they would have led them away by the hands. The gunsmith is very busy mending their rifles, two of which are irreparable, and the men are having holidays in consequence.

---

[*] A term commonly used to refer to an African township or village; in this case the 'Fingo' (or Mfengu) village (see note 9).

Our ears cannot stand anything like the back of a door: the rat-tat of some stones nearby shakes one inwardly. All of these things have assumed the attitude of death-dealing instruments and they almost invariably resemble Mausers or Dutch cannons. We often hear the alarm and run outside to find nothing wrong; and such alarm was often the motion of the pillow if one was lying down. David was yesterday grumbling: 'Oh, what a restless life; if I knew that things were going to turn out this way I would never have left Aliwal North.'

After I left Mr Mahlelebe yesterday I came through the gaol yard on to the Railway Reserve's fence. Mauser bullets were just like hail on the main road of our village. I had just left the fence when one flew close to my cap with a 'ping' – giving me such a fright as caused me to sit down on the footpath. Someone behind me exclaimed that I was nearly killed and I looked to see who my sympathizer was. When I did so another screeched through his legs with a 'whiz-z-z-z' and dropped between the two of us. I continued my journey in company with this man, during which I heard a screech and a tap behind my ear: it was a Mauser bullet and as there can be no question about a fellow's death when it enters his brain through the lobe, I knew at that moment that I had been transmitted from this temporary life on to eternity. I imagined I held a nickel bullet in my heart. That was merely the faculty of the soul recognizing (in ordinary post-mortal dream) who occasioned its departure – for I was dead! Dead, to rise no more. A few seconds elapsed after which I found myself scanning the bullet between my finger and thumb, to realise that it was but a horsefly.

It is very difficult to remember the days of the week in times of war. When I returned from the river early this morning I found David still in bed, and he asked me if there is any sign of their advance. He was dumbfounded when I said that they were not likely to advance as today was Sunday. What, Sunday? He thought it was Thursday (Ha! Ha!).

Wednesday, 1st November

Nothing happened during the day but in the evening my dear friend Mr E.G. Parslow was murdered by Lieut. Murchison – mentioned in the official publication yesterday. This murder has not only deprived me of a good friend but it has wrecked me financially. He paid for my little assistance[10] so liberally that I never felt the prices of foodstuffs that [have] reigned here since the commencement of the siege. The cause of the murder is incomprehensible; but then reasons are hardly tangible.

Sunday, 5th November

Guy Fawkes' day. The usual prayers and thanksgivings. Late last evening about 1,000 Boers were seen crossing from the southern laars* over to the north of the town, but as it soon became dark we lost sight of them. Just about the time 'Au Sanna'[11] always fires her 'bad-night' shot we heard the report coming from the north instead of the south; we, however, thought little of it as it might have been that our ears were mistaken. This morning, however, it was discovered that it was a dynamite explosion that went off.

The railway line being on a gradient a few miles north of the town, the Boers filled the trolley with dynamite, tied a fuse to it, lighted the fuse, and pushed it down the reclining line into town. Their intention was apparently to wait until the dynamite exploded somewhere about the railway station and killed everybody, when they would walk in and then publish to the civilized world that they had taken Mafeking at the barrel of the Mauser. But God forbade it and their determination had been frustrated. The dynamite exploded a half-mile beyond the graveyard, smashed the trolley that carried it, tore up the line and blew up the ground. While some of us were paying homage to the All-Father in places of worship, some were busy arranging the line to prevent a re-occurrence. A very fine day. Soft and pleasant rains till eve.

2

Handwritten report to C.G.H. Bell, 7 November 1899[12]

Morena,†

20 Barolongs, under Paul, accompanied 80 troopers of the Protectorate Regiment during the small hours of the morning and went to about 400 yards from the laager down Molopo, from where they maximmed and musketted it. They nearly put down every tent and many of the Boers fled up Lothlakane. By that time a large number of them was returning from the eastern camp and our men retreated slowly with only one trooper badly wounded. It was the wish of the Barolongs to go for no other purpose than capturing their cannon but the whites would not do that. They subsequently discovered that they could have found it very easy indeed if they had prepared for it when they

---

* A form of 'laager', or camp, sometimes pronounced as spelt here.
† A Tswana word equivalent in this context to 'sir', conveying respect for a person in authority; used in relation to both blacks and whites.

started. They were very ably assisted by a '7-pounder' from the Refugees' Camp. They consider the enemy's loss enormous.

Sol T. Plaatje
7.11.99.

Sunday, 12th November

We have a black Sherlock Holmes in the person of Manomphe's son, Freddy. He arrived from Kanya with some despatches this morning in company with Malno's brother-in-law: the latter was on horseback, which is very risky to cross the enemy lines with. On Friday the horseman remained behind and Freddy came across a party of 60 Boers at Tlapeng.[13] He hid the letters and went straight up to them. They searched him for letters, and on finding nothing on his person, they became very friendly – more so when one of the party recognized him as an old good servant of his. They gave him a quantity of mutton which he roasted on the spot and had a fine repast at the same time as his Dutch friends. They left the place at 5 p.m. giving him an opportunity of fetching his letters. He reached his home (Ga-molimola)[14] in the evening and hid his letters in an ant-heap close by. Our friend the horseman, who met no Boers, arrived the same evening. Freddy advised him to return to the bush and hide his horse all day next day (yesterday) until dark, when they would plan the best way of getting into town. Freddy became doubtful of the man's aptitude and requested him to hand over his letters to him for safekeeping, which he did.

In the morning a party of 40 Boers rode past Modimola and asked Freddy where the cattle were. Subsequently another party (of 90 this time) also came past. After leaving Freddy's place, this last party observed the spoor of a horse. They traced it to a small village a little beyond. (Instead of going to where Freddy showed him, our foolish friend went to this village.) When the inhabitants perceived a party approaching along the horse's spoor, they decided to give them to understand that it belonged to the owner of the village, and that his son had been riding it looking for stray goats. There was an interpreter of some sort who promptly advanced to meet the ephemeral conquerors of Mafeking and related to them the history of the horse. The head of the village – the old fool – overhead this, and blurted out that he was lying. This infuriated the Boers, who sentenced the interpreter to receive 55 cuts with a stirrup leather for his lies, and made a prisoner of our foolish friend while the interpreter was undergoing the sentence. When Malno's brother-in-law got arrested he whined and begged the Boers not to take him alone as he was not the only offender: there was another man, ahead with the Magistrate's letters, and they came from Kanya together.

The Boers returned to Freddy, who lied so classically, and with such thoroughness and serenity, that they disbelieved their prisoner's statement. They searched his person, his house, nay everything, but failed to find them; and Freddy walked calmly in here with both dispatches this morning. From Freddy's information, the reason why we are having such quiet days is because the Boers have gone in different parties to loot our stock. We hope that by the beginning of next year they will be purging them back to us in much the same manner as they did 14 years ago.[15]

We spent this day in church. The pulpit was occupied by Mr Lefenya,[16] who warned his hearers to be very careful in their prayers, and remember that their God was the enemy's God; we, however, have the scale in our favour as we have never raised our little finger in molestation of the Transvaal Government, or committed an act that could justify their looting our cattle and shooting our children in the manner they are doing. The weather was fair and as shelling and Mausering were conspicuous with their silence, we wished that Sundays would come a little more often.

Saturday, 18th November

What a pleasant morning. One often wishes that it could be mutually agreed that both sides should lay aside their guns and go out picnicking, and not resume operations until Monday morning, January 1st, when the troops will be in the country for certain. When I reached the rocks, I found the people arguing over the meaning of the unusual movements of the people in the laager down at Koi-koi.[17] My field-glasses discovered that it was the enemy trekking, from one neighbourhood towards Lothlakane. Oh, how we wish them God-speed and a safe departure across the border. Everybody is so pleased at the laager dispersing that very little attention is paid to Big Ben's outbursts. I went out for a ride for the first time since the siege; enjoyed it so much that the sun set whilst I was still on horseback.

We have just got definite information that the troops landed at Cape Town on the 4th instant and that they are given six days rest prior to proceeding north. There is a general dismay in fool's paradise where their movements were not being studied before telegraphic communications were cut between this and the civilized world. Bets were freely entered that they would be here on the 30th *ultimo*, then the Sunday after, etc., etc; and bets are still pending that they will be here day after tomorrow. I have the honour of not sharing this dismay for, having expected them to reach here on the 20th, I prolonged my period to the middle of December, when October went past and we had heard nothing of their whereabouts.

The prices of foodstuffs ran up to a very high degree: meat from 10d to 2/0d per pound, bread from 11/2d to 6d a loaf, and groceries and other necessaries in similar proportions. The office closed the stores on 12th *ultimo* and did not even open to pay us at the end of the last month: the probabilities are that we will receive October's pay together with November's and December's at the end of the year, as relief appears to be as far as ever. The forage also rose from 4d to 1/6d per bundle and I was lucky enough to get free Government rations from the military authorities for our pony, who now feeds on Scotch hay and oats – and he is as fat as a slaughter-pig. He has, since the siege, been working only with his teeth and I think it is his wish that Mafeking should be besieged a little more often: this, and the fact that I keep pace with the hard times by means of earnings from newspaper war correspondents who (though not quite like my late lamented friend) are fairly liberal, are good reasons why I should sing the twenty-third psalm.

Sunday, 19th November

I have forgotten to mention that some time ago the church bells, which were heretofore used for no other purpose than to remind the public that it was time to worship their creator, have been turned to some other service; they ring in case of an alarm. The church bells, which have always been a comfort to Christians, are now a nuisance as they signify the advance of the enemy. During the first week of hostilities the alarm was sounded by a bugler, galloping from one end of the camp, blowing the bugle with all his force, while others echoed the strain to all corners of the camp. Since the arrival of this big thing[18] galloping is an impossibility and the church bells are substituted. One has to depend on this timepiece for Divine Service, which we very seldom attend as we do the whole week's work today. But in spite of all that humiliation, prayers and thanksgiving offered to the All-Father are of such far greater sincerity and deliberation than on an ordinary occasion.

It sounds much like a sabbath morning when after six days of terror and shuddering (as though one had no right to live in this world) one has the liberty of breathing freely and enjoying the calm atmosphere, which gives the Sunday a more different and blessed aspect than the other days of the week. Saints and sinners alike thank God for the leisure and wish that there were three Sundays in every week.

David trampled the back of a big snake with his booted foot last night. When the brute made for his leg he picked up a stick and killed it.

The Government have started a cheaper grain store for the benefit of the poor in the stadt.*

Saturday, 25th November

The summary jurisdiction courts are not as particular as our divisional courts about punctuality. Night before last I was warned to be at the office at 7 p.m. I misunderstood the warning, and went to the courthouse until they sent for me half-an-hour later. Last night I was told to be at the office at 6.15. I misunderstood the time this time and turned up at 7.00. I thought that these warriors would pistol me as this was my second offence but they viewed the matter with total unconcernedness. This morning I turned up ten minutes late. The shorthand writer was also 15 minutes late. The officers, finding me an irresolute, unreliable wobbler, engaged the services of a white man as the witnesses and prisoners were principally Boers – but the fellow being an amateur interpreter was completely flabbergasted when it came to cross-examinations, and I took his place to immense advantage. This lateness appears to be a disease with which I am infected and I will see it does not occur again as I feel very uncomfortable in consequence.

This evening they gave me an opportunity of realizing what it is to wait for others. They all turned up at 6.15 sharp but the presiding officer failed to put in an appearance. At 7.20 he was sent for and his excuse was that he had forgotten all about it. My patience was so exhausted that I would have knocked him down if I had the means. I was very restless in court, for 'Sanna's 'bad-night' shot always comes between 8.00 and 9.00 p.m. The court was over at 8.55 p.m. When I left it flashed towards the town. I, however, had my doubts and wondered if this evening they may not prefer to knock spots out of the B.S.A. camp. Then the whole plain I was to traverse would just lie in the course of the shell. I ran in order to cut quickly across this risky ground. I had no sooner reached the outskirts of the stadt when a big red flame was visible to the east – and imagine my joy of the forethought, for around came the usual row, then the loud hum which turned to the side of the town and went to knock bits of brick out of the B.S.A. buildings. Thank God I ran and it didn't fly over my head.

---

* Dutch, 'town', the name given to the central area of Mafikeng.

Thursday, 7th December

A lovely morning. After I got up I rode in the direction of Meko's to enquire where last night's shot fell, as it burst in the stadt. I found that it had fallen on the ground near a wagon wheel to which a cow was tied, whence the broken shell made for the cow, despatched it to eternity, splintered the strong wagon and severely wounded a chappie that was playing on the other side of it. Bits of cow's meat were scattered in every direction. When I was there, shelling proceeded very briskly from 'Sanna' and the smaller artillery which are of minor importance. Only 'Sanna' is our 'ingwe'.* I went up to town and just after I crossed the railway line, the alarm bells chimed. The pony knows them already and he became infuriated and bucked like a dam cow while I tried to make him stand on the lee of Whiteley, Walker & Co's store. He was still bucking when a shell flew overhead with a sharp loud hum and burst in the direction of the railway. Things were too serious to permit of a fellow hanging about the streets of Mafeking and I turned round the stadt way as fast as his legs could carry me. The next shell burst just as I reached the outskirts of the village.

During my short stay in town I learned that the first shell of this morning burst near one of the railway cottages and killed a young fellow by blowing off his belly and pitching his intestines on to the opposite roof.

The man Phil-june has been allowed to go so Lady Sarah Wilson reached here this morning.[19] She says the Boers at the laager say that their forces are slaying thousands of the English everywhere – at least so they are told – but they are puzzled as to how Lord Methuen managed to reach Kimberley if that was the case.

I wonder why the Boers are so 'kwai'† today. During the last few days we seldom had a 'Sanna' shell during the forenoon, and then a day's complement was only between two and four, but this morning we had seven between 7.00 a.m. and 8.00 a.m. from 'Sanna' only, besides a heavy thunder from the smaller artillery and a shower of Mausers which played the accompaniment. The middle of the day was somewhat quiet but operations were resumed at 3.30 p.m. with great vigour. I was obliged to stop going to town this afternoon despite urgent private affairs. The afternoon fire lasted till sunset but 'Sanna', just to show that she is older and mightier than the lot, kept up her part as long as the moon was shining – till 8.30 p.m. It will be a serious business if the

---

*   Xhosa-Zulu, 'leopard'.
†   Dutch: 'angry' or 'hot-tempered'.

Boers are going to give us not more sleep while the moon is shining. We always had only one shell – the 'bad-night' shot – fired into use between 8.00 and 9.00 p.m.

This single one we find very inconvenient as it makes everyone imagine, at sunset, that he is either going to have his legs shattered or a few ambulatory escapes – if he is not annihilated to death; but if we are going to have them as regularly as we had them this day we might as well expect to be throwing up the sponge soon. Our patience is altogether exhausted. When the trouble commenced no one dreamt that we would still be beleaguered at the end of November: others gave the troops only up to 30th October to arrive here; I, however, gave them up to 30th October to reach Kimberley and to arrive here on 20th November, which was the most liberal of the lot. But here we are today, December 7th, losing people daily and not even able to tell where the troops are. Surely if everybody knew that this was going to be the case we would never have had the forbearance to start it. The result of yesterday afternoon's 'Sanna' outrage was two whites and a Native killed, and two whites wounded. If we are going to die at this rate I am sure there will only be wounded people hopping about single-armed and with amputated legs to tell the history of the siege.

One of the killed was in Mr Riesle's bar (Mafeking Hotel). They are dead against our poor ex-Mayor. When they shelled us with 12- and 7-pounders, on the 16th October, Mr Riesle was the only person who got his windows smashed; I have already described how they went for his sitting-room and wrecked the piano and goods therein being, but have not mentioned that when 'Sanna' (before she was christened) gave her debut in Mafeking on October 23rd Mr Riesle was the first victim. It went for him in a quaint manner; some flames had to be put out, which has never been the case with any other explosion up till this day. They have since been going for his outhouses, back-cottages, servants' rooms and W.C.'s time after time in a most merciless manner.

I have never before realized so keenly that I am walking on the brink of the grave. It is really shocking, while still meditating how one of your fellow creatures met his fate at the shell of the Dutch cannon, to hear that many more had their legs and 'sinqes'* shattered somewhere; and it is an abominable death to be hacked up by a 94-pounder. People say the reason is that shells being less frequent, the inhabitants are less particular about taking the necessary precautions. I, however, attributed the ludicrous failure of 'Sanna' during the months of October and November to the fact that people are

---

*   Xhosa, properly *isingwe*, meaning 'back'.

considerably alarmed, and sighed to their creator – of whose possession they were then perfectly certain nearly every second. Their soliloquies were so far retrenched by the perilousness of their position that in their cogitation there was only room for the one word 'God'; and they yearned for the company of his angels more than they cared to meditate sin. But now we have so far forgotten ourselves as to imagine that this failure was attributable not to providential protection but to Cronje's[20] misfortune and our good luck, or to his cowardice and our valour – what an odd notion.

Saturday, 9th December

Too little, if anything, has been said in praise of the part played by that gallant Britisher – the Barolong herdboy. Cattle are now grazing on what may be termed 'disputed' territory, just where the Dutch and English volleys cross each other; and it is touching to see how piccaninnies watch their flocks, and how in the bright sunshine along the wide plain south and west of the stadt – especially when after filling his belly with a lunch of black coffee and beef – the Dutch artillerist would turn his attention to them, and sate his iniquitous whims by sending a shell right in the midst of a group of them. God would guide it flying over their little heads and it would kindle a mortal fire near them: it is an imposing sight to see them each running after a fragment and calmly picking it up. They would quietly mind their stock or drive them home under a severe shell fire with the tenacity of the African in all matters where cattle are concerned. The chappie killed by that shell that struck the hospital last month was turning goats on the rushes at the back of the hospital. The Boers made a small retort within easy range of a Martini south of the stadt. They had intended to snipe the stadt from there, but the stadt folks made it hot for them. Last week a few herds* went straight up to it and brought home some tinned beef biltong and two spades.

Two other herds went out last night. They went out as far as Jackal Tree, where they lay down on the grass near the Boer camp, when the enemy were busy outspanning. It was raining at the time and the oxen were tied up to the yokes. They waited until the owners sheltered themselves from the rain, then advanced and successfully loosened four of the oxen without detection. One of the smart thieves led them away by their riems,† while his confederate drove their loot behind.

---

*   Herdsmen.
†   Dutch: 'straps' or 'thongs'.

There is a regiment composed of a mixture of Zulu, Shangaan, Tembu and other Transkeian breeds under one McKenzie, styled the Black Watch. These are camped just where the railway passes Bokone.[21] Some of these fellows on sentry duty saw their Barolong brethren advancing with their highly prized but 'nqabile'* possessions. The party was made and an eruption, such as nearly started a revolution in the whole place, ensued. Their row was such as could have attracted considerable attention if 'Au Sanna' was not the lawful claimant of our attention. The case was 'sticking up'† and the Colonel judged against the Transkeians, as the Barolong could substantiate their claims by the riems they carried in their hands. The Zulu swore that they brought the cattle from the Boer laager. The Colonel gave the Barolong the third ox and as they were abnormally fat animals he bought the others off them.

This cattle theft has put the Boers on the alert. On Thursday I sent out a man to Kimberley for Vere Stent;[22] he and his companion tried to cross along the railway line but they found the country so excellently guarded by the Boers that to get through was an impossibility. They tried the north-west with the same result and they are now planning a scheme for a fresh try tomorrow. The Barolongs had a brush in miniature with the enemy this morning.

About 90 Boers were observed a half-mile to the south of the stadt waiting for our cattle. When the cattle were cleared away from the stadt range the Boers stormed the herds who, finding it impossible to drive the cattle, ran home for arms. Uncle Cornelius[23] happened to be about and he alone managed to keep the Boers until his bandolier was empty. Just then about 40 men came up and drove the Boers off. One of our men got a slight wound and the Boers wounded three cows and a donkey. We only hope we have given them something in return.

Tuesday, 12th December

'Sanna' never moved till 5 p.m. when she sent five shells into the location. The thinner artillery and Mausers were very mild.

We had a civil court today. A lot of boys of the firm of Julius Weil are suing their employers for wages. Mr Spencer Minchin, LL.B., solicitor (now Lieutenant Minchin, Bechuanaland Rifles), appeared for all the plaintiffs, and Mr. J.W. de Kock, attorney (now member of the Town Guard), appeared for the defence. It was a novel court: only the parties concerned looked as usual,

---

*   Xhosa, 'scarce'.
†   Robbery.

Plaatje at work as court interpreter during the siege of Mafeking. 'Myself in knickerbockers and without a jacket,' Plaatje wrote, 'looked more like a member of the football team or a village cyclist than a court interpreter.'

but not the court. The plaintiffs' attorney was in military attire; lawyer for the defence, never shaved since the siege, all hairy and dressed in a third-hand suit without a collar, looked more like a farmer than an attorney. Myself in knickerbockers and without a jacket, looked more like a member of the football team or a village cyclist than a court interpreter. All of the Natives, but one, carried their cases.

Sunday, 24th December[24]

Christmas Day. I am not yet able to turn out but I hear that a good many people are going to keep it up as high as is practicable.

I remember my low state with an afflicted sense. To think that this is the second Christmas of my wedded life and I have to spend it, like the first one, so very, very far away from the one I love above all: it is becoming too big and I wish I could drive the thought from my mind. Still, I remember last year when I spent three lengthy, solitary days in old Ma-Diamond's[25] beautiful garden and she fed me with the first issues of her fructuous grove in fruits and

greeneries. I told her how happy we would both be if my kind little wife, whom
she very much longed to see, was with us; we were consoled, however, by the
knowledge that she was on that day presenting my first-born to his saviour
under a magnificent Christmas tree somewhere, and that she would soon or
later bring us our little darling boy who would positively be the happiness of
our hearts next Christmas (today) in the same garden, the cultivation of our
aged lady friend. But here I am today so very far from having that expectation
of our calming meditations fulfilled. I am not even graced with as little as a
congratulatory missive from both of them, but am nailed to a sick-bed with
very poor attention – worst of all, surrounded by Boers. I had expected a ready-
dressed chicken from my friend Meko as I have developed a dire hatred for all
other food, and (indeed) was almost starving when David came from him with
two. Hence I discovered that despite my mental tribulations I was not
absolutely friendless. I sent back to them St Leger's[26] cream coloured lappie*
and 'seo sa buti'† for their little boy, for which they returned hearty Christmas
thanks.

I saw little of the open air but all that reached my ears was full of merriment
so there must have been some happy things going on. It was raining somewhat
pleasantly all the evening.

Tuesday, 26th December
Early this morning we were aroused by the sound of big guns, muskets and
Maxims towards Game Tree.[27] It lasted for nearly an hour, then all was quiet
again. It was a good number of the garrison endeavouring to capture a Dutch
fort at Game Tree. FitzClarence[28] figured among the ringleaders again and
everyone was sure that – bullets failing – he would capture the Dutch fort at
the point of the bayonet, but they unfortunately found it a tough business.
They got up to the fort and were preparing to jump right into it amongst the
Boers. But the walls were so high that only a few managed to get on top. Even
here they could do nothing as the trench was too well roofed and the Boers,
who meanwhile had their rifles through the loop-holes, played havoc with
them until they hoisted the Red Cross. FitzClarence alone got inside and
stabbed two or three. They shot him once but he proceeded to bayonet
another when they shot a second time and he dropped down – though not
dead. (Three who went to the door of the trench were taken prisoners.) He is

---

*   Dutch: 'a small rag, or cloth', possibly an item of clothing.
†   Tswana/Nguni: 'the thing that belongs to my elder brother' – precise meaning unclear.

now in the hospital improving. I think the wounding of FitzClarence incapacitates an eminent 'moguli'* from taking part in future operations against the Transvaal, when the troops cross the border. The Boers never hit so hard a blow on Mafeking since they besieged us. Altogether we lost 23 men killed and 26 wounded. The rest of the day was quiet.

Wednesday, 27th December

A very quiet and pleasant day, fair and cloudy. I was able to get up this morning and hope to be about soon. Nothing happened during the day. In the evening David entertained me with some Lenkoaniacs,[29] which I enjoyed very much. He once found Hyena Jones covered with a thick blanket in his room in the daytime. David's lips were just about to part when he hushed him in a faint voice and informed him that his time was extremely short – so short that the devil already knew how many notches of the tape-measure it will 'lingaana'.† I presume it is to be inferred from this that Jones' soul will go to the devil when it departs this life. David, however, took to himself the liberty of putting to him certain abridged interrogations concerning his ailment in the most sympathetic manner, and to his surprise every one of his queries made Hyena 'weller'. He was travelling so accurately, though slowly, along the part of recovery that he was eventually able to remove the thick blanket off his body with the extraordinary remark that his respect for David was as great as his astonishment at his piousness. For David was among the very rare specimens of Christianity on the face of the globe able to cure a dying person simply by motion of their lips; and he stood up and started tidying the room with his usual healthy and civilized way of doing things.

Besides a lot more he [David] told me how Hyena once determined to settle the love question with his rival with a thing a little more deadly than his tongue – for which purpose he procured a rifle. He took a companion with him and bragged as they went along – but he forgot to shoulder the rifle, and took to his heels immediately the rival put in an appearance. On one occasion (shortly after his arrival) Jones nearly assaulted him for having told an enquirer that Mrs Lenkoane was at work, instead of which she had gone out for a walk – he told some such lie. 'Mma, ke tseba bora ba batho ba jwale ka bo Phooko.‡ When ach yue khoing to atopt the wase of sophilised people? Ke sa

---

*   Tswana for 'leader' or 'distinguished one'.
†   Zulu-Xhosa, meaning 'equal to'.
‡   Sotho: 'Look here, I know the enmity of people such as Phooko.'

tsua chata hona jwale.* What will the chentleman think of me to hear that my wife is at work?'

Our Civil Commissioner[30] is a white Lenkoane. His acumen in fixing sarcastic phrases and aptitude in putting comical jokes is beyond description. His mere silence gives him a very ferocious appearance.

On Sunday he sent word to all hands that his servants – he had about a dozen of them – should all turn up on Monday to a grand Christmas dinner he was going to give them. They rolled up en masse, but were surprised to find everything in much the same manner as when the pudding party in no. III Royal Reader[31] got some pudding – except that these poor fellows received not even the aroma of a grand Christmas dinner. The officers came for their meal at the usual hour, and when they departed the ole buck† quickly retired to his bomb-proof for his after-lunch siesta – leaving the disappointed menials to take their way, with dismay written on their faces in bold letters. This is Wednesday already, and he has not yet offered them the slightest excuse for the inopportune treatment.

1900

Friday, 5th January

It was raining softly all night, and the result is a fair and lovely morning.

The presiding officer at the trial of the girl Bezuidenhout, his honour Major H.J. Goold-Adams, being indisposed, she was remanded sine die.‡

Poor Ngidi came in for a very rough time. He was before the court yesterday on a charge of being asleep while on sentry duty the previous night, and was sentenced to be dismissed. He appeared again this morning on a charge of failing to hand over a bag of kaffircorn. The sentence of the court: seven days H.L.§ and the confiscation of the kaffircorn.[32] Hard luck on poor little Alfred.[33] The following is the cause of his trouble: during the month of November the authorities, deeming it expedient in view of the approaching hard times, forbade the sale of grain of any sort by the storekeeper. All grain belonging to storekeepers was commandeered, and the government had it retailed cheaply – on economic lines – to the public.

------

* Sotho: 'I have just now (got) married'. For fuller notes on these allusions, see n. 83, p. 156 of Mafeking Diary.
† Charles Bell.
‡ Latin: literally, 'without day', i.e. indefinitely.
§ Hard labour.

For this purpose they have established a grain store in the stadt, one at the location, and Lippman's in town. Early in December orders were issued to private owners as well that they were to state the amount of grain in their possession, as this drain got a grip of us; and it became imperative that all grain should be collected from private people, and everybody be allowed to buy so little as not to have the slightest chance of wasting anything. It is only by dint of a favour that I was allowed to buy a steen brood* per diem. Therefore it is criminal to have in your possession any quantity of grain beyond what the regulations permit you to purchase from one of these stores run on economical lines.

Rice, barley, oatmeal, and sugar have also been included and their sale is restricted unless one has an order which regulates the quantity he can purchase in a certain shop to last him a certain period. A common person would be enriched by this arrangement, as cash cannot procure whatever one requires – he being allowed to purchase so much worth and the balance all remaining in his till. But our case is different: the regulation diet is cheap enough as the purchase price is also regulated, but it is too small to keep a decent man alive. One can only increase his diet by various unrestricted luxuries, the prices of which rule higher than the clouds.

From an official's viewpoint, this restriction is a wise policy, as it prevents the decrease of our supplies from passing faster than the days of the siege. To the merchant it is a boon, in as much as it enables him to demand whatever he desires for his unrestricted dainties. It is a curse, however, in that the money is circulated at the expense of the private individual's pocket. From a Seolong† point of view this whole jumble is more annoying than comforting. For this they may be excused, as the arrangement is in the hands of young officers who know as little about Natives and their mode of living as they know about the man on the moon and *his* mode of living.

It came to their notice that some Barolongali‡ were selling kaffir beer the other day. They look upon it as wasting, or if the scale of this luxury was to continue, they were going to make a case against the party and would have, had the Civil Commissioner not been what he is – a white Native.

They do not know that kaffir beer to a common Morolong is 'meat, vegetables and tea' rolled into one, and they can subsist entirely on it for a

---

*   Dutch: literally, 'a brick (loaf) of bread'.
†   Serolong, the language of the Barolong.
‡   Sotho-Tswana, 'Barolong women'.

long time. If ever you wish to see the sense of the word economy, observe the kaffir beer by the amount of water poured on to the corn to what is yielded. If prohibited, I wonder what is to become of the bachelor, who is a fighting man and soldier and can therefore not brew it for himself, as it is not sold in any of the three.*

The collection of grain is now going on in the stadt unlike at the location. There it is carried away by the chiefs. The officers are under the impression that when the chiefs reach a hut they take away the last crumb they find in possession of the owner, who would henceforth survive on what they purchase economically from the store. The store has been shut for the last five days, because when the regulation was struck down to 6d a time, Barolongali told the storeman he could go to H[ell]. This was last Sunday. The store has since been shut. I believe the storeman has gone to Hopetown in obedience to the Black Petticoat Ordinance.[34] I presume the truth is that the officers are either under the impression the Barolongs are able to purchase from a closer store, or that they can live a week without – for otherwise I cannot comprehend. This causes me to believe that they liken Barolongs to the man in the moon, who is at his place every time there is a full moon. The full moon is always at night, when the store is closed, and the man in the moon could not possibly come down for any grain; and it is their belief that Barolong can do the same: for while this 'every-morsel-economical-collection' is in progress, the store shows no sign of reopening – God help these poor beleaguered people.

Ebie[35] has a very bad chest. He has had it for the last few days and he shows no sign of improving. His people 'ncoma'† his coughing as that which was never heard in the hut before. Most of the children are down with fever. Further, Molema's cattle and many others have the rinderpest.[36] Mafeking[37] has 'setlhabi'‡ – she can hardly breathe. Sickness has formerly not troubled us very much during the siege; sickness was so rare that I have never heard anyone complain of toothache.

With Selabi all the afternoon. He told me of the welfare of my family. If he is not the boldest 'cheat' in Bechuanaland, I owe him an apology.

Since the middle of the last month we have been tasting to see if the Civil Commissioner's grapes are ripe; so far we have only been able to discover that they are sweet, but we cannot yet tell if they are ripe or green. There is,

---

*   Any of the three grain stores.

†   Xhosa-Zulu: 'recommend', 'praise', in this context, 'particularly remark upon'.

‡   Tswana: 'a sudden piercing pain in the chest'.

however, no likelihood of this being found out until there are no grapes to taste!

This morning I went round for another taste. I tried to pick only as much as necessary for tasting, when a whole bunch came down on my hand – rather a heavy weight. It weighed about three pounds, but I was not the fool to replace it, although it was far too much more than I required. In the afternoon I saw the 'baas'* filling his little basket and I went round for another 'discovery', viz., what they taste like. Just when I came in, I heard 'Do you know who steals my grapes, Patrick?'[38]

I carried on bravely. 'No, Sir, I don't.'

'Do you know, Plaatje?'

'I am Plaatje.'

'Do you know who always steals my grapes?'

'No.'

'To steal is no answer ... By Jove! It is you who always steals my grapes. Can't you fellows do without stealing?'

I thought that the next question might be too unpleasant and I tried to modify the flowing tide before it grew worse, so I began:

'I have only been eating ('eating' mind you and not 'stealing') those in front of the stable, Sir.'

'I don't see why you should steal them even if they were at the back of the stable, for your father didn't steal any grapes.'

I successfully stemmed the tide when I interpolated:

'Well, my father didn't work for the Magistrate.'

He turned around and went on with his business. He was still smiling when he eventually gave me the sweetest bunch in the garden!

3

Letter from Barolong chief and headmen to the Civil Commissioner and Resident Magistrate, Mafeking [undated][39]

Sir,

We, the undersigned, chief and headmen of the Barolongs, have the honour to submit the following matter for your immediate consideration.

When you first intimated to us the intention of the authorities to open a grain store in the stadt for the benefit of our people we prepared the

---

* Charles Bell.

schoolroom for the purpose. This Mr Francis[40] refused as being insecure; and, without giving us the slightest chance of reconsidering the matter, he opened the church building and used it on his own account.

The action has interrupted divine services much to the dissatisfaction of the tribe, who do not consider that matters have reached such a serious turn as to warrant the suspension of divine services. Seeing the discontent of the people we have prepared a good and spacious house (Josiah's[41] new house) and placed it at Mr Francis disposal but we are sorry to say that Mr Francis does not feel inclined to move the grain into it.

We may also draw your attention to a grievance by our people that the shop is conducted in a most irregular manner. It must be understood that the people in the stadt are so many that during good times there always was a crowd in nearly every shop in town, and when all the people have got to be satisfied by one shop, as is the case at present, it becomes necessary to make provision for 4 or 5 persons to be served at once. As instances have been brought to our notice where some people had to await their turn for 3 days, in consequence of their having to be served one by one, we hope that you will also endeavour to have this matter satisfactorily arranged.

We have the honour to be
Sir,
Your obedient servants

The Civil Commissioner
Mafeking

Sunday, 21st January
Today is the celebration of the 100th day of the siege. People are having all sorts of pleasure in honour of the occasion, and one can almost fancy it is their desire to celebrate a 200th day.

Teacher Samson is very ill at the location. He has the rheumatic fever – the result of a bad cold his foot contracted while guarding on a rainy night.

This afternoon the Civil Commissioner held a meeting of the Barolongs in the stadt. Reuters and London *Times* war correspondents were also there. Things went on very smoothly until Wessels[42] commenced to speak. He threw a different complexion on the otherwise excellent harmony which characterized the commencement of the proceedings. He misunderstood, misconstrued and misinterpreted everything said and an undesirable scene ensued.

I think he took serious exception to the suggestion by the Civil Commissioner that whoever desires to leave the place for the time being should be permitted to do so, as our supply of food is too limited. They both kept on talking, and scarcely gave each other a chance, each expecting me to translate his hot beans first. Whoever can interpret for Wessels correctly ought to consider himself a professor. Fancy having to either make an English speech, or to turn every word of the following half-sensible, broken Setswana parts of sentences and phrases, offered after peculiar intervals, into English:

'E' – 'ke a utlwa' – 'ke utlwa sentle' – 'kala a bua' – 'ke re, morena' – 'a re …'*
Every one of these sentences causes him to assume a more serious attitude. He will wave to and fro and occasionally change position and chair, or stand up to demonstrate his injured feelings. It is an excellent thing that the C.C. is so patient or else things could happen that would cause great joy in the Boer laager when they become known there.

4
Letter to Lord Edward Cecil, 26 January 1900[43]

Lord Edward Cecil
Chief Staff Officer

My lord,

I beg to apply for an appointment to the Courts of Summary Jurisdiction as an interpreter. As a member of the said court you will remember that, at its formation, the staff interpreter was called on to perform that duty: he being incompetent in Dutch my services were procured, and I have since been the 'unattached' interpreter of the court. I have not previously drawn attention to this fact for I hoped that you would in the course of time remember me, as in colonial courts interpreters have the consideration of heads of department to a certain extent and are paid at the rate of 4/6 per hour if not permanently attached to the court, and permanent interpreters are paid at that rate 'extra', when they are engaged in other than criminal cases, besides their usual salary.

I hope your lordship would remember that except during the week of my indisposition (last Christmas) I have never failed to act to the satisfaction of the officers of the court in that capacity; and also bear in mind that, although

---

* Sotho-Tswana: 'Yes … I understand (hear) … I understand well … the way he speaks … I say, Sir … he says …'

it would do me an amount of good, it will not hamper the Government in any way if you felt pleased to grant my request.

Your obedient servant,

Sol T. Plaatje

Solomon Tsekisho Plaatje
Civil Commissioner's Department
Mafeking
January 26th, 1900

5
Letter to C.G. H. Bell, 30 January 1900[44]

The Civil Commissioner

Sir,

With reference to the attached paper,[45] I beg to state that I exceedingly regret the irregularity and humbly request that you will overlook it and kindly have the matter fixed up satisfactorily. You might kindly mention to the Chief Staff Officer that, if he felt pleased to grant it, such appointment may only be stipulated to interpreting during each session of the Summary Jurisdiction Courts and such other assistance as I am able to render the staff, without prejudice to my civil duties, the same as I have been since the commencement of the siege.

Your obedient servant

S. T. Plaatje

30-1-00

Thursday, 8th February
There is a little rain about 4.00 this morning, and the weather is very enjoyable this morning.

Runners came in from the north. They bring good news as far as concerns Plumer's forces[46] up north; but nothing fresh from east and south.

'Au Sanna' went off during the middle of the morning but was quiet all day. I hear they were working at her all day. From today no Natives are allowed in town without a pass. There are three classes of Natives, viz. permanent employees in town; permanent employees outside town; and stadt folk. The former (class one) are registered in the same manner as in Kimberley (the contract ticket) and walk about with a red ticket. I don't understand the procedure in class two. Class three receive a yellow ticket from Lekoko and hand it back every time they return from town.

I have started keeping an official diary from today, all of the doings in connection with Native affairs. This is somewhat bothersome as besides this one I am typing Mr Bell's, Dr Hayes' and Capt. Greener's simultaneously.[47] I cannot refuse the new gratis job as I am using the office typewriter and share the pay with no one; particularly as I heard the chief tell the Mayor that every member of this staff from his chief clerk down to the interpreter and every one of them [are] not only disinclined to do any work during the siege, but generally lodge a solemn protest and wish each to know the reason why he in particular, and not someone else, has to do that work.

The people are now receiving oatmeal for food instead of grain which, it is feared, will run short if sure steps are not taken to save it. The oats were intended for horses, but as the horses could eat grass when things grow serious, it is being thought of as human food. There is a general grumble all round here also. The pang has been felt all round, just at this time when folks had appetites. I have developed a marvellously strong appetite. I long for food every evening at 10.00 p.m. and after taking my supper at 7.00 I nearly die during the night if I do not take a cup of cocoa and a few biscuits before going to bed. Things are getting serious and I consider myself lucky for having thought out the thing at the beginning and stuffed my pants with matches and such things as were likely to be called in when things grow serious. I trust I will not number among those who will eat horses if we are not relieved by the end of March.

Ganankoto[48] was for a little time the Civil Commissioner's great favourite. As he was often called: Hanangkutu; Mr One-Leg; Have-no-Nkutu; Habanab's or Have-no-Legs (from heav'n-o-legs).

6

'Our beef providers', *Mafeking Mail Special Siege Slip*, 16 February 1900[49]

The appearance of some under-cut, juicy and succulent, on certain breakfast tables made us curious in this time of siege as to its origin. We learned it was 'Native beef', and the following account, which we prefer to give in its own picturesque language, is interesting in connection with the subject of our meat supply:

'Mathakgong, the leader of the expedition of 10th, whose loot was captured by the enemy a fortnight ago, said he would not have a quiet night until that fiasco had been blotted out; so on Friday he took four men with him to go and make another trial. Yesterday he and his companions were coming in with what appeared to be a span (12 head) of oxen they had captured close to Batho-Batho's, near Maritzani, at 5 p.m. They brought them down safely until they reached the Magogo valley, where the Boers fired at them. The Boers first of all fired from their right and before they had time to reply another volley came from their left. They replied calmly, four men went to the right (where the heaviest fire was) and one to the left. The Boers soon shut up but not until they had wounded two oxen. One fell amongst the Boers and one just outside our advance trench, and 10 came in safely.

Night before last (Saturday) 12 armed Barolongs left our advance trench, south of the stadt, to go and annoy the Boers. They crossed their lines without being observed and were only fired at on their return. As soon as they returned the fire the Boers ran back to their trench and were silent for the night.

These people attacked the homestead of a Native farmer at Maritzani and exchanged shots, but the farmer made a vigorous defence and they retired.'

7

Letter from Plaatje to unknown recipient, undated [late February 1900][50]

Please oblige Mr [unclear] (if you know where he is now) and send him the following message:

'Are still beleaguered. I never wrote by this route before as I have been thinking Kimberley would have been relieved long 'ere this for there have always been signs of the arrival of the troops; in fact the time of our relief never appeared to be more than 30 days off and we are still expecting to be relieved very shortly. However, if this reaches you before the line clears up please write via Gaborones and state how Elizabeth and Sainty[51] are. I have sent them messages and funds to Kimberley through Reuters, and once through another agency,[52] but I wonder if any of them reached them as you don't seem to be bothering yourself about keeping me informed about you and our people.

We hear folks are eating horseflesh in Kimberley. We are not eating any just yet and pray for relief before we have occasion to do so. They are not shelling us nearly as much as they used to do before. All of their guns appear to have gone up north except the big siege gun and a 5-pounder, the former only give us 3 or 4 (of her shells) per diem, a striking contrast to what we were subjected to a month or two ago. Our people here (excepting Taylor's mother-in-law, who died of natural causes, and young Sidzumo's wife blown up by a 94-pounder shell before Christmas – my pony was dittoed in the Civil Commissioner's stable 3 weeks ago) are still well. I have never felt better in my life. Altogether life is worth having even after being besieged for 4 months without hearing of one's wife. Hope you are all well. Goodbye.

You might please also remember me to Mr and Mrs Cronwright Schreiner.[53] I hope the effects of this maze have not ramified [sic] their way. Thanks in anticipation.

Yours etc

Wednesday, 21st March

Myself, Philemon[54] and Mr Gates are taking a census of the stadt. The latter and an assistant are taking it across the river. Phil starts at Tloung, myself at Bokone, and we'll meet in the centre. It is a tedious, bothersome job. We commenced at 7.00 and at 10.00 I was knocked up. The people are vexing me exceedingly: one would ask me what I wished to do with the name of the owner of a place, another would object to the repetition of the census as they were counted (registered) twice already during the present siege. Another would say: 'No wonder the present, unlike all previous sieges of Mafeking, is so intolerable for the unfortunate beleaguered people are counted like sheep.' Another would stand at the door, empty herself of the whole of her stock of bad words, then threaten me to 'just touch my pen and jot down any numbers of her family'. The so-and-so!

Another would give a cordial reception – so cordial that I would fancy that she will offer me a pipe full or a cigarette. She will act to my greatest satisfaction throughout in every way, except giving me the proper answer. I never knew that my store of patience was so bottomless – until the evening when I came home and found I had no fewer than 1,677 persons on my list.

I have not been to town all day today – the first day for three months. I hear 5 miles[55] has been captured by the Cape Boys[56] from the Boers at the brickfields. The Kromdraai lager is moved away from here. Two runners who were bound for Kimberley failed to leave owing to the long train of Boer waggons from Kromdraai circuiting round to the Transvaal side of the place – the first dawn of liberty.

Mathakgong left with nearly 30 men on another cattle-raiding expedition – his fourth during the present siege.

I have not seen my siege friends (the beggars) today. There were always scores of them every day at the residency and they were relieved by the soup kitchen. They are made up of the blackish races of this continent – mostly Zulus and Zambesians.[57] They venerate the Civil Commissioner and call me a 'ngwana's molimo'.* It is really pitiful to see one who was too unfortunate to hear soon enough that there was a residency in Mafeking, and, being too weak to work, never had a chance to steal anything during the last six days, and so had nothing to eat. Last month one died in the Civil Commissioner's yard. It was a miserable scene to be surrounded by about 50 hungry beings, agitating the engagement of your pity and to see one of them succumb to his agonies and fall backwards with a dead thud. Surely these Transvaal Boers are abominable. I really do not think they are children of the same Dutchland as the inhabitants of the O.F.S. No wonder their president was a judge while Oom Paul was a 'schaapwachter'.†

I wonder where is Gates: my total for today is 1,677, Philemon's 734. They were getting on much worse than I. Keshupile was his 'moshupatsela'.‡ He went with him till dinner-time and then started grumbling that he did not estimate that the trouble of this work was a tenth of what it is. Tshipithata[58] is away cattle-raiding.

Plaatje continued to keep a diary until 30 March 1900, the date of the last entry, though the siege itself was to continue until 17 May. Since there were over 20 sheets of blank paper remaining in the notebook in which the diary was written it seems very unlikely that the remainder of the diary was completed but subsequently lost. Why Plaatje did not continue with his diary can only be speculated upon but it may simply have been a matter of the pressure of work on him, and perhaps also the effect of the growing sense of pessimism in the town as food grew shorter, and relief still failed to materialise.

8

Letter to the Civil Commissioner and Resident Magistrate, Mafeking, 6 June 1900[59]

With the ending of the siege Plaatje returned to more routine office duties, but found it increasingly difficult to survive on his salary of £96 per annum. In these two letters

---

* Sotho-Tswana: correctly, *ngwan'a molimo* (a contraction of *ngwana a molimo*), meaning (literally) 'child of god' or 'young god'.
† Dutch: 'shepherd'; 'Oom ('uncle') Paul was a familiar term for Paul Kruger, President of the Transvaal Republic.
‡ Sotho: 'guide'. Keshupile is Keshupile Tlatsana.

*– the first applying for an increase in salary, the second for a special local allowance –
Plaatje presents his case for improved remuneration. On both occasions he was
supported in his application by Charles Bell: in response to his first claim his salary
was increased by £12 to £108 p.a., and in response to his second letter by a further
£12. On the covering note supporting Plaatje's letter, Bell wrote that 'he is a
painstaking, hardworking man; a thoroughly efficient interpreter, and rendered
invaluable service during the late Siege'.*

Office of the Civil Commissioner
and Resident Magistrate
Mafeking
6 June 1900

Sir,

Application for increase of salary

1. I most respectfully beg to apply that my salary should be augmented by
the addition of a local allowance, in order to enable me to cope successfully
with the high prices of life necessaries ruling here.

2. I had been studying to try the Service examinations in such special
subjects as are essential for this office, viz., Dutch, Sechuana, Sesutu and
typewriting; and in order to qualify myself for promotion I registered as a
candidate in those subjects, for last December's examinations; unfortunately
war broke out in October and my intentions were completely defeated, and I
hope you will bear me out as to how far studies deteriorate with the class of
shelling we were subjected to, for upwards of six months of the siege.

3. I think it impossible from the very nature of things that a man, dressed in
a chord suit of clothes, dwelling in a Native hut and living on mealies and
kafircorn could make a suitable person for the medium of speech between a
magistrate and a community as we find locally; but I am sorry to say that this is
the only mode of living that a man in receipt of my salary can manage to
provide for himself and family, without the liability of falling into debts as is
often the case.

4. Nothing can improve an employee much more than recognition of his
services, on the part of the head of his department, by way of stern
encouraging remarks and by way of increase of emoluments. My present salary
is £96 per annum. I have been in receipt of this since the beginning of 1897,
when I was still a bachelor, and engaged at more inferior duties, in a post

office. I have now got to perform higher duties, on a better situation, to keep a wife and child as well as an old mother of 60 years at the same salary.[60] This is almost an impossibility in Mafeking, unless one adopts a mode of living which may render him objectionable to the sight and presence of his senior officers.

5. In one office in the Colony we have an interpreter,[61] very well known to me, who does not even know how to read (or much less translate) a Dutch letter, and who does nothing beyond barely interpreting in the Kafir[62] and Sesutu languages, receiving £200 per annum: this ought to be an example that you would be well within your rights to ask for a substantial increase for your interpreter who, besides being a faithful oral and documentary translator in the Dutch and Native languages, does the office typewriting and as much of shorthand writing as is within the requirements of your office.

6. I have no doubt that up to the present, especially during the trying times we both had to endure for upwards of six months of the siege, you are aware that I have always endeavoured my utmost to perform my duties to your satisfaction: that you will feel pleased to give my application a favourable recommendation; and I am sure it will be the best incentive to better zeal, in improving myself for duty, in future.

I have the honour to be, Sir,
Your obedient Servant
Sol T. Plaatje

9

Letter to the Civil Commissioner and Resident Magistrate, Mafeking, 18 July 1901[63]

Office of the CC and RM
Mafeking
July 18th 1901

Sir,

Application for local allowance

I have the honour, most respectfully, to submit for your recommendation, an application that my salary should be supplemented by a local allowance, if only temporary, in order to enable me to cope with the high prices ruling here for the necessaries of life, owing to the disorganised state of railway communication with the coast.

From the commencement of the siege, until April this year, my salary was supplemented by an Imperial allowance, for services rendered; now this has ceased and I am compelled to apply to the department.

I am given to understand that at Kimberley, where living is much cheaper as that town is nearer the coast ports, the two interpreters of the Resident Magistrate's Court receive £150 p.a. each; and the nearest magistracy, of Vryburg, has both a Dutch and a Native Interpreter at £150 and £100 p.a. respectively.[64] These latter combined duties I carry out in this office and as the necessity for a better Dutch interpreter did not arise in July of last year (when the treason cases were first brought before the court)[65] the fact speaks for itself as regards my competency.

I have had more than seven years' continued service and in December of last year I presented myself as a candidate for the Civil Service examination in such subjects as I am mostly called upon to perform in this office, viz., typewriting, Dutch, Sechuana and Sesutu. For official reasons I could not be examined in the two latter.[66] I was, however, successful in obtaining a pass, at the head of both lists of successful candidates, in the two subjects I sat for (typewriting and Dutch). Besides the Civil Service certificate I hold one by Major-General Baden-Powell and one by H.H. Goold-Adams, the present Governor of the Orange River Colony, for services rendered to the Imperial Government, in that connection, during the siege of Mafeking.

The present high prices ruling for foodstuffs and necessaries of life are known to yourself and, if only on these grounds, I trust my application will receive your favourable recommendation.

I have the honour to be
Sir
Your obedient servant
Sol T. Plaatje

The C.C. and R.M.
Mafeking

10

'The Essential Interpreter' [manuscript][67]

'The Essential Interpreter' forms part of a hitherto unpublished manuscript of Plaatje's, written in late 1908 or early 1909, in which he writes about both the nature of court interpreting and the case of the deposed Batawana chief, Sekgoma,

'Essential interpreters' – Plaatje and friends. Plaatje is standing, centre, with Isaiah Bud-M'belle, his brother-in-law, to his left. Sitting at the front (left to right) are Patrick Lekhoane and Philemon Moshoeshoe.

who was detained without trial by the British Imperial authorities between 1906 and 1911. Plaatje began writing about the Sekgoma case in his notebook, expanded upon the nature of court interpreting as a result of its centrality to this subject, and then partially separated out the two components of his account. For present purposes, in view of the essentially self-contained nature of these two parts of Plaatje's account, this separation has been completed, and 'Sekgoma: The Black Dreyfus', relating as it does to the period 1906-1909, appears on pages 104 to 119.

The administration of justice in South Africa is something entirely different from the same thing in Europe, where judge, plaintiff, defendant, counsel and witnesses all speak the same language. In South Africa, where the inhabitants are Englishmen, Dutchmen, and Kafirs of various races, there is hardly any court of law without its interpreter.

I was at one time employed in the magistrate's court, Mafeking, under the Cape authorities, as an interpreter. The Resident Commissioner's office, which is also the court of appeal for the Bechuanaland Protectorate, is situated in the same town. A messenger from the Resident Commissioner's office called at our office one morning and stated that his honour needs the services of an interpreter. I went over as soon as my time allowed, and officiated. In due course, I rendered my account for the service to the Imperial Government. Later in the day I was called by my chief, the colonial magistrate, who produced my account, returned in a note by the Resident Commissioner, his honour expressing surprise that I should claim any remuneration for the service, a claim that was never put forth by any of my predecessors. My chief supported his view and added that as an employee of the Cape government, I should render my services free as the Cape was bound to assist the Imperial Government whenever necessary.

I told him of my inability to appreciate the logic of this contention; that it was monstrous, from my point of view, that he could be called upon to go out, adjudicate upon Protectorate cases in the Imperial office, or that any of his subordinates could be ordered to go and do clerical work in the Imperial headquarters, without emoluments, as in that case his staff, and not the Cape government, would be assisting the Imperial Government; that if the Imperial authorities were to run offices on charity, and other people were giving their labour free, I also could go and do my share of free labour. But I could not, I told him, go and render free services to facilitate the work of well-paid officers any more than I could afford to work in his office without a salary. I did not press my claim, however, and the matter lapsed.

A few days later, the same messenger came for the services of an interpreter. The message being passed over to me, I declined to attend and I am told that this most important adjunct of the correct administration of justice went about begging for a hand until a street boy was obtained to interpret 'anyhow'. It seemed to me a lamentable state of affairs that a high court of justice should have no interpreter and it betrays a culpable indifference, on the part of the authorities, to the interests of a community which should enjoy the protection of a civilised state, in practice as well as in theory.

It is said that in the course of the hearing, by the same Resident, of the dispute, which culminated in the separation of Chief Khama and his son, several amateurs took turns at this office.[68]

One of the most painful things which it is possible for anyone to endure, is to sit and watch some faulty interpretation in a court of law; and when there hangs in the balance the liberty of a man – especially in courts like those of the Bechuanaland Protectorate which are seldom if ever attended by the public, and the proceedings of which are scarcely ever reported in the public press – it becomes a very serious matter.

To avoid this kind of thing, every magistrate's court in Cape Colony has its resident interpreter, and when the circuit judge comes along to adjudicate upon cases which are beyond the jurisdiction of the magistrate, he brings with him his own interpreters, who, coming from a distance, are more likely to be disinterested and least likely to have any bias towards any of the local contestants.

One not acquainted with local forensic procedure will not so easily appreciate the gravity of the subject under discussion, but I cannot too strongly emphasize the importance of this office in any South African court of justice; and this is my only apology for wandering from the subject and going rather deeply into this subject of court interpreters. It is essential that every judge should clearly understand the evidence in any case upon which he sits in judgement, and the only means he has of attaining this in Southern Africa is by possession of a good interpreter.

By this I do not mean that interpreters are infallible. I have often noticed during my term that a witness would fail to drive home a point by stopping short of uttering a small suffix which could at once decide the issue, and I have seen, in minor instances, interpreters make use of their own knowledge of the circumstances and add such missing links not expressed by the witness in evidence, and this apparently insignificant addition become the subject on which counsel based their disquisition, and decided a momentous issue.

The greatest offenders in this regard are the white men who interpret in Native cases in the Transvaal courts. They carry into the courtroom an exhibition of the extreme superiority of their race over that of the unfortunate wretches for whom they have to interpret, and their translations are then just a matter of form regardless of the interests of justice or the consequences of their callousness. I have found a reason for the indifference of some of them but I am at a loss to understand the cause of the following glaring solecism.

This was at the great and historical trial of Dinuzulu at Greytown in Natal, in a court presided over by three of His Majesty's judges, who apparently thought that they had at their disposal the services of an infallible translator, if infallibility was among the things that be.[69] By his name, I gather that he was a European and the judges' task was made more difficult by the necessity of deciding an issue through such solecisms.

The law guarantees protection to the man with a black skin as much as it does to the man with a white skin, and until you get black interpreters to translate for black prisoners, that guarantee exists in theory only and not in practice.

The writer had the fortune of serving his apprenticeship as interpreter under the late Mr C. G. H. Bell, a magistrate who had a clear grasp of the English, Dutch, Kafir, Sesuto, Zulu and Sechuana languages, in all of which I was constantly called upon to officiate. I always made my translations with a perfect security, believing that he could rectify my errors, if any. I cannot express the satisfaction this gave me – always – not only because of the correctness of my renditions but on account of the knowledge that the chances of a miscarriage of justice were *non est*. My satisfaction was always as great as my anxiety when I found myself interpreting for a magistrate who was not himself a linguist.

Each court of law has its audience. In South Africa it is composed of a motley crowd of white men, Kafirs and Hottentots, males and females, clean and unclean. Some of these audiences are very intelligent and can appreciate a legal point – good, bad or indifferent – as quickly as any member of the court and there is often a distinct, yet respectful, bid for the plaudits of this 'gallery' by 'budding' lawyers and court attendants.

On one occasion, I had to officiate through two languages – the German and the Koranna – with both of which I was less familiar and in which the magistrate was absolutely unversed. Mr Bell's abilities as a linguist were often the byword with the motley crowd and on that morning I found an impression among them that the proceedings had given me the greatest satisfaction since for the first time I was able to exercise a free hand, having to perform a role in which I was not subject to criticism, but my mind was working in the opposite direction. It seemed to me that the magistrate, prisoner, prosecutor and spectators could really not believe that I was doing my best in a difficult position, and that it was a very good best. As mistakes are very common in these matters, I left no loophole for the slightest error. I took much pains in eliciting my facts and getting the deponent to revise his sentences if they contained a phrase, the meaning of which I was not quite certain. This retarded the proceedings in an unmistakable manner and my renditions, usually noted for their expeditiousness, were clearly boring. I felt that it was a tedious performance, taking up the time of the court to ascertain minute details which could easily be left unresearched; however, I threw the approbation of the court and its loafers to the winds and centred my attention in

Charles Bell, Magistrate and Civil Commissioner in Mafeking, whose staff Plaatje joined in 1898:
'His acumen in fixing sarcastic phrases and aptitude in putting comical jokes is beyond description,'
Plaatje wrote. 'His mere silence gives him a very ferocious appearance.'

the correct administration of justice only, determined to tell the magistrate so should he remonstrate against me for delaying the court more than is my wont.

It transpired in the end that this did deserve the approbation of the court, for in a conversation with his lordship the mayor the magistrate expressed his satisfaction with his new interpreter, who, unlike some that he had had, preferred to be understood when he translates and who visibly feels grave and took extraordinary pains when interpreting into and from languages not known to any others, and when he knows that the course of justice depends on him entirely. Others, he said, considered it *infra dig* to invite correction, and seem to fear that patient eliciting of obscure facts will be mistaken for incompetence and are happier if they can easily gloss over mistakes in an inaudible tone. Needless to say I was highly elated at the testimony.

Mr Bell informed me, when I first came to his office, that interpreting in court and interpreting at the sale of a cow were two different things entirely, and that it was as necessary to cultivate the art as to acquire a knowledge of the respective languages. I found this out very soon, as the reader can imagine, from the following description of the proceedings of a South African magistrate's court:

Let us say the prisoner is a Zulu. At the commencement of the trial an interpreter's first duty is to turn the indictment from English – the language of the court – into Zulu for the information of the prisoner at the bar, and then call on him to plead. The accused man will do so in his mother tongue, and the interpreter has to give a correct translation of the plea for the benefit of the court and the audience therein.

This recorded, the first witness will be called.

He will be a Dutchman, let us say. Then the same interpreter has to turn the familiar forensic oath into Dutch, pointing out confidentially for the benefit of the witness alone (before, during or after this translation) the attitude demanded by the dignity of the court, which is rarely understood except by court frequenters. He should point out gracefully that in saying, 'So help me God,' he should say so hand raised or whilst kissing the Bible. All instruction is conveyed in such a manner as to be observable to the witness only and others should scarcely notice that anything had taken place besides the bare translation of the oath.

The following trialogue will next take place:

Prosecutor: 'You are a farmer and you live at Donkerhoek?'

Interpreter: Ditto (in Dutch).

Witness: 'Ja ik ben.'*

---

* Dutch: 'Yes, I am.'

Interpreter: Ditto (in English). And while the magistrate is taking down this question and answer, the interpreter repeats in Zulu the whole of the foregoing for the benefit of the Zulu prisoner.

This translation, re-translation and cross-translation is kept up by the interpreter in an audible voice so rapidly and intelligently that, although he is carrying it on through three languages, he should keep nobody waiting; the only person whose convenience is studied being the occupant of the bench. This law, however, is not in the statute book and there is nothing to prevent an interpreter taking three times as long as, and translating say only half of what should be 'interpreted' by a good one; and the tug-of-war will be reached when the prisoner cross-examines the witness.

Prisoner at-the-bar: 'Mlungu, uti.'*

Interpreter: Ditto (in English, for the benefit of the court and audience), straight away.

Interpreter: Ditto (in Dutch for the benefit of the witness).

Witness: Replies (in Dutch).

Interpreter: Translates the Dutch answer, first into English then (whilst the magistrate writes) hands back the answer to the Zulu in his (the Zulu's) mother tongue, and so on, and so on, *ad infinitum.*

The prisoner will continue his cross-examination, the witness replying, the questioner rejoining and the interpreter translating. It is evident that unless an efficient linguist is kept, justice may easily be miscarried in the course of this trilingual colloquialism [sic].† Its true inwardness can only be understood by those who, besides understanding the respective dialects, have at some time or another watched the proceedings of a case in one of the South African courts of law. It is thus apparent that each such court should have not only a human tool who can reproduce a Kafir or Sechuana sentence in English but one whose conscience will never permit of any augmentation or garbling in his renditions. To add anything from the interpreter's own knowledge that would lead the court to liberate an unfortunate prisoner is as bad as the other way about it. If such knowledge exists, and he fears that an unfortunate person was likely to suffer on account of his ignorance, it would be better for the interpreter to enter the witness box and give evidence on it. Additions by an interpreter to secure the discharge of a prisoner are as deplorable as incomplete translations by which the innocent suffer.

---

* Zulu: 'Yes, Sir.'
† More correctly, colloquy (conversation).

A familiar phrase, too often slaughtered by interpreters, is one which at the close of a preparatory examination the magistrate says to the prisoner, 'You are committed for trial.' It appears that some interpreters, finding this sentence so short in the official language, consider it tiresome to explain its meaning in too many words. They prefer to cut it short at the expense of the prisoner's information. I heard one interpreter tell a prisoner what would literally be, 'The magistrate says that you will wait for the judge' – truly a serious error.

My own difficulty when I was still a fresh attaché of the court was the finding out of the real meaning of most of the least known of forensic phrases, including commitment for trial, and how to express them in the vernacular. I found out that this was too difficult a phrase to render into intelligible Dutch or any of the Native languages in half-a-dozen words. A literal translation of it will be beyond the reach of the intellect of a person of mediocre intelligence, so I found the following rendition rather round-about but more satisfactory because better understood:

Magistrate: 'You are committed for trial.'

Interpreter: 'Kgetse ea gagu yaka e koaliloe e tla romeloa koa masekising eo mogolo koa Teemaneng, fa a sena go e bala ke ene o tla holeang fa u tla sekisioa ke magesetrata kgona ke liyoche eo o tla tlang, lefaele gore ga nke n sekiosioa gope.'

- 46 words to explain 5.

I have often found English prisoners, after being told in this pithy official language, and despite the fact that the phrase is in their mother-tongue, that they scarcely understood their fate as they did not know if 'committed for trial' was something round or square. My translation just quoted would, if retranslated into English, read: 'Your case as recorded will be sent to the crown prosecutor at Kimberley. After reading it he will say if you are to be tried by the magistrate, by the next circuit judge, or if you are not to be prosecuted at all.'

Some interpreters appear to think that they can best serve the convenience of the public and save the court's time and money by cutting things short; but I think that economy of time and public money is no concern of the interpreter. He is only to translate what is going on to moderate length, repetition or impertinence of speech being the duty of the magistrate. Many a Native prisoner, unacquainted with the procedure in European courts, when asked to plead, will often plead guilty with a 'but', and a hasty interpreter will at once translate the plea without mentioning the qualification, with the result that once a plea of 'guilty' is entered the Native is practically debarred from calling his witnesses, and this guiltless man will be convicted on the plea as rendered by the interpreter.

Such pleas are often given in this form: 'I am guilty, because the law (police) says so;' or, 'It would appear that I am because I am here (in the dock);' or,

Prisoner: 'I am guilty, my lords, in the strictest sense of the law (for which I am deeply sorry) but ...'

Interpreter: 'The prisoner pleads guilty.'

Prisoner: '... but not in fact, nor in God's honest truth.'

I once heard one magistrate, an experienced old bencher, look askance at the interpreter and say, 'Surely he has said much more than that?'

A slight confusion ensured and thanks to the acumen of the magistrate, a plea of 'not guilty' was entered, and what appeared at the beginning like a very short case, lasted three-quarters of an hour and resulted in the dismissal of the charge.

What the prisoner really meant is that he is 'not guilty'; but his notion, which I make bold to say is a laudable one, is that to say so in two words in reply to a charge in which the British crown contends against him, is tantamount to calling his sovereign lord King Edward the Seventh – whom God preserve – a liar.

I think I have shown that it is impossible for the South African courts to mete out substantial justice without the aid of good interpreters, but even where this rule is observed there is still room for improvement, for the salaries offered are in many instances so small as to attract but few good men. That in itself is not a very bad thing but its worst feature is that an interpreter, like a judge (of whom he is the mouthpiece), when once appointed is interpreter for life; with this difference, however, that he has little prospect of an increase of salary. Even where an appreciating magistrate fought hard for it, there is practically no chance of a promotion. Applications for recognition of long and valuable services have in almost each instance failed, in spite of strong recommendations by the magistrate. I never knew that they (interpreters) were so badly paid until I left the colonial service.

After leaving the service, several offers were made to me of similar appointments in other parts of South Africa and the pittance wage offered was in one instance less than half of what I was paid towards the end of the term of my interpretership at Mafeking – clearly showing that the Cape government was not the worst offender in this connection. When I told my would-be benefactor that I had left a similar post at £130 p.a. on finding that figure a waste of time, he blushed, adding that he could not dream of paying that. I told him what would happen if he did not offer at least £100 per annum with increments for good behaviour and proficiency – that he would get the wrong fellow. He got him at £50 p.a. He served him some months then forged the District Commissioner's name on a cheque and got 4 years' hard labour.

I could go on enumerating such painful instances, whereby a niggardly pittance was attached to a highly respectable appointment. All respectable Natives naturally give it the go-by, and when a gross miscarriage of justice resulted, nemesis overtook an innocent victim and not the administrator who encompassed it indirectly by employing the wrong man and directly by withholding a reasonable wage when a good man was about.

You pay a good sum for the best horse to do your work. You do not get the scum of the British bar to adorn the bench, you get the best blood, so why then should you get the refuse of Native society to act as his [the judge's] mouthpiece? Is that not an undue stultifying of his forensic abilities, seeing that they have in the main to be carried out by and through the interpreter? In India they employ Native masters of arts and professors of literature – men of education and character – to act as interpreters and the opposite policy almost universally pursued in this country is in the main responsible for Sekgoma's unfortunate position. It is a series of faulty interpretations which, I think, the Imperial government, being in a measure responsible, should investigate and feel pleased to make ample reparation.

I am told, though I cannot say with what amount of truth, that towards the end of 1906 when Mathiba, the newly installed Chief of the Batawana, came to interview his honour the Resident Commissioner, Sekgoma's people also claimed and were accorded a hearing.[70] Scenes were the order of the day in the respective interviews and in the end his honour decided that they should proceed to Pretoria and there interview the High Commissioner. They went, I am told, and each time they spoke to His Excellency, Sekgoma's men had to speak through Mathiba's secretary who acted as interpreter between Lord Selborne[71] and the Natives. Where was His Excellency's interpreter? And if he had not one, why were not the services of a disinterested person procured for the occasion?

Experienced colonial magistrates born in the Native Territories,[72] who speak and write the vernacular, cannot do without their interpreters, and how can an Imperial officer, who knows as much Sechuana as the man in the moon, expect to mete out substantial justice to the Native tribes without the aid of an unbiased interpreter?

The staff of Koranta ea Becoana (Bechuana Gazette). *This photograph was probably taken soon after the opening of the Bechuana Printing Works in Mafeking in August 1902. Plaatje is sitting centre left; Silas Molema (holding a piece of paper) is sitting, front right.*

11
Editorial, 'Equal rights', *Bechuana Gazette,* 13 September 1902

This editorial appeared in the third issue of the Bechuana Gazette, *and was reproduced again on 21 December 1904. In the pieces from the* Bechuana Gazette *which follow the distinction between an article and an editorial was often not a very meaningful one, but where I have applied the term 'editorial' these appeared immediately beneath the editorial masthead; where I have applied the term 'article', they appeared elsewhere in the paper.*

Plaatje's motto was taken, appropriately enough, from the Song of Solomon (Chapter 1, verses 5-6), and he carried it beneath the editorial masthead on most issues of the Bechuana Gazette *following its first appearance on 6 September 1902. Later, it also appeared in Plaatje's newspapers in Kimberley after he moved there in 1910.*

Koranta ea Becoana,

"BECHUANAS' GAZETTE."

Only Authorised Medium for publishing Government Proclamations addressed to Natives by Colonial, Protectorate or Imperial Military Authorities.

No. 1.   MAFIKENG, MATLHACO, PHATO 16, 1902.

The Art Metropole.

 # Mo Tlung ea Kgatisho!
Mo Tlung ea Kgatisho!!

Likgetsana tsa Marifi---le Pampiri TSE LI NTLE tsa go koalela litsala tseno. Li nale bo Almanaka ba monongoaga le ba isago. Re ka go gatisetsa leina ya gago mo go cone fa u rata.

Likoalo tsa Serolong, Setlhaplag, Seshotho le Setebele, Libelbele, Litestamente le likopelo li santse li laelicoe,

Tse li Gorogileng ke tse:

Marang, Loeto loa Mokresete,
   Dilo tse di chwanetseng go itsewa,
      Dikaelo, Arithmetike, Dipeleta,
         Dipoconyana le LINOTO TSA LONDON,
Secoana fela.

KITSISHO.

Eo o ese a amogeleng KORANTA ea gague o locoa gore a rialo re itsise re bone go e romela.

Faele Babali ba ba agileng mono Mafikeng rare fa ba tsile go luelela Koranta tsa bone pele, e tlane ere li sena go gatisioa li romeloa koa matlung a bone.   Eo o sa luelelang pele a tie go e itseela.

The first pages of the first issue of Koranta ea Becoana (Bechuana Gazette), *printed at the Bechuana Printing works, Mafeking, 16 August 1902.*

MAITOKO.

Re nga a ba lelo mo babaling ba rona ka tiego e kgolo ea "Koranta," Re nga tsa kamele, le gone re sa lire ka banoa. Matbata a re lekanyeng mananyale magolo, me gompieno re a lentse, re gotisa "Koranta" mo Ligatisi ong tsa rona tse fa babali ba ka li tsheg tsa li tla emelang ruri.

Ntso e re e tlhabanyeng enz ele boket ra re e fents ka thusho ea hart a to ba molemo le Magosi ya a ratang no rafe ea one.

A Re uhile la tlhoko thata re tume re a n gela likoranta tsa ba ba aeonyeng le rona, me rona re sena go ba batse tsa kananyo tsa bone. E ntse sellhahi se se batlh a e mo go rona re choeue mola a boamegedi, me re sena go ba b delebi mafoko a a votshe a kagis ho, lea pi delo e e gar dung p ho ee tshen yeg e ea Molebo ea Seredo, ka kgo di ea Seetebosigo, ka ntata ea baloetse you Kgosi, e yaanong re lebogang Molin o ka e fetile. Re choobile segolo go amogela tiro tsa kgatisho, tse li nang le tlhoatlhoa, re li lebelela bong ha esae ba tlhazegq ka eone, ka golo mko ea eone e feta Mashini tsa rona bi sa dir.

E botbata re kile na ba bona mo nobaong ea Noa ko go itsa Mashini rona e megolo go tla kouna; me erile fa rere n thogedor, lipase tsa e n ka pelo, tsa ba tsa ea go fidla loa Barekising ka motshe gatong. Me ha, ke nobato oa ga mang?

Lipampiri le litlhaka le lilo tse ling e tse lintsi tsa kgatisho, li reen ile malatsi ale matlhaeo fela go roa ko Kapa go tla k uma; me foele anobitniyann en m nyenyaue ro re gatisang k'uno le ka ene, go rou kou Port. Elizabeth, (tsela e khutelwane go feta Kapa) o chotse u seka na ngatega! kgweli lile peli. O kabo a sa tlega yalo fa re re go golegile koloi en likgoni ra es go tso tsasa.

Nako e sale teng sa nyafaleng ruri! Los gopole gore yaanong fa re rekile Likgatisho gare tlhole re tlhoka mali; rea tlhoka fela yaka gale. R e nale barutegi ba ba tsamaisang tiro, ba ba lopang tlhoatlhoa tse b golileng. Re reka lipampiri, lienke l: lithoto tsa lingoe tse li senyegang ka kgatisho ngoe, tse fa baba li ba sa ikurine litla tlhokafalang, kgatisho e esae. Me rare se nya faleng; re lo beatse motheo tiru ke eo he, e tsamaisung.

South African Spectator

KE kbane e e gatisiosng koa Kapa ka English le Setebele. E batoa ke tlhoga. cotlhe tsa kata tsa Lipaaho tsa Kapa le Natal.

Segosta mo go buelereng tiehoa do tsa Banche.

Tlhaotlhong: 6s. fela ka ngoaga.
F. Z. S. PEREGRINO,
Mong. le Moralagani,
Box 370, Cape Town.

Romdi Cheoge fle Paro la a rata ga e bon.

The King Crowned.

TO MY PEOPLE.

On the Eve of my Coronation, an event which I look upon as one of the most solemn and important in my life, I am anxious to express to my people at home, and in the Colonies and in India, my heartfelt appreciation of the deep sympathy which they have manifested towards me during the time that my life was in such imminent danger.

The postponement of the Ceremony owing to my illness caused, I fear, much inconvenience and trouble to those who intended to celebrate it, but their disappointment was borne by them with admirable patience and temper.

The prayers of my people for my recovery were heard, and I now offer up my deepest gratitude to Divine Providence for having preserved my life and given me strength to fulfil the important duties which devolve upon me as the Sovereign of this great Empire.

(Signed) EDWARD R. AND I.
Buckingham Palace,
8th August, 1902.

It is with deep thankfulness to Almighty God that we are able to record that to-day week witnessed the Coronation of the Ruler of this mighty Empire.

It must have been a bitter pill for Their Majesties to think of how shocking it was to the millions of their loyal subjects, who spent their earnings with the intention of celebrating in some form or other, the Enthronement of their Sovereign, and on the eve of the event to learn that it has been postponed, because the King was too ill. It is therefore, a relief to the King and the Nation, that the Ruler has now been crowned and that, despite his recent indisposition, His Majesty went through the difficult programme of this august ceremony with a brave and manly spirit.

The felicitations of the black races inhabiting this land are second to none in their sincerety, and we have the authority of the chieftains of the various tribelets to record their unswerving loyalty and their high respect for the Throne and person of Victoria's Son; and to assure the wise statesmen whose duty it is to guide the destinies of the Empire that nothing whatsoever, which is within their strength to avert, will as long as they live, serve to endanger the humane prestige of the British power, the supremacy of which has now been declared the only factor throughout the length and breadth of South Africa.

We join in with the other subjects of His Majesty, of all nationalities, white and black, old and young, male and female, in wishing Edward the Seventh a peaceful and prosperous reign.

GOD SAVE THE KING.

Publisher's Note.

We owe a further apology to our readers for the sparseness of news matter in this, our first issue, and also to a number of businessmen who sent us advertisements for to-day's paper. The machine was only fixed up yesterday and, as this is our trial number, we could hardly be expected to produce a full sized paper in one day. Their advertisements therefore, though already made up had to stand over for want of space.

Bechuana's Gazette.

. SATURDAY, AUGUST 16, 1902.

OUR APOLOGY.

We regret the causes of the delay in the opening of the Bechuana Printing Works and the issue of this paper. We trust that our contemporaries will appreciate the difficulties under which we laboured and understand how deeply we deplore the fact that, although in regular receipt of their exchange copies, we were unable to keep up the journalistic equilibrium from this end.

It has been a trying time for us to hold our subscribers' monies and yet be unable to give them, in print, the joyful tidings of the peace declaration as well as the shocking intelligence of the frustration of His Majesty's Coronation, owing to the King's ill-health, which latter incident is now thank God a thing of the past. Still more disappointing has it been for us to accept remunerative printing and advertisement engagements,

then have them withdrawn because their time had expired and our machinery was not coming forward.

Who is to blame for all this? Tis true we had some difficulty with Martial law restrictions, under which our large printing machine could not be indented for; but on that item being struck off, the permits were immediately granted and they reached the coast in May last.

It took the Cape Government Railways 5 days to bring our stationery, type, &c., 15,000 lbs. weight, from Capetown; but to come from Port Elizabeth on the same Railways (a lesser distance by 70 miles), the small jobbing machine on which this paper is printed took don't get a bit! two months.

It could not have delayed much longer had we misjudged our ox-wagon and personally went to fetch it.

THE Kimberley Saddlery Co.

(Late C. Greaves & Son),

WHOLESALE & RETAIL SADDLERY, &C.

All requisites connected with the trade supplied.

Orders promptly attended to.

Address :
P.O. Box 170,
Market Square,
KIMBERLEY.

Telegrams,
SADDLERY

Notice of Removal.

T. A. LEWIS ROBERTS, D.D.S., DENTAL SURGEON KIMBERLEY, may now be consulted permanently at COHEN'S Buildings, opposite Public Library.

Hours of CONSULTATION:
Daily 9 a.m. to 5 p.m. Sunday mornings by appointment.
Ckerodays, a.m.
Roberts, Dental Kimberley.

B. FERRARIS & Co.,

(Ramochankana le Ramonnana.)

Ntlo ea bagolegadi ea lilo tse li rekoang ke Bancho.

Lithoto tse li Thakanyeng tsa ngaro tse li segeroeng ruri, marokgoe le lipaka tsa setofo, Forubele le Kasmere. Aparo tse li choeu tse litshetlha tse li ncho le tse li makasa. Bo Yase, Mahempe, le khai tsa kafa teng tsa methale eotlhe. Bo setele le eng, le eng.

LILO TSA METHALE, TSE LI TLHOPHEGILENG KA TLHOATLHOA TSE LI MOLEMO.

Likobo, Bocale, Liprinte tsa Germane le tse lingoe. Litlhako tsa banna le basali, &c., &c.

Mabele a Sesvona, Mili le lilo tse lingoe, li ramelou go goo gor, lefa ele ka teroua, kou motho o ratang li ea gone.

GAKOLOGELOANG RAMOCHANKANA,

B. FERRARIS & Co.,

"THE CORNER."

Pniel Road and Thompson Street,
P.O. Box 155.
Kimberley.

Telegraphic address :
" Ferraris"
Kimberley.

> I am BLACK but comely, O ye daughters of Jerusalem, as the tents of Kedar and the curtains of Solomon.
>
> Look not upon me because I am BLACK for the sun hath looked upon me; my mother's children were angry with me; they made me the keeper of their vineyards; but my own vineyards have I not kept.

We do not hanker after social equality with the white man. If anyone tells you that we do so, he is a lunatic, and should be put in chains. We do not care for your parlour, nor is it our wish to lounge on couches in your drawing-rooms. The renegade Kaffir who desires to court and marry your daughter is a perfect danger to his race, for if his yearnings were realised we would be hurrying on the path to the inauguration of a generation of half-castes, and the total obliteration of our race and colour, both of which are very dear to us.

For this reason we advise every black man to avoid social contact with the whites, and the other race to keep strictly within their boundaries.

All we claim is our just dues; we ask for our political recognition as loyal British subjects. We have not demonstrated our fealty to the throne for the sake of £.s.d., but we did it to assist in the maintenance of the open door we now ask for, so it cannot be said that we demand too much.

Under the Union Jack every person is his neighbour's equal. There are certain regulations for which one should qualify before his legal status is recognised as such: to this qualification race or colour is no bar, and we hope, in the near future, to be able to record that one's sex will no longer debar her from exercising a privilege hitherto enjoyed by the sterner sex only.

Presently under the British Constitution every MAN so qualified is his neighbour's political equal, therefore anyone who argues to the contrary, or imagines himself the political superior of his fellow subject, is a rebel at heart.

12

Article, *Bechuana Gazette*, 13 December 1902

We understand that the Native chiefs of this division have signed a petition for presentation to Mr Chamberlain[73] praying for annexation to the Transvaal. Good lord! This is by far the most appalling information we have heard since the war broke out.

They say that a rolling stone gathers no moss, and never has this saying been more exemplified than in the working of the cruel Annexation Bill, which wrenched us from crown colony government and attached us to the responsible Cape.[74] Our leaders were formerly in direct communication with the High Commissioner, and the chiefs were in constant touch with Downing Street. Our appeals to Mr Chamberlain against annexation found his mind already made up and our friends in the Cape parliament, with the exception of the then member for Namaqualand (Mr Merriman) all yielded to the desire of the late Mr Rhodes and we had to go. The connection between us and the High Commissioner was cut off and we now find ourselves in an entanglement of red-tape with no possible prospect of extrication.

One should have thought that the chiefs having been 'once bitten' would naturally be 'twice shy' but it appears that in order to please our white friends they are willing to seal their own doom, and have offered to swallow another dose.

In the face of the eighth clause of the final peace terms[75] this action on their part is nothing but a terrible leap in the dark and never was there a more flagrant case of wilful political suicide than there is in this movement; and we earnestly trust that for the sake of themselves the chiefs will see to its early withdrawal before it is too late. The matter may be re-opened when there is any justification from within but all present accounts from that colony show that the treatment of the black subject is second only to Rhodesia.

13

Editorial, 'Mr Chamberlain', *Bechuana Gazette*, 10 January 1903

The visit of Joseph Chamberlain, the British Colonial Secretary, provided the focal point for a wide variety of individuals and organisations, black and white, to express in a formal way their views, aspirations and grievances in the aftermath of the Anglo-Boer War. His tour lasted three months, during which time he visited all four South African colonies, gathering information to help him to shape, in conjunction with Milner, post-war reconstruction policy.

His Majesty's Secretary of State for the Colonies is now in the Transvaal and his powerful and pointed speeches have, besides showing the people that he is after all only human, demonstrated in full the fact that those who have expected the best of results from his visit will not be disappointed.

Deputations will interview him in the Transvaal about labour controversies and also on such matters as taxation and compensation.* To some of these he

---

* For losses suffered during the Anglo-Boer war between 1899 and 1902.

has already given us – and by us we mean every member of the Empire, from all corners of which his visit is being followed with the keenest interest – an inkling of the statesmanly policy he means to pursue. Deputations will meet Mr Chamberlain and lay before him complicated matters affecting the welfare of the Dutch subjects of His Majesty, and yet another deputation will ask the Colonial Secretary to put his thumb on the bitter blot of South Africa, this continued misrepresentation of the honest intention of the coloured subjects of His Majesty – this demon of misrepresentation and imbecility, which threatens to turn South Africa into a regular sty.

We have demonstrated our fealty to the British throne on the battlefield long before and since we became Britons, and yet we are charged with conspiracy, and intentions to rebel, by a set of speculators who are encouraged by the leading Progressive press, and their only claim to British fellowship is that they vividly imagine that the pigment of their skins is the same as the Sovereign's, and we will be excused for saying that they have evinced greater interest in money-making than in the protection of the flag. We would inform these men that they had better sweep their own floors before finding faults with us, and if they do not in the near future exhibit a striking improvement in their character we are going to ask for, and we mean to have, a special legislation making it a criminal offence in South Africa for *soi-disant* politicians or journalists, who would still charge members of another race with disloyalty unless he can prove it in a court of justice.

We wish that those who travel a long distance to interview the right honourable on the labour question would speak the truth and inform him that their mission in South Africa is a money-making one, and as such they find it awkward to pay the labourers as their greed will only allow them to grab but not to regard the merits of those who brought their coveted treasure within their reach, and that for this reason the Natives who are free men and not slaves, refuse to work for them.

We deeply sympathize with the intentions of any syndicate or individual to develop the mineral resources of South Africa, but it is hardly fair to expect us to swell to overflowing the pockets of any capitalists unless our services are also considered. We are willing to work, but for nothing less than a living wage. One shilling a day may be good pay in Europe and India where we are told that one can obtain a decent meal at a penny, but it is quite the reverse in this country where one cannot obtain a meal at anything less than one shilling. Pay and we shall belt up!

14
Article, 'Haikona annexation', *Bechuana Gazette*, 17 January 1903

The white population of this country still believe that their salvation lies in the annexation of Bechuanaland to the Transvaal Colony. The alleged merits of the proposal have been explained to us but we regret to have to confess that after studying the pros and cons of the movement we have found that the game is not worth the candle.

It is therefore with pleasure that we are able to state that the Barolong chiefs, who previously signed a petition in favour of annexation, have discovered their mistake, as clearly explained to them in these columns, and that they have withdrawn in time for the arrival of Mr Chamberlain, before whom they are now preparing to sing a totally different song. Attempts have since been made to obtain the signatures of the Ra-Tlou chiefs and headmen in the further ends of the district. Acting on our advice these chiefs have stoutly refused to associate themselves with the movement and it is right that such should be the case.

The chiefs of the division have considerable difficulty in the collection of the annual hut-tax, as some of the tribesmen grumble about money being so scarce. And it is a puzzle to us how they expected to get on in the Transvaal without surrendering their estates to the possession of mortgages and their relinquishment for the benefit of the tax-gatherer, which would ultimately mean the enslavement of their young men to the mining capitalists at a wage to be dictated by the Rand Mining Association. And where does the benefit come in?

The Cape government tax is only ten shillings per year, on each head of a family, while Sir Godfrey Lagden[76] demands two pounds per year from each male member of every family across the border, so that families hitherto used to paying only two shillings per annum would, in the event of annexation, be fleeced to the tune of £6 to £8 and even £10 according to the number of male Natives composing each family. How could we find these amounts, and whence will we scoop them in this arid desert they call Bechuanaland?

Joseph Chamberlain was presented with a petition from a group of whites requesting him to consider the question of annexation to the Transvaal, but it carried no African support, and nothing came of it in any case.

15
Editorial, *Bechuana Gazette*, 31 January 1903

During the week Mafeking had the distinguished honour of being first[*] to entertain the Empire's statesman. At 4.30 p.m. on Tuesday a blare of hooters and bells heralded the approach of the Colonial Secretary's cavalcade when about five miles outside town. Every shop was closed and nearly everybody made for the street. Seldom before were such throngs witnessed in our town, which was never so beautifully decorated. Considering the facilities afforded all sections of the community to see the distinguished visitor one could not help feeling proud of the privilege of belonging to this most British of towns, under the mayoralty of that rising statesman, J.W. de Kock Esq.

The programme of the Reception Committee as originally drafted read inter-alia: 'During Tuesday it is expected Mr Chamberlain will receive in private deputations and addresses from the chamber of commerce, annexation committee, the Location Natives, Indian and Chinese communities and such other deputations as may desire.' The whole of Wednesday morning and forenoon was originally set apart for Natives.

How unlike your Durban and Johannesburg, where our readers write to say they are shown out of the receptions for the sake of their colour, as facilities were offered only to barbarians who played the Zulu dance and gave the visitor an impression that all the Natives could do was dance. Oh no, this is a British town in a British colony and our visitors felt it too; they shook hands, read papers edited and printed by black hands, in the stadt they took seats over carpets spread for them by black hosts. They not only sat down but introduced us to their friends, and Mrs Chamberlain also spoke in glowing terms of the beauty of our address.[77]

A brass band of a number of Mashona youngsters came down to provide music for the drills of the Bulawayo Cadets. We invited them to play at our home but the Europeans in town gave them such prominent position on their programme that they soon became everybody's favourite and the African Choir[78] could not have had a more cordial reception in London than these half-naked little black piccaninnies of instrumental musicians from the north, received in Mafeking. All they could do for us, with considerable inconvenience to themselves, was to come down and play 'God save the King' when our visitors arrived, then hurry back again to carry out their many important engagements and appointments in town.

---

[*]   In the Cape Colony.

Mafeking welcomes Joseph Chamberlain, Secretary of State for the Colonies: awaiting his arrival in town (above) and in the Barolong stadt (below).

Our visitors departed at ten on Thursday morning by Special trains from Kimberley, carrying away the best wishes of everybody. We wish them God speed and a most successful and enjoyable tour. His Worship the mayor and the presentation committee are to be heartily congratulated on the accomplishment of a most successful ceremony.

No one can grumble at the reception arrangements which left absolutely nothing to be desired.

16
Article, *Bechuana Gazette*, 14 February 1903

Amongst the thousand and one obnoxious disabilities under which the Transvaal people are suffering is one which directly obstructs the spread of the Christian religion in South Africa. Under the regulations of this religion, no man and woman can be admitted into the full membership, unless they be legally married according to the usages of its doctrine. Among the various congregations in the Transvaal colony there happens to be a number of elderly families (married, of course, but according to Native rites) who spent their last years on Dutchmen's farms, earning something like £3 per annum, which is scarcely sufficient to clothe their bodies.

The time came when such people desired to become Christian converts, and they were enrolled as members on probation. They have been on probation for a number of years, and although they have attained to the necessary qualification stages, they have been debarred from the fellowship until they have gone through a Christian marriage ceremony. This they are willing, but unable, to do as for this luxury they are bound to pay into the Transvaal treasury a penalty of £3.

Now, £3 sterling for a happy marriage may be a moderate sum for newspaper editors, merchants and clergymen, but it is cruelly expensive for old farm servants who earn much less in a month than some townspeople do in a single day. In the interests of this class of people we should have thought that a combined appeal from the ministers of the various religious denominations should have been organized, praying for a repeal of the impediment.

In the Cape Colony a man may be legally married without paying a brass farthing, and we cannot understand why a sense of respect for relics of a defunct republicanism should be allowed to prompt British administrators to thus maintain the ostracism of certain people from a brotherhood which, in the other dependencies of the Empire, are entered free, gratis.

We are disappointed to find that while everybody was trying to show Mr Chamberlain his claims to relief, nothing was done by the clergy – especially those who minister to the spiritual needs of the blacks – in this most important matter, on behalf of their flocks. It would be a humane deed if someone would commence a movement to bring the matter before the notice of the High Commissioner and he, or she, will earn their thanks by securing the salvation of a number of souls, whose spiritual positions at the present time are well nigh intolerable.

17
Article, *Bechuana Gazette*, 4 April 1903

We, as the mouthpiece of the Natives of Bechuanaland and the Transvaal colony, are surprised to find the people of the Transvaal inclined to ignore the grand axiom, 'Equal rights for every civilized man south of the Zambezi', by one of Britain's greatest statesmen, the late Cecil John Rhodes. The solution of the Native problem lies in the carrying out of this principle, which we believe is the essence of the British constitution. But the policy of deliberately boycotting and ostracizing the Native African and the British Indians, as persisted in by the selfish newcomers of the Rand, leaves a dark future for the generation to take the place of the citizens, both white and black, who inhabit this subcontinent.

Our motto as Native Africans is Africa for all law-abiding citizens, naturalized British subjects and all those foreigners in whose countries we would be treated with respect and political equality. Equal rights for all of them, regardless of race, colour, creed or sex.

18
Article, 'Bogwera',* *Bechuana Gazette*, 11 April 1903

In some pity we record that during this, the fourth month of the third year of the twentieth century, the Barolong have revived the ancient circumcision rites which had long since gone down beneath the silent prayer of Christian civilisation. Scores of young men have during the week been taken away from their profitable occupations into the veld to howl themselves hoarse and submit to severer flogging than is usually inflicted by the judges of the Supreme Court.

---

* Tswana: 'circumcision ceremony'.

Silas Molema, Barolong headman and proprieter of the Bechuana Gazette: *'an outstanding character in the history of Bechuanaland', Plaatje wrote later.*

The fact that in the year A.D. 1903 the sons of Montsioa can safely solemnise a custom the uselessness of which was discerned by their fathers, and which the rest of Bechuanaland has for years relegated to the despicable relics of past barbarism, shows that someone has not been doing their duty. A startling state of affairs is that there are still to be found such a large number of youths who, being accustomed to dress like Europeans and live on three meals every day, and others who have again been living under luxurious circumstances behind shopkeepers' counters and in white men's kitchens, willingly surrender their contentment and volunteer to expose themselves to all kinds of weather, in the open air, besides the thousand and one other tortures forming part of this ceremony, the nature of which ex-pupils of the weird hedonism are not permitted to tell us.

19

Letter from Silas Molema to Sir H.J. Goold-Adams, Lieutenant-Governor of the Orange River Colony, 11 April 1903[79]

Although this letter was sent in the name of Silas Molema, it was clearly typed and written by Plaatje, and even Silas Molema's signature was in Plaatje's hand. To all intents and purposes it may be considered as Plaatje's letter, and significant as a clear statement of the policy of the Bechuana Gazette.

To His Excellency Sir H.J. Goold-Adams[80]
Lt.-Governor of the Orange River Colony
Government House
Bloemfontein

May it please Your Excellency
    I most respectfully beg to address Your Excellency on the following subject, in the interests of the Natives of the Orange River Colony.
    I think that Your Excellency is aware that I am publishing a weekly newspaper, the object of which is to enlighten the Natives on what is going on amongst them. It is published in two languages and is the only advertising medium for reaching Sechuana-speaking customers throughout South Africa. To the Natives it inculcates loyalty to the Throne, support to the upholders of the law, obedience to its administrators and assistance to their European neighbours in the pursuit of their various trades and callings, which makes up the industry of this land.

To the European readers it advocates fair treatment to their Native servants, equal political rights to their Native neighbours and the absolute social segregation of the white and black races of South Africa, which latter alone – while preventing the inauguration of a generation of half-castes – will keep and maintain the purity of our race and colour, both of which we are as proud as our European educators are of theirs.

I have not yet had reason to regret the adoption of this policy. I have a long list of exchanges among the English, Dutch and Native press of South Africa (daily, weekly and otherwise) and this policy has often been commented on by many of the Progressive press[81] and some of the Dutch.

As the majority of the aboriginal Natives of the Orange River Colony are Bechuanas, the paper has a large circulation throughout the Colony. To mention one instance, Thaba Nchu district alone takes more than 600 copies of every issue. The readers of that district have repeatedly asked me why Government Notices and Proclamations, having reference to them, are not promulgated in the columns of their own paper, by their Government, as is done by the Government of the Cape Colony and His Honour the Resident Commissioner of the Protectorate. I have, after receipt of these complaints, addressed an application to the Native Department, and one to the Honourable the Colonial Secretary at Bloemfontein; and as I have not received an answer to any of them I now crave leave to most respectfully request that Your Excellency may kindly oblige the Natives under your administration, by directing such instructions as will place *Koranta ea Becoana* among the authorized mediums for the promulgation of Government Notices, addressed to the Native inhabitants of the Orange River Colony.

I beg to remain,
Your Excellency's humble Servant
Silas Molema

Office of the Koranta
P.O. Box 11
Main Street
Mafeking

No record of any reply to this letter has been found. Minutes attached to the letter in the government files, however, suggested that a reply be sent to Silas Molema to the effect that whilst the Bechuana Gazette could not be considered an 'official' medium for the promulgation of government notices, there was nothing to stop notices being sent to the paper for insertion as and when considered appropriate by the authorities.

20

Article, *Bechuana Gazette*, 23 September 1903

We have often heard it asserted by Native travellers, just from the Transvaal, that a rooted animosity for the British authority lurks within the breasts of the ex-burghers of that colony, and that if they could find any instrument likely to overthrow this power they will not hesitate to use it. For our part we have always doubted the truth of such statements but here we have it hot from a Boer general's lips. In giving evidence before the Labour Commission[82] on the 15th inst. General Louis Botha[83] advocated the breaking up of the Basutoland and Swaziland Native reserves, placing compulsion on the owners to pay rent.

We are satisfied that the quixotic proposal is not so much due to a vaulting ambition on Mr Botha's part to disinherit the Natives, as to coax the British to tempt providence indirectly. Having failed to 'drive the British into the sea' by force of arms, the general plans this neat provocative to fan the flame of black humanity against the crown, under the guise of a desire to help a solution of the so-called labour difficulty.

Our conclusions would not be so decisive had Mr Botha been a little less specific. But he mentions as instances the Basutos and the Swazis – two powerful nations that were never subdued by any living power – and innocently requests the British government to dispossess them of their reservations. He goes further. The provoquont shall not only be limited to those territories but should be applicable to all Natives from the coast to the Rand. There is the whole case in a nutshell, and he is intellectually blind who misconstrues such a clear and outspoken statement. But the suggestion is too temerarious and foolhardy for any British official to entertain, and the admirers of Mr Botha's leadership of the Afrikaner cause in the Transvaal must feel disappointed to find that a proposal so dangerous should have found room in his scheme to solve the labour question.

In another column we reproduce from the *Diamond Fields Advertiser* a valuable contribution on the labour discussion, from the pen of Mr Russell Harding[84] of Kimberley. In the words of a supporter, in a subsequent issue of the same paper, Mr Harding has 'not only hit the right nail on the head, but he has driven it home'. We have heard of similar disclosures being made in Johannesburg but strange to relate their authors have invariably failed to substantiate them when called upon to do so by representatives of the press.

Mr Harding mentions many startling exceptions taken by the Labour Association[85] to the nature and looks of the labourers supplied by him, and he is prepared to hand over his correspondence to the Labour Commission. We sincerely trust that he will be true to his word, as we are prepared to support him to the presence of the commissioners.

We are amazed to learn that one of the Association's peculiarities is an affection for Bechuana labourers while its *modus operandi* proves the contrary. The mines of this and adjacent colonies (excepting only those of the Rand) advertise in the Native papers. The Association's local representatives will admit that they never found as many labourers in Bechuanaland and the Orange River Colony as during last autumn when the Transvaal government (through our columns) did the advertising; but the Association never stirred. And we have before us a letter from Koffyfontein which asks us to temporarily withdraw their advertisement until they have some vacancies at their mines. It had 'answered so well that our compounds are full at present'. And it is the third letter, received by us during the last two months, to the same effect.

For the Association to profess to make a special hobby of Bechuana labourers, and not to advertise for them in the Bechuana's *only* paper sounds as queer as if they had told us that 'black was white'.

In fact there is no evidence that General Botha's recommendations before the Labour Commission were designed to provoke Africans into rebellion: his motive was rather more straightforward, namely to increase the supply of African labour, for white farmers particularly, by preventing Africans in Basutoland and Swaziland from being able to make an independent living.

21
Article, *Bechuana Gazette*, 23 September 1903

We often wondered if the commissioners were particularly anxious to hear Native witnesses. But we must contradict the reverend chairman[86] when he charges somebody with failing to ask 'a single Native to give evidence before the Labour Commission'. The Commission advertised in the *Imvo*[87] and the *Koranta*, asking the readers of those two papers to voluntarily come forward and give evidence, at the same time offering to defray their reasonable travelling expenses; and if the reverend gentleman reads none of those two papers, then he is totally unfit to give evidence on behalf of anybody, and should not blame others for his personal dereliction of duty.

Thus far the more correct conclusion is that the commissioners have a just cause for complaint against Native lethargy; and until we hear of the rejection by the Commission of a qualified Native witness, the leaders of the black races (including the reverend complainant) stand condemned, in our opinion, of a most callous indulgence to the welfare of their people, and a stoic inertness to assisting the authorities to clear up at least one of the thousand and one race complications in the political air of this country, even when the government disburses the cost of invitation and transportation.

22
Article, *Bechuana Gazette*, 14 October 1903

Although the Bond[88] is putting forward no candidates for that constituency, it would appear that Vryburg is going to be the scene of a hot contest. Some of the candidates have already circularized the electors pressing their claims on the electorate for alleged services rendered. But, to make a serviceable choice, a liberal voter should remember that, in such important matters, it would be folly to act the selfish.

There are three sections of the community, viz., English, Dutch and Native. Socially, the former two are one, and the last named separate; thus the three sections are metaphorically fused into two distinct parts – white and black – but the whole is politically inseparable. The white race can no more do without the black, and the black without the white, than the right hand can do without the left. In fact, if all the Natives of this country had the option and they were willing to migrate to the planet of Mars, the whites would stop them even if they had to use machine-guns, just the same as the Natives would do, were the whites to rise *en masse* and attempt to leave for Europe.

So you cannot possibly do justice to yourself without considering the welfare of the whole community. Choose two staunch imperialists who are going to work for the progress of the land. Vryburg has had sufficient sleep already. And a pair of hard-working men are wanted to support Mr Smith from the lower house. We have spent much time and thought over this matter, and after comparing the records of the different candidates before the electorate, we have come to the conclusion that the first man is FLYNN. We have got enough reasons to fill more than a whole issue of this paper; but we will enlarge hereon subsequently. At present we are busy in correspondence with the oldest inhabitants, to ascertain about the second-best man, as you know that we must have two. In the meanwhile take this as a hint and sign a requisition for FLYNN.

23
Article, 'The late Chief Wessels Montsioa', *Bechuana Gazette*, 16 December 1903

A great Bechuana departed this life when Wessels Montsioa, Paramount Chief of the Barolong, breathed his last.

The deceased chief was born at Selokoida in the Protectorate in the year 1856. As a youth he took very little interest in politics as the probabilities of his ever succeeding his father were very slight. One after the other of his brothers were killed in one or another of the bloody struggles between the Stellaland and Goshen filibusters and the Barolong, the forces of the enemy being subsequently strengthened by the addition of the Marico burghers against this little village, which was besieged on several occasions for years before the advent of the British. When Sir Charles Warren's Imperial expedition proclaimed a Protectorate over the country in 1885, an end was put to these struggles, the oldest son of Chief Montsioa being Kebalepile. He was recognised by all – British, Boer and black – as a valiant chieftain who would make a creditable successor to his dearly beloved and highly respected father. The popular disappointment was bitter when, during the autumn of 1891, Kebalepile died after a brief illness, during the lifetime of his father; and Wessels became heir to the chieftainship which he attained in October 1896 when he father died.

He had a very quiet reign, being laid up for weeks at a time by a gouty knee. He could not [...]* (and during the siege the command of the Barolong levies was held by Lekoko as Acting Paramount Chief under the military). His health has since been failing, and during the best part of last year he was laid up at the farm near Ramatlhabama where he died peacefully on the afternoon of the 2nd instant, after ruling the Barolong for 7 years and a month.

Deceased visited England in 1895, accompanied by his secretary, Mr Stephen Lefenya, and attended the reception of the Prince and Princess of Wales in Cape Town, with Josiah Motshegare, Tau Tauana and a few other headmen, in 1901.

The funeral
When the message of the chief's death reached Mafeking, the councillors at once proceeded to Tlapeng and fetched the body, which reached the stadt in a

---

*   Some words are missing in the original newspaper article. Plaatje clearly intended to convey that Montsioa was unable to carry out his duties as Paramount Chief effectively.

wagonette drawn by twelve red bullocks followed by wagons, cars and mounted men. The arrival was heralded by the pitiful lamentations of the women which sounded dolefully from every quarter of the stadt. It was a sorrowful dirge: in fact nothing like it was heard since one afternoon in April 1900, when ex-General Snyman sent a message into the garrison to say that every one of a band of young Barolong raiders (which turned up on the following day, with the loss of only one killed) had been massacred by his burghers.

Arrangements were at once made for the burial to take a place at 3 p.m. At that hour the coffin was carried to the church, the cross-shaped building being packed to the doors, several hundred of people remaining outside, not able to gain admission.

At that time a thick cloud ascended the skies and when right over the town it burst forth into a heavy deluge of hailstones and water which soon flooded the whole place and continued for nearly two hours. Many Europeans in the town intending to proceed to the funeral had to turn back to shelter and some of them to stay away altogether as the flood that rushed down afterwards, at the rate of 12 miles an hour, was 'unfordable'. The magistrate was very near the stadt with Mrs Green when their carriage stopped in a sluit which had become a perfect river – to turn back being as dangerous as to go forward. Carcases of sheep and goats coming down the stream, got mixed up with the carriage wheels and contents of the butts near 'Morena's' cart that night. It was only with some difficulty that he managed to extricate the cart, and come back.

Thousands of Natives and Europeans thronged the houses and verandahs near the chief's circle, separated by the rain in the air and the running streams on the ground. They knew not what went on in church and it was impossible to ascertain that the body had ever left the house for the chapel. Thousands remained indoors and took it for granted that the funeral service was postponed for a day as a burial under the circumstances looked like an impossibility.

When the first shower came down the water was drained off by a trench of watercourse dug around the grave. During one of the brief intervals it was found that the grave was filled to overflowing by water and hailstones that fell direct from the clouds, which had to be baled out.

In the meantime the funeral service had been completed in the church and when the shower was lighted the crowd followed the cortège knee-deep – and much deeper – across the streams that rushed between the huts and the remains of the late chief were conveyed to its last resting place in his late cattle kraal where, according to the custom of the tribe, his father and mother

Wessels Montsioa, Chief of the Tshidi Barolong, 1896-1903: 'He had a very quiet reign,' Plaatje wrote, 'and died peacefully on 2 September 1903.'

lie buried. The service was conducted by the Reverend Supt. Geo Weavind, assisted by the Reverend Molema Moshoela of the Methodist church, in the presence of many people, though more were kept back by the waters.

Amongst those present were His Honour Ralph C. Williams, CMG (Resident Commissioner of the Bechuanaland Protectorate), who braved the storm, drove to church and joined the procession, from there accompanied by Mrs Williams and an escort of the Bechuanaland Protectorate Mounted Police (European and Native) under Lieut. C. Hannay; S. Minchin, esq., JP; Messrs Joseph and W.M. Gerrans, E. and J. Rowland, S. Sargent , Capt C. Goodyear, the principal headmen and councillors, Chief Massibi of Jan Massibi's, and many ladies and gentlemen.

The pall-bearers were chieftains Badirile, Joshua, Silas, Officer and Ephraim Molema; Andrew, Joseph and William Saane, Tiego Taoana, and others of the chief's kinsmen.

The rain

Such heavy rains as fell that afternoon, after the severe drought, came like a comforter to the people and is regarded all round as a good omen. When Chief Montsioa's first wife died in 1891 and her son, Kebalepile, shortly after, their death was followed by incessant rains. In fact the Molopo formerly was but a streamlet. Its waters ran during the rainy season – December to April – and ceased to flow in May. Crops were so plentiful that year that grain sold at 5s per bag. That this is going to be the case this occasion everybody hopes, though nobody knows. The chief, we are informed, died a peaceful death and the floods bore eloquent testimony. The strangest part of this rain is that it only fell within a perimeter of 15 miles round the town. Travellers from Zeerust, the north and the west were surprised when they approached the town in the evening to find Mafeking in flood. At Molimola they could not make out what filled the river.

24

Constitution of the South African Native Press Association, January 1904[89]

This copy of the constitution of the South African Native Press Association was sent by Plaatje for information to the Principal Native Commissioner, Orange River Colony, on 1 February 1904. Plaatje and Peregrino seem to have been the main instigators of the association, which may well have been modelled in part on the Negro Press Association in the United States (Plaatje had been in correspondence with J.E. Bruce, one of its leaders, at this time). The Association does not seem to have survived actively beyond 1904, but it nevertheless represented a pioneering attempt to help formulate the notion of 'native opinion'. See also Plaatje's remarks about the objectives of the Association in his evidence to the South African Native Affairs Commission, pp. 91-96.

The South African Native Newspaper Press Association
Motto: Defence, not Defiance

Name
1. This Association shall be known as the South African Native Press Association.

Objects
2. The aim and objects of the South African Native Press Association shall be:
   (a) To form a combination for mutual defence and protection.
   (b) The conservation of the best and legitimate interests of the Native People's Newspaper Press of South Africa.

Principles
3. The principles of this association will be, to encourage and to seek to aid all who are engaged in the laudable work of diffusing knowledge and in legitimate educational work among the Natives of South Africa, to seek to cooperate with the Government in the solution of the many difficult race problems by which they are confronted, and to help to bring about understanding, and to establish amiable relations between the various Governments of South Africa, and the Native population.

Eligibility
4. The membership of the South African Native Press Association shall (with the view of avoiding complications, and preventing any misconstruction of the duties of the promoters), be confined:
   (a) To Native Africans who are British Subjects, and engaged as Editors, Publishers or Compositors, on newspapers devoted to the interests of the Native races of Africa.
   (b) Any teacher in a recognized school, any regularly ordained pastor, of a recognized church, evangelists, or others engaged in the promotion of educational work, and in the propagation of religion, and who possess the qualifications of eligibility referred to above, may become members of this Association.

Officers

The officers of the South African Native Newspaper Press Association shall consist of a President, Vice-President, Secretary, and Treasurer.

President: Mr A.K. Soga, Ed., *Izwi* , East London.[90]
Vice President: Mr F.Z.S. Peregrino, Ed., *South African Spectator*, Cape Town.[91]
Treasurer: Chief Molema, Mafeking.
Secretary: S.T. Plaatje, Editor, *Koranta ea Becoana*, Mafeking.

Central Office: Office of the *South African Spectator*, Cape Town.

25

Article, 'The High Commissioner', *Bechuana Gazette*, 23 March 1904

The most abused man in South Africa at the present time is Viscount Milner of St James and Cape Town.[92] One could stomach these abuses in silence when expressed by organs and writers of pro-Boer proclivities; but when an Imperial organ, like the Kimberley *Free Press* for instance, declares that he has been 'tried and found wanting', one wonders where it will all lead to. Convinced as we are that His Excellency is perfectly able to take care of himself, we cannot pose as his defender; but we would like to know of any one British statesman that was ever entrusted with a task of the magnitude of the present problem before Lord Milner.

Given a staff, seemingly of the most British Englishmen with whose assistance it was expected he would effect a re-settlement of the country, it is perplexing to find that after all, his lordship could not have been more at sea, had he been sent out to pacify the Native Affairs Department, including numbers of the most rustic malcontents displaying characteristic anxiousness in instilling contempt for British rule in the Native mind, by carrying out their duties with undue excess and convincing the latter that the Dutch code was preferable to the present. What with disappointed malcontents, who, instead of bringing British honesty entered the new colonies determined to out-Boer the Boer by revolutionizing matters and to turn the Transvaal into 'a white man's country'.

Nature and nature's God has painted this country black, and any mortal could easier cause the sun to rise in the west and set in the east than make the Transvaal a white man's country. The Native, recognizing the acknowledged benefits accruing from the modern scramble for Africa – a boon that was not even dreamed of in the philosophy of Downing Street – are contented to live with and assist the immigrants to amass riches. This contentedness has remained inviolate, although the behaviour of the immigrant forces us to the conclusion that if he discovered the means to exterminate the blacks he would not hesitate to use it on the masses, taking good care, however, to leave a sufficiency of menial tools to sustain his indolence; yes, laziness, although he makes the most noise, and the world is apt to believe that the truth is the other way about.

What's up with them?

The divisional bench of the new colonies has in many instances not scrupled to lay aside the law if only to press the heavy yoke of oppression on the black man's neck. The railway administration was signalised by the most brutal tyranny, in all cases where black passengers sought to make use of their tickets, until the chief traffic manager shouted, 'Stop!' It should be remembered that not every department is presided over by a Hoy.[93] Men in authority have deliberately misinterpreted the statutes and carried out one law for the white subject and another for the black, so that while at Government House a policy is being shaped for the proper government of the conquered territory, paid servants of Government House outside its walls are 'making things hum'. It required your sympathy as much as at present. He had your support in halcyon times when he did not need it, but now that his cruiser has struck troubled waters he needs your assistance all the more as forsooth, *on connait l'ami au besoin.**

We want a black consul

When the Native question gets solved, the Transvaal political problem will have advanced fifty per cent. We have very few representatives as against the army of misrepresentors. And the High Commissioner needs a black adviser on the black question. One who would report things with his pen and not with his prejudices. Testimony obtained directly from Native sources passes through so many channels that when they finally land at Government House they have undergone so many changes and alterations that they scarcely represent the original version. Somebody should be appointed to supply the High Commissioner with the news of the black man, first hand.

There is nothing new or extraordinary in such a request. It has solved the problem in the British colonies in West Africa, and the antipodes. French, German and American governments carry out their administration by the aid

---

* French: 'One knows the friend in need.'

of black statesmen. To come nearer home, the Afrikander Bond did remarkably well during the last election; considering the wholesale disfranchisement of their supporters[94] they should have had a minority of 12 instead of 4. And surely if the Progressives in the Eastern Province had not at the last moment awakened to the fact that the South African Party[95] were having tremendous successes through the use of black men to further their principles [they would not have secured so many African votes]. We repeat that if the Progressives had not realised this and adopted similar tactics (which adoption we regret to say was undertaken very reluctantly by the Progressives), Mr Merriman[96] would have been premier. And we would recommend the same remedy for the Transvaal chaos.

26

Editorial, 'The Central South African Railways', *Bechuana Gazette*, 30 March 1904

We publish elsewhere the proceedings of an interview with the traffic manager of the Orange River Colony.[97] Our Bloemfontein correspondent informs us that the interview has done a lot of good. 'From the following day Native passengers moved about the station with the freedom of folks who were entitled to the use of what they paid for, and for which they hold tickets. The booking clerk at the Bloemfontein station is civility itself'; and so mote it be.

In thanking Mr Barrett for this change, we must draw the attention of the management to the fact that in all probability there are a number of black sheep in the railway flock, and that not many miles away from Springfontein. We have heard for a long time that Natives dread taking return tickets. They complain that (presumably) the return half is always given them on completion of the forward journey. On resuming the return journey, this return (?) half would be taken away from them with a 'no good'! We tried to make enquiry, but have only found one instance where a passenger discovered that the wrong half was given to him. He was fortunate enough to discover this, and he returned it to the department asking for a refund of the extra fare paid in consequence of this mistake. Departmental investigations disclosed the fact that the return half, collected in error by the official, *had since been used.*

Springfontein is apparently a fine field for dishonest officials (or someone in the guise of an official). Third-class passengers (mostly Natives) are often detained in this station for about four hours. Whilst in waiting there, a ticket examiner would call round on an inspecting business. Two or three Natives in the crowd would be told that their tickets are 'no good' and they would be made to pay their fares over again.

It is undoubtedly the misfortune of these Natives that they cannot read English, but it is certainly not their fault; and they deserve the protection of the administration from the ravages of unscrupulous impostors, who take mean advantage of their ignorance.

In the interview above referred to, the traffic manager struck the right note when he expressed his belief that Natives have no desire for the company of Europeans in railway compartments, as *vice versa*. There appears to be an idea abroad that Natives seek not only equal privileges but that they, in addition, want to rub shoulders with white passengers. And we take this opportunity to inform everybody that no Native (except he be crazy) has a desire for the company of the whites. We seek not to sit and exchange cigars with you. Unlike you. We say this without difficulty, as we believe that you will find it difficult to explain your inconsistency. You tolerate the presence of a black servant in your first-class compartment, while you cannot stomach his presence when he is nobody's menial. We have no desire for your company in a first-class or any other compartment, whether you are a servant or a master; and it will be interesting to know from you, the particular charm possessed by the black servant, which renders his company more delectable than that of the black gentleman.

27
Editorial, 'What are equal rights?', *Bechuana Gazette*, 20 April 1904

When a fellow resides in Mafeking, he will hear very little about this *thing* or *things*, and although it is never preached, he will find that it is practised to perfection. On going down to Kimberley he will experience a bit of difference; but not much worth speaking about. On going to the Eastern Province, in the direction of Port Elizabeth, he will suspect some humbug in this doctrine for there will arise a change, decidedly in favour of the crank and opposed to the wishes of right-thinking people, who wish to apply the term in its proper sense, and he will find that its practice is somewhat theoretical. But when he gets to East London, he will find the white people trumpetting it forth, but practising the direct opposite, and notwithstanding the fact that it is preached by everybody, the very suggestion of its practise is repugnant to the ideas of both Bond and Progressive thinkers.

For this and sundry reasons a Natal contemporary[98] was obliged to say that the phrase might be reduced to 'equal rights for all civilized men south of the Orange', and we may add – 'to say nothing of the Vaal, but let alone the Zambesi'. The *Native Eye*,[99] on the one hand, thinks that the rank and file of the Progressive Party sing this chorus without an idea as to its meaning; *Izwi*, on the other hand, is of the opinion that the *Eye* knows not what it is thinking about. We ourselves are benighted, and would be glad indeed to be enlightened on the point. What are *equal rights*, in East London and Johannesburg, anyway?

28
Letter to Attorney-General, Transvaal, 13 May 1904[100]

The Attorney-General, [101] Pretoria

Sir,

Abuse by South African Constabulary

I have the honour to report that on passing Lichtenburg (the first magistracy from Bechuanaland) on the 30th *ultimo* on my way here, I called at the police station to ascertain if my Cape passport wanted renewal by Transvaal officials before I could proceed with it. Standing near the door of the police station I could see a policeman writing at a table near the door. Further in the room there was seated a man in the constabulary, with three stars on his shoulder. I spoke to the policeman from the door. I think he said,'take off your hat'. Of this I am not quite sure, however, for just then the man with the stars yelled at me, in a furious manner which, apart from my personal injury in consequence, would amount in the Cape Colony to a distinct contravention of the Police Offences Act, 27, of 1882.[102]

In order that there should be no misunderstanding I stepped aside of the door and noted his abuses of me in my pocket book, from which I now copy them as follows:

> 'Take off your hat off you damned, bloody, dirty black swine!'
> 'And always wait till you are spoken to!!'

I may add for your information that I am not quite sure whether or not I am 'damned', but of the following I am quite certain, viz., (1) I had no blood stains on me, at the time; (2) I was not dirty, while I need hardly add that (3) I

Sir Richard Solomon, Attorney-General of the Transvaal from 1902-1906, to whom Plaatje complained about his treatment by the police in Lichtenburg in 1904.

was not a pig. I transacted business with half-a-dozen businessmen in Lichtenburg, directly before and after this episode, none of whom objected to my appearance. Not having an amplitude of time at my disposal I waited – but not 'till spoken to'. I had perforce to bide my time with the enquiry until I reached Klerksdorp, where it came off satisfactorily unaccompanied by thunder.

I may also add that it is unnecessary to make 'my hat' the *raison d'etre* of an official's indulgence in a butt of vulgarity at my expense. I have been in police offices, and also in the private offices of heads of similar departments, in this, the Cape and Orange River Colonies and never gave cause for such extraordinary treatment as I know exactly when and where to 'take off my hat'.

I think, Sir, you will agree with me that it is lamentable that a stranger should be treated kindly by the villagers and that he should regret ever having set his foot at a public office, and for this reason I trust that you will enquire into the matter.

Yours obediently
Sol T. Plaatje

P.O. Box 185
Johannesburg
May 13th 1904

Sir Richard Solomon forwarded Plaatje's complaint to the Inspector-General, South African Constabulary, his private secretary commenting, 'Sir Richard feels sure that you will enquire into the matter and if the story told is true deal with the officer capable of using language such as is reported.' No record could be found to reveal what, if anything, happened subsequently.

29
Article, *Bechuana Gazette*, 22 June 1904

There is a movement on foot to start an agitation on the Vaal River diggings, for the repeal of the new Liquor Proclamation, no. 147 of 1904. It is to be hoped that the Government will not lend an ear to so monstrous a demand, as the ravages of the white man's fire water, when brought in contact with the black man's stomach, are too well known. Our only regret is that the proclamation does not go far enough. It provides for the prohibition of the supply of the damning drug to Natives, but the Native voter may still obtain it as the franchise has placed him on a political equality with the white man.[103] Nothing pleases us better than to find the government refrain from applying class measures to the civilized Native voter. Viscount Milner has instructed the South African Constabulary to practise this preferential treatment in dealing with civilized Natives in the streets and on the railway carriages. This only renders the labour districts of the Transvaal habitable for the civilized Native; and, we are sure, it will wake black humanity from its present educational lethargy, and keep them a bit less apathetic when they are face to face with serious progressive problems.

But an exception is really essential when we have to deal with a vile stuff that was accursed as long ago as in the days of Noah. An equivalent to the Bechuanaland Proclamation, no. 64, of 1889 is what is necessary for the whole colony. Here, voter or no voter is debarred from its procurement by serious pains and penalties, except for medicinal (?) purposes, and that even is more than enough.

One of the most glorious sights in the city of Johannesburg can be seen at the Rand Club and similar institutions. Lords of creation drugging their lilywhite selves, with that product of their own civilization, whilst their sable brethren are denied a similar process. Re-cross the border and you will find instead of a sober industrious coloured man, in many instances a drunken wretch, scarcely fit to live. Oh, for a bit of martial law! During the reign of the sword our people were hard-working, sober, thrifty and honest. No sooner were the doors of the bars thrown open and we were pushed back for 40 years. No! we have too much rum already and don't require any more, even if it were to please Vaal River diggers.

Plaatje was a committed teetotaller. In Kimberley and in Mafeking (where being drunk and disorderly was one of the commonest offences in the magistrate's court at which he interpreted) he had witnessed at first hand the devastating effects that liquor could have on his people. 'Sobriety', indeed, was one of the four principles to which the Bechuana Gazette *declared itself committed, and it was an issue that was to concern Plaatje for the rest of his life.*

30

Article, 'Whae's yer pass?', Bechuana Gazette, 13 July 1904

One of the plagues with which South Africa, of all countries on the globe, is cursed, is the sickening humbug which they call a pass. The man who first conceived it – bless his pious heart! – wanted to stop vagrancy and stock-thieving among Natives; but his followers have rendered it suitable for every kind of emergency, and it is now applied for (1) the degradation of respectable black men; (2) maintenance in office of white men on Native money; (3) the vulgar demonstration of European superiority, and (4) fifteen different purposes such as, by some administrations, a means of raising revenue, etc., etc.

Mr C.K. Mokgothu of Johannesburg draws attention to one form of the administration of the reprehensible system, which, if it does not amount to it, at least borders very dangerously near to robbery. If a Native asks for a monthly pass say on the 29th of June, he is furnished with one for which he has to pay the monthly fee of 2s. Of course, it is not printed in his language but as the 'speckled sheet', as he identifies it by general appearances, is given by a government official, he is simply satisfied. This Native would be arrested soon after the 1st of July (three days afterwards) for being minus his badge of degradation, and sent to prison, the one in his possession having expired with the month of June.

In other colonies a pass is obtained on any day of the month for any number of days, and there is nothing in the laws of the Transvaal to entitle anyone to this noxious breach of equity at the expense of the Natives. And it is for the Native Affairs Department to see that this injustice is promptly put a stop to.

The benefit of the pass law is that thousands of useful, unoffending black men, than whom His Majesty has no more law-abiding subjects, are daily sent to prison without having done any harm to anybody, and they die as regular goal-birds even though they had never during their lifetime dipped the tips of their fingers in the cup of criminality. It is revolting to anyone who comes from districts like Mafeking for instance, where the jailer has no such share and where revenue is raised by honest and lawful means. The writer met an inhabitant of this place in Johannesburg last month, who looked at one of the 'blessings' of the pass law and said: 'Well, if this is British then our colony is certainly not'. Here, no such horrors are licensed and in no spot on earth do whites and blacks live as peacefully together as they do in Mafeking. And we are sure that if there is any Native unrest in existence, it is the outcome of the callous and oppressive administration of the pass law.

31

Evidence of S. T. Plaatje to South African Native Affairs Commission, 12 September 1904[104]

The South African Native Affairs Commission was a large-scale enquiry which took evidence from many hundreds of witnesses, black and white, throughout the four

South African colonies and the High Commission territories between 1903 and 1905. Chaired by Sir Godfrey Lagden, Governor-General of the Transvaal, the Commission enquired into various aspects of 'native affairs' 'in view of the coming federation of the South African colonies', concentrating particularly on questions of political rights and landholding. Its report, published in 1905, reflected a growing consensus in governing circles in favour of segregation, and many of its recommendations provided a blueprint for legislation enacted after the Union of South Africa in 1910 – in particular the Natives' Land Act of 1913.

Plaatje had earlier (Bechuana Gazette, 21 October 1903) criticised the constitution and membership of the South African Native Affairs Commission as unrepresentative, and argued that its membership should have included 'some prominent natives', that the Bechuanaland Protectorate was unrepresented on the Commission, and that it should have been chaired by a judge on the grounds that such a person was likely to be impartial.

37,698. *Mr Sloley*: Do you belong to the Native Press Association? – Yes.

37,699. What are the objects of the Native Press Association? – It is simply to improve the press of the Natives generally.

37,700. Did you go to the last meeting? – No, I was not able to go at the time.

37,701. Who writes the articles in your paper? – I do.

37,702. The English? – Yes.

37,703. And the Sechuana also? – Yes.

37,704. You have no white writers? – No.

37,705. What are your views on the franchise? – Just as the franchise is.

37,706. What are your views as to the representation of Natives, about which the chief was asked, that is as to Natives electing their own members? – Separate representation?

37,707. Yes? – They say, 'The proof of the pudding is in the eating.' I have never seen it done, and do not know how it would work amongst our people.

37,708. Do you think the present system works well? – Yes; I have seen it work, and I have not seen any harm in the present system.

37,709. Do you not think that the time of election stirs up hostile feelings between black and white people? – No, not in these parts – from Kimberley upwards.

37,710. Did you vote yourself? – Yes; and I have only seen elections between this and Kimberley, and I have never seen any hostility between the whites and blacks.

37,711. You did not find, when you went to record your vote, that there was any difficulty in getting to the proper office and recording your vote? – No; at that time everyone was only too anxious that every voter should record his vote.

37,712. You have separate political meetings for Natives addressed by the candidates? – The candidates usually go out to our meetings and those of us who understand English attend the white people's meetings too, because at our meetings we use interpreters; we attend nearly every one of the meetings that are held by the white people in their halls.

37,713. What attitude do your people take towards the African Methodist Episcopal Church?[105] – I have not seen it do any good and it has certainly not done any harm. That is as far as I know.

37,714. What are your views on land tenure? – What land tenure, individual?

37,715. There are two systems, the individual and tribal? – The tribal one works all right up here, though I do not know how it works in other parts. For instance, anyone in the district of Mafeking can go out and buy a farm. Some Natives do hold farms, which they have paid for, and there are four or five farms which were bought together, belonging to the tribe, and registered in the name of the chief; and there is this Native location in the Cape Colony. Besides that, there is the Native Reserve in Bechuanaland Protectorate, where our people also have land, and they also hold land in the Protectorate – farms given to different headmen by the late Chief Montsioa before he died.

37,716. *Captain Dickson:* You have written rather strongly in your paper about the treatment of Natives in the mines; can you give us any individual cases?[106] – In the mines?

37,717. I think you mentioned our chairman's name and said if he could not find cases you could. – There were some people who came here and made complaints about bad treatment they had received but they have been redressed since.

37,718. You took up a challenge from our chairman and said you could find a case if he could not. – There were some at that time, but they have been redressed since.

37,719. All the cases you have written of in your paper have been redressed. – Yes, it was at the time the statement appeared in the paper that Sir Godfrey Lagden in the Transvaal said he did not find a single case in six months of grievance on the part of the Natives. There were at the time some of these Natives in Mafeking coming over from the Transvaal and one gentlemen read in the paper that we could tell him of some cases, and he took up the matter and the matter was thoroughly gone into, and the cases of the Natives were taken up and they got their money back.

37,720. All the cases have been redressed? – All those I knew of.

37,721. Have you altered the attitude you had a little while ago towards the Ethiopian Church; you wrote rather strongly a little time ago? – It was against the individuals that I took up the attitude, not against the Church.

37,722. You had very strong antipathy towards many of the leading individuals in the Church at the time? – Not leading individuals, ministers of the Church.

37,723. It is the ministers of the Church you have antipathy against? – Yes.

37,724. You hold the same opinions as you held six months ago? – Yes; I told the bishop that some time ago when he was here.[107]

37,725. You think that several ministers of the Church are doing a great deal of harm? – Yes, a great deal of harm.

37,726. *Mr Campbell:* Do you think that a polygamist, say with a dozen wives, should be allowed the franchise? – If the man is otherwise qualified I do not see why he should be deprived of the franchise because he has more than one wife.

37,727. You do not think the law ought to be altered to stop a man who has such a lot of wives voting? – I do not think it ought to be altered if the man is otherwise qualified.

37,728. You do not think so? – No.

37,729. *Mr Samuelson:* Have you a Native Vigilance Association here? – Not here; anything that crops up, or anything affecting the Natives here, we first advise the chief about and ask him to take steps in the matter.

37,730. Have you any Native Political Association? – No, excepting the Press Association.

37,731. What is the name of your paper? – The *Koranta ea Becoana* (*Bechuana Gazette*).

37,732. Are you married? – Yes.

37,733. Were you married by Christian rites? – Yes.

37,734. Under what law is the estate of Natives married by Christian rites administered? – Under the laws of the colony. The minister solemnizes the marriage and it is registered in the Colonial Office.

37,735. When a man who is married by Christian rites dies, under what law is his property administered? – If he has made no will his eldest son is the heir.

37,736. It is administered under Native law? – Yes.

37,737. He can make a will depriving his children of his property and willing it to somebody else? – He can do that if he likes as far as that goes, but they have not generally gone in for that on a large scale.

37,738. Can they do it under Native law pure and simple? – I do not think so. I have never seen it done.

37,739. You think whilst Natives cling to their customs, their usages, their polygamy and their 'bogadi'* they should be entitled to ask for and to have the highest privilege of civilized nations – the franchise? – While he has his obligations to the state as well as any other civilized man he is entitled to it.

37,740. What do you mean by industrial training; what do you include in that term? – In the same way as was explained by the chief here a little while ago, and also with regard to ploughing the land and also advice as to the best way of putting their produce on the market and so forth.

37,741. What do you mean by industrial training? – I mean that they should be taught any kind of work, agriculture and everything else.

37,742. Building, carpentry, saddlery, and so forth? – Yes.

37,743. Is there much superstition amongst your people? – Yes, but it is dying out now, like polygamy. There are very few people going in for polygamy.

37,744. Are many of your people being trained in the use or practice of European medicines? – No. There is one young man in the training institution at Lovedale, where they teach them how to dispense medicine.

37,745. Do you think it is a good thing and that it would get rid of a good deal of superstition with regard to medicine men? – Yes, I think it is a very good thing.

37,746. *Mr Thompson*: Are you a Barolong? – Yes.

37,747. Were your father and mother? – Yes.

37,748. You have answered your cross-examination very fearlessly and well. I want you to answer me equally honestly on the question of the franchise. Do you think that all the Natives who have the franchise among the Barolongs are fitted for it and can use it intelligently and honestly? – There are not many who have it; there are only one hundred who have it, which is the number of those who are able to use it honestly.

37,749. Those that have it can use it honestly? – Yes.

37,750. And have as intelligent a view of the franchise as the chief? – A better view of it than the chief, some of them.

---

*   Tswana: 'brideprice', the custom among the Tswana (with equivalents among a number of other African peoples in southern Africa) of the bridegroom paying cattle to the family of a bride on her marriage.

37,751. *Mr Stanford*: It seems the chief[108] is under a wrong impression with regard to the appeal? – Yes, he was making a mistake.

37,752. The people know they have an appeal? – Yes, the people do, although as a matter of fact no one has appealed as yet.

37,753. They accept his decisions? – Yes.

37,754. Legally they have an appeal? – But according to the Act they have no appeal in civil cases.

37,755. Yes, there is an appeal in civil cases. – I mean in civil cases his jurisdiction is exclusive, although criminal cases can go before the Magistrate before they go to him.

37,756. Section 33 of the Act says: 'It shall be lawful for any person party to any dispute civil or criminal before any Native chief exercising his jurisdiction under the provisions of sections 31 and 32 of these regulations to appeal from the decision of such chief,' etc., 'provided that in all cases appeal shall be from the decision of any such court as herein provided to the Chief Magistrate.' – His jurisdiction is exclusive.

37,757. It says so in the first instance but it goes on as I have read. – That had escaped my notice. [...]

32

Article, 'Native affairs', *Bechuana Gazette*, 21 September 1904

The Inter-Colonial Commission on Native Affairs sat here last week. They took the evidence of Chief Khama of the Bamangwato, Chief Badirile of the Barolong, and also that of our editor. The commission sat in camera; but there is nothing very shocking in the commonplace questions put to the witnesses, or anything that would nauseate the ears of any listener, however sensitive.

Sir Godfrey Lagden presided. With the exception of the Protectorate, every South African colony and dependency is represented, amongst the representatives being Mr Sloley, under whose administration the Basuto are justly contented; Sir Thomas Scanlen (formerly of the Cape now of Rhodesia); Capt. J. Quayle Dixon (principal Native Commissioner of the Orange River Colony), etc, etc. The Cape is represented by Colonel Stanford (Cape Secretary to the Native Affairs Department), and the versatile, yet none the less determined, Matebele Thompson.[109]

The Commissioners came here unawares and took us by surprise. Our editor was only able to attend at a sacrifice; some of our friends who were prepared to give evidence only heard about them when they were leaving. If the commissioners wanted useful evidence, they surely should have notified the public about their coming. The commissioners arrived on Wednesday night, took evidence on Thursday, had a good look round the place on Friday, and left Mafeking again on Friday night.

Important visitors to Mafeking always go down to the stadt, hold a *pico** and see the homes of the Natives but the Native Affairs Commission apparently had not time for that. This office is not far out of the way from Dixon's Hotel (where they lodged) to the Town Hall (where they assembled). It is just opposite the Standard Bank – a fact perhaps accountable for our impecuniosity – yet a Native Commission did not evince that eagerness always shown by English visitors to this town of visiting to see and encourage a small band of Bechuana, editing, printing and publishing their own newspaper under their own vine and fig tree.

33
Article, *Bechuana Gazette*, 5 October 1904

By 1904 proposals to grant a form of representative government to the Transvaal, a British colony since its occupation by British forces during the South African War, were under active consideration by the Imperial authorities. Responsible government was eventually granted to the Transvaal in 1906 and to the Orange River Colony in 1907, no provision being made for African voting rights in either case.

There is a desire on the part of Downing Street to retain a control of Native Affairs when the mooted representative government is accorded to the Transvaal. In this matter the home cabinet is actuated by nothing if not by humanistic motives, considering that (with but few exceptions) the colonists of both the Transvaal and Orange River Colony are not sufficiently enlightened to be entrusted with the destinies of an inferior race. They have flatly refused to grant any form of voting rights to their very few civilized Natives, and how can they rightly claim to have a control over Native Affairs?

The Transvaal government first desired to take the Cape as a basis on colour legislation, with the result that they were stoutly opposed. The heads of the government were further weakened by the *modus operandi* of some of the Native Commissioners of the Transvaal, moulded by popular sentiment. These gentlemen defeat the very object for which they were appointed. Some

---

*   Or *pitso* (Tswana), 'meeting' or 'gathering'.

of them force Natives to take off their boots, and leave them across the street when they have to enter the commissioner's office for any purpose, or be flogged. Under these circumstances how can anyone blame the Native for moaning that the Boer fieldcornets – however capricious – were not so bad?

In the Orange River Colony the Lt.-Governor once advised a white audience to do their best and make this 'a white man's country'. His assent to the Brandfort Town Council regulations[110] shows that he clearly means what he said. Look how often their juries differ from the judges if Natives are to benefit by the verdict, and when asked why they return with a verdict that is at variance with the evidence, they coolly tell the judge that they consider it their duty not to do justice but to protect the white people. The only place where our people can get justice is in the High Commissioner's office and the high courts but it is so expensive to reach both these palaces. If Mr E.E. Watkeys[111] was not on the Bloemfontein Town Council, it would be impossible to find a more solid band of rank negrophobe legislators on any part of the globe, except the Farmer's Congress of the colony.

Not only are they satisfied to maltreat their own Natives, but they had the nerve to suggest to the Cape government to disfranchise us. Such then are the people into whose hands the home government rightly hesitate to commit the Natives. And we sincerely pray that they will hesitate until the colonists inaugurate a more enlightened Native policy. With us it is different. On this side of the border we have that expensive little asset, the franchise, which to us is worth a Jew's eye. We ourselves are too few to do anything with it, but knowing that we possess it, the colonists treat our people very well.

34

Article, 'Half a loaf is better than no bread', *Bechuana Gazette*, 19 October 1904

The Native Affairs Commission, which has being *doing* South Africa now for fully a year, is about to accomplish its mission. They sit very tight over their proposals, but it has leaked out somehow that they are going to recommend the New Zealand form of separate parliamentary representation for South Africa. So far so good.

Now let us briefly examine the motives underlying this separation. New Zealand has a population of 800,000 whites and 40,000 blacks. The upper house is composed of 43 white and 2 black members, and the lower house of 72 European and 4 Native members.

The Transvaal, on the other hand, has a white population of 300,000, while its black population number no fewer than a million persons – about 25 times as many as the Maoris. Are they prepared therefore to elect a numerically proportionate number of representatives as white New Zealand, and give the blacks a proportionate number, which will be about 150? We are afraid that they will be in a hurry to 'separate' like New Zealand, but will shrink from its attended obligations.

In New Zealand the Natives are the landowners. They may only lease, but cannot legally sell ground to the whites. The latter have adopted many subterfuges to browbeat the prohibition, one of these being marriage with Native girls (not so much for love as for the purpose of dispossessing the Natives of their land) regardless of the grave consequences with which the process is fraught, showing at once the level to which a white man is capable of being dragged, by avarice. Thus a number of Maori women died, leaving white husbands to inherit their estates, until the practice was countermanded by legislation prohibiting inter-marriage.

In the Transvaal on the other hand, the whites are the landowners. Legally they may sell land to the Natives; but the Transvaal Native Affairs Department has stoutly opposed every such transaction, for fear that investment in fixed property will make the Native independent. But why the Natives have not yet availed themselves of Lord Milner's suggestion, of running the department before the Supreme Court, for thus interfering with a legal transaction, 'no fellah can understand'.[112]

Again, in New Zealand the loyalty of the Maoris was nurtured by a British population, while the so-called public opinion of the Transvaal is wielded by American and French Republicans, loyal subjects of the Kaiser and Czar respectively, Spanish democrats and Italian socialists, Belgian Jews and anarchists at heart; to all of whom the Native can give points in real loyalty to the British throne.

Again, in New Zealand, on the one hand, the 'separate representation' was introduced in order that black men should sit in Parliament. It was found that if mixed voting was allowed, the Maoris would always be out-voted by the whites, and they would perhaps never be able to return a black representative. In the Transvaal, on the other hand, it is being introduced because the above-mentioned heterogenous internationalists (conglomerated for the sake of convenience under the term *white*) would not have black voters under any consideration, not to speak of black MPs.

In New Zealand the 'separation' was prompted by humane motives, while in the Transvaal it is compromise between humanity and its counterpart. In short, New Zealand's separation is purely British, while that of the Transvaal is transatlantic and continental. A quaint sarcasm, which has apparently also leaked out, is attributed to the commissioners. They are going to recommend, so says the Pretoria correspondent of the *Diamond Fields Advertiser*, that the Natives elect their members separately, but *they must be white*. Goodness gracious alive! We cannot believe the report, we have not such a low opinion of the commissioners, for anyone who thinks that way cannot be credited with any degree of political intelligence. White Bethnal Green returns Sir Mancherjee Bhownaggree to the House of Commons, because they consider him the *best* person, who is *best* suited to guard their *best* interests. And if the Transvaal Native is going to get his vote, and that vote is separate from that of the white community, he will naturally be the *best* judge as to whether his *best* representative should be white or otherwise. His franchise will be a hoax if it is to be accompanied by official dictation as to whom he should nominate, and you would have to call it by another name, for that is no franchise.

No sir, the Cape's is the only statesmanlike representation, which (under the peculiar and exceptional circumstances of South Africa) is least likely to wound any side. Here we have a franchise which is unconditional and untrammelled. It protects us from the onslaughts of white exploiters without Downing Street interference. We have not yet elected a black member, but we have no 'black peril' and no white intimidation, and our labour difficulty is no greater than that of any other country. The fact that on the re-opening of Kamfersdam last month, the manager could insert a notice in this paper and get more labourers than he required, speaks well for our colony. Here the Native question is settled and the recommendations of the commission cannot affect us to any great extent, but we would fain ask our people in the new colonies to accept New Zealand's franchise, as however unsuitable for this country, it is better than nothing at all.

35

Article, 'Rev. W.C. Willoughby of Tigerkloof', *Bechuana Gazette*, 2 November 1904

The Reverend W.C. Willoughby was a well-known missionary of the congregationalist London Missionary Society, and principal of the newly founded Tigerkloof Institution, near Vryburg in the northern Cape. Plaatje was often critical of the inadequacy of the work of the LMS in the educational field in the Bechuanaland

Protectorate in particular, and Willoughby for his part resented the influence of the Bechuana Gazette, *which he associated with the rise of 'Ethiopianism'. Willoughby subsequently described Plaatje's articles as 'the irresponsible utterances of the youth at the* Koranta ea Becoana (Bechuana Gazette) *office'. Willoughby was undoubtedly very much in Plaatje's mind when he criticised some missionaries in Bechuanaland for 'trying to ignore the Native press' in his Introduction to his* Sechuana Proverbs, *published in 1916 (see pp.212-20).*

In our Sechuana columns appears a communication by a Serowe correspondent, who states that while addressing a meeting at Chief Khama's court, pressing the claims of his society to a piece of land on which to build a school, the reverend gentleman in our title said that Lovedale had only produced drunkards and other things too bad to mention; but as for Morija, she was no better than the poor day school at Serowe. Not having been privileged with the scholastic education provided for Natives in this country, we will leave it to others to answer Mr Willoughby from personal observations drawn, whilst they were in some other school, if not actually in one of these two missionary institutions.

But the fact that we have never been within 100 miles of these two educational establishments will not prevent us from stating authoritatively that Lovedale and Morija[113] are to our people what Oxford and Cambridge have been to the Englishman. We have often had enemies of Native education tell us that we owe our little success entirely to the fact that scholastic training was not among the forces we requisitioned to our aid; but we invariably succeeded to get them to realise that commercial South Africa is indebted to the several educational establishments in the country, and more particularly to the two pioneer civilizing agencies – Lovedale and Morija.

We have no objection to white men exchanging complimentary shots within their own camp, but we do most strenuously object to a missionary trying to educate our people up to the laudable cause of charity, in the interests of his society, and supporting his supplications by slanders on two missionary institutions, without which our people would drop a 100 years down the progressive ladder; and this in the presence and hearing of a large number of Natives in *kgotla** assembled. It has often reached our ears that Mr Willoughby always induces Natives to send their boys to his school, by urging that he is going to put all existing institutions in the shade. If the London Missionary Society desire that their project, near Vryburg, should become

---

* Tswana: 'court', or 'decision-making gathering'.

something other than a *kloof*,* they had best send a president to organize the work. For a beginner to cast aspersions on the work of his seniors (like the present principal of the school) is a sure step towards failure.

Plaatje's article was noted by the Bechuanaland News (Vryburg) *in its issue of 17 December 1904, which criticised what Plaatje had to say as 'extremely discourteous, if not offensive', 'slanderous' and 'inspired by the Ethiopian ideals which are abroad, and becoming so prevalent, in Native society'.*

36
Article, *Bechuana Gazette*, 9 November 1904

The case of Paulus Malaji vs. Kensington Township syndicate, along with that of Tsewu vs. Registrar of Deeds, 4 April 1905 (also in the Transvaal Supreme Court), appeared to affirm the right of Africans in the Transvaal to purchase land in their own names, in the face of opposition from both white opinion and the Department of Native Affairs. It led to strong pressure on the Transvaal government to prohibit this by ordinance, initially disallowed by the Imperial authorities but eventually enacted after Union in the Natives' Land Act in 1913.

The Transvaal Native Affairs Department received a crushing blow through the mandatory order of a Supreme Court judge. Since the British occupation, this department, especially those of its able representatives who are stationed far away from civilization, have consistently made it their business to oppose every sign of progress discernible amongst the Natives. Whenever he heard that a Native was negotiating for the purchase of a farm, the sub-Native Commissioner would misuse his authority and come down upon the parties like a regular nightmare; and as the word of each such functionary is law within his district, he would invariably use his unlimited powers to frustrate the proceedings.

Consequently the Natives have been swindled of thousands of money in the course of futile attempts to effect purchases without the knowledge of these merciless potentates. Just the other day a lawyer lost an action against him for £900, instituted by a Native chief at Pretoria. Just now another lawyer stands committed for trial at the Pretoria sessions, charged with defrauding a Native in the sum of £1,500, while acting as his agent in a land purchase; and

---

* Afrikaans: 'deep ravine', 'gully', referring to the *kloof* in Tigerkloof, the LMS educational institution.

as two more lawyers were recently struck off the roll for minor malpractices (owing no doubt to the meddling of Native Commissioners) it would therefore follow that some more lawyers may have similarly fleeced unfortunate Natives and have succeeded to evade the clutches of the law.

When questioned as to why they interfere, the sub-Commissioners say that the laws of the late republic prohibited the transfer of land to Natives. We have searched the Transvaal law book from cover to cover but have failed to find in it a single ordinance prohibiting the sale of land to Natives. We have had the greatest difficulty to convince our people of this; even the high court action that led up to the present consummation was undertaken in a half-hearted spirit, as the Natives had the written word of a snow-white government official to the effect that the laws of the country were against us.

Early in 1903 a large number of Natives secured stands in the new Kensington township. Money was duly tendered and accepted, and in the end (apparently yielding to public prejudice), the sellers refused to pass transfer, and offered to refund the money instead. The more timid ones amongst them accepted the refund, but acting on our advice the majority would not be intimidated. Mr Paulus Malaji, chairman of the Basuto Association, made a test case, which has been in court since early this year, but was adjourned again and again, to enable the defendants to find the last straw on which to base their contention.

Mr Justice Curlewis very truly remarked that he personally knew of no legal impediment, but as there was a general impression that 'a Native could not hold land, except in the name of a Native Commissioner', it is as well that the defendants should be given an opportunity to establish their defence; but the court was not going to be guided by impressions. To the discredit of the department, be it said, they have in the interim been assisting the defence with whatever official papers they thought would be of any material use, and openly opposed another syndicate which was offering more stands to the Natives, but the die is cast and the mandate has gone down on the civil records of the Transvaal Supreme Court.

The best letter that has ever reached us by the Johannesburg mail, since the declaration of peace, reached us last week from Messrs Bell and Tancred, Solicitors, Exploration Buildings, Johannesburg, and is as follows:

Paulus Malaji vs. *Kensington township syndicate*

This case came before the Witwatersrand High Court today, when Mr Justice Wessels gave judgment, ordering the defendants to transfer the plots Nos. 315 and 316 to Paulus Malaji, subject

> to the conditions of sale. He also gave judgment for interest on
> the £55 at 6 per cent from 3rd June 1903, to date of transfer, and
> awarded costs to Malaji. We have not yet seen the conditions of
> sale, and therefore cannot yet state what they contain. We saw
> them for the first time when they were put into the court by Mr
> Short and we have not had any opportunity of reading them.

Probably the conditions are that none but 4-storey villas should be erected in Kensington, but be that as it may, the judgment of Mr Justice Wessels, who was himself a member of the late republican bar, clears the air and settles for ever the question that a Native may hold land in his own name, even in golden Transvaal, provided he can find the money to purchase it. At one stage of the proceedings, the defence obtained an adjournment, in order to instruct Counsel; he also obtained an adjournment to do something else. Presumably he advised his clients that they had not a leg to stand on, for according to the *Rand Daily Mail* of the 31st October, Mr Short (one of the directors) appeared in person; and *he attended in order to tender transfer* and deny damages. The beauty of sub-Native Commissioners is slain upon high places: how are the mighty fallen! Tell *it* not in Gath, publish *it* not in the streets of Askelon.

37
'Sekgoma – The Black Dreyfus' [manuscript][114]

Sekgoma Letsholathebe (1873-1914) was the fourth son of Chief Letsholathebe I of the Batawana, who lived in the north-western part of the Bechuanaland Protectorate. Following the death in 1890 of Chief Letsholathebe's son and heir, Moremi II, Sekgoma was appointed regent for Moremi's infant son and heir, Mathiba. Over the next few years Sekgoma sought to establish himself, with considerable success, as the legitimate chief of the Batawana. Opposition to his rule nevertheless grew, and by 1906 he was opposed not only by a number of his sub-chiefs and people, but also traders, missionaries (Sekgoma did not convert to Christianity), and Khama III of the Bamangwato. As a result the British administration was persuaded to depose Sekgoma and install Mathiba in his place. It was at this point that Plaatje picks up the story.

Plaatje's account is in the form of an unpublished manuscript, written in late 1908 or 1909, and linked in its conception to 'The Essential Interpreter' (see pp.51-61). From internal evidence it seems likely that Plaatje may have been writing for a British rather than just a South African audience, given his concern to explain the workings of the South African judicial system to a readership he assumes to be unfamiliar with it. Possibly he set out to write about the case for publication in Britain at the time of the Privy Council hearing in December 1909, and to be used by a deputation, composed of three of Sekgoma's supporters, which travelled to Britain in support of his case earlier that year.

The significance of the whole episode, in Plaatje's view, was to highlight the lack of accountability of the Bechuanaland Protectorate authorities and the absence of the rule of law, and any machinery for appealing against arbitrary government decisions.

The manuscript is entirely handwritten, and seems to be a first draft: it has the appearance of having been written in some haste, and several gaps were left for the insertion of extracts from documents which Plaatje intended to be included, but which he evidently did not have to hand when he was writing it.

Sekgoma – The Black Dreyfus

Detained for three years at Gaberones prison without trial, by orders of the Earl of Selborne, His Majesty's High Commissioner for South Africa

Sekgoma, the Chief of the Batawana, reached Mafeking on the 15th day of March 1906, on his return from Kimberley whither he had gone to consult a medical adviser.

At the railway station he found Lt. Surmon of the Protectorate police, who stated that he had come to see if the chief was passing through or breaking his journey at Mafeking. His friends and relatives met him at the station and took him home to Montsioastad.[115]

A police sergeant called at his quarters at noon, and asked him not to fail to inform the Resident Commissioner of the date of his departure for the north. He assured the officer that he would personally call and see his honour, and tell him when the arrangements for his departure were likely to be completed. It should be remembered that the country of the lake is not only a good [many] degrees from civilization but that it is some 200 miles or so of sandy, difficult road to the west of the railway line. This makes supplies very expensive at Lake Ngami. Flour costs £7 per muid of 200 lbs and sugar £4.5s. per 100 lbs and prices of clothing and other commodities rule proportionally. An inhabitant of regions where foodstuffs command such prohibitive prices would naturally take advantage of the opportunity when he visits a place where flour sells at 30s. instead of five times that figure, and gather as much supplies as his purse will purchase; and it took Chief Sekgoma fully 14 days to prepare for his journey.

Sekgoma, Chief of the Batawana, arrested by the British colonial authorities in March 1906 and detained without trial for five years: Plaatje labelled him 'the black Dreyfus' after the famous French cause célèbre.

Official visitations became decidedly officious during his stay. A police sergeant called in the forenoon and called in the afternoon; he called in the day time and called in the evening; he called during his presence and called in his absence; in fact the monotony of his queries and his ostensive solicitude for the welfare of the chief made him a perfect nuisance to the women folk, who felt that there was a screw loose somewhere, and were consequently alarmed.

In the meanwhile, messengers had arrived from Ngamiland and told Sekgoma that his recent divorce proceedings against his wife, Bitsang, had incensed Dithapo, his principal councillor, against him. That Dithapo had secured a considerable following amongst the tribe, who were working for his overthrow. Dithapo's eldest son Wetshootsile was co-respondent in the divorce suit against Bitsang.

Sekgoma duly called at the residency and paid his respects to His Honour Ralph C. Williams, Resident Commissioner.[116] The latter told him – I quote Chief Sekgoma, not the Resident Commissioner – that there was a disturbance in Ngamiland: that some of the Batawana did not want him, because they say he is not their rightful chief. The rightful chief, his honour told him, they said, was Mathiba, his nephew, and that Sekgoma had been acting as regent, and Mathiba being of age they said that no time should be lost to install him in the chieftainship.

This was news to the hearer, as it would naturally be to any student of Bechuana laws and customs under which no chief ever claimed, or was installed in, the chieftainship during the regent's lifetime. (A minor waits for the regent's death just as patiently as a prince waits for the death of his own father.)[117] However, his honour was pleased the disturbance took place during Sekgoma's absence as that made him feel certain that he had not been its cause. The whole matter, his honour added, would be inquired into in due course.

His purchases having been effected and consigned to the north, the usual formality – offerings of expressions of loyalty to the chief, and promises of protection, in His Majesty's name, by his honour – having been gone through, Chief Sekgoma and [his] following left on the 1st April by the Rhodesian train for the north.

Their movements right into the train were watched by officials and they say that Lt. Surmon, the first officer who greeted the chief on their arrival from Kimberley, travelled to Gaberones by the same train. They say that on his arrival there, he conferred with two policemen who joined the train when Lt. Surmon alighted and travelled with it as far as Palapye where the Chief

Sekgoma and party disembarked. Throughout the journey it had become evident that the British authorities were bent on doing something to the chief. And they were already anxious to know the exact shape which that 'something' was going to take.

It soon broke out, however, for more officers came over to the railway station and offered him free quarters for the night. These he declined with thanks. He spent the night with his people, and the next morning they came with a greater determination than on the previous day. It is difficult to ascertain if a warrant of apprehension was served, but all things being possible under the Protectorate process which presumably cared little for legal formalities, force could be used by the police with or without a warrant.

They took him in a cart to Khama's town, Serowe, about 540 miles to the west, his men following on horseback. There he was offered accommodation in a tent but preferred his covered wagon which was placed at his disposal in a guarded enclosure.

The justice of thus luring a man into a trap is not apparent. It is as obscure as the reason for his arrest. He was coaxed away from a colony whose subjects enjoy the King's writ, a country where black men pay rates and taxes, and exercise the franchise – away into a country under the despotic rule of one man, a well-administered country but without any judges and whose provincial courts are of a quasi-military nature, presided over by the despot's own subordinates who sometimes sit in judgement over their own acts.

Having no immediate means of obtaining legal advice which in the Protectorate is as scarce as hen's teeth, he commended himself to the magnanimity of his captors and hoped for the best. He was told to await the arrival of the High Commissioner who would on his arrival settle the whole question of the Ngamiland chieftainship in dispute.

By permission of Sir Ralph Williams, the then Resident Commissioner, I had the honour of accompanying the High Commissioner's entourage to the protectorate during Easter week 1906, in the interest of my journal.[118] The only other journalist of the party was Mr Scruder, the fine-fingered tableauist who represented the *Diamond Fields Advertiser*, Kimberley's only daily.

Saturday of the holy week was spent with the Natives of the southern protectorate. There were representative numbers of the Bakwena with their Chief Sebele, the Bangwaketse with their Chief Bathoen (both these tribes were originally under one chief and their totem is the crocodile); the Bakgatla, whose totem is the baboon, with their Chief Linchwe; the Bamalete, with their late Chief Mokosi, whose totem is an ox (I may mention that here is a poser as the Bamalete cherish beef as heartily as any other nation and with Bechuanas it is an abomination for any tribe to eat the flesh of its sacred animal, but this is by the way); and the Batlokwa whose sacred animal is the [wild boar].

His Excellency received gifts of karosses and other souvenirs from the Natives. Chief Linchwe presented an English address of welcome which was artistically illuminated by the Sisters of St Joseph's convent, Mafeking, and his daughter gave Lady Selborne a choice bunch of ostrich feathers. No rule was observed as to how many followers shall accompany each chief, and the Bangwaketse's camp included 157 wagons, 100 horsemen and eight mule-carts while Chief Gaborone's camp had but five wagons, no horsemen and no carts; and when it was His Excellency's turn to 'hlabela' * the Natives he gave them 21 fat oxen. Each of the first-named four tribes received five bullocks, and Gaborone's tribe only one with the result that the one was almost sufficient for Gaborone's people, and the five each for the Bakwena, Bakgatla, and Bamalete were almost sufficient for the respective recipients, [but] the five for the Bangwaketse was scarcely half enough.

At the close of the interviews His Excellency returned to attend the Easter service in St. John's Church at Mafeking, and reached Palapye siding on Monday morning, resuming his duties there with an interview with Khama's son, Sekgoma.[119] The latter had expressed a desire to see His Excellency while at his father's town, Serowe, but his father forbade him the honour.

The same morning His Excellency's 'special' train was left at the station and Earl Selborne and party proceeded by mule carts to Serowe. There they were enthusiastically received by Chief Khama and the Bamangwato nation, and for the first time in my life I witnessed a sight unknown in South African gatherings (though a frequent occurrence in Europe) of two persons being crushed to death by the jolly crowd. The spacious *kgotla* was thronged all morning by a mass of humanity who vociferously cheered Lord Selborne's speech. A garden party by the European inhabitants concluded the day's proceedings. The next morning Chief Khama arranged a hunt for Earl Selborne. Some 15,000 beaters went out in opposite directions and encircled numerous herds of big and small game and herded them towards the

---

*   Tswana, to slaughter (oxen, as a form of tribute or thanks).

Ralph Williams, Resident Commissioner of the Bechuanaland Protectorate, addressing the Bamangwato at Serowe, 1906.

distinguished party, who had some excellent and very easy shooting. During the hunt His Excellency, mounted on one of Chief Khama's stately chargers, was attended by the court interpreter who is a brother of the present paramount chief of Basutoland.

While these festivities were taking place, a subject of His Majesty the King, who until then ruled a brave and daring people, a crack shot and a horseman of no mean standing; who slays a lion at sight; who once hunted down and killed eight elephants in one afternoon; to whom and whose people protection had been guaranteed by Earl Selborne's predecessor in a letter and personally 'by word of mouth' by His Majesty's Secretary of State for the Colonies – was cogitating in prison at the Serowe police camp simply because there happened to be a claimant to his seat.[120] I have read in newspapers about rival claims to baronetcies and such likes but have never heard it contended that that was sufficient justification for the authorities to imprison the sitting party. The only reference to this brave man, in the whole of His Excellency's account of the trip, is the following: 'The remainder of my time at Serowe was occupied in investigating the question of the Batawana chieftainship. The matter proved to be even more complicated than I expected, and I spent many hours in hearing all that Sekgoma and Mathiba had to say, and in questioning them and in discussing the points raised with Khama himself, who is closely related to both claimants.'[121]

One would have thought that the easiest way out of the difficulty would have been to send the ruling chief back to his seat, and to call on his rival to substantiate his claim, or to appoint a court to determine the validity of Mathiba's claim. Instead I am told that His Excellency left Sekgoma in prison, joined the train at Palapye, and proceeded north on a hunting expedition.[122] On his return Earl Selborne accorded Sekgoma an interview at Palapye Road station and conveyed to him the comforting information that he was imprisoned for his own good and for the benefit of his tribe, as it is feared that if he was allowed to return to Ngamiland there may be fighting. He claimed his release and assured His Excellency that he would maintain law and order in his country until the whole business had been enquired into, and pending any settlement that may be arrived at by the authorities of the British Imperial government to which he had sworn allegiance. This offer was rejected so he next asked that Mathiba should also be imprisoned. The answer was that he could not so be as he was staying with his friends – with Khama. 'Well', said the captive to the captor, 'I too have got some friends! Could I not be permitted to go to them?' This last request was not granted and so with a bow

His Excellency boarded the special train and returned to his gubernatorial duties in Transvaal, leaving Sekgoma, unmanacled yet a captive.

This was the final [act] in Sekgoma's arrest. Efforts have been made to get the authorities to bring him to trial or accept bail but they have stubbornly refused to vouchsafe either.

———————

Life imprisonment, in this enlightened age, is the lot of political ringleaders who have been [convicted]. Surely no such judgement was ever passed on any but inveterate felons and murderers, whose death sentences have been commuted. Is it larceny to have a rival in one's post? Surely if the existence of a rival in any walk of life exposed one to such a terrible fate then no man would be free from its consequences. Prime ministers from Pitt down to Asquith would have died in St Helena as for sure each leader of the opposition is the rival in office of the prime minister of the day.[123]

A civil dispute is nothing strange or extraordinary in Bechuanaland. Raditladi, Mphoeng, Sekgoma gora Kgama[124] – each had his differences with Chief Khama. They left the village with their respective followings – not exactly in peace – but nobody was put in gaol. And why single out Sekgoma for such barbarous treatment? In answer to this the Bechuanas would say when Kgari parted with Sebele, Pula with Ikaneng, and [Bathoen] with Masoupa.[125] Sekgoma was placed in the next train and conveyed south to Gaberones, where he was put in a cottage in the police camp along with three of his attendants. And he has remained there ever since. That his arrest was illegal is manifest in the following proclamation issued shortly after his arrest, and which, the author thinks, was issued in order to legalise his illegal arrest:

PROCLAMATION

By His Excellency the High Commissioner[126]

Whereas by the Order-in-Council of Her late Majesty dated the ninth of May 1891 the High Commissioner is empowered to provide for the peace, order and good government of all persons within the limits of the said Order including the prohibition and punishment of acts tending to disturb the public peace;

And whereas it is expedient to the peace, order and good government of that portion of the said limits which is known as the Bechuanaland Protectorate (hereinafter called the Protectorate);

Now therefore under and by virtue of the powers in me vested I do hereby declare, proclaim and make known as follows:

1. The Proclamation of the High Commissioner dated the thirtieth of June 1891 shall be and is hereby repealed.

2. The High Commissioner on its being shown to his satisfaction that there are reasonable grounds for believing that the presence of any person within the Protectorate is dangerous to its peace, order or good government may instruct the Resident Commissioner to issue an order under his hand directing such person to leave the Protectorate within such time after service of the order on such person as may be specified therein and if on the expiration of such period such person shall be found within the Protectorate he shall be guilty of an offence and may be arrested without warrant by any police constable or officer and brought before a Resident Commissioner, Assistant Commissioner or Resident Magistrate and shall be liable on conviction to imprisonment with or without hard labour for a period of not less than one month and not exceeding six months and with or without a fine not exceeding one hundred pounds and in default of payment to a further term of imprisonment for a period not exceeding six months.

3. Any such person as in the last preceding section is described may at or before the end of any period of imprisonment mentioned therein by warrant under the hand of the Resident Commissioner (which warrant shall only be issued on the written instructions of the High Commissioner) be removed from the Protectorate and shall be deemed to be in lawful detention during the course of such removal and if any person who has been so removed from the Protectorate be thereafter found therein he shall be guilty of a further offence and may be arrested without warrant and shall be liable on conviction to a period of imprisonment not less than six months and not exceeding twelve months with or without a fine not exceeding five hundred pounds and in default of payment to imprisonment with or without hard labour for a further period not exceeding six months and at or before the expiration of such sentence he may again be removed from the Protectorate and the provisions of the last preceding section relative to removal shall again apply to such further removal.

4. Any such person as is described in section one of this Proclamation who at the date of the taking effect thereof is detained in the Protectorate shall be deemed to have been since the commencement of such detention and to be for three months after the date of the taking effect of this Proclamation lawfully detained and to have been

imprisoned without hard labour under section two hereof and the
provisions of section three of this Proclamation relative to such
removal shall apply to any such person.

5. This Proclamation shall have force and effect from the date of its first
publication in the Gazette.

GOD SAVE THE KING
Given under my Hand and Seal at Mbabane, Swaziland,
this Fourteenth day of September One Thousand Nine Hundred and Six

SELBORNE
High Commissioner
By Command of His Excellency the High Commissioner

C.H. RODWELL
Imperial Secretary

If I have a correct comprehension of legislative phraseology, this practically
means imprisonment for life without hard labour. The authorities were
implored to at least [say] under what charge they justify this action, and all
that was said is he is 'detained' by order of His Excellency the High
Commissioner who declines to give reasons.

While Sekgoma professed the highest regard and appreciation for British
sense of justice he has never hesitated to claim a fair trial and so in the month
[of November 1906] he summoned the Resident Commissioner to show cause
before the High Court.

The case was argued with exceptional ability by Mr Advocate Phear. The
following is an epitome of the learned counsel's speech and the court's
decision as reported in the *Diamond Fields Advertiser*.[127]

It was a mistake for his friends in the first instance to bring the case before
the court as the result might have been anticipated. Similar disappointments, I
am told, had been experienced by them as a result of petitions to the High
Commissioner, and when the judgement was made known to them they were
so disheartened, particularly by the bill of costs, as to give up all hope of ever
succeeding to get their friend's release.

The same thing occurred [when] the Bechuana were governed by British
statesmen and not by members of the royal family. They would say further that
if Sekgoma were the first victim of such cruel circumstance, he was certainly
not the last as it would seem that as long as a cousin of His Majesty was sent

away to leave his share of the King's *malito*,* and rule over black men in Africa, there will always be that terror.

And it would almost seem as if the last-named is the correct surmise. His Excellency's succession to the High Commissionership was synchronized by the publication of the Proclamation ... empowering him to expel from the Protectorate anyone found likely to be of danger to the public peace.[128] A similar proclamation in Basutoland was the subject of a petition and a deputation is leaving for England to ask the King for its repeal.[129] How did your Rosmead, Loch and Milner[130] manage to rule the Protectorate and rule it successfully without recourse to such legislative expedients?

The Bahurutse, an important section of the Bechuana, were separated by the ... barriers from Bechuanaland and included in the Transvaal. During the Republican regime they had a faction fight in which several lives were lost. The Boer government mediated between the two sections and placed Gopane and about 7,000 Bahurutse at the Maandane and left Ikaleng at Linokana with 7,000. They continued to cultivate this most fertile spot in the possession of any Bechuana tribe until a decision by Lord Selborne caused such a stir amongst them [that it led] indirectly to the exodus of some 4,000 of them who left their homes in protest. Results do not appear to have justified His Lordship's experiment for it caused untold misery and privation to women and children, thousands of whom are to become homeless wanderers in the wild woods and are being driven by pillar to post by the white farmers of the Marico district. It is to be hoped that this will do them some kind of 'good'.

His Lordship's idea of what is good for black men is curious and original. At the time of the British occupation it was presumed that the Republican statutes contained a law prohibiting the registration of land to a Native.[131] When it was discovered that no such law was in existence the nominated legislature passed an Ordinance prohibiting the registration of land to a Native. A Native deputation waited upon His Lordship asking him to refuse to sanction the outrageous enactment. His Lordship soothed them and asked them not to be alarmed as the act was passed 'for their own good'. Thanks to the Rt. Hon. Alfred Lyttelton the measure was vetoed, and in spite of an

---

*   Tswana, 'property', conveying an implication of entitlement. The Earl of Selborne was not literally a cousin of the reigning monarch, King Edward VIII, and Plaatje's use of the term in this context conveys the more general sense of his being the King's representative in southern Africa.

Ordinance ' for their own good' the Native may still purchase property in the Transvaal and register it in his own name – but I am wandering.

We last saw our subject in a cottage in the police camp at Gaberones, guarded alone with his three attendants by armed policemen. We should, however, record a curious allegation on the part of the authorities who, it is alleged, alleged that they never imprisoned Sekgoma at all, but have merely subjected him to detention. These palliative platitudes fall to the ground in the face of the legal definition of the term imprisonment, which is ...

It is complained that his estate was compulsorily sequestrated.

In the preceding pages we have seen that a man set up a claim to a position in the possession of another. Instead of calling on the claimant to prove his bona fides and giving the defendant leave to furnish his pleadings, the authorities threw upon the defendant the onus of disproving that which had never been proved, and rendered his task impossible by detaining him in prison, removing him so far from the scene of the hearing as to completely nullify his defence.

British sense of justice has here been trampled under foot, for since when was it criminal to have a rival in any position; and of which law, pray, is it a contravention to have one's position claimed by someone else? It is not Roman-Dutch law which obtains in all South African colonies. It is not the common law of England which often supplements but never supplants Roman-Dutch law in South Africa. It is not common sense, so what is it? It is the absence of a clear charter of justice for the protection from their rulers, of the inhabitants of that portion of the British empire known as the Bechuanaland Protectorate. This indeed is one branch of the Protectorate administration which calls for immediate consideration.

In the Cape Colony the laws are administered by the magistrates, who exercise jurisdiction over their respective divisions. Some cases are tried by summary process. A preliminary examination is held by the magistrates, in all serious cases, at the completion of which the records are forwarded to the Solicitor-General, who either 'declines to prosecute' (if there is no *prima facie*[*] case), remits the case back to the magistrate under a given process, or indicts the accused, who are thereupon committed to prison until the arrival of the circuit judge, who tours the districts twice annually.

---

[*]   Latin: 'at first sight'.

Every judgement by the resident magistrate involving the sentences to imprisonment for any period exceeding *one month* and a fine exceeding *five pounds*, as well as all corporate punishments, are subject to review by a judge of the nearest superior court with jurisdiction in the district.

There is also an appeal from the decisions of each magistrate or assistant magistrate to the superior court, and from the latter to the Supreme Court and Court of Appeal, and finally to the Privy Council. Ample opportunity is given to the accused to prepare a defence and every facility is given them to subpoena their witnesses, and the chances of a miscarriage of justice are very remote .

Only a bare valley – the Ramatlhabama – divides the Bechuanaland Protectorate from colonial Bechuanaland,[132] where the above judicial machinery obtains. In the former the magistrates are also sub-administrators and exercise over these divisions their extensive judicial powers which include some very serious cases – cases which in other [countries] are usually tried by judges and handled by well-trained barristers. Up to the time of Sekgoma's arrest, there was not even a law agent resident in the Protectorate.

An appeal lies from their [magistrates'] decisions to the court of the Resident Commissioner – a capable administrator but without any legal training – who also reviews their judgements and whose court is the highest tribunal in South Africa for the determination of civil and criminal appeals in the Protectorate. Rhodesia and other possessions of the British South African Company are in possession of the best judicial machinery in the country. They have magistrates and judges in Rhodesia, and they may appeal from the courts of the latter to the Cape Supreme Court. In the Protectorate one's case is decided by a layman, from whose decision he may appeal to another layman whose court is the highest in the land. From this lay court there is no appeal to any South African high court of justice, but the Privy Council in London.

Now let us see if the administration of justice under this system can be said to be adequate for the safeguarding of the persons and properties of His Majesty's subjects in the dependency.

If an inhabitant of the Cape colonial Bechuanaland were similarly dealt with he would instruct a solicitor to retain a barrister, and apply to the nearest judge for a rule *nisi** restraining the authorities; and it is our experience that

---

*   Latin: 'unless'. A rule *nisi* was a legal limiting term indicating that, as in this case, the judge's rule, whilst not fixed or absolute, was to take effect unless some cause is shown, or reason arises, to prevent this.

British judges are jealously strict against any tampering with the liberty of the subject.

Under the Protectorate law there are no such provisions. To do that a Protectorate subject would have to send to England by land and sea at an enormous cost, and the indignant protests so naively and feebly uttered by Sekgoma, which were scarcely heeded, constitute the entire legal remedies of the Protectorate.

The sanctity of civilized rule is the liberty of the subject, and as this is usually safeguarded by the law courts under an inflexible yet just charter of justice, and as it would seem that such judicial machinery does not exist in its entirety in this Protectorate, the protection of the subject in the said Protectorate exists in shadow only and not in substance.

The highest court of justice in the land is that of the Resident Commissioner, and it would be crediting his honour with almost super-human powers to expect him to veto his own acts.

The order for Sekgoma's detention was presumably an administrative *fiat* by His Excellency the High Commissioner on the advice and recommendation of his representatives on the spot, who, I take it, believed that they were doing nothing but right. The law courts of the Protectorate are presided over by the same administrators, who, it is presumed, advised His Excellency to take that step. Now, could there be a bigger farce than to compel a man to appeal to a court presided over by the same individual against whose acts he has a reason to complain? A man in such circumstances can expect but scanty protection from the court; as in the words of Dr Kenny[133] 'there would be more judges than justice, and the quality of impartiality would be distinctly strained'. Indeed, if the laws of the country really expect an administrator to veto his own acts, then I submit that they are about as absurd as some of the greatest achievements of Don Quixote.

Following his arrest Sekgoma embarked upon a long and expensive series of appeals as the British authorities, fearful that his release would precipitate civil war, kept him imprisoned in Gaberones. In 1909 his case reached the High Court in London, which refused to make a ruling on the grounds that under the Foreign Jurisdiction Act of 1890 the High Commissioner's power in the Protectorate was absolute. Early in 1910 the Court of Appeal finally decided against Sekgoma, rejecting his application for a writ of habeas corpus *and dismissing his appeal, arguing that the inhabitants of the Protectorate were 'uncivilized', and that British officials would be unable to rule* effectively if the inhabitants of the Protectorates were to enjoy the full legal rights and protection accorded to British citizens.[134]

Sekgoma was made, but declined, offers of land for himself and his followers in the eastern Transvaal, and on the Molopo River in the southern part of the Protectorate, provided he renounced his claim to the Batawana chieftaincy. He was finally released from detention in 1911, but died two years later. See also Plaatje's article, 'Annexation and the Protectorates' (Pretoria News, 16 January 1911 [pp.136-40]) where Plaatje sets the Sekgoma case in the context of the debate about the incorporation of Bechuanaland into the Union of South Africa.

PART TWO
1910-1923

'Champion for the cause of our peoples'

Previous page:
Plaatje as editor of the Bechuana Friend, *c*. 1912

'*Now let it be known that Mr Plaarje has performed the part of an intelligent and energetic champion for the cause of our peoples.*'
From an editorial entitled 'A worthy defender', *Ilanga lase Natal*, 6 April 1917.

Introduction and Commentary

South Africa's four colonies came together in the Union of South Africa in 1910. African views and concerns had not figured prominently in the deliberations which led up to the creation of the new Union, and the non-racial Cape franchise was not extended to the other provinces of the Union. But it had at least been preserved in the Cape, and Plaatje was amongst those who initially took an optimistic view of African prospects in the new Union, hoping that the liberal influence of the Cape would spread northwards to Natal, the Orange River Colony and the Transvaal. Plaatje had hoped that J.X. Merriman, a former Cape prime minister, would become the first Union prime minister, but he was not wholly disheartened by the fact that General Louis Botha was elected to this position, and he was encouraged by the presence of a number of well-known Cape liberals in the first Union cabinet.

Plaatje's personal circumstances were also rather more encouraging than they had been for some years. In Kimberley he was now the editor of a new newspaper, *Tsala ea Becoana* (*Bechuana Friend*), financed largely by a group of relatively wealthy African farmers in the Thaba Nchu district of the Orange Free State. This paper was to appear from 1910 to 1912, and then – after a short break – emerged with a new name, *Tsala ea Batho* (*Friend of the People*), and continued publication until 1915. Not that these papers were Plaatje's only platform during these years: between 1910 and 1914 he also contributed regularly to the *Pretoria News* (generally under the heading, 'Through Native Eyes'), and his articles appeared from time to time in the other major English-language newspapers, particularly the *Diamond Fields Advertiser* in Kimberley. Plaatje had become perhaps the best known African journalist and political spokesman of his day.

In the immediate aftermath of Union a variety of concerns are evident in Plaatje's published writings and correspondence. One was the matter of the discriminatory treatment of Africans on the railways to which Plaatje returned (Doc. 42, pp.143-47). Another was the question of the future of the High Commission Territories (Bechuanaland, Swaziland, and Basutoland), whose status was addressed in a schedule to the Act of Union on the understanding that they would in due course be incorporated into the Union of South Africa: Plaatje's view, coloured as it was by his views on the autocratic nature of the Bechuanaland protectorate administration, was that this would be preferable to continuation of the status quo (Doc. 40, pp.136-40).

Another issue was that of landholding rights for the Barolong of Thaba Nchu, whose cause Plaatje took up, publicly and privately, in a campaign to secure an amendment to existing legislation and thus to ease the restrictions which existed on the transfer of land between them (Docs 38, pp.133-34; 39, pp.134-61; 43, pp.147-48).

But within a year of the creation of the Union one overriding issue was becoming increasingly central: the question of segregation, the key element in the comprehensive 'native policy' which the new government now began to formulate. Plaatje had addressed the issue in a prize essay on the subject which he had written in 1910, and was eventually published in January 1911 – the first extended statement of his upon the subject since his comments on the work of the South African Native Affairs Commission six years earlier (Doc. 41, pp.140-43). His scepticism is plainly evident. During the course of 1912, with Hertzog as the Minister of Native Affairs, the practical and political implications of a policy based upon the idea of segregation were spelt out and Plaatje's views in response were even more forthrightly expressed (Doc. 44, pp.148-51).

At the same time as he sought to represent African views on the political issues of the day, Plaatje was by now heavily involved in the affairs of the South African Native National Congress (SANNC), the united African political organisation which was formed in January 1912. He was elected its first General Secretary, and along with its first President, the Reverend J.L. Dube, shouldered much of the burden of establishing an effective national organisation, seeking to represent the views of the African people as a whole.

Soon after its formation Congress was to be galvanised by the government's plan to introduce new legislation to separate African from white landholding, and thus to implement a major plank in a segregationist solution to the so-called 'native problem'. The central provision to this new legislation was to deprive Africans of the right to acquire land outside their existing areas of occupation, and to prohibit whites from acquiring land within these areas, now defined as 'Scheduled Native Areas' – the effect of which would be to confine African landholding to less than 10 per cent of the land surface of the Union of South Africa. The legislation contained, moreover, a number of other provisions which sought to meet the insistent demands of white farmers for more cheap labour. In particular it responded to the demands of white farmers in the Transvaal and Orange Free State to have sharecroppers on their land transformed into farm labourers or servants.

Plaatje was appalled by the provisions of this Natives' Land bill, as it was known, and it was to dominate the next few years of his life. Included in this selection are examples of his immediate response to the legislation in the columns of the *People's Friend* (Doc. 45, pp.151-54); a speech he made to the Kimberley branch of the APO (African People's Organisation, a predominantly coloured organisation, of which Plaatje was a member) in which he addressed the question of the Natives' Land Act and its wider context (Doc. 49, pp.163-72); correspondence challenging John Tengo Jabavu, the well-known Cape politician, to debate the question of the Land Act (Doc. 48, pp.159-63); and finally some extracts from *Native Life in South Africa*, published in London in 1916, appealing to the British public for support in securing the repeal of the Natives' Land Act (Doc. 52, pp.184-210), and a devastating indictment of the entire direction of the policy of the South African government towards the African people of South Africa.

The SANNC protested vigorously to the South African authorities about the Natives' Land Act, but to no avail, and the legislation was duly enacted in June 1913. In its aftermath Plaatje's life was dominated by the task of monitoring the effects of the Act, and he was horrified by what he saw, and subsequently wrote about, in the Orange Free State in particular, where white farmers took advantage of the legislation and forced many Africans to leave their homes in search of new places to live. Early in 1914 the SANNC, at a meeting held in Kimberley in February, decided to send a deputation to England to protest to the British Imperial Government, and if necessary to the British public, to seek the repeal of the Natives' Land Act. Plaatje topped the poll of votes in a Congress committee appointed to elect the deputation, and preparations were made to travel to England.

In fact opinion within the SANNC was not unanimous about the wisdom of sending a deputation of this kind to Britain. A minority within the organisation favoured resorting to strike action as a means of remedying their grievances, a course of action to which Plaatje in particular was strongly opposed. Such caution in political issues is paralleled in his response to more personal forms of discrimination, for example in the letter he wrote to the General Secretary of De Beers after encountering discriminatory treatment on one of Kimberley's trams (Doc. 46, pp.154-56). Contrast this with the action of Pixley Seme, Congress's treasurer and a newly qualified barrister, in drawing a revolver when threatened by two whites for travelling in a first-class railway compartment.

Plaatje departed for the United Kingdom as Secretary of the SANNC deputation to England in June 1914, leaving the affairs of the *Friend of the People* in the hands of his brother-in-law, Isaiah Bud-M'belle. In the somewhat light-hearted account of the sea voyage to England Plaatje revealed that he spent much of his time aboard ship compiling 'a little book on the Natives' Land Act and its operations which I hope to put through the press immediately after landing in England' (Doc. 51, pp.174-84). In fact it was to be nearly two years before the book appeared in print, and nearly three before Plaatje was back home in South Africa.

When they arrived in England the advice given to the Congress delegates by the Anti-Slavery and Aborigines' Protection Society, the leading humanitarian organisation concerned with colonial affairs, was that they should refrain from public agitation until they had had an interview with the Colonial Secretary, Lord Harcourt. This they accepted, but the interview with Lord Harcourt provided no encouragement whatever. He simply repeated what they had been told by the Governor-General of South Africa, Lord Gladstone, before leaving South Africa: that is to say, South Africa was now a self-governing dominion within the empire and the Imperial Government was not in a position to intervene on their behalf even if it wished to do so.

After the interview the Congress delegates resolved to take their case to the British public, a pamphlet (drafted by Plaatje) was printed, meetings were arranged and their campaign began. But within a couple of weeks war broke out, and – with differences already emerging between some of the delegates – it was decided to call off the campaign, and four of the five men departed for South Africa. Plaatje, however, decided to remain in England in order to complete and to publish the book he was writing, and to continue the campaign single-handed.

Over the next two years Plaatje addressed over 300 meetings to publicise the case against the Land Act, and worked hard both to complete his manuscript and to raise funds to get his book published. It was a hard struggle, not made any easier by the hostility of John Harris, the Organising Secretary of the Anti-Slavery and Aborigines' Protection Society, the one organisation in England from which Plaatje could have reasonably have expected a degree of material support. Harris, however, supported the principle of segregation which he believed to be embodied in the Natives' Land Act, and did his best to dissuade people from supporting Plaatje's campaign.

Plaatje met with a far more encouraging response, however, at the hands of the Brotherhood movement, an inter-denominational religious organisation whose members sought to promote the practical implementation of Christianity in everyday life – an aim which Plaatje supported wholeheartedly. The movement declared its support for the cause of the Congress delegates, and then provided Plaatje with both a public platform and a network of friends and supporters: over half the meetings he addressed in England, indeed, were under the auspices of the Brotherhood movement.

Plaatje achieved his main objective in England with the publication of *Native Life in South Africa* in May 1916. In many ways the book represents one of his crowning achievements – not in the matter of the book alone but in overcoming so many of the obstacles which lay in the way of its publication. *Native Life* ended up as a book of more than 400 pages, considerably larger than the 'little book' Plaatje had envisaged whilst aboard ship. Much of the reason for this was due to Plaatje's perception of the need to link the presentation of his case to the British public with the war against Germany: his account of the Land Act and its effects thus became subsumed within a wider and much more comprehensive political and historical commentary upon South Africa, his overriding aim being to demonstrate the loyalty of the African people to the cause of the Imperial Government, past and present, in the hope that this would ultimately move the authorities to due recognition of their political rights, and the redress of their grievances; and to secure, above all, the repeal of the Natives' Land Act. Hence, too, the addition of a detailed account of the Boer rebellion of 1914 (sparked off by South Africa's entry into the war and invasion of German South West Africa) in order to contrast Boer 'disloyalty' with African 'loyalty'.

One of the most striking chapters of *Native Life in South Africa* (part of which is reproduced here in Doc. 52, pp.202-10) is his 'Report of the Lands Commission: An Analysis', written after the remainder of the book had been completed, and added in to its second printing. The Natives' Land Commission had been set up under the provisions of the Land Act with the objective of finding more land for the African population, and thus to remedy the gross imbalance evident at the time of the passage of the original Act when less than 10 per cent of the total land surface of the Union of South Africa was set aside for the African population. As Plaatje had predicted, the Commission failed in its task, confirming Plaatje's worst fears about the likely impact of the Land Act on the future course of South Africa's history.

Plaatje's period in England between 1914 and 1917 was significant also for the opportunity it afforded to write on other matters, for he was able to complete two further books – *Sechuana Proverbs with Literal Translations and their European Equivalent* and *A Sechuana Reader in International Phonetic Orthography (with English translations)*, the latter written together with Daniel Jones, then a lecturer in phonetics at University College, London. Both books were the product of Plaatje's fascination with his native Tswana language and culture, and his concern that they should be preserved in the face of the onslaught, as he saw it, of European culture and civilisation.

For the former, Plaatje succeeded in compiling over 700 Tswana proverbs, drawn from memory, which he then presented together with literal translations and the closest European equivalents he could find. Had he embarked upon the task thirty years earlier, he said, he believed this total could have been three times as great. In his Preface and Introduction to these proverbs (Doc. 54, pp.212-20) Plaatje had much of interest to say about his own perceptions of the Tswana language and its development, its capabilities and limitations, and in particular about the problem of orthography from which Setswana had suffered so grievously. All of these issues Plaatje was to return to in the 1920s.

The *Sechuana Reader* arose from a chance meeting with Daniel Jones in 1915 which led the two men to collaborate on the task of providing a phonetic reader in Setswana (Plaatje's Preface is reproduced in Doc. 55, pp.220-22). Plaatje was impressed by the capacity of the International Phonetic Alphabet to reproduce the exact sounds of the Tswana language, and immediately saw in this a means of preserving the true pronunciation of his native tongue from the onslaught of European influence about which he elaborated in his Introduction to the *Sechuana Proverbs*. In this sense, and in terms of Plaatje's broader perceptions about the importance of preserving his native culture, the one book is linked very closely to the other.

The third piece dating from Plaatje's time in England is his contribution to Professor I. Gollancz's *A Book of Homage to Shakespeare* (Doc. 53, pp.210-12), published in 1916 to commemorate the 300th anniversary of Shakespeare's death. Plaatje's contribution was entitled 'A South African's Homage', and relates in an amusing manner his courtship of Elizabeth M'belle, his future wife, in 1897 and 1898, linking this to the fascination for Shakespeare which he developed at the same time. 'A South African's Homage' reveals much about the reasons for Plaatje's enthusiasm for Shakespeare, and helps to explain why Plaatje was subsequently to devote so much time and effort in translating Shakespeare's plays into Setswana, and in raising the funds necessary to get them printed.

Plaatje returned to South Africa in February 1917 with plans to develop the Brotherhood movement in South Africa, and with a political reputation considerably enhanced as a result of the publication of *Native Life in South Africa* and the impact it was making. On several occasions, indeed, the book was mentioned in debates in the South African House of Assembly, and it was widely reviewed and noticed in both England and South Africa. Sadly, his newspaper, the *People's Friend*, had ceased publication in 1915, the victim of financial pressures as well as the effects of Plaatje's extended absence overseas, and he was unable to resuscitate it. But he found a forum for his views on the issues of the day in the daily press: included here are letters to the press on the Native Affairs Administration bill (Doc. 59, pp.228-32), and on the manner in which the casualty list for the troopship *Mendi*, lost in February 1917 with the loss of over 600 African lives, was compiled and published (Doc. 56, pp.222-24).

In two personal letters to Jane Cobden Unwin (Doc. 57, pp.224-25; 58, pp.225-28), one of his supporters in England, Plaatje describes the family circumstances to which he returned, and also the difficulties now faced by the South African Native National Congress. At its meeting in Bloemfontein in May 1917 the President, the Reverend John Dube, was forced to resign due, so it was said, to the 'careless correspondence' that his secretary, R.V. Selope Thema, had allowed to be sent to John Harris, Organising Secretary of the Anti-Slavery and Aborigines' Protection Society, which Harris had then proceeded to use for his own purposes, and against the expressed position of the organisation.

In fact John Dube had already lost the confidence of many of the other leading figures in the organisation, and the issue of the correspondence with Harris provided a suitably convenient pretext for forcing him out. Plaatje was then offered the presidency of the organisation, but declined on the grounds, he said, that 'the deterioration of his business made the idea impossible'. The position was taken instead by S.M. Makgotho, president of the provincial Transvaal branch.

These differences within the leadership of the SANNC were symptomatic of a wider ferment within African political and social life, much of it attributable to the impact of rapid industrialisation which had occurred during the war years, particularly on the Witwatersrand. For here a new urban proletariat was coming into being, its members concerned more with the immediate reality of inadequate wages, the high cost of living, and poor living conditions, than the wider political and constitutional issues with which the SANNC had been predominantly concerned. They were far less responsive to the older generation of Congress leaders who tended to draw their support from the rural, chiefly societies. Instead, they were much readier to exploit their new-found collective strength in seeking remedy for their grievances.

The resulting tensions had played their part in the divisions which were already emerging within the SANNC. They were also central to a revealing episode in Plaatje's own life during the course of 1918. In January that year, on returning to Kimberley from a trip across the Transvaal and Orange Free State, Plaatje noticed that demolition work had just begun on an old tram shed, owned by the De Beers company. He immediately saw in this the opportunity of using this as a meeting-hall for use by Africans in Kimberley, and in particular as an ideal headquarters of the new inter-denominational Brotherhood organisation which he was now seeking to establish in Kimberley.

The correspondence which then ensued (Docs 60-63, pp.232-37), culminating in the Governor-General of South Africa agreeing to formally open the new Assembly hall in August 1918, provides a fascinating example of the ways in which Plaatje was able to take advantage of the prevailing political and social tensions to persuade De Beers to support his work in Kimberley. For Plaatje the successful outcome was material support in his work: for De Beers, if the effect was to help keep Kimberley free of the strikes and disturbances taking place on the Rand, then it was cheap at the price. At the same time it was, for Plaatje, a dangerous game to be playing, and an indication of the fact that the position and influence of Plaatje and many of the other SANNC leaders was no longer what it had once been.

With the ending of the Great War in November 1918 Plaatje and the SANNC leadership addressed themselves once again to the wider constitutional position, and the grievances of the African population, and resolved to send a second delegation to England. Plaatje was initially reluctant after all the difficulties he had encountered in England between 1914 and 1917, but in the end he agreed to go, this time as its leader. He arrived in England in July 1919 with J.T. Gumede, the Natal representative on the delegation, joining three other delegates (Richard Selope Thema, Levi Mvabaza and Henry Ngcayiya) who had arrived earlier.

As with the first deputation Plaatje and his colleagues were bedevilled by shortage of funds. He did succeed in raising the funds to print a pamphlet he had written called *Some of the Legal Disabilities Suffered by the Native Population of the Union of South Africa and Imperial Responsibility* (Doc. 67, pp.250-57), which provided a comprehensive statement of the case they were presenting, and, as before, he addressed a wide variety of meetings to gain support for their cause. They secured interviews, too, with the Archbishop of Canterbury and, most notably, the Prime Minister, David Lloyd George. Plaatje and his colleagues managed to make quite an impact on Lloyd George (Doc. 68, pp.257-64), and in many ways this episode represented the apogee of Plaatje's ability to impress highly placed politicians and statesmen with the strength of his cause and the force of his personality. At the same time it emphasized the ultimate futility of a strategy so heavily dependent upon personal appeals of this kind. Even a concerned Prime Minister, who fulfilled his promise to communicate about the matter with Jan Smuts, by this time the South African Prime Minister, would never undermine the work of years of careful cultivation of South Africa as part of the empire.

Plaatje remained in England until September 1920, much of his time blighted by the aftermath of the notorious *Edinburgh Castle* incident, where three Congress delegates, seeking to return home, were ejected from the ship while it was in Southampton docks (Doc. 66, pp.247-50). But Plaatje continued with his campaign. As well as seeking to raise public support for Imperial intervention in South Africa, he established a branch of his Brotherhood organisation in the United Kingdom, and managed to write an historical novel, *Mhudi* – eventually to be published in 1930. In September 1920 he departed for the United States on a mission to extend what had by now become a one-man campaign, and to raise funds to support the work of his Brotherhood organisation in South Africa.

The two major documents from Plaatje's visit to the United States are his address to the 1921 Pan-African Congress in Europe (Doc. 69, pp.264-74), delivered on his behalf by W.E. B. Du Bois, since he could not raise the funds to travel himself ; and the *Mote and the Beam* (Doc. 70, pp.274-83), a pamphlet which Plaatje wrote and published early in 1921 in order, he wrote subsequently, 'to pay my way through the United States'. Plaatje's response to a review of the pamphlet by Hubert Harrison, a well known black political figure, provides a revealing indication of his motives and objectives in travelling to the United States (Doc. 71, pp.283-87); and a letter he wrote, towards the end of his time in the United States, to Mrs Sophie Colenso, provides a candid summary of what he felt he had learnt (Doc. 72, pp.287-89).

Before leaving the United States Plaatje travelled south to visit the famous Tuskegee Institute, then northwards to Chicago and on to Ontario in Canada, and thence to London in 1922. Here he completed a substantial, albeit very selective, account of his experiences in North America for the friends and supporters who had contributed financially to the costs of his trip to America (Doc. 73, pp.289-99). Finally, after a fruitless period of nearly a year in England between 1922 and 1923 Plaatje returned to South Africa, re-united with his family after a period of four and a half years' wandering.

Selected Writings

38

Letter to Henry Burton, Minister for Native Affairs, 8 November 1910[1]

This letter – together with documents 39 and 43 (pp.134 and 147) – formed part of Plaatje's campaign on behalf of a group of relatively prosperous African farmers in the Thaba Nchu district to secure a lifting of the restrictions governing their ability to purchase land. Plaatje enjoyed a close relationship with Henry Burton, the first Minister of Native Affairs in the Union government, having known him since both were in Kimberley in the 1890s. Plaatje's objectives were eventually achieved in 1924 (see pages 320-23.)

Tsala ea Becoana/Friend of the Bechuana
Corner of Brett Street and Shannon Street,
Kimberley
8th November 1910

H Burton, Esq., K.C., M.L.A.
Parliament Street
Cape Town

Dear Sir,

The Native Farmers' Association of Thaba Nchu desire me to attend at Cape Town and lay before you the hardship they are subjected to under Chapter XXXIV of the Laws of the Orange River Colony. Under this law a Native can only transfer land to a white man but not to another Native. In the republican days land was sometimes transferred by special permission of the President but since the British occupation it is enforced with the utmost rigour; and the matter calls for urgent redress just now as two young men are debarred from holding two farms they inherited from their uncle; under the law only sons and brothers can inherit and (apparently) not nephews.

As the Native mind has been indoctrinated with the idea that only Unionists[2] could help them it is our duty to teach our people that friendship could be shown to them by any, and that justice is not the monopoly of any party. For this reason I would strongly urge your approval of my going down with a view to giving particulars which will enable you to introduce a short measure abrogating the oppressive chapter. Coloured people and Hottentots[3] may buy or lease land but not aboriginal Natives and I feel certain you will not approve of a system under which the Natives of the Free State are subjected to a hardship which obtains nowhere else in the Union.

If complete abrogation is not practicable the law could be so amended as to exclude the Moroka district (which is in every sense a Native district) from its operation.

Your immediate reply will oblige.

Yours respectfully

Sol. T. Plaatje

Editor

Henry Burton passed on Plaatje's letter to Edward Dower, the Acting Secretary for Native Affairs. In replying to Plaatje, Dower indicated that 'Mr Burton proposes to visit the Native Reserves of the Orange Free State in the near future when he hopes to have an opportunity of enquiring personally into matters affecting the Natives of the Orange Free State'. On Dower's recommendation, an enabling bill was drafted, and eventually submitted to the Minister of Native Affairs for his approval in November 1911 (see pp.147, 150).

39
Letter to W.P. Schreiner, 7 December 1910[4]

Hon. W.P. Schreiner, K.C., C.M.G.[5]
South African Chambers
Cape Town

My Dear Sir,

As I will not see you before Tuesday and you will in the meanwhile be seeing the other three Native Senators[6] on my behalf, I think that I should mention to you that I wrote the Rt. Hon. J.X. Merriman at the same time as I wrote you and Col. Stanford,[7] and if you think that his influence will help us you might ask him also to see me on Tuesday morning so that I may request him to reinforce us and help us to induce the Prime Minister to see the justice of introducing a short relieving bill.

Henry Burton, first Minister of Native Affairs in the Union government – in Plaatje's view
'a friend of the Natives' and of the Barolong in particular.

I was very much struck by the tactics of General Hertzog[8] 20 years back when he addressed a Dutch jury at Fauresmith in favour of two Native prisoners. I was but a youngster then but I will never forget the episode and I have carried with me a warm admiration for the General all these years and I will be very much surprised if he also does not see the justice of our modest request for immediate relief.

With such a combination I am sure we could favourably impress the Rt. Hon. the Prime Minister (who knows me) and the Minister of Lands;[9] for it will be a pity having regard to what has been done for the participators in Bambata's rising,[10] if the law-abiding Barolongs of Thaba Nchu cannot get the ear of the government in a matter which (judging from the gazette I showed you) the Free State government was also anxious to redress.

Yours respectfully
Sol T Plaatje

119 Loop Street
Cape Town
17.12.10.

P.S. For the present I am not seeing any of my friends about this for if it were raised abroad the opposition press will make political capital out of it and do our cause more harm than good. S.T.P.

40

Article, 'Annexation and the Protectorates: The pros and cons', *Pretoria News*, 16 January 1911

This was the first of a series of articles which Plaatje wrote between 1911 and 1914 for the Pretoria News, *edited by Vere Stent, for whom he had worked during the siege of Mafeking. In an accompanying editorial Stent provided a biographical outline of Plaatje's life and career, commending his views and opinions to his readership, and underlining 'the importance of knowing what the Native thinks before we legislate for him'. 'We commence today an experiment,' Stent wrote, 'which will prove a success if only we can persuade the more rabid negrophobes to adopt a more moderate and sensible attitude.'*

The fiat has gone forth, and with a single stroke of His late Majesty King Edward's pen, the Union of South Africa has become an accomplished act.[11]

The same reasons which impelled the whites of South Africa to combine under one legislative and administrative authority should force the Natives of the territories of Basutoland, Bechuanaland and Swaziland to abandon their present separate forms of administration and come under one umbrella.

From the statesmanly speeches of His Royal Highness, the Duke of Connaught to the Basuto chiefs at Bloemfontein and the Bechuana chiefs at Gaberones, it is clear that that umbrella could under no circumstances be planted at Downing Street. It must be on this side of the Atlantic.

The Natives of the protectorates were strongly and persistently against any idea of being included in the Union. Having regard to their old relations with the Boers of the Free State and the western Transvaal, and, taking into consideration the fact that leaders of the old commandos against them or their descendants are now holding prominent positions in the Union, their fears are not unreasonable, but what alternative have they? They are not ruled from Downing Street at the present time. They are governed by resident commissioners who are responsible to the High Commissioner, now Governor-General of the Union of South Africa. So that their seclusion is more imaginary than real.

An analogous state of affairs arose in 1895 when the Barolongs of Mafeking protested against the annexation of their then crown colony of Bechuanaland to the Cape Colony. The late Sir Sidney Shippard visited them and assured them of the benefits of the change. The common Native peasants – always against changes – were not disposed to accept his assurances, but their wise Chief Montsioa, said, 'It is indeed true that the change will be for the better. For what do we know about England or imperial rule? We sacrificed much to resist the attempt of the Boers to annex Bechuanaland to the Transvaal Republic, because we loved the Queen of England, having seen how well her officials treated our people in Cape Colony.'

The Ramatlhabama valley which divides Cape Colony from the Bechuanaland protectorate runs across Montsioa's territory and today, after 15 years' comparison of the two administrations, none of the Barolongs on the south side of the valley will vote for the *status quo ante*. Why should they? They were paying a wheel-tax of 10s. per wagon per annum. This tended to restrict Native industry, as the owner of six wagons, before annexation, paid the government £3 per annum for his enterprise. All that ceased with annexation. They have liberal school grants ranging from £20 to £60 per individual teacher per annum in return for half the tax, whilst their fellows in the protectorate send their children to the Cape side as they enjoy no school grants on the north side of the boundary. The Cape magistrates have sometimes sentenced Natives to many months of imprisonment with hard labour and some lashes, and four days later a telegram has come from Kimberley ordering the release of the prisoners as the judge had quashed the sentences.

On the north band of the valley the magistrate's word is final. An appeal lies from his decision to the Resident Commissioner who is in some instances not quite as competent a lawyer as the magistrate who presided over the lower court; in fact, an appeal is the biggest farce in the quasi-military administration of the indeterminate constitutions of those Cinderella dependencies which allow administrators of no legal standing to decide momentous causes which no judge will attempt without the aid of counsel and jury. One of the effects thereof is that a harmless and innocent chief of the Bechuanaland protectorate has now languished in gaol for nearly five years on the orders of Lord Selborne. Thanks to the absence of an independent tribunal to which to apply for his freedom, he is still there, although his innocence has been more than proved. Lord Selborne imprisoned him presumably on the advice of the resident, who according to the protectorate judicial practice is also the judge of appeal; and I think it is too much to expect him to give judgment against his own advice.

During the period of his incarceration inconsiderate agents have squandered his estate valued at over £6,000. No wonder that the Bechuanas hesitated to accept Lord Selborne's assurances concerning Union as it is not unreasonable to doubt the assurance of a governor-general who is capable of imprisoning a guiltless man for five years, even though the imprisonment is unaccompanied by the customary 'hard labour'; and the Natives of Mafeking (under the jurisdiction of the Supreme Courts) are aware that a wrong of such magnitude will be impossible on the south side of the Ramatlhabama.[12]

I have no information regarding Swaziland, but in Basutoland, one tenth of the population, the enlightened few – is strongly in favour of annexation to the Union. Their reasons are that the imperial code is just the same as their old chief Moshoeshoe's and has outlived its usefulness; and that it favours the chiefs at the expense of the liberty of the subject. They say, moreover, that the civil service is hereditary; ability is no recommendation for public appointments. A young white man will be pitch-forked into any sinecure just because he is the son of his father, and regardless of his ability to govern the Natives justly. That is one-tenth of the population. One-tenth again is strongly against annexation. Unlike the other tenth, they have not reduced their reasons to writing, and I will proceed to do so for them.

Primarily they are horribly afraid of a change just because it is a change; in the next place, they reason (not unreasonably perhaps) that England sacrificed thousands of her sons and hundreds of millions of money to conquer the Boers, and that for some reason or other which from a Native point of view no number of explanations can successfully clear, they not only gave back to the Boers their old republics, but gave them the two colonies of Natal and the Cape of Good Hope in addition. Is it not possible, therefore, that the main object of the annexation movement is to pursue the peculiar magnanimity of England and give the Boers a bonsella in the form of three protectorates? Moreover, according to the schedule to the South Africa Act, the prime minister has a bigger say than anyone else over Natives; and the present Prime Minister of the Union has not always used guarded terms in his references to the protectorates. Again, they have been told that some one by the name of Hertzog is engaged in a monster scheme, the effect of which will be that Germans will stop speaking German, English stop speaking English, Frenchmen stop speaking French, Xhosas stop speaking Kafir, and that it will be a criminal office for a Mosuto, Zulu or white man to speak anything but Dutch.

Bechuana, Sesuto and Swazi are just as dear to us as the Irishman's language is to him and his home, and as the loss of one's language is too dear a price to pay for annexation their fears are also reasonable. But ask the opposing tenth for any safeguards under the present system which could be regarded as being better for the Natives than clauses 1, 20, 24 and 25 (legislative) 14, 15 and 16 (administrative) and 23 (judicial) of the schedule to the Act of Union, and they will not cite any.[13] Eight-tenths of the population 'do not care two straws' whether the country remains as it is, attached to Downing Street, or annexed to the Union.

I do not contend that the last work in human wisdom has been said in the schedule to the Act of Union, but I maintain that if the protectorates have to come under one umbrella, that umbrella should without doubt be the Union of South Africa; and I am satisfied that if the authorities had dropped red-tape for once and given the Natives a true interpretation of this liberal schedule they would, instead of opposing it, have been as anxious as their white neighbours to be included in the Union. It is true that the Dutch element preponderates in the Union, but, like their English colleagues, they have to subscribe to the oath in section 51 of the Union Act,[14] and abide by its terms.

The Resident Commissioner will share his responsibilities with the Prime Minister and territorial commissioner, the Supreme Court will relieve him of all the legal work, giving him sufficient time to devote to his administrative duties. To the magistrates, the continual rendering of periodical returns will perhaps be an irritating innovation. They will sometimes give fair and conscientious judgment to be subsequently told that as they were not in accordance with real and substantial justice they have been quashed on review. But magistrates of civilized countries have to put up with that, and it is in the interests of justice.

Instead of making representations and financing expensive sea voyages to England on serious tribal affairs, the chiefs will apply to the Union government and get an answer within a month. In my opinion the jurisdiction of the Supreme Court alone warrants the change as it will give to the common people the King's protection in practice as well as in theory. Neither chief nor commissioner will be a law unto himself. Whatever the state requires from the Natives and vice versa, is distinctly laid down, and everybody will know where he stands exactly.

41
Article, 'Segregation: Idea ridiculed', *Friend of the Bechuana*, 18 January 1911[15]

This is part of an essay (the remainder has not survived) written by Plaatje in 1910 as his entry in a competition organised by C.F. Tainton, a prominent pro-segregationist from Johannesburg. Plaatje's essay was awarded third prize, worth £1-10s. 'Greater care in the arrangement of his arguments,' Tainton commented, 'would have added much to their value. His paper is a clear but bitter protest against our present native policy, and throws much light on the effect of a repressive policy on educated and able members of the Native races.'

Geographical separation is not without its allurements. What a glorious millennium! A city of black folks where, Europeans being excluded, the havoc wrought in the Native territories by attorneys' fees will be things of the past. With black postmasters, black carpenters, black tax-collectors, and black shopkeepers, making money! In fact, black everything, with a British resident reporting to the Governor-General (in the words of a recent imperial blue book on the Gilbert Islands in the South Pacific):

> Wars have ceased, the districts are in perfect order, extreme poverty is (almost) unknown; every man is secure in the

possession of his piece of land; taxes are light and arouse no complaint. The Native police are efficient and the Native officials admirably honest; the houses are good; the roads clean; and the hospitals have been established.

Resistance by whites

But all this is visionary. Has it ever occurred to the thousands of white officials that when the segregation idea becomes an accomplished fact they stand three chances to one of being retrenched? I think it has; and I am satisfied that when the Natives begin to move the whites will stop them even if they have to use Martini rifles for the purpose.

Go to Kingwilliamstown and see the flood of black peasantry pouring through the streets, walking up and down the thoroughfares, meeting and gossiping with friends, staring at the shop windows, purchasing groceries, farming implements and clothes; then imagine these Natives all far away in Katanga and ask yourself the question: 'What will become of the merchants of Kingwilliamstown without the Kafir? – the Kafir as a labourer, the Kafir as a transport rider, the Kafir as a customer?', and only one possibility suggests itself, namely, that they will be bankrupt. And what is patent in regard to Kingwilliamstown is equally so in regard to Port Elizabeth, to Kimberley, Bloemfontein and Johannesburg, in spite of all that has been urged in the latter two cities in favour of 'a white man's country'.

Native objections

On the other hand let us imagine the government succeeding in locating these Natives in an area where the whites are prevented from living; that transported to fountains of new justice and laws, they dwell in a monotony of lonely looking forests of Kafir corn or mealies, wasting time through lack of bicycles and silver watches. Confusion will reign supreme at the Native settlement; the educated ones striving to enforce a progressive code for the maintenance of law and order; hereditary princes on the other hand always regarding the action of educated Natives with suspicion, will scheme and manoeuvre for their overthrow. Blood and brains will often be at loggerheads and you know,

> When two raging fires meet together
> They do consume the thing that keeps their fury.

This is not an empty saw. It was exemplified at the close of the last century when differences between the Boer and Hollander officials and those of the burghers and uitlanders* resulted in the overthrow of the two republics. However, after taking those drawbacks into consideration, and weighing the possible gains and losses, I find the balance of advantages decidedly in favour of the blacks, provided, of course, their areas are reduced by reason of their unsuitability.

Economic disadvantages

Living in a place whence exotic influences are banished, the Natives will develop a civilization along a separate groove without treading on the white man's land; intermarriage and criminal conversation between white and black will be next to impossible; the sons of their well-to-do will have no way of squandering their fathers' substance in the bar; and the side-bar will be debarred from continuing the relentless forays which it so ruthlessly inflicts upon Native estates in the territories but – is it practicable?

They will not pay any taxes unless, like in Basutoland, the money is devoted solely for their uses. This will result in a net loss to the Union treasury of £2,000,000 annually and a large sum to the respective municipalities. Europeans will make the rude discovery that the Kafir was handy not only as a water-carrier, but as the gold mine from which local and general exchequers drew heavily and paid the fancy salaries which helped to educate white children and keep white families in comfort. Millions of money now circulating amongst Europeans will be withdrawn to pay black officials and feed black storekeepers; the effect whereof will be the wholesale dismissal of many white men and then the trouble will begin. Oh no! Earlier still, for I am sure that when you tell the traders of the Transkei to relinquish their holdings and seek fresh pastures in white areas, they are not the Englishmen I took them for if they do not resist the order at the point of the bayonet. The ideal is sound but how will you attain it?

Before the war an imperial officer doubted my loyalty because I predicted that 150,000 soldiers would take over 12 months to conquer the republics. He was prepared to wager that 50,000 troops (leaving alone the 100,000) would within six months have made such a complete business of it as to have almost forgotten that there ever was war. I need hardly add that I would have won the bet if gambling was in my line. Today I venture to predict that if the High Commissioner started a segregation department with a vote of £20,000,000 within eighteen months the vote would be overdrawn and the work only

---

* Dutch, 'aliens' or 'foreigners', a term applied to British and other nationals living in the Transvaal prior to the outbreak of the Anglo-Boer War.

partly done. By that time the Union Parliament will receive petitions from Europeans praying for the repatriation of the suggested Natives.

Some concrete cases

Look how boldly the Alice municipality fought the principal of Lovedale last year, when Mr Henderson wished to segregate the 1,000 students of the famous institution. Could it be contended, in the face of that, that Alice or any other town would tolerate legislation with the object of removing every Native family along the Chumie and Gaga?[16]

I was in Johannesburg in the winter of 1904 when the Rand municipality cleared its Natives to Nancefield, 12 miles away. I saw the misery and hardships which attended the enforcement of the measure, and heard Native viragoes loudly lamenting the downfall of Kruger and cursing the new administration, which they termed 'remorseless tyrants' (*batana i-eitibeg*, lit: cruel birds of prey.) No measure was more popular in white Johannesburg, but before the month's end the result was effectively felt by the townspeople and when I visited Johannesburg I found the town full of black colonies and a movement was on foot to move the location from Nancefield to Sophiatown, much nearer the town. So how can we effect a separation, and how can we cross the troubles between our present conditions and segregation? That is my difficulty. The odds are unsurmountable. Commerce will be dislocated; to meet the interest on the segregation loss every conceivable tax will have to be doubled; the labour market will be disorganised and many commercial houses will be ruined, and we will gain very little from such a sacrifice.

It cannot be said that with his one thousand years' civilisation, his heritage of a cultured home, his high school advantages, facilities for employment and superior emoluments, the white man fears competition on the same ground with the handicapped black son of a black father with scarcely a generation's training; who is trammelled by colour, language, environments and low wages. Two things you need to give the Native, and two things only you must deny him. Keep away from him liquor and lawyers, give him the franchise, and your confidence, and the problem will solve itself to your mutual advantage.

42

Article, 'The "Kaffir Mail": Discriminating fares', *Pretoria News*, 3 March 1911

I mentioned in my last letter[17] that we had no 'Jim Crow'[18] cars in South Africa, but that the C.S.A.R. had 'Jim Crow' compartments. I should have mentioned that among the innovations inaugurated by the Central South African Railways is a whole 'Jim Crow' train. Officially, it rejoices in the respectable name of 'Kafir Mail', but it is known among railway officials as 'nigger train'. This train was a kind of separate conveyance for the use of Native passengers – a mild sort of segregation. I have often wished to travel by this slow train, so as to study it from within, but I have never yet been able to spare two clear days which are necessary for a journey by it between Bloemfontein and Johannesburg. My knowledge of it is based upon observations and conversations with its passengers at such stations and junctions as Smaldeel, Bloemfontein, Springfontein, Burghersdorp and Queenstown. It is composed of the old wooden-bunked carriages of the *Spoorweg Maatschappy*, discarded Cape Government Railways and Natal old coaches. Sometimes these coaches are varnished, but they often looked sooty and insanitary.

I am told that fares paid to travel by this train were the same as per the ordinary express, and passengers by the 'Kafir Mail' had to put up with the following disadvantages:

(a) Its table of arrival at, and departures from, stations appears in none of the official timetables. They have to rely on enquiries for fares, distances and time; (b) it pulls up at the goods sheds and at outside sidings where there are no platforms, and women with babies behind their backs have to go in for jumping exercises when boarding or alighting from the train; (c) passengers by this train are herded together in any old way regardless of sex, condition or numbers; (d) It took over 30 hours to reach Bloemfontein from Johannesburg – a distance covered by the express in 11 hours; (e) passengers by it miss connections at Smaldeel, Bloemfontein, Springfontein, which are joined by the ordinary trains which leave Johannesburg 10 hours later.

What must be the feelings of Native passengers when, packed sardine-like in unclean compartments, they see first one and then another express fitted with electric lights and modern conveniences, drawn by similar looking engines, dashing past them with white passengers who, though not overcrowded, paid the same fares or much less, as will appear from my observations on excursion fares?

I would put better carriages on the 'Kafir Mail'; I would run them at scheduled times so as to overtake the connections. I would give them platforms to facilitate their ascents and descents. I would insert a timetable in a translation of the tariff book so as to deprive them of any reason to complain, and I would not keep them for three days on a journey which white passengers accomplish in only one. The question is, are not these guards and firemen wasting public time and money, and delaying rolling stock by occupying 72 hours to Queenstown, where others taken only 23? As these 'Kafir Mails' are run daily, could not a saving be effected by accelerating their movements, for in the circumstances it would appear that three guards are engaged for the slow service where the daily express uses only one?

There is an idea that anything is good enough for a Kafir. That being so, why not give him an inferior article, but at an inferior price? Europeans scarcely even consider the harm that they do to themselves by engaging in a business which is so flagrantly chicane as to look at the colour of a customer's skin and, if it is not white, sell him a fourth-hand article at a first-class price.

It will perhaps surprise your readers to learn that many Natives would be strongly in favour of segregation if only they were assured that it is going to be carried out on equitable lines. If the Johannesburg post office, for instance, which has a 'Jim Crow' department, had rented a separate little office, or had placed the Fraser Street post office at the disposal of coloured people, they could have little reason to complain. Why does the Postmaster-General dig a cellar at the bottom of his office, and send his Native customers down it for stamps, whilst his white-skinned customers get them at face value on the ground floor of a sky-scraper? If I found it necessary to serve some of my customers in a dark cellar, I would give them a liberal discount for the inconvenience.

The Native's dread of territorial segregation is that in pursuance of this policy of favouritism, the government will select the most arid and fever-struck districts for the 'black belt' and that you will tax them almost as heavily as white men for the privilege of going to die there of fever. They fear that you will give them a train with ramshackle coaches and over-charge them for its use.

In America an hotel-keeper runs tremendous risks in refusing accommo-dation to a negro; at Jacksonville one forfeited his licence for the same reason. In South Africa, however, you want segregation without its responsibilities. In America the cleaning of 'Jim Crow' cars is attended to with as much diligence as the others. A white man entering a coloured compartment and refusing to leave it when warned to do so is liable to fine and imprisonment, just as much as the black who refuses to leave a white carriage.

But here in South Africa it appears that the whites claim separate accommodation for the Natives, but would like the Natives to give it up on demand. In plain English, then, you want every available accommodation for yourselves. Is it fair to the men you found in the country, and who have since your arrival loyally assisted you to build and improve your homesteads, villages, towns and cities all over the subcontinent?

Last week a Johannesburg paper lashed itself to fury over the heavy charges to passengers on the South African Railways, and absence of concessions. Your contemporary concluded a vehement leaderette with the following partial yet suggestive sentence, 'There are special concessions for coolie-produced sugar, but the white man who pays the piper hasn't the ghost of a chance of calling even an occasional tune.' This view is generally held by white men all over the Transvaal. They firmly believe that they are the only sufferers. Ignorant of the fact that the Native is their faithful helpmeet in every turn, they would violently dispute a suggestion that in some branches of taxation the Native actually pays a bigger share of the bill. It may surprise them to hear that some Natives actually take out letters of exemption just for the privilege of being taxed as lightly as white men.

The old Cape Government Railways used to arrange their fares according to classes, so that a man received exactly what he asked for and paid only for what he received. Their fares were 3d., 2d., and 1d. per mile for 1st, 2nd, and 3rd classes respectively, and a liberal discount was made in each class for prepaid return fares. In the Transvaal and Orange River Colony, however, the fares were 2d., 1½d. and 1d. respectively. It will be seen that the C.S.A.R. carried 1st and 2nd class passengers (mainly whites) at a cheaper rate than the Cape administration, but treated third-class passengers (mainly Natives) no better. Reductions were made in favour of 1st and 2nd class return passengers, but not the third. This discrimination was carried to undue lengths when the holidays came along. The C.S.A.R. carried 1st and 2nd class passengers at one single fare plus one tenth for the double journey, in which concession the third-class Natives did not participate; they continuing to pay full fare out and full fare back. The result was that during the holidays the third class was the most expensive as well as the most inconvenient and overcrowded of the three.

Last Easter I paid 5/- for a first-class excursion ticket, Johannesburg to Pretoria and back, and Natives were at that time paying 7/6 for return tickets between the same stations. At the last Congress of the Native Convention,[19] two delegates came from Bethlehem in a third-class compartment, paying 31/2 each. They were amazed to learn on arrival at the Congress that their fellow-delegates (who travelled 2nd class) had paid only 22/-, over 9/- less. These inequalities should show you how you managed to travel cheaper than passengers over Cape lines, and yet maintained your improvements and high salaries. It was because your faithful Natives were loyally footing the bill, while you called the tune and enjoyed cheap family excursions. Surely the devotion of such people deserves some consideration at your hands. The attention of the railway board is respectfully invited to above anomalies.

43

Letter to Henry Burton (Minister of Native Affairs), 3 May 1912[20]

Plaatje's letter was in response to the news that the government had decided not to proceed with the Barolong land relief bill in view of the plans, then under discussion, for a more comprehensive bill on African land tenure — what became the Natives' Land Act of 1913.

3rd May 1912

The Hon. H. Burton, K.C., M.L.A.,
Minister of Native Affairs,
Cape Town.

My dear Sir,

I beg respectfully to inform you that I have been to Thaba Nchu and reported the result of our recent mission to Cape Town on the Free State farms bill.

The news has caused a bitter disappointment at what the Natives call their shabby treatment by the Free State ministers.

The Minister of Justice has never hesitated to extend acts of clemency to proved criminals in Natal found guilty of serious crimes by superior courts of justice and they in Thaba Nchu get 'stank voor dank'* for their life-long loyalty to the Orange Free State.

They do not ask that the law should be broken but all they ask for is the continuation of the *status quo*. They only ask that the Governor-General should retain the same discretion which was beneficially exercised by the State President in the early days, when they were not, as now, interfered with in the enjoyment of their possessions. The President never to their knowledge refused a single request for transfer, and they are beginning to suspect that it is not so much the law as that the present government are designedly oppressive.

In 1886 the farm Somerset, formerly the property of the Free State government, was transferred and registered in the name of Abram Setlogelo, a Native. In 1889 Stephanus Makgothi, a Native, bought from A.H. Wells,

---

* Dutch: 'get small thanks'.

European, the farm Bastardspost and got transfer. In 1891 Joseph Masisi, a Native, exchanged his farm Langebewond for the farm Thaba Patchoa, till then owned by James Robinson, European, merchant of Jammersbergdrift district, Wepener. In 1893 John Sebitloane purchased the farm Tuinbult from the estate of Marete Likgolo and in 1894 Mongane Ramagaga, a Native, purchased the farm Tafelkop from Thabaki Marete. Joseph Masisi, a Native, bought of Olive Isabel Eleanor Addams, European, an erf in Thaba Nchu town and got transfer. I have carefully enquired and can hear of no instance where the President refused an application and I am sure that any relief extended to them at the present time will allay a lot of bad feeling.

Yours respectfully,
Sol T. Plaatje

44

Article, 'Native view of General Hertzog's scheme', *Pretoria News*, 23 October 1912

The reshuffling of portfolios has handed the most important state department of the Union to the Free State.[21] A Free State minister controls the 5,000,000 Natives of the Union, and his recent speeches would seem to indicate that the fears which permeated the Native population, when the change was announced, were justified. The same minister has charge of the police force and all the courts of justice. The Department of the Interior is in the hands of the father of the Free State. (Like the Jews, the Americans had their Abraham, but, with due respect, one has to add that Right Hon. A. Fisher has still to prove his fitness for the title 'the Abraham of South Africa'). He is moreover the Union Minister of Crown Lands and it seems that the Free State very nearly 'conglomerated' all the portfolios.

The result

General Hertzog has announced a big scheme which he has up his sleeve: he unfolded it at Nylstroom and elaborated on it at Smithfield and it is to segregate the white and black inhabitants of the Union. I purposely waited to see the full reports in the Free State ministerial newspapers, but, after reading the Smithfield outline, one would be inclined to say, in the words of Luscombe Scarelle's Ikey, that 'the shcheme wouldn't vork very vell.'

The modus operandi

The speech has alarmed the Native population much more than the Europeans and they are anxious to know how it will work. I quote from the speech: 'In other parts of the Union the Natives were educated and had all the white man's rights, but when they came to me for situations I had no room for the Natives. I want my officials among the whites. That was perhaps unfair to the Natives, but I had to do it as long as matters remained as at present. We have to be unfair to the Natives because we have to defend ourselves and at the same time defend the Natives.' This is the first time in the history of South Africa that a crown minister expressed the view that he can advance the cause of the whites by being unfair to the Natives; but the inconsistency is more sickening. Not once, but twice to my recollection, when questioned in Parliament, General Hertzog flatly denied the dismissal of Native civil servants or colour discrimination of any kind. On other occasions he sent the Minister of Mines and the Minister of Native Affairs to read the denials for him. If the whites can be defended by repressing the Natives, why did he not tell Parliament that?

Coming events cast their shadows before them and the persecution of Native farm tenants which recently characterized the action of some police officers in the Free State and Transvaal, and also that of white farmers who appear to be imbued with the new spirit, assured the Natives that there was something drastic in store for them. The Labour Party may now congratulate itself for the Minister of Native Affairs has declared in favour of territorial segregation – their favourite theme.[22]

The Rev. Mr Postma asked the Minister of Railways for his opinion on the subject, at Burghersdorp last week, and Mr Burton declared that he was not in favour; but then the Minister of Railways and Harbours is not likely to deny in Parliament anything he told his constituents and he received, after this negative reply, as enthusiastic a vote of confidence from the burghers of Burghersdorp as General Hertzog did from the burghers of Smithfield when he propounded his segregation proposition. It would be useless to ask the Prime Minister for an explanation of these divergent views of two members of his cabinet as General Botha would probably reply that 'a great deal had been said by the one minister which should not have been said, and by the other minister things had been said which should have been said in a different way'. 'Both are slightly mistaken and … both are more or less right.' So the Labour Party may draw what comfort it can from this inexactitude.

Free State Native policy
All that is clear is the promise of some sort of territorial segregation and we are going to get it on Free State terms. Just one instance of the Free State territorial policy:

Moroka's Barolongs resided in Thaba Nchu long before General Hertzog was born in Cape Colony. They had an alliance with the Free State republic under which they fought all of that republic's wars against Basutoland with their own horses, their own guns and their own rations. Indeed but for the bravery of these people in the field, at a time when the gallant general was still in his pinafores, a large portion of what is now known as the province of the Orange Free State (including a large slice of the Smithfield district) would have been part of Basutoland today.

Of course, it would be too much to expect republicans to thank black men for any services rendered or sacrifices made. Their fellow Europeans of British descent have spared neither expense nor energy in developing the country and educating the old republicans. They are still lavishing British capital on spanning a network of railways over the country, connecting centres hundreds of miles distance from the backveld; and by bringing the markets right up to the farmers' doors they have enhanced the value of landed property, provided profitable employment for young burghers in their industrial areas and improved the lot of the burghers generally; but so far from thanking Providence for the spread of British enterprise in South Africa, like the two daughters of King Solomon's horseleach, they are always crying, 'Give, give.'

Similarly the thanks received by these Barolongs for purchasing the enlargement of the Free State with their own goods and the blood of their best sons was Chapter XXXIV of the Free State law book under which no Native can obtain title to land when white men can freely purchase land from Natives. The absurdity of this law came into prominence two years ago when two Barolong young men inherited a farm each, and the registrar of deeds was debarred, by this law, from giving them transfers in terms of their deceased uncle's will. The injustice was so flagrant that the Minister of Lands gazetted a bill which promised some kind of relief. That bill never reached Parliament, and the fact remains that, in a British colony, these aboriginal Afrikanders, whom the Boers found in the country and with whose assistance they retained the Free State, cannot even inherit their own property under Free State-made laws. What right has any man to talk of segregating the white and black inhabitants of the Union when in his own house he has proved incapable of redressing such a palpable wrong? Surely one has first to bank his own money to the best advantage before aspiring to act as banker for other people, and he will at least be expected to master his arithmetic and be *au fait* with the banking laws and fluctuations of the money market.

45
Editorial, 'The war of extermination', *Friend of the Bechuana,* 10 May 1913

Kruger never placed anything so barbarous before the Transvaal Volksraad

Is Abdurahman a reliable prophet?

It may be very easy to steal a pin, but the Union government should realise that to steal a whole subcontinent is not quite so easy. A bill with a very long name[23] sneaked into the Union Parliament through some back window this week, which proposes to hold up the real estate market for an indefinite period until a commission of five had reported on it, and General Hertzog's segregation idea is crystallized into law. Till then (which may probably be in 1950) no Native can buy land.[24]

Now, since the Union, every bill has been sent to us by the government's printing contractors in a gazette extraordinary: but nothing of the terms of this legislative monstrosity has ever leaked out. It sneaked into Parliament as quietly as an evil deed of which its perpetrators are ashamed. But for the kindness of three members of Parliament, each of whom very kindly posted to us a copy of the bill, we would know nothing of its contents beyond the bare fact that some such measure had found its way into Parliament. Thanks to the three members referred to, we are able to tell our readers what we are likely to be in for.

Worse than Hertzog's

Compared with this bill, General Hertzog's segregation scheme, which our people (ourselves included) condemned as it sought to separate the British family in this country 'on the rotten and indefensible ground of colour' – to use Lord Milner's phrase – was a more humane and statesmanlike proposition. General Hertzog propounded his scheme to a Native deputation (our editor among them) last year. He drew a ring on a Free State map round Moroka with slices of the adjacent districts, and stated that his commission would be definitely instructed that that should form the Free State black area, where Natives will freely buy land, live and develop along their own lines, and have Native clerks in government offices, where they could be raised under government control without any interference from white susceptibilities. This bill distinctly lays down that Natives who are at present debarred (as in Chapter XXXIV of the laws of the Orange Free State from buying land) will continue to be so debarred – sub-Section (a) of Section 15.

General Hertzog told us that in Native areas, Natives would purchase, hire and occupy land as freely as they wish. This bill prohibits Native syndicates from buying land in any area, while no such restrictions are placed on white syndicates (section 10).

General Hertzog clearly recognised that the Native locations are full and stated that land will have to be indicated outside the locations where they could buy. Section 5 of this bill lays down that no person except a Native will be permitted to purchase land in the scheduled Native areas. On reference to the schedule we find that 'scheduled Native areas' are nothing but the present Native locations and inalienable reserves which are so crowded that, for upwards of a quarter of a century, Natives have been flowing over to find a resting place for the hollow of their feet, on the vast areas which, till then, have been peopled only by snakes and scorpions. Until the segregation law is passed, these Natives are to be squeezed back into the locations and forced to leave their present holdings in the possession of mice and rats.

General Hertzog clearly said that under his scheme no European trader, missionary or school master will reside in Native areas until the Natives satisfied the government that they need him: but just as though the present congestion in the Native territories is not enough for our one-sided authorities, this bill lays down that the Governor-General will approve of the establishment of towns, mission and trading stations on the reserves, apparently without reference to the Native occupants.

General Hertzog proposed to give free title to owners whether white or black in their respective areas. Section 9 of this bill empowers the government to expropriate your land by force. And the penalty for contravening any section of this bill is to be a fine of £100 or six months with hard labour with £5 per day for every day as long as it takes you to prepare to comply: and in addition you are exposed to a civil suit for damages.

No comparison

Those people who have for months back been sneering at Mr Sauer[25] on the ground that he will be too mild with the Natives and not deal with them as rigidly as General Hertzog certainly owe an apology to Mr Sauer, for the present minister has gone a good deal further than the member for Smithfield.

The Hertzog scheme, harsh because of its physical and geographical wildcat discriminations, was, nevertheless, a debatable legislative proposition: but the Sauer bill is ruinous and too repressive for an assembly of honourable men, who can claim to be British and who daily open their meetings with prayer.

General Hertzog promised us a segregation which would guide the activities of both races and develop the potentialities of each in its separate area, through its own people for the benefit of each, providing separately in each area all the outlets for the economical, industrial, professional, educational and religious aspirations of each – in fact, the emancipation of the blacks by creating for them a place where they could enjoy the fruits of their possessions free from European interference. But this bill seeks to deprive them of what little they possess today and make them roving wanderers and potential criminals. It therefore deserves to be hurled out of Parliament as rudely as it was sprung into it.

We appeal to the Natal members, and would like to remind them that in spite of all temptations, they have remained Englishmen and loyal to Queen Victoria's constitution which granted them self-government in 1842.

We appeal to the Unionists, to that rising star of Natal who punished Sir Frederick Moor[26] for joining the Boer party.

Lord Milner's South African Native Affairs Commission is accused of foisting this thing upon us: but we appeal to the Hon. Marshall Campbell[27] to remind Natalians that the Natal members of that commission flatly refused to identify themselves with such an un-British recommendation, and if Mr Sauer can protect Cape Natives from its operation (sub-section 2 of section 15 of this bill)[28] they have a greater claim to protect Natal Natives from its operation because of the minority report signed by the two Natal commissioners.

We appeal to the Rand representatives. We wish to remind them that they were not represented in the Milner commission. The Transvaal was represented by republicans only, and if any of the British Transvaalers were represented on that commission we venture to say the Transvaal commissioners would most probably have signed a minority report on the lines of a paper recently published by Mr Patrick Duncan.[29]

We appeal to the Cape members. We ask them to remember that it was never their intention, when consenting to Union, that the 'Free' State was to be allowed to run amok with Native legislation.

We appeal to them to redeem their election pledges, to the effect that, as long as they have voices in the House, they will see to it that Natives throughout the Union do not get any disabilities in addition to what they had before. This has not been redeemed; for while Free State Natives and coloured people bought land by permission of the President during the republican days, we cannot now buy land under any circumstances.

We appeal to the Free State members to put an end to the reproach brought about by the irritating tendencies which belie the name of their province, and virtually reduce it to the slave state of the Union.

Finally, we appeal to the Rt. Hon. Louis Botha, Prime Minister of the Union. He kicked General Hertzog out of the cabinet, partly because that General thought to be a successful minister of the crown was to pamper one's party at the expense of other sections of the community; and we beg to remind him that that was no more a ministerial crime than fostering one's own colour at the expense of other coloured subjects of the crown. If General Hertzog could be kicked out for the one thing, some other general might be kicked out for the other. We have not yet lost faith in the good sense of the South African Parliament, and (in spite of this bill) we have no reason to feel despondent. Let the right thing be done and no man will be better pleased than Dr Abdurahman[30] to find his prophecy is falsified!

46
Letter to the General Manager, De Beers, 17 July 1913[31]

Office of the *Tsala ea Batho*
c/o Shannon and Selby Streets
Kimberley
July 17th 1913

The General Manager
De Beers Consolidated Mines Ltd
Stockdale St
Kimberley

Dear Sir,

I am too appreciative of the financial support accorded me by the De Beers Company, ever since I started newspaper work,[32] to worry them over trifles but I would respectfully call attention to my treatment on their tram cars.

As an instance, yesterday I was going to the mayor's meeting with the Greenpoint Natives and wished to leave by the 2 p.m. tram out. The seat allotted to Natives at the back of the car was fully occupied but for three white passengers in uniform, inside the car was empty so I wished to take a seat near the motor-man in front (a seat which on the Gibson cars[33] is used by raw

Natives)* but the motor-man objected and directed me to the back which, as I say, was fully occupied; and, Sir, you can understand that after working at top speed, with the lunch-hour thrown in, in order to be off at a certain time, it is not very comfortable to pay a shilling for the privilege of standing on an empty car, so I preferred to walk and take a cab further on. I would but add that although I and one of my friends are allowed to ride on the Gibson cars I always take the last seat inside the car – no matter where the Coloured people and Indians sit – so as not to be in the way of European passengers; moreover, I make it a rule to avoid full cars and it is not likely that I would abuse a similar privilege were it extended to me by the De Beers tramway management.

It is not very pleasant to me, as a citizen of Kimberley and supporter of De Beers Company, when I show round a highly placed Native visitor from, say, Durban or some other town where there are no restrictions against respectable and well-behaved Natives, to feel compelled to avoid taking him near the De Beers trams to give him a favourable impression about Kimberley and De Beers Company.

Please understand, Sir, that I lay claim to no rights whatever but as a paying tenant on the company's estates I would humbly and respectfully request but a share of the large-heartedness which has made this company famous and that is to be treated by the tramway employees with the same consideration, which they at all times extend to the Coloured and Indian passengers, including those Indian and Coloured people who acknowledge me as their superior.

Apologising for taking up your time with a personal matter.

I beg to be, Dear Sir,

Yours very respectfully

Sol T. Plaatje

Editor of *Tsala ea Batho*

Plaatje received a reply to his letter from the Secretary of De Beers on 29 July, inviting him to visit his office to discuss the matter, but no record of what transpired has survived.

---

*   A term in common usage by whites in late nineteenth and early twentieth-century South Africa, often used in a derogatory sense, signifying Africans who had not been exposed to Western forms of behaviour.

47
'With the kids' [manuscript], 1913[34]

Plaatje's children were St Leger ('Sainty'), born in 1898; Richard, born in 1901; Olive, born in 1903; Violet ('Oliviet', or 'Teto'), born in 1907; Halley, born in 1910 and named after Halley's Comet which appeared that year; and Johannes, born in September 1912, who died in infancy, following an attack of whooping cough, in January 1914.

Working from 8 a.m to midnight and often till later than 3 a.m next day (with only short intervals for meals and 5 or 6 hours sleep in 24 hours) we cannot have the same time we formerly devoted to the children. When we were in the public service there was 7 hours work, 8 hours sleep and nine hours at our disposal. The greatest part of the nine were spent with the children and it was often as good as a play to watch them struggling with life's initial problems; but not one interested me so much and so often as Olive with whom, by the way, the easiest time of our life was spent.

Sainty

Writing in our little library one day Sainty, when scarcely three, came in with an air of satisfaction. 'Papa', he said rather pleasantly, 'I am told that my cow at the cattle-post has *calved*.' It is perhaps necessary to explain that the Sechuana verb to *tsala* (the noun *tsala* means friend) applied to all viviparous animals means to breed, and when orifarous animals are referred to it means to lay (eggs), so *tsala* was the verb he used for 'calving'.

'Good,' we said, 'that's very nice; but do you know what your cow produced by *tsala*-ing? He scratched his head and muttered in Sechuana: 'She has produced, she produced – er- er- eggs.'

Sainty was a bilingualist from the time he commenced to speak. Growing up amongst purely Barolong children they would always surround and pester him with all kinds of curious questions as to what he meant by this, that and the other Xhosa phrase. Quaint were the Sechuana interpretations he would sometimes give for Xhosa words, of which the following are a few:

'There's a monster – Take care.'
'Goodbye – I am going.'
'Get out (*suka*) – I dislike you (I am tired of you).'
'Come here – Hurry up this way.'
'Never – Don't do it again.'
'What is good morning, sir? – I greet you.'

'There, you've done it – I will tell mama.'

'Look out – I will beat you.'

'Nothing today – Come tomorrow.'

At our family worship, evening and morning, of which he is now the leader, he used to be perceptibly sorry for being unable to read. He used to stand alongside someone precisely as if he could also read and this ambition made him a good reader from early childhood. He could read as well as Standard VI children when he was still reading his II. The teachers had a lot of trouble trying to balance his ability because his weakness in arithmetic was a strange contrast to his advanced stage in reading English, Dutch and the vernacular, and he always tried hard to understand what he was reading.

We saw him and some older boys apparently debating the contents of a daily newspaper. The problem was evidently insoluble for he came straight up to us, and asked, 'What is "Rowdy Natives?"' We gave him the Sechuana equivalent, at the same time asking how he would render it in English, and he said, 'Noisy Natives'. We had to admit that his English was much more refined than the headlines of Johannesburg newspapers. While I on the other hand had got so accustomed to reading them that I had come to the conclusion that slang was good English.

We will never forget his clanger on the morrow of his passing his Standard V with flying colours. He had $4^1/2$ sums right, he proudly told his sister to inform us. His disappointment was so intense that one could almost hear him thinking when his sister came back with the retort: 'Papa wishes to know what about the other half and why all the sums were not wholly right?'

Richard

Richard never stayed with us. He went to grow up among relatives when he was only 20 months and never lived with us for more than 6 months in 1909. When he was three years old we visited our uncle's old home at Bethany right across whose water dam the train from Cape to Bloemfontein is running. It was so quaint to hear him call me uncle and telling me how his mother and father and Sainty would come from Mafeking. The train would bring them and he longs to see them, but the train was very long about it. A Bloemfontein Wesleyan minister called there one day and Richard had the time of his life. His father had turned up.

Olive

Since she was three years old Olive would perform any task or do any class of menial work to deserve the title of lady. Strongly across the grass one day we espied a strange youngster to whom we called to deliver a [unclear]. The boy refused [to let us in], and Olive looked at us and said: 'He's not a lady, you know, he's not a lady.'

Her uncle used to come to Mafeking with the Circuit Court.[35] They arrived with the early morning train and went to court immediately after breakfast.

Late in the afternoon Olive asked, 'But what is uncle doing in town?'

We: 'Working'.

Olive: 'Working at what?'

We: 'Cases (The Sechuana for a court case is the same as a 'bag').

Olive: 'Are these bags of mealies or bags of corn?'

We roared, and Olive continued more seriously,

Olive: 'What is there to laugh at? Surely he is not working at empty bags!'

One afternoon they went to a Sunday school at Beaconsfield where we were visiting. She was asked for her name which she gave as, 'Olive, Sir!' The teacher wanted the full name and after a little consideration she gave it, serene and seriously, as Olive Schreiner.[36] Naturally the class rocked with laughter at the serious yet funny answers of the newcomer.

As she passed on in years from 6 to 7 our work was increasing in leaps and bounds. I had not the same amount of time to devote to the children and Olive's attentions became almost burdensome. She would walk in just when we cannot afford to be interrupted and gently stroke us.

'What can we do for you, dear?'

Olive: 'Have a cup of tea.'

'No thanks, dearie, very busy just now.'

Olive: 'But it is made by me, pappa.'

'Indeed! Well lets have a cup.'

At times when she hears that I am cleaning the bicycle to ride into town she would come up and solemnly hand me a clean muffler which she desired to see round my neck because knowing Papa would go to town I had washed and carefully ironed it for you. Let us hope these industrial habits will increase. She is nearly 10 now and they certainly do not develop as fast as the years.

Her cousin Winston died when she was three. For months after when she heard of someone's death she would say: 'Oh, what a pity we did not know of it before. I would have gone there and sent a message to Winston. Why doesn't someone come from there and tell us of Winston?'

One evening after prayers she asked Mama whether God has a big house in heaven. On receiving an answer in the affirmative she said: 'I am sure that house must be full of the bread in the Lord's Prayer because wherever you go people are always asking for that bread.'

48

'Imvo and the Natives', *Friend of the People*, 6 December 1913

In November 1913 Plaatje embarked upon a tour of the eastern Cape as part of the South African Native National Congress campaign against the Natives' Land Act, gathering evidence of the impact it was making. Plaatje was appalled to discover that Tengo Jabavu, the editor of Imvo, *supported the Land Act. The following article then appeared in the* People's Friend, *responding to an earlier article in* Imvo *which had commented disparagingly on a meeting Plaatje had addressed in King-williamstown.*

After our editor's recent visit to the Eastern Province when the editor of *Imvo* refused to see and explain to him the 'beautiful' principles that he reads into the Natives' Land Act, principles that are not printed in the Act, the *Imvo* – which squealed because, under the Act, its editor is not allowed to borrow money – had the impudence to say that the Natives who composed Mr Plaatje's meeting were a handful drawn by curiosity. This statement drew the following challenge from our editor:

A challenge

To the Editor, *Cape Mercury*,

Sir,

Please let me thank you for your personal attendance at, and lengthy report of, our meeting at Kingwilliamstown last week, and also for your sympathetic reference in a leading article to the difficulties endured by our people under the tender mercies of an unprecedented law.

How unlike the callous indifference of the alleged Native paper of Kingwilliamstown, edited by a gentleman, who, I am told, never attends Native meetings and has to depend on Englishmen for information about the life of his (?) people. The *Imvo* is trying to discount the importance of the meeting, and belittle its representative character, as it has for months past endeavoured to underrate or ignore the hardships of our people under the harsh provisions of the Natives' Land Act. They have told me that the editor of *Imvo* is the embodiment of selfishness. That this quality is not wholly foreign to his nature is demonstrated in the current issue of *Imvo*. After bolstering up the Act for all it is worth, and railing the Natives for organising an appeal against it, your acrobatic contemporary tells its readers that the only

John Tengo Jabavu, editor of Imvo Zabantsundu *– the leading African politican of his day. Plaatje wrote that he 'knows absolutely less than nothing about the Natives' Land Act and its principles'.*

flaw in the Act 'which is occasioning a manifest hardship through harsh administration is that relating to lending money'.

Now, I am informed, and have every reason to believe, that three months ago Mr Tengo Jabavu wished to raise a loan of £200 and could not get it under the restrictions of the Natives' Land Act. Consequently that is the only hardship which manifests itself under 'an otherwise useful (!) Act'.

Cattle belonging to Natives may be hounded out of their grazing areas, and widows may be driven from home with their belongings on their heads by this Act, but so long as such provisions do not conflict with Tengo Jabavu's personal interests the Act is useful from *Imvo*'s point of view.

I shall never forget the scenes I witnessed in the Hoopstad district during the cold snap of July – of families living on the roads, the numbers of their attenuated flocks emaciated by lack of fodder on the trek, many of them dying while the wandering owner ran risks of prosecution for travelling with unhealthy stock. I saw the little children shivering and contrasted their condition with the better circumstances of my own children in their Kimberley home; and when their mothers told me of the homes they had left behind, and the privation and exposure they have endured since eviction, I could scarcely suppress a tear. But because these were not its editor's children, *Imvo* can refer to their suffering in a manner that will bruise a wound in one's heart and cause it to bleed when it was healing.

Imvo comments disparagingly on Monday's meeting and adds that 'Reuter's correspondent at Kingwilliamstown is not aware that there are Natives and Natives, as well as King and King, there being town and district.' Sir, if you will be kind enough to let me use your columns for the purpose, I challenge *Imvo*, or Mr Tengo Jabavu, to call a series of three public meetings anywhere in the district of Kingwilliamstown. Let us both address these meetings immediately after the Natives' Land Act has been read and interpreted to each. We could address the meetings from the same platform, or separately, but on the same day and at the same place. For every vote carried at each of these meetings in favour of his views on the Act, I undertake to hand over £15 to the Grey Hospital (Kingwilliamstown), and £15 to the Victoria Hospital (Lovedale), on condition that for every vote I carry at any of the meetings, he hands over £15 to the Victoria Hospital (Mafeking) and £5 to the Carnarvon Hospital (Kimberley). That is £30 for charity if he will accept.

I will not place difficulties in his way by inviting him to meetings up here, but leave him to call meetings among his own people (if he has any) in his own district, and I will attend at my own expense.

Yours,

Sol T. Plaatje,

Editor of *Tsala ea Batho* and
Secretary, S.A. Native National Congress
14 Shannon St., Kimberley.

Imvo's reply

Dear Sir,

I am instructed by the editor of *Imvo* to acknowledge the receipt of your letter, and to inform you that as he has not been reading and following your writings, etc., he cannot understand what you mean by it. In short, to let you know that he takes no interest in the matter.

I am, Sir,

Yours truly

A.M. Jabavu.[37]

Imvo Office, Kingwilliamstown
24th November 1913

It is a disreputable confession for a leader – even if he be self-appointed – to declare that he takes no interest in a measure that hobbles his people's hands, limits their activities and muzzles the country's cattle and prevents them from eating wild grass, unless they belong to white men.

However disreputable it may sound for a journal to advise ignorant people to support a law concerning which its editor knows nothing, the confession is comforting as it dispels the horrible idea that there was one black man who wilfully preferred slavery to freedom. We were ashamed to think that a journal printed in our own language – even it if belonged to the party at present in power – could deliberately support a satanic measure denounced by all Christian churches in the country. So we felt relieved to hear that when *Imvo* extols the Native Lands Plague to the skies, it praises a law about which its editor knows nothing, and in which he takes no interest.

We honestly believe that this ignorance is not assumed for no black man who knows English or Dutch could, after reading 'The Natives' Land Act,

1913', try and borrow money from white people under the circumstances and in the manner Mr Tengo Jabavu tried to do, only to meet with the rude shock that under a law exalted by his paper – a law in which he takes no interest – he could not borrow money.

These and similar eccentricities which characterised the tone of the *Imvo* editorials of late, confirm the view expressed by his son, that Mr Tengo Jabavu knows absolutely less than next to nothing about the Natives' Land Act and its principles; but our sleepy friend will wake up to gather some sense one of these days.

This episode was widely publicised in the South African press, black and white, and contributed substantially to the demise of Tengo Jabavu's political reputation. Plaatje subsequently wrote more about this episode in Chapter 13 of Native Life in South Africa.

49
Lecture entitled 'Along the colour line', reproduced in Kimberley *Evening Star*, 23 Dec 1913

The passage reproduced below is the first part of a lecture by Plaatje to the Kimberley branch of the African Peoples' Organisation (APO), a predominantly but not exclusively coloured organisation, of which he was a member. The Kimberley Evening News *decided to reproduce it in full, it said, 'because we consider it advisable for European readers to be informed of present Native opinion on legislation lately passed, and on other matters which are now stirring the country'. The paper wanted it 'distinctly understood, however, that publication does not necessarily imply that our views are in accordance with those of the speaker'.*

'My difficulty,' said Mr Plaatje in introducing the topic, is to condense my experience as to lead you for one hour 'Along the colour line', giving personal observations only and avoiding hearsay evidence as far as possible. I depend upon whites as on our people, and can as little afford to do without either as I can dispense with the use of either of my hands. I have seen the coloured man from right to left, and from top to bottom. I have seen him from the Basuto in his mountain home, where villages are built between rocks that are inaccessible to vehicles; where goods are conveyed up and down mountain slopes and on ponies' backs. I have seen him right across the country to the thirstland of the Kalahari. I have seen him from the Atlantic shores in the western province to the Indian

Ocean in the east, and clear across the country to the northern Transvaal and Southern Rhodesia. I have dined at the sumptuous tables of our eminent coloured doctors at the Cape and our solicitors in the Transvaal; I have frequently enjoyed the hospitality of chiefs and princes, and also taken shelter in the primitive home of a bush herd in the employ of a Dutch farmer.

Speaking of the colour line, one old man up the country had a dream some years ago. He dreamt that he had been to

The 'Nether Regions'

He was very much upset about it next morning as people asked him all sorts of funny questions. 'What does the place look like?' they asked. 'Were there any coloured people?' 'Oh yes,' said the old man, 'the place is full of white people too.' 'What were they doing?' 'Every white man had hold of a coloured man, holding him between him and the fire,' but, he added, 'there were not enough blacks to go round.'

So then it seems that it will pay the white man to treat us well as we are not only serviceable to him here, but the presence of a few of us in the next world may also prove very useful to him. If that be our allotted task there should be some method in its performance and, seriously, our loyalty cannot benefit us except by co-operation. Every Native should belong to the Native Congress, and every Cape Afrikander* should belong to the APO. The same reason which impelled South African governments to combine under one central administrative and

Legislative umbrella

should bring us together into these associations. It we are to profit by our experience, there should be a little less sport and a little more serious study; fewer tea parties and a few more serious meetings; a little less of the liberties of the club and a little more of the restraint of the church, for Dr. van Dyke[38] very truly says:

> We need a more sane and hygienic life, and above all we need to get back to the old-fashioned idea that purity of life is demanded by God, and is a duty that we owe to him as well as the crown of a noble manhood and womanhood. It is a great misfortune that we have drifted away from this, and that children are growing up without the knowledge of the truth that God will surely punish uncleanness.

---

* Of coloured descent.

Immediately after Union the party in power gathered to distribute the loaves and fishes of Africa. An ingenious Nationalist hit upon a brilliant plan of perpetuating the benefits. They gave their leaders and some of their generals free first-class railway passes for life so that one who was lucky enough to be a leading Nationalist at that time can travel on our railways and go wherever he chooses for the rest of his natural life without paying a brass farthing. A few members of the opposition were also thought of. But nobody seems to have remembered the services of

General Tengo Jabavu,

the one man who helped to install the Merriman ministry at the Cape and arranged things so that when we got Union it was under Boer terms. Even today when his former following has practically deserted him, he is loyally trying to prove the impossible theory that the sins of the present administration are their virtues, and if gratitude was a fibre in the composition of the ruling party, the brilliant services of such a useful party man would not have been overlooked; but his colour was too deep for the fruits of his own heroic achievements at the polls. It is the story over again of a coloured man acting as a shield between the whites and the fire. It seems ironical when one considers that his late friend, Mr Sauer, was Minister of Railways when the free passes were handed out.

Let me say again, at the risk of repetition, that without combination we will never be recognised; but we must endeavour to work twice as many hours and sleep half as long as a white man. With the wages paid to Cape Afrikanders in Kimberley there is no reason why more coloured people should not live in their own houses. More thrifty ratepayers and less picnic-goers will enable us to resist the republican encroachments upon our rights. Indolence will never do it. An effort should be made to retain in this poor country the thousands of pounds posted in India, Russia and China by every mail, and if we combine and stand by our leaders there is some hope of doing it.

Legislative changes

If things had remained exactly where they were at the commencement of Union, our complaints would be somewhat narrow. But take the 'Free State', whose coloured population was so badly treated that it was pretty generally admitted that their condition could not possibly be any worse. Additional difficulties and insults have been created since Union. If you hold a first-class railway ticket and come to Bloemfontein by train, they will put a label on a third-class carriage and put you in there. Unless you are prepared to offer physical resistance and fight like a bandit for your money's worth, you will travel third-class with that first-class ticket. Yet before Union, when Mr Barrett was traffic manager, a coloured passenger was nowhere better treated than in the Orange River Colony.

Again, in the 'Free' State, ordained Native ministers are no longer allowed to solemnize marriages. Members of their congregations and Christians with their own minister on the spot are subjected to the indignity of being married by a magistrate's clerk. That rude excommunication of religious ministers in the 'Free' State on the ground of colour is a wholly illegal business. No Parliament ever armed anybody with such highhanded usurpations, but the Right Honourable the Minister who died recently appointed himself a sort of Pope and disrobed ordained Native ministers of recognised religious bodies, including two trusted colleagues under Mr Pescod,[39] who were marriage officers in the 'Free' State before Union. Of course, Native and coloured people there were not allowed to buy land, but a Native with a thousand sheep could always hire a farm; moreover, he was allowed to plough and graze his flocks. Today he dare not do it under a law passed since Union. Two violent republican laws repealed by the crown colony government have been re-enacted since Union, placing every coloured man under the behest of his white neighbour, whether or not he works for him.

In the Cape

There were certain openings in the public service for coloured men. Today they not only refuse new applicants, but they are fast weeding out the old hands, replacing them with whites. In some instances, where the white man, drawing nearly three times the salary of his coloured predecessor, was inefficient, a second white man was assigned to a post previously held by one coloured man. The tax-gatherer has continued to charge us to meet the printing and painting bills, to satisfy the ridiculous provision that everything should be printed in two languages, but the painting contractor has been ordered to keep black painters, however good, away from the work. The Cape government never paid attention to the selfish white labour agitation against skilled coloured labour, but now a coloured carpenter can only find work with a private employer and not on government contracts. The new Maitland railway station, used by the large Native population of Ndabeni, is one of the latest government buildings erected entirely by lily-white labour. A coloured man could only work at mixing clay, but not at laying bricks. In

Three provinces in the Union

you could buy land anywhere, up till this year, but now you can neither hire nor buy land. Paul Kruger had a law under which Indians could not buy land in the Transvaal, but he never proposed anything half so wicked as to fine you £100 for allowing a landless Indian to plough or graze his horse on your land. All those things happened while I was getting Dutch telegrams from the Prime Minister promising us just treatment and all the rest of it.

The Natives' Land Act

I have already written and said much about that wonderful law which has hounded Natives out of their homes and put many to flight. Some are still roaming about the country and others are under notice to clear. Under the tyrannical provisions of that law, the moment those notices expire they are homeless, as there is a £100 fine on anyone who accommodates them. Others have sold their stock in Bloemhof and Klerksdorp, at prices that the white buyers could fix. Some have found a precarious accommodation in Basutoland; those of us who know the congestion of Basutoland and how petty chiefs are constantly shooting each other over small patches of arable land, can understand the kind of life they are getting.

I was one of those who criticised Dr. Abdurahman's Johannesburg speech, when he prophesied a war of extermination in this country, and if at the beginning of this year someone had told me that the South African Parliament was capable of passing a law like that, I would have considered him a fit subject for the lunatic asylum; but not only has the doctor's prophesy proved true, but when we told the government of people living on the roads under the drastic provision of that law, of that process of extermination that they were subjected to, in a manner that was never previously associated with British rule in this country, the information was received by the government with manifest satisfaction.

But it is an ill wind that blows nobody any good and that act has united the Native races in a way which was never dreamt of in the philosophy of Meintjes Kop.[*] In the far away corners of this Union, the mutual understanding and fellow feeling of the black and coloured people is surprising. They have stood up as one man, and are collecting funds to despatch a deputation to the Imperial government, to protest against this treatment at the capital of the empire. Amongst the largest contributors towards the fund are Natives who, at the beginning of this year, would have scorned the idea of contributing towards the fund of the Congress not wholly composed of members of their tribe.

---

[*] Meintjes Kop (Afrikaans, Meintjes Hill) is the site of the Union Buildings, Pretoria, the central government buildings.

Tribalism and clanishness is melting away under the heat of our bungling misgovernment, and a bond of sympathy and co-operation is being automatically weaved amongst the coloured races of South Africa.

Mr Dube,[40] the Zulu president of the Native Congress, is welcomed among Xhosas with an enthusiasm as great as that among the Basutos; he is hailed among the Bapedi and Bechuana as heartily as he is among the Swazis, and he is as much at home among Cape Afrikanders as he is among his own people in Natal. And when a man like him, the chief executive of a Congress composed of many South African tribes, who speak seven or eight different languages, refers to Dr. Abdurahman as 'my leader', then one begins to understand what the *Transvaal Leader* meant when it said 'the Natives' Land Act is combining the Native races of this country on an unprecedented scale'. Still, I maintain that we could have combined under happier auspices than the tyrannical provision of the law which prohibits dumb animals from eating wild grass because they have a black owner.

The government's 'sympathy'

In the midst of all these difficulties, the only sympathy received by our people from the government is the paternal advice that they must not appeal to England. We have been to Parliament and also to the Governor-General before the Act was passed, and got no sympathy. Since the Act came into force, we have been to the ministry with desperate appeals for help under the harsh provisions of that remarkable Act, and got no sympathy. So we turn our eyes to England as a last resort. The effect of the government's advice against an appeal to England is likely to land this country into serious disaster, if wiser councils do not prevail in time. When I was in Transvaal last week, I found some prominent Natives favouring an abandonment of the deputation, but for different reasons than those intended by the government when they gave the advice. Some of our people are advised that a more rapid way of obtaining redress and a speedy abrogation of the measure would be to

Organise a general strike

amongst the Native labourers in Johannesburg. The women and some of the chiefs are strongly in favour of a strike and when the Native women of the Transvaal are bent upon a thing, you may depend upon its ultimate success. After a small quarrel with some Indians last year, 12 Native women took upon themselves the task of preventing Native man, woman or child from buying at an Indian store. They did it so systematically, yet rapidly and effectively, that the Indian traders had to put up their shutters and seek fresh pastures. I was surprised, when I visited Boksburg last May, to find not a single Indian trader.

What used to be a prosperous Indian bazaar was now a row of ruins, and if the government persist in advising against an appeal to England, they are paving the way for an alternative which will shudder this country.

But, remember that the compounds of Johannesburg are not enclosed and when the strike is declared, and those women begin to jeer at pusillanimous labourers who hesitate to join, we will have the whole quarter million out on strike. Numbers of them will strike without knowing what they are striking about. Serious conflict is bound to ensue. Our government, which is incapable of any statesmanship, where colour is concerned, will not fail to call out the burghers. Many of the strikers will be shot down, and much innocent blood will be spilled.

I agree that the blood of the victims will be upon the heads of the persons responsible for the passing of the Act. But have we exhausted all bloodless means? Let our delegates tell the Imperial Government that we have appealed to the highest authorities in South Africa and both our appeals, and the church's representations on our behalf, have been ignored; and let the Imperial Government inform our delegates that His Majesty's kingship over us ceased with the signing of the Act of Union and that whites and blacks in South Africa can do what they please; then only will we have the alternative, and I too will agree that we had better have a general strike, and 'damn the consequences'. Till then I will maintain that the consequences of a strike are too serious and the probable complications too dreadful to contemplate.[41]

The social pest

I do not think we need waste time over what is called social equality, as, even amongst ourselves, there is no such thing. I must, however, emphasise that I have never heard any expressions of sympathy among my people for cranks who assault women; but can we say the same about the other side? When we see the liberties on the part of their men folk with our women, which they seem to tolerate; when we hear them disclaim against onslaughts by black men upon the purity of white women, and when, at the same time, we see the evidence of the sins of white men written upon thousands of coloured children; then the insincerity of their reproofs stands demonstrated.

Take for instance the hypocritical attitude of those 'good' people of the 'Free State' who imagine that they can uphold the morality of their province, by bits of paper carried by one section of the community, paying for it at the rate of one shilling per month, per capita. Just now they are incensed because two days ago the judge gave a black peril monster 15 years and did not sentence him to be hanged. These bloodthirsty 'Free' Staters had nothing to say against two white peril cases which took place about the same week as the Bethany outrage. One was a white man alleged to have outraged a Native woman, and nobody knows anything about the circumstances as the case was conveniently tried behind closed doors, and the man was discharged. About the same time another white man of the 'Free' State attacked a defenceless white woman and took the precaution to paint his face black so that the outrage may be debited against us. I have scanned their paper in vain for any condemnation of the outrageous deceit. We must advise the people to keep strictly within their circle, but we can never suppress crime, as long as the authorities think that they can run the show without our co-operation.

To mention one instance: the people of Thaba Nchu had been very much concerned about the liquor traffic in their location, but the government, as usual, could not stop it. Last month, the Women's Christian Association banded themselves together and made a house-to-house visit, and spilled hundreds of gallons of liquor. They warned one sinner in particular that if he did not desist, they would themselves effect his arrest. As he was incorrigible they actually led the police to his brewery and he and his associates got long terms of imprisonment. But for the action of these women, those breweries which are now many years old would still be distilling liquor and dispensing it among young people with the usual baneful results.

Finally, I will refer you to a leading article in the *Congo Star*, a paper published in Elizabethville in the far interior. It says: 'We are deliberately coming down from our raised position to grovel in the dirt with the beasts. We come down to the level of the black by taking possession of his womankind. The Native is possessed of a strong sense of justice and his resentment of this treatment, apart from his loss of respect for the white man through his degrading conduct, will sooner or later come into play. The evil instead of diminishing is on the increase. One now sees white men accompanying their black concubines openly in the public streets. There are more black female cyclists about than ever and the climax was reached the other day when a white man was seen driving his black amourette in a trap in the public thoroughfares.'

The central African white peril monster is playing the game and atones for his sins by his honesty. The last thing in the world that the South African white perilist will do is to go for a spin with his black concubine. He meets her on the quiet so that the only evidence you have against him is the indirect written one in ineffaceable blood on the foreheads of thousands of half-caste children nursed by black mothers. He does not drive her in a trap in the public thoroughfares.

He abandons his black amourette after saddling her with the white man's burden and then joins the campaign of respectable people against the black peril.

Unfortunately, these are the people who conduct Native education in every walk of life. But when the imitative blacks respond to their teaching, they affect to be infuriated. Hampered as we are by the demon of colour prejudice with its obstructive environments, low wages and other limitations and disabilities, we have no means of counteracting their mission.

Segregation

I have always had my doubts about the practicability of segregation for I thought it would involve both white and coloured in tremendous and unnecessary sacrifices. But I must confess that I never suspected that their first attempt at segregation would inflict upon our people the ruin that it has done during the past four months. Nine years ago, the Native Affairs Commission had before it a number of 'Free' State Natives and asked them if it would not be better to separate the white and coloured inhabitants of one district with a boundary along the railway line to Natal, putting the coloureds on the side furthest from Basutoland. One of the Natives, Mr Mokitlane Nyokong, stood up and seriously proposed a fence along the railway line all the way up from Port Elizabeth right through to Johannesburg, putting the Natives to the East and the Europeans to the west of that line. Naturally, this serious proposition convulsed the commissioners who burst out into loud peals of laughter.

But, considering the size of the country, the numbers of Natives and Europeans, and the stock owned by both, and the preponderance of both colours on both sides of the line, I consider it by far the most sensible suggestion ever put forth by any person who has discussed the segregation question. And if such a logical segregation proposition can amuse the government commission, the absurdity of the whole segregation scheme stands demonstrated.

One commission passed through here the other day with the object of bringing the question to a head, but, if what it told was true, it would seem that they also had a hold of the wrong end of the cane. We are told that they want to create a Native area somewhere between Boshof and Hoopstad, where the population is about 50 per cent white and 50 per cent coloured. Now, there is a well-known black belt in the 'Free' State where the population is about 90 per cent black and only 10 per cent white, in some cases. Why not have the Native area there? The chessboard proposal, with which dame rumour is crediting the segregation commission, will end in disintegration instead of separation, and we will have the Cape Afrikander as a buffer between the two.

In Natal, today, he is told that separation is extant and he cannot buy land from them. When he offers to buy some land from a Native, the government tells him that, under the provisions of the Natives' Lands Act, he cannot buy land from a Native. When these things are taking place, coloured people are wasting valuable time discussing the progress of the M.C.C.* They need to wake up before it is too late and help us to demand complete segregation, or nothing at all. There can be but one reason why we could not get the right thing and it would be to prevent our managing our own affairs, thus arresting our development and keeping us as an easy prey for exploitation by the other colour. It would be to prevent our making, on a large scale, the progress that is made by the handful of our people in Basutoland and the Transkei.

If, with all the millions we are giving them annually, the Union government can barely make ends meet, it is certain that without us the white administration would be in a very sorry plight. Under proper segregation every one of them would have to prepare for double taxation and public servants would have to do with half their present salaries. They will pile up deficits as we pile up surpluses, and to save the white administration from bankruptcy, the mines will be so heavily taxed that only a few of them would be able to work and many a white South African will be glad to clear out of it. By that time, the Union ministers of finance will ask Parliament to forcibly appropriate our accumulated surplus and then the black man's burden, about which it is inexpedient to speak at present, will appear in all its nakedness and the action will be known by its proper name, viz.: robbery of the deepest dye. Still, you will agree that the government could segregate, or congregate and aggregate without subjecting anybody to the unrelenting cruelty which our people are now going through under the tender mercies of the Act known as the foretaste of segregation. [...]

50
Editorial, 'A happy new year', *Friend of the People*, 3 January 1914

Another year has gone by, and what a year! It is doubtful if since the British occupation of this country a section of the white community ever received such a free licence to do what they please with their Native fellow-subjects as was done during the year of troubles, 1913. Other parts of this planet have had their share of the misfortunes associated by superstition with the number 13.

---

*   Marylebone Cricket Club, responsible for running the English national cricket team.

We can speak with authority on the troubles that came our way, misfortunes we have endured, such as droughts, pestilence, deaths, economic troubles, industrial wars, tribulations and anxieties due to legislative horrors dictated by the demon of colour prejudice – all those have been allotted to us during the last year. Even Jeremiah, the pessimistic plaintiff of old, complaining of persecution in bondage, under strangers, says: 'We have drunken our water for money, our wood is sold unto us.' But we, the Natives of South Africa, have by a law passed in 1913 been deprived of the right to pay in money for our water, and tyrannical penalties have been fixed under section 5 of the Lands Act on any alien who sells our wood unto us. We can by law receive such wood and water only provided they form part of our rations when we are serfs in the employ of such aliens.

But it does not appear that the oppressor himself is reaping any satisfaction, for his house is rent in twain. His time has been so fully occupied with vain attempts to reconcile himself with himself that he often forgot to use the scourge he forged for our backs; and if he does not relent in time we shall be the last to laugh when we see him swept off like the obdurate Pharaoh in the waves of a political Red Sea.

The year is over and, let us hope, the troubles with it, and also that 1914 will bring with it showers of rain, alleviation of disease amongst men and beasts, the emancipation of coloured women in the 'Free' State, who are constantly sent to prison for refusing to be outraged by men armed with authority; and the repeal of the Native Land Plague, 1913.

Three Native papers ceased publication during 1913, but we are still here to tell the story. It is not through any valour on our part, as much as through the liberality of advertising firms throughout South Africa, who stood by us when our natural customers, the Native peasants of the 'Free' State and Transvaal were driven from pillar to post under the cruel provision of an unprecedented law, and could not send us money. We wish to thank these merchants for their liberality, and hope they will be rewarded with the commercial success they deserve.

It is doubtful if, even with the aid of commercial people, we alone could have survived without the aid of the proprietors and staff of the two English papers of Kimberley – the *Diamond Fields Advertiser* and the *Evening Star*. With their concern for the welfare of the weak, they have consistently guided our footsteps both in the typographic and journalistic spheres. For this guidance we express our heartfelt thanks and beg to assure them that many years will roll before we are able to do without it.

We cannot conclude without placing on record the heartfelt thanks of the suffering Natives for the outspoken support of missionary bodies, and more especially for their unceasing protest against the physical wrongs and other injuries to which our people have been subjected by Parliament under the drastic provisions of the Native Land Plague, and we wish for them an abundance of the master's promised grace in their noble work. To all our friends, supporters, and sympathisers we wish a happy new year and amelioration of these difficulties, plenty of rain and better crops for the people during the new year. We are sorry to have no special prayers to offer on behalf of the oppressor. All we wish for him in his persecution of our people is may God 'confound their politics and frustrate their policies'.

51
Article, 'Native Congress mission to England', *Diamond Fields Advertiser*, 14 and 17 July 1914

In February 1914 the SANNC convened a special conference in Kimberley on the Natives' Land Act, and resolved to send a deputation to England to request the British Imperial Government to disallow the legislation. Plaatje was elected a member of the deputation, and made preparations to depart. Last-minute meetings with the Prime Minister and Governor-General in Cape Town produced no concessions, and the five delegates (the Reverend John Dube, the Reverend Walter Rubusana, Thomas Mapikela, Saul Msane, and Plaatje himself) departed for England in May 1914.

Plaatje's account of the voyage, and his impressions of England once he and his colleagues had arrived, appeared in the Diamond Fields Advertiser *on 14 and 17 July, the first under the headline, 'Native Congress mission to England: first impressions of a sea voyage'; and the second, 'The Native Congress Deputation: last week of the voyage, the arrival in Great Britain, first impressions of a Native visitor'.*

1

Overloaded with the final cares – not to say anxieties – preceding a sudden, yet long, absence abroad, I was attacked by a splitting headache on the eve of our departure from the Cape. Nasty forebodings about sea-sickness, of which I heard too much, did not allay the sick headache, so that I broke down during the preparations in the morning, and had to be laid to rest immediately in the ship. I do not know when they had luncheon, or when the steamer sailed, but

The South African Native National Congress deputation to England, June 1914. Left to right: Thomas Mapikela, Rev. Walter Rubusana, Rev. John Dube, Saul Msane, Sol Plaatje.

a quiet rest had a curative effect during the afternoon, and, after tea, I went on deck to catch the last glimpse of the African shore, with the hilly district to the east, off what used to be Hottentot's Holland. Away back, the majestic Table Mountain was receding in the distance; and Cape Town, which hitherto had always represented the end of the world to me (or, as the Native is wont to say, 'Where the clouds do end') was out of sight. I have always admired the waves of the briny deep from the solid rocks of Camp's Bay, or elsewhere, but from the deck of the *Norseman* one has a bird's-eye view, so to say. And – oh, if that wretched sea-sickness would only come and go – I would adjust myself to these strange surroundings.

An uneventful night

The monotony of the surrounding blues was relieved in the evening by the brilliant lights of the P&O liner *Borda*. The spectacle, as she passed some three miles to east of us on her maiden voyage to the Cape, reminded us that we were not the only tenants of the deep blue sea. The rest of the night passed off uneventfully, from my personal viewpoint.

Next morning I was up on deck early to see the *Norseman* steaming to the north-west, under a brilliant sky, with the flag of the Aberdeen line fluttering overhead. To a maritime novice like myself she had the appearance of a strange sea monster of gigantic proportions. She must have been sailing opposite the mouth of the Orange River at that time.

In the same direction the crimson hue of daylight indicated that the sun's rays were preparing to shoot. I drank deeply of the soft balmy air, which was emphatically pure, because – 200 miles from the nearest coast – the sea breeze contained not a particle of dust. Hitherto my travelling experience extended from the mountain ranges of the Transkei and Basutoland to the northern protectorate and Kalahari forests, and it never used to occur to me that I would live to soar through dustless tracks; but these meditations were repeatedly disturbed by unpleasant expectations of my oncoming attack of *mal-de-mer*, of which, it just be confessed, I stepped on board with rather exaggerated ideas. It had been my sorrow to see and hear old stagers like Mr Mapikela,[42] and other passengers who had crossed the ocean many times, croaking and squirming during the night. The plight of the lady passengers was particularly doleful, as it seemed to me that some of them would never recover. I shuddered in anticipation of the impending onslaught of an inexperienced greenhorn like myself.

A lucky escape

Just at this time a ragged-looking veteran of the seas came on deck and asked how I fared. It was with a sign of relief that I listened to his to me interesting conversation, especially that part of it (which was afterwards over-corroborated), wherein he assured me that, having survived the first day and night, I need no more expect any trouble with sea-sickness. I felt like a discharged prisoner and prepared for my work with extra freshness and security.

I am compiling a little book on the Natives' Land Act and its operations which I hope to put through the press immediately after landing in England.[43] It keeps me busy typewriting in the dining-saloon all forenoons and evenings: the afternoons I spend on deck, making notes, etc. With such a regular daily programme I can afford to sympathise with our fellow passengers who are always very busy doing nothing. Their inertia must be well-nigh maddening, and, as I see the heavy loads of time hanging down their weary necks, it is to me strange how they can stand it so long. I think that the reason why three of them got fainting fits is that they had nothing else to do ; but I will be sorrier for them when, after landing, they endeavour to re-attune themselves with the normal life of toil.

They give you four meals a day on board, which I consider 'one too many'; consequently, I ignore the supper bell, and limit myself to three square meals a day. Lost in my daily work, and selecting my food in that manner, I completely forget at times that we are in mid-ocean. Thanks to the renowned steadiness of this boat, it sounds for all the world like toiling on terra firma. While thus engaged, I would some day notice, by the quick movement and unusual gait of the male passengers, as well as the strange demeanour of the ladies, that something is amiss; and when eventually I go upstairs for a spell and stand face-to-face with the breakers of the briny deep on the deck side, it will then occur to me that the 'billows are inclined to toss', and, incidentally, how fortunate it is for a working-man on board to be insensible to *mal-de-mer*.

Native incredulity

The Kaffir in me would not allow me to touch one or two regular condiments, which I hesitate to mention by names for fear of affecting their sales in Native territories. My drastic Native disposition was suspicious of the freshness of the fresh milk on board, and would not be persuaded that it found its way into the steamer's refrigerating house direct from Cape dairies. Its colour, at any rate, was not very reassuring, and I have done remarkably well on black coffee and tea.

Writing about Native conduct reminds me of an incident on my last railway journey down from Kimberley. A Hottentot came to the carriage window at one of the stations selling bottles of milk. 'Have you washed your bottles clean?' asked a Dutch passenger, in the taal. 'Ja baas', replied the Hottentot. 'Did you add plenty of water?' returned the Dutch gentleman. 'Ja baas', repeated the Hottentot, in naive Native innocence.

Australian and other passengers

The advantage of travelling on an Aberdeen liner is the opportunity one gets of meeting with Australians and other colonists from the antipodes. I have never seen so many since the war, but then the Bushmen* did not have their merry widow and kiddies with them. The old farmers especially are very nice, and never so happy as when they are imparting useful information. They told us much about the Native of the Fiji and Samoan Islands, and their peculiar language.

The Fiji alphabet

Their vowels sound just like the vowels in the various languages of the South African Natives, but the components differ very widely from ours. For instance B, C, and D sound like 'Mb', 'th', and 'ad' respectively.

----

*   The Australians

The children were at first inclined to be terribly afraid of us, but satisfied now that we are not cannibals, they never tire of admiring Mr Msane,[44] the stalwart Zulu member of the deputation, and his powerful voice. The saloons of the *Norsemen* being all of one class, one has the free run of all parts of the ship, and can promenade the deck from stem to stern. This reminds one of an old plantation song descriptive of a journey to the land of Beulah. It says:

> The fare is cheap and all can go,
> The whites and blacks are there;
> No second-class on board the train,
> No difference in the fare.

There are over 30 white South Africans on board, and it is a pleasure to see them combatting what Mr Merriman calls 'the South African besetting sin of snobbishness'. The Australians are perfectly colour blind; but colour prejudice overcame a few South Africans one day along the voyage.

It happened in this way. On our second night out Mr Msane joined some white passengers at chess. He took them in turns, and invariably swept the board with them. This did not look nice to our countrymen. Next day, one of our party was silly enough to join a sweep, and he came out with a trump. For a three-penny piece he walked off with half-a-sovereign, gathered from forty of his white fellow gamblers. The sight of his black hands pocketing the 'splosh' was too bad for the few white South Africans who joined the game, and they told the Bushmen that they have decided never to join a sweep again with a Kaffir. At the same time we considered the decision a colour bar of the right kind, and good for his moral perception; and considering the result of his first 'sweep', decidedly to his pecuniary advantage.

We have long since lost the company of the Cape penguins and other sea-birds which used to follow our ship. We see the whales no more, nor the smoke-like spray which they shoot in the air from beneath the surface of the water. Their places have been taken by the flying-fish, which rise from the ocean in scores, fly away from the ship like a swarm of house martins, and drop in again no sooner their pinions are dry. The bulky porpoise also show now and again to relieve the monotony [...].

2

At Tenerife we had the first stoppage of our voyage, after sailing incessantly for 4,444 miles. It was to me a long stretch, and a silence in the machinery department of our floating island was more than welcome. I had the novel experience of landing in a community who did not know any of the languages I speak, and who only know enough English to fix prices for what they can 'sell' you. They looked like coloured people, those Spaniards of the Canary Islands. To think that Spain formerly ruled the seas from east to west, and the Canaries are all that they possess hereabout! The castles and fortifications on the mountain tops around the island show that if the Anglo-Saxons did not also gobble and retain these Grand Canaries as a calling place to the colonies, it is not entirely their fault.

We saw the divers, of whom we had heard so much, jumping out of their little boats, following penny pieces dropped by the passengers from the ship into the bay – 200 feet deep – overtaking it before the coin had gone a dozen feet, and returning with it to the surface. One of them swam with only one leg. His one thigh and the whole of the lower limb had been bitten off, they say, and eaten by a shark in the course of one of his diving feats. The divers' boat was in the form of a motor-tender driven by an elderly coloured man, who gave the divers thunder and lightning in Spanish. The latter promptly vociferated with similar gusto in reply, but we could not understand a word.

There was not quite a general scramble for land, but I found myself in the first passenger tug making for the island. As we left the steamer, she was boarded by a number of Spanish merchants loaded with fruit, ice-creams, cigars, cigarettes, picture postcards, and many nick-nacks, with which they 'sold' the passengers who remained on board. I looked forward to a long draught of fresh cow's milk on land, after fasting for 16 days, but in a two hours' drive around the town I failed to see a single cow, or goat, only donkeys, mules, and horses, so my Native nature again exerted itself against touching any Spanish milk, and I prepared for another week's abstention.

Incidents on land

We saw their rich banana fields, from which the British and foreign merchantmen at the port were receiving cargo for England and the continent. At the fruit market we were given choice selections of figs, apricots, mandarins and other things to sample; they were not bad, by a long way, but to taste them was to understand why a single Cape peach costs 1s., and sometimes more, in England. To say that their cigarettes would not hold a candle to our Eureka or Springbok, why, the very comparison is to grossly flatter the Spanish weed. We purchased for 3s. and 4s. boxes of good cigars, which cost from 12s. to 15s. a box in Johannesburg, but they were the Havana leaf from foreign factories, and not from the island.

It was a relief to get back to the steamer, which, for the best part of a week, was still to be our home, and up the ladder as the Spanish merchants descended and returned to Santa Cruz. Not content with fleecing the passengers and charging them 100 per cent dearer on the boat for articles which we obtained on the island at half the price, we found out later, when Tenerife was far out of sight, that some of the boxes purchased on the boat and not on the island had two layers of good cigars on top and two or three very inferior articles underneath.

Our excursion tickets cost 3s., which, besides the return trip from the ship to the island, included a two hours' drive around Santa Cruz, in landaus drawn by three mules side-by-side. Mr Msane was the centre of interest on the island. Women beckoned to each other, and little girls shouted to one another to look at the big stout 'Morena'. By the way, ethnologists should enquire how the Sotho-Chuana group of languages in South Africa came to share that word, and its meaning, with Spaniards.

Nelson's flag

We visited the arena, where bullfights are taking place once every other month. They are putting in a cinematograph installation, to kill two birds with one stone, so to say. We also visited the town hall, the theatre, the fruit market, and the cathedral. We saw some marvellous hand-carving at the cathedral, and a lofty altar made entirely of silver, some of these works being nearly 500 years old. We also saw Lord Nelson's flag, taken by the Spanish troops in the British reverse of 1797, when the daring admiral unfortunately lost his arm. The flag is enclosed in a silver cross-shaped casing, and preserved in the cathedral.

At each of the places visited, the porters never failed to pass round the hat. No fewer than three collections were taken at the cathedral. When we remonstrated with them for this barefaced rack-renting of innocent visitors, the Spanish caretaker told us in his best English that the takings at the door were for the sole benefit of the cripple who passed round the hat. The collection in front of the altar was for the church, and we were left to infer for whose benefit the third and last impost was demanded at the exit.

I am told that we visited the general post office of Santa Cruz also; I remember buying some stamps at a tobacconist's stall, and posting picture post-cards in a box hard by, but I cannot remember seeing the Tenerife branch of the Spanish post office; this, however, may be due to the fact that the postmaster, if there was one, may have forgotten the inevitable collection plate.

At Tenerife we heard of the shocking news of the marine disaster on the Canadian coast the week before, when the *Empress of Ireland* forestalled any rescue work by sinking within a few minutes after collision with the *Storstad*, within full view of relief, and carried down a thousand souls to eternity. It was a staggering blow to us, and our own prayer was that the story might turn out to be a gross exaggeration. Unfortunately it only proved too true.

Strange stars

The days are growing longer, and our nights are very short. We fail to see the southern cross, and the familiar winter constellations of the south, signifying the ripening of Native grain in South Africa. Summer stars, which usually mark the ploughing season, have taken their places. The polar star is visibly near since we crossed the line, and the heavens look totally strange for this time of the year. It is not generally known, perhaps, that the South African Natives have no fixed names for the various planets, but call them by their position in the sky during the night. Our fair friend Venus, whom the South African Natives now call the 'harbinger of the morning', occupies a different position for where we are. From here the Bechuanas would call her 'Kgoga-masigo' (or 'leader of the nights'); Jupiter and Sirius are nameless amongst the South African Natives, because they are day stars, both of them, at present. Here they illumine our evening skies, and the Bechuana would call them 'Kope-dilalele', or 'guests of the evening meal'.

Skimming along a smooth, rippleless sheet of water, we had the steadiest part of our voyage opposite the Portuguese coast, but a change of the most disagreeable nature took place when we encountered the 'roaring forties', after passing Finisterre. The Bay of Biscay was very angry, although old sailors thought that it could have been worse. Ripples swelled into billows, and the larger swells into a constantly moving mountain-shaped formation, with swinging hollows in between, and, although our ship negotiated them with commendable pluck, it must be confessed that the pitching and rocking as she ascended and descended the huge waves was enervating to one's whole system. Work was utterly impossible for two days, and many of the passengers who were susceptible to that kind of illness had return attacks of *mal-de-mer*. Old seafarers had a bad time of it, while raw Kaffirs like myself and another member of the deputation remained immune. Some white men flattered me by saying they wished they had my constitution, but I must confess that I had never felt so intolerably near death – except, perhaps, during the war, when I could almost touch him – as during those two days across the bay.

It was here that the mastery over nature of the white man's science, which usually inspires security, even in the darkest hour, at sea as well as on land, manifested itself; for as the sea raged and the passengers were unwillingly swinging in a sea-saw for two full days, felt sick and suffered from sea scare, we had these indomitable sons of the seas, two of them, perched in a roost – the crow's nest – halfway up the mast, while the officers collectedly read the compass on the upper deck, and guided the ship forward with its heavy load of human beings and cargo.

Coming to the dining saloon one morning, we found a group of stewards lining up for duty. Out of sheer admiration the four of us burst forth with the singing of the sailors' chorus 'Sons of the Sea', the stewards responding by joining us in the chorus as heartily as only sailors can; and it is safe to say that white and black never sang with a deeper meaning in harmony as we sang with those sailors on the Bay of Biscay:

> They may build the ships, m'lad, and think they know the game,
> But they can't build the boys of the bulldog breed,
> That made old England's name.

In the evening, the flashlights of Ushant, some 40 miles to the east, brought back recollections of the ill-fated *Drummond Castle* and its last voyage. It was nearly two decades ago, and yet that sea catastrophe is still green in our minds. How quickly time flies.

Arrival in Great Britain

One night, more on towards morning, the green shores of Merry England could be seen through the light mist. The enrapturing eagerness to get on land was stimulated by the sight of the snow-bleached islanders who bade us welcome to the home of John Bull, and to his island. A glorious landscape appeared in view as we steamed nearer the Devonshire coast, and sighted Plymouth sound. A tender came for us, and it was quick work through the customs, and on to the spring cushions in the special ocean train of the Great Western Railway.

To me it was a railway journey of intense interest, more so, even, than my first railway ride from Kimberley to Modder River in 1886. The distance from Plymouth to London is exactly the same as that from Beaconsfield to Mafeking. The speed of the South African trains has been accelerated since the dining-cars were introduced, and they now do that distance – 225 miles – in from twelve to fourteen hours. Gliding through a panorama of the most picturesque scenery, on Friday we covered that distance in exactly four hours, which is something over 56 miles an hour, including a short halt at Exeter; but thanks to the broad gauge and spring carriages, one hardly appreciated the breakneck speed. The fog lifted as we left Plymouth, and gave us a grand view of a well-populated and thoroughly cultivated country. From the carriage windows we saw herds of beautiful cattle on both sides of the line, but, strange to say, all the cattle in Devonshire and Somerset were red in colour, while those through the Berkshire and Surrey counties were more of less speckled, and the saying about a black sheep in every flock does not apply to cattle, apparently.

London through Native eyes

After arrival at Paddington station, it seemed a pity to part with the Australians who had befriended us on the voyage. However, we were received by home friends, and some retired colonists who have now come back to swell the millions who comprise John Bull's family. The latter are amazed at the tyrannical provisions of the Natives' Land Act; they are surprised to read the weighty arguments of Messrs Merriman, Theo. Schreiner, Meyler, Sir Bisset Berry, and Sir Edgar Walton, in our possession, against the measure, as well as the desperate appeals of missionary bodies. The late Mr Sauer's whitewashing of his Act, and General Botha's faint praise of it, had led them to believe that it was a fair measure, which met with the unanimous approval of every thinking European and the majority of the Native people. Mr Lewis Harcourt[45] has written us for further particulars, which we have furnished, and we are still awaiting his convenience before deciding upon a definite plan of campaign.

Oh! what swarms of people, and myriads of trams, 'buses, motor-cars, overhead and underground railways. To think that there is in this one city more people than in the whole Union of South Africa is to marvel how the authorities manage to avoid collisions and accidents. The Metropolitan Police Force is composed of nature's gentlemen, who seem to know everything, and it is difficult to conceive how one can get lost in London, unless he himself wanted to get lost; these swarms of humanity in the capital of the world give one a near idea of what the regulation in heaven will be like after the resurrection of the souls of all ages. There, being supernatural, they will not be hampered by such trifles as the feeding and housing problem.

There is a Native adage, 'Never measure your straw hut with great places'. I happened to be engaged to interpret in a case in a South African court one morning, and to my surprise the magistrate stepped on the bench wearing a shirt of the same line and pattern as my own. I quickly disappeared into one of the ante-rooms and hid the offending garment before I returned to officiate. But this Sechuana adage troubled me again when I arrived. I booked to put up at the Buckingham Hotel, in the Strand. In an hour's conversation at the station, I noticed that some friends repeatedly confused my address with a more august residence of that ilk, and I promptly changed quarters and accepted one of several invitations to stop with friends in the suburbs, which is very welcome, as it is a relief to get out of these moving crowds of an evening after a full day.

Writing of Buckingham reminds me that a young fellow's escapade landed him in the servants' quarters of the royal palace on the eve of our arrival in London. He was promptly handed over and charged. His Majesty the King, to whom news of the trespass was communicated, sent to the magistrates on behalf of the prisoner, and pleaded for the utmost leniency under the law [...].

52
Native Life in South Africa (1916)

Native Life in South Africa was published in May 1916. Formulated as an appeal to the British public, it consisted of 24 chapters, ran to over 350 pages, and sold at 3s 6d a copy. Native Life provides an account of the events leading up to the passage of the Natives Land Act, the effects it had when implemented, the campaign mounted by the SANNC to secure its repeal, and an account of several historical episodes designed to illustrate the loyalty of the African people to the cause of the Imperial Government – strengthening the case for support from the British public. In the last two chapters of the book this is then contrasted with the events leading up to the Boer rebellion of 1914.

The chapters reproduced here are Chapter 1 'A Retrospect', Chapter 4 'One Night with the Fugitives', the Epilogue, and part of a section entitled 'Report of the Lands Commission: An Analysis'. This commission, set up under the original provisions of the Natives Land Act, and chaired by Sir William Beaumont, a Natal High Court judge, was published shortly after Native Life in South Africa was printed, but Plaatje's supplement was then added to a second printing of Native Life before the end of 1916. The book was reprinted on a number of occasions over the next few years, and one edition was published in the United States in 1922 by W.E.B. Du Bois's journal, Crisis (see below pp.131-32).

Plaatje at his writing desk – this photograph appeared as the frontispiece in Native Life in South Africa, *published in London in May 1916.*

CHAPTER 1
A Retrospect

I am Black, but comely, O ye daughters of Jerusalem, as the tents of
    Kedar, as the curtains of Solomon.
Look not upon me because I am black, because the sun hath looked upon
    me: my mother's children were angry with me; they made me
    the keeper of the vineyards; but mine own vineyard have I not kept.
                                                    – The Song of Songs

Awaking on Friday morning, June 20, 1913, the South African Native found himself, not actually a slave, but a pariah in the land of his birth.

The 4,500,000 black South Africans are domiciled as follows: one and three quarter millions in locations and reserves, over half a million within municipalities or in urban areas, and nearly a million as squatters on farms owned by Europeans. The remainder are employed either on the public roads or railway lines, or as servants by European farmers, qualifying, that is, by hard work and saving to start farming on their own account.

A squatter in South Africa is a Native who owns some livestock and, having no land of his own, hires a farm or grazing and ploughing rights from a landowner, to raise grain for his own use and feed his stock. Hence, these squatters are hit very hard by an Act which passed both Houses of Parliament during the session of 1913, received the signature of the Governor-General on June 16, was gazetted on June 19, and forthwith came into operation. It may be here mentioned that on that day Lord Gladstone signed no fewer than sixteen new Acts of Parliament – some of them being rather voluminous – while three days earlier, His Excellency signed another batch of eight, of which the bulk was beyond the capability for any mortal to read and digest in four days.

But the great revolutionary change thus wrought by a single stroke of the pen, in the condition of the Native, was not realized by him until about the end of June. As a rule many farm tenancies expire at the end of the half-year, so that in June 1913, not knowing that it was impracticable to make fresh contracts, some Natives unwittingly went to search for new places of abode, which some farmers, ignorant of the law, quite as unwittingly accorded them. It was only when they went to register the new tenancies that the law officers of the Crown laid bare the cruel fact that to provide a landless Native with accommodation was forbidden under a penalty of £100, or six months' imprisonment. Then only was the situation realized.

Other Natives who had taken up fresh places on European farms under verbal contracts, which needed no registration, actually founded new homes in spite of the law, neither the white farmer nor the Native tenant being aware of the serious penalties they were exposed to by their verbal contracts.

In justice to the Government, it must be stated that no police officers scoured the country in search of lawbreakers, to prosecute them under this law. Had this been done, many £100 cheques would have passed into the Government coffers during the black July, the first month after Lord Gladstone affixed his signature to the Natives' Land Act, No. 27 of 1913.

The complication of this cruel law is made manifest by the fact that it was found necessary for a high officer of the Government to tour the provinces soon after the Act came into force, with the object of 'teaching' magistrates how to administer it. A Congress of Magistrates – a most unusual thing – was also called in Pretoria to find a way of carrying out the King's writ in the face of the difficulties arising from this tangle of the Act. We may add that nearly all the white lawyers in South Africa, to whom we spoke about this measure, had either not seen the Act at all, or had not read it carefully, so that in both cases they could not tell exactly for whose benefit it had been passed. The study of this law required a much longer time than the lawyers, unless specially briefed, could devote to it, so that they hardly knew what all the trouble was about. It was the Native in the four provinces who knew all about it, for he had not read it in books but had himself been though its mill, which like an automatic machine ground him relentlessly since the end of the month of June. Not the least but one of the cruellest and most ironical phases – and nearly every clause of this Act teems with irony – is the Schedule or appendix giving the so-called Scheduled Native Areas; and what are these 'Scheduled Native Areas'?

They are the Native locations which were reserved for the exclusive use of certain Native clans. They are inalienable and cannot be bought or sold, yet the Act says that in these 'Scheduled Native Areas' Natives only may buy land. The areas being inalienable, not even members of the clans, for whose benefit the locations are held in trust, can buy land therein. The areas could only be sold if the whole clan rebelled; in that case the location would be confiscated. But as long as the clans of the location remain loyal to the Government, nobody can buy any land within these areas. Under the respective charters of these areas, not even a member of the clan can get a separate title as owner in an area – let alone a Native outsider who had grown up among white people and done all his farming on white man's land.

If we exclude the arid tracts of Bechuanaland, these locations appear to have been granted on such a small scale that each of them got so overcrowded that most of the population had to go out and settle on the farms of white farmers through lack of space in the locations. Yet a majority of the legislators, although well aware of these limitations, and without remedying any of them, legislate, shall we say, 'with its tongue in its cheek' that only Natives may buy land in Native locations.

Again, the locations form but one-eighteenth of the total area of the Union. Theoretically, then, the 4,500,000 natives may 'buy' land in only one-eighteenth part of the Union, leaving the remaining seventeen parts for the one million whites. It is moreover true that, numerically, the Act was passed by the consent of a majority of both Houses of Parliament, but it is equally true that it was steamrollered into the statute book against the bitterest opposition of the best brains of both Houses. A most curious aspect of this singular law is that even the minister, since deceased, who introduced it, subsequently declared himself against it, adding that he only forced it through in order to stave off something worse. Indeed, it is correct to say that Mr Sauer, who introduced the bill, spoke against it repeatedly in the House; he deleted the milder provisions, inserted more drastic amendments, spoke repeatedly against his own amendments, then in conclusion he would combat his own amendments, by calling the ministerial steamroller to support the Government and vote for the drastic amendments. The only explanation of the puzzle constituted as such by these 'hot-and-cold' methods is that Mr Sauer was legislating for an electorate, at the expense of another section of the population which was without direct representation in Parliament. None of the non-European races in the provinces of Natal, Transvaal and the 'Free' State can exercise the franchise. They have no say in the selection of members for the Union Parliament. That right is only limited to white men, so that a large number of the members of Parliament who voted for this measure have no responsibility towards the black races.

Before reproducing this tyrannical enactment it would perhaps be well to recapitulate briefly the influences that led up to it. When the Union of the South African Colonies became an accomplished fact, a dread was expressed by ex-Republicans that the liberal native policy of the Cape would supersede the repressive policy of the old Republics, and they lost no time in taking definite steps to force down the throats of the Union legislature, as it were, laws which the Dutch presidents of pre-war days, with the British suzerainty over their heads, did not dare enforce against the Native people then under them. With the formation of the Union, the Imperial Government, for reasons which have never been satisfactorily explained, unreservedly handed over the Natives to the colonists, and these colonists, as a rule, are dominated by the Dutch Republican spirit. Thus the suzerainty of Great Britain, which under the reign of Her late Majesty Victoria, of blessed memory, was the Natives' only bulwark, has now apparently been withdrawn or relaxed, and the Republicans, like a lot of bloodhounds long held in the leash, use the free hand given by the Imperial Government not only to guard against a possible supersession of Cape ideals of toleration, but to effectively extend throughout the Union the drastic native policy pursued by the province which is misnamed 'Free' State, and enforce it with the utmost rigour.

During the first year of the Union, it would seem that General Botha made an honest attempt to live up to his London promises, that are mentioned by Mr Merriman in his speech (reproduced elsewhere) on the second reading of the bill in Parliament. It would seem that General Botha endeavoured to allay British apprehensions and concern for the welfare of the Native population. In pursuance of this policy General Botha won the approbation of all Natives by appointing Hon. H. Burton, a Cape minister, to the portfolio of Native Affairs. That the appointment was a happy one, from the Native point of view, became manifest when Mr Burton signalized the ushering in of Union, by releasing Chief Dinuzulu-ka-Cetywayo, who at that time was undergoing a sentence of imprisonment imposed by the Natal Supreme Court, and by the restoration to Dinuzulu of his pension of £500 a year. Also, in deference to the wishes of the Native Congress, Mr Burton abrogated two particularly obnoxious Natal measures, one legalizing the 'Sibalo' system of forced labour, the other prohibiting public meetings by Natives without the consent of Government. These abrogations placed the Natives of Natal in almost the same position as the Cape Natives though without giving them the franchise. So, too, when a drastic Squatters' Bill was gazetted early in 1912, and the recently formed Native National Congress sent a deputation to interview Mr Burton in Cape Town, after hearing the deputation, he graciously consented to withdraw the proposed measure, pending the allotment of new locations in which Natives evicted by such a measure could find an asylum. In further deference to the representations of the Native Congress, in which they were supported by Senators the Hon. W.P. Schreiner, Colonel Stanford and Mr Krogh, the Union Government gazetted another bill in January 1911, to amend an anomaly which, at that time, was peculiar to the 'Free' State: an anomaly under which a Native can neither purchase nor lease land, and native landowners in the 'Free' State could only sell their land to the white people.

The gazetted bill proposed to legalize only in one district of the Orange 'Free' State that sale of landed property by a Native to another Native as well as to a white man, but it did not propose to enable Natives to buy land from white men. The object of the bill was to remove a hardship, mentioned elsewhere in this sketch, by which a 'Free' State Native was by law debarred from inheriting landed property left to him under his uncle's will. But against such small attempts at reform, proposed or carried out by the Union Government in the interest of the Natives, granted in small instalments of a teaspoonful at a time – reforms dictated solely by feelings of justice and equity – ex-Republicans were furious.

From platform, press, and pulpit it was suggested that General Botha's administration was too English and needed overhauling. The Dutch peasants along the countryside were inflamed by hearing that their gallant leader desired to anglicize the country. Nothing was more repellent to the ideas of the backveld Dutch, and so at small meetings in the country districts resolutions were passed stating that the Botha administration had outlived its usefulness. These resolutions reaching the press from day to day had the effect of stirring up the Dutch voters against the ministry, and particularly against the head. At this time General Botha's sound policy began to weaken. He transferred Hon. H. Burton, first Minister of Native Affairs, to the portfolio of Railways and Harbours, and appointed General Hertzog, of all people in the world, to the portfolio of Native Affairs.

The good-humoured indulgence of some Dutch and English farmers towards their Native squatters, and the affectionate loyalty of some of these Native squatters in return, will cause a keen observer, arriving at a South African farm, to be lost in admiration for this mutual good feeling. He will wonder as to the meaning of the fabled bugbear anent the alleged struggle between white and black, which in reality appears to exist only in the fertile brain of the politician. Thus let the new arrival go to one of the farms in the Bethlehem or Harrismith districts for example, and see how willingly the Native toils in the fields; see him gathering in his crops and handing over the white farmer's share of the crop to the owner of the land; watch the farmer receiving his tribute from the Native tenants, and see him deliver the first prize to the Native tenant who raised the largest crop during that season; let him also see both the Natives and the landowning white farmers following to perfection the give-and-take policy of 'live and let live', and he will conclude that it would be gross sacrilege to attempt to disturb such harmonious relations between these people of different races and colours. But with a ruthless hand the Natives' Land Act has succeeded in remorselessly destroying those happy relations.

First of all, General Hertzog, the new Minister of Native Affairs, travelled up and down the country lecturing farmers on their folly in letting ground to the Natives; the racial extremists of his party hailed him as the right man for the post, for, as his conduct showed them, he would soon 'fix up' the Natives. At one or two places he was actually welcomed as the future Prime Minister of the Union. On the other hand, General Botha, who at that time seemed to have become visibly timid, endeavoured to ingratiate himself with his discontented supporters by joining his lieutenant in travelling to and fro, denouncing the Dutch farmers for not expelling the Natives from their farms and replacing them with poor whites. This became a regular ministerial campaign against the Natives, so that it seemed clear that if any Native could still find a place in the land, it was not due to the action of the Government. In his campaign the Premier said other unhappy things which were diametrically opposed to his London speeches of two years before; and while the Dutch colonists railed at him for trying to anglicize the country, English speakers and writers justly accused him of speaking with two voices; cartoonists, too, caricatured him as having two heads – one, they said, for London, and the second one for South Africa.

The uncertain tenure by which Englishmen in the public service held their posts became the subject of debates in the Union Parliament, and the employment of Government servants of colour was decidedly precarious. They were swept out of the railway and postal service with a strong racial broom, in order to make room for poor whites, mainly of Dutch descent. Concession after concession was wrung from the Government by fanatical Dutch postulants for office, for Government doles and other favours, who, like the daughters of the horse-leech in the Proverbs of Solomon, continually cried, 'Give, give'. By these events we had clearly turned the corner and were pacing backwards to pre-Union days, going back, back, and still further backward to the conditions which prevailed in the old Republics, and (if a check is not applied) we shall steadily drift back to the days of the old Dutch East Indian administration.

The bill which proposed to ameliorate the 'Free' State cruelty, to which reference has been made above, was dropped like a hot potato. Ministers made some wild and undignified speeches, of which the following spicy extract, from a speech by the Rt Hon Abraham Fischer to his constituents in Bethlehem, is a typical sample:

'What is it you want?' he asked. 'We have passed all the coolie[46] laws and we have passed all the Kaffir laws. The 'Free' State has been safeguarded and all her colour laws have been adopted by Parliament. What more can the government do for you?' And so the Union ship in this reactionary sea sailed on and on and on, until she struck an iceberg – the sudden dismissal of General Hertzog.

To the bitter sorrow of his admirers, General Hertzog, who is the fearless exponent of Dutch ideals, was relieved of his portfolios of Justice and Native Affairs – it was whispered as a result of a suggestion from London; and then the Dutch extremists, in consequence of their favourite's dismissal, gave vent to their anger in the most disagreeable manner. One could infer from their platform speeches that from their point of view, scarcely anyone else had any rights in South Africa, and least of all the man with a black skin.

In the face of this, the Government's timidity was almost unendurable. They played up to the desires of the racial extremists, with the result that a deadlock overtook the administration. Violent laws like the Immigration Law (against British Indians and alien Asiatics) and the Natives' Land Act were indecently hurried through Parliament to allay the susceptibilities of 'Free' State Republicans. No minister found time to undertake such useful legislation as the Coloured People's Occupation Bill, the Native Disputes Bill, the Marriage Bill, the University Bill, etc., etc. An apology was demanded from the High Commissioner in London for delivering himself of sentiments which were felt to be too British for the palates of his Dutch employers in South Africa, and the Prime Minister had almost to apologize for having at times so far forgotten himself as to act more like a Crown Minister than a simple Africander. 'Free' State demands became so persistent that ministers seemed to have forgotten the assurances they gave His Majesty's Government in London regarding the safety of His Majesty's coloured subjects within the Union. They trampled underfoot their own election pledges, made during the first Union General Election, guaranteeing justice and fair treatment to the law-abiding Natives.

The campaign to compass the elimination of the blacks from the farms, was not at all popular with landowners, who made huge profits out of the renting of their farms to Natives. Platform speakers and newspaper writers coined an opprobrious phrase which designated this letting of farms to Natives as 'Kaffir-farming', and attempted to prove that it was almost as immoral as 'baby-farming'. But landowners pocketed the annual rents, and showed no inclination to substitute the less industrious 'poor whites' for the more industrious Natives. Old Baas M – , a typical Dutch landowner of the 'Free' State, having collected his share of the crop of 1912, addressing a few words of encouragement to his Native tenants, on the subject of expelling the blacks from the farms, said in the Taal: 'How dare any number of men, wearing tall hats and frock coats, living in Cape Town hotels at the expense of other men, order me to evict my Natives? This is my ground; it cost my money, not Parliament's, and I will see them banged (*barst*) before I do it.'

It then became evident that the authority of Parliament would have to be sought to compel the obstinate landowners to get rid of their Natives. And the compliance of Parliament with this demand was the greatest ministerial surrender to the Republican malcontents, resulting in the introduction and passage of the Natives' Land Act of 1913, inasmuch as the Act decreed, in the name of His Majesty the King, that pending the adoption of a report to be made by a commission, somewhere in the dim and unknown future, it shall be unlawful for Natives to buy or lease land, except in scheduled Native areas. And under severe pains and penalties they were to be deprived of the bare human rights of living on the land, except as servants in the employ of the whites – rights which were never seriously challenged under the Republican regime, no matter how politicians raved against the Natives.

CHAPTER 4

One Night with the Fugitives

Es ist unkoniglich zu weinen – ach,
*Und hier nicht weinen ist unvaterlich.**

– Schiller

'Pray that your flight be not in winter,' said Jesus Christ; but it was only during the winter of 1913 that the full significance of this New Testament passage was revealed to us. We left Kimberley by the early morning train during the first week in July, on a tour of observation regarding the operation of the Natives' Land Act; and we arrived at Bloemhof, in the Transvaal, at about noon. On the river diggings there were no actual cases representing the effects

---

* German: 'It is ignoble to weep – ah/And now it would be unfatherly not to'.

of the Act, but traces of these effects were everywhere manifest. Some fugitives of the Natives' Land Act had crossed the river in full flight. The fact that they reached the diggings a fortnight before our visit would seem to show that while the debates were proceeding in Parliament some farmers already viewed with eager eyes the impending opportunity for at once making slaves of their tenants and appropriating their stock; for, acting on the powers conferred on them by an Act signed by Lord Gladstone, so lately as June 16, they had during that very week (probably a couple of days after, and in some cases, it would seem, a couple of days before the actual signing of the Bill) approached their tenants with stories about a new Act which makes it criminal for anyone to have black tenants and lawful to have black servants. Few of these Natives, of course, would object to be servants, especially if the white man is worth working for, but this is where the shoe pinches: one of the conditions is that the black man's (that is the servant's) cattle shall henceforth work for the landlord free of charge. Then the Natives would decide to leave the farm rather than make the landlord a present of all their life's savings, and some of them passed through the diggings in search of a place in the Transvaal. But the higher up they went the more gloomy was their prospect as the news about the new law was now penetrating every part of the country.

One farmer met a wandering Native family in the town of Bloemhof a week before our visit. He was willing to employ the Native and many more homeless families as follows: a monthly wage of £2 10s. for each such family, the husband working in the fields, the wife in the house, with an additional 10s. a month for each son, and 5s. for each daughter, but on condition that the Native's cattle were also handed over to work for him. It must be clearly understood, we are told that the Dutchman added, that occasionally the Native would have to leave his family at work on the farm, and go out with his wagon and his oxen to earn money whenever and wherever he was told to go, in order that the master may be enabled to pay the stipulated wage. The Natives were at first inclined to laugh at the idea of working for a master with their families and goods and chattels, and then to have the additional pleasure of paying their own small wages, besides bringing money to pay the 'Baas' for employing them. But the Dutchman's serious demeanour told them that his suggestion was 'no joke'. He himself had for some time been in need of a Native cattle-owner, to assist him as transport rider between Bloemhof, Mooifontein, London, and other diggings, in return for the occupation and cultivation of some of his waste lands in the district, but that was now illegal.

He could only 'employ' them; but, as he had no money to pay wages, their cattle would have to go out and earn it for him. 'Had they not heard of the law before?' he enquired. Of course they had; in fact that is why they left the other place, but as they thought that it was but a 'Free' State law, they took the anomalous situation for one of the multifarious aspects of the freedom of the 'Free' State whence they came; they had scarcely thought that the Transvaal was similarly affected.

Needless to say the Natives did not see their way to agree with such a one-sided bargain. They moved up-country, but only to find the next farmer offering the same terms, however, with a good many more disturbing details – and the next farmer and the next – so that after this Native farmer had wandered from farm to farm, occasionally getting into trouble for travelling with unknown stock, 'across my ground without my permission', and at times escaping arrest for he knew not what, and further, being abused for the crimes of having a black skin and no master, he sold some of his stock along the way, beside losing many which died of cold and starvation; and after thus having lost much of his substance, he eventually worked his way back to Bloemhof with the remainder, sold them for anything they could fetch, and went to work for a digger.

The experience of another Native sufferer was similar to the above, except that instead of working for a digger he sold his stock for a mere bagatelle, and left with his family by the Johannesburg night train for an unknown destination. More Native families crossed the river and went inland during the previous week, and as nothing had since been heard of them, it would seem that they were still wandering somewhere, and incidentally becoming well versed in the law that was responsible for their compulsory unsettlement.

Well, we knew that this law was as harsh as its instigators were callous, and we knew that it would, if passed, render many poor people homeless, but it must be confessed that we were scarcely prepared for such a rapid and widespread crash as it caused in the lives of the Natives in this neighbourhood. We left our luggage the next morning with the local mission school teacher, and crossed the river to find out some more about this wonderful law of extermination. It was about 10 a.m. when we landed on the south bank of the Vaal River – the picturesque Vaal River, upon whose banks a hundred miles farther west we spent the best and happiest days of our boyhood. It was interesting to walk on one portion of the banks of that beautiful river – a portion of which we had never traversed except as an infant in mother's arms more than thirty years before. How the subsequent happy days at Barkly West, so long past, came crowding upon our memory! – days when there were no railways, no bridges, and no system of irrigation. In rainy seasons, the river used to overflow its high banks and flood the surrounding valleys to such an extent, that no punt could carry the wagons across. Thereby the transport service used to be hung up, and numbers of wagons would congregate for weeks on both sides of the river until the floods subsided. At such times the price of fresh milk used to mount up to 1s. per pint. There being next to no competition, we boys had a monopoly over the milk trade. We recalled the number of haversacks full of bottles of milk we youngsters often carried to those wagons, how we returned with empty bottles and with just that number of shillings. Mother and our elder brothers had leather bags full of gold and did not care for the 'boy's money'; and unlike the boys of the neighbouring village, having no sisters of our own, we gave away some of our money to fair cousins, and jingled the rest in our pockets. We had been told from boyhood that sweets were injurious to the teeth, and so spurning these delights we had hardly any use for the money, for all we wanted to eat, drink and wear was to hand in plenty. We could then get six or eight shillings every morning from the pastime of washing that number of bottles, filling them with fresh milk and carrying them down to the wagons; there was always such an abundance of the liquid that our shepherd's hunting dog could not possibly miss what we took, for while the flocks were feeding on the luscious buds of the haak-doorns and the blossoms of the rich mimosa and other wild vegetation that abounded on the banks of the Vaal River, the cows, similarly engaged, were gathering more and more milk.

The gods are cruel, and one of their cruellest acts of omission was that of giving us no hint that in very much less than a quarter of a century all those hundreds of heads of cattle, and sheep and horses belonging to the family would vanish like a morning mist, and that we ourselves would live to pay 30s. per month for a daily supply of this same precious fluid, and in very limited quantities. They might have warned us that Englishmen would agree with Dutchmen to make it unlawful for black men to keep milk cows of their own on the banks of that river, and gradually have prepared us for the shock.

Crossing the river from the Transvaal side brings one into the province of the Orange 'Free' State, in which, in the adjoining division of Boshof, we were born thirty-six years back. We remember the name of the farm, but not having been in this neighbourhood since infancy, we could not tell its whereabouts, nor could we say whether the present owner was a Dutchman, his lawyer, or a Hebrew merchant; one thing we do know, however: it is that even if we had the money and the owner was willing to sell the spot upon which we first saw the light of day and breathed the pure air of heaven, the sale would be followed with a fine of one hundred pounds. The law of the country forbids the sale of land to a Native. Russia is one of the most abused countries in the world, but it is extremely doubtful if the statute book of that empire contains a law debarring the peasant from purchasing the land whereon he was born, or from building a home wherein he might end his days.

At this time we felt something rising from our heels along our back, gripping us in a spasm, as we were cycling along; a needlelike pang, too, pierced our heart with a sharp thrill. What was it? We remembered feeling something nearly like it when our father died eighteen years ago; but at that time our physical organs were fresh and grief was easily thrown off in tears, but then we lived in a happy South Africa that was full of pleasant anticipations, and now – what changes for the worse have we undergone! For to crown all our calamities, South Africa has by law ceased to be the home of any of her Native children whose skins are dyed with a pigment that does not conform with the regulation hue.

We are told to forgive our enemies and not to let the sun go down upon our wrath, so we breathe the prayer that peace may be to the white races, and that they, including our present persecutors of the Union Parliament, may never live to find themselves deprived of all occupation and property rights in their native country as is now the case with the Native. History does not tell us of any other continent where the Bantu lives besides Africa, and if this systematic ill-treatment of the Natives by the colonists is to be the guiding principle of Europe's scramble for Africa, slavery is our only alternative; for now it is only as serfs that the Natives are legally entitled to live here. Is it to be thought that God is using the South African Parliament to hound us out of our ancestral homes in order to quicken our pace heavenward? But to go from where to heaven? In the beginning, we are told, God created heaven and earth, and peopled the earth, for people do not shoot up to heaven from nowhere. They must have had an earthly home. Enoch, Melchizedek, Elijah, and other saints, came to heaven from earth. God did not say to the Israelites in their bondage: 'Cheer up, boys; bear it all in good part for I have bright mansions on high awaiting you all.' But he said: 'I have surely seen the affliction of my people which are in Egypt, and have heard their cry by reason of their taskmasters; for I know their sorrows, and I am come down to bring them out of the hands of the Egyptians, and to bring them up out of that land unto a good land and a large, unto a land flowing with milk and honey.' And

He used Moses to carry out the promise He made to their ancestor Abraham in Canaan, that 'unto thy seed will I give this land'. It is to be hoped that in the Boer churches, entrance to which is barred against coloured people during divine service, they also read the Pentateuch.

It is doubtful if we ever thought so much on a single bicycle ride as we did on this journey; however, the sight of a policeman ahead of us disturbed these meditations and gave place to thoughts of quite another kind, for – we had no pass. Dutchmen, Englishmen, Jews, Germans and other foreigners may roam the 'Free' State without permission – but not Natives. To us it would mean a fine and imprisonment to be without a pass. The 'pass' law was first instituted to check the movement of livestock over sparsely populated areas. In a sense it was a wise provision, in that it served to identify the livestock which one happened to be driving along the high road, to prove the bona fides of the driver and his title to the stock. Although white men still steal large droves of horses in Basutoland and sell them in Natal or in East Griqualand, they, of course, are not required to carry any passes. These white horse-thieves, to escape the clutches of the police, employ Natives to go and sell the stolen stock and write the passes for these Natives, forging the names of magistrates and justices of the peace. Such Native thieves in some instances ceasing to be hirelings in the criminal business, trade on their own, but it is not clear what purpose it is intended to serve by subjecting Native pedestrians to the degrading requirement of carrying passes when they are not in charge of any stock.

In a few moments the policeman was before us and we alighted in presence of the representative of the law, with our feet on the accursed soil of the district in which we were born. The policeman stopped. By his looks and his familiar 'Dag jong'* we noticed that the policeman was Dutch, and the embodiment of affability. He spoke and we were glad to notice that he had no intention of dragging an innocent man to prison. We were many miles from the nearest police station, and in such a case one is generally able to gather the real views of the man on patrol, as distinct from the written code of his office, but our friend was becoming very companionable. Naturally we asked him about the operation of the plague law. He was a Transvaaler, he said, and he knew that Kaffirs were inferior beings, but they had rights, and were always left in undisturbed possession of their property when Paul Kruger was alive. 'The poor devils must be sorry now,' he said, 'that they ever sang "God Save

---

* Dutch, 'Good-day'.

the Queen" when the British troops came into the Transvaal, for I have seen, in the course of my duties, that a Kaffir's life nowadays was not worth a ——, and I believe that no man regretted the change of flags now more than the Kaffirs of Transvaal.' This information was superfluous, for personal contact with the Natives of Transvaal had convinced us of the fact. They say it is only the criminal who has any reason to rejoice over the presence of the Union Jack, because in his case the cat-o'-nine tails, except for very serious crimes, has been abolished.

'Some of the poor creatures,' continued the policeman, 'I knew to be fairly comfortable, if not rich, and they enjoyed the possession of their stock, living in many instances just like Dutchmen. Many of these are now being forced to leave their homes. Cycling along this road you will meet several of them in search of new homes, and if ever there was a fool's errand, it is that of a Kaffir trying to find a new home for his stock and family just now.'

'And what do you think, Baas Officer, must eventually be the lot of a people under such unfortunate circumstances?' we asked.

'I think,' said the policeman, 'that it must serve them right. They had no business to hanker after British rule, to cheat and plot with the enemies of their Republic for the overthrow of their Government. Why did they not assist the forces of their Republic during the war instead of supplying the English with scouts and intelligence? Oom Paul would not have died of a broken heart and he would still be there to protect them. Serve them right, I say.'

So saying he spurred his horse, which showed a clean pair of hoofs. He left us rather abruptly, for we were about to ask why we, too, of Natal and the Cape were suffering, for we, being originally British subjects, never 'cheated and plotted with the enemies of our Colonies', but he was gone and left us still cogitating by the roadside.

Proceeding on our journey we next came upon a Native trek and heard the same old story of prosperity on a Dutch farm: they had raised an average eight hundred bags of grain each season, which, with the increased stock and sale of wool, gave a steady income of about £150 per year after the farmer had taken his share. There were gossipy rumours about somebody having met someone who said that someone else had overheard a conversation between the Baas and somebody else, to the effect that the Kaffirs were getting too rich on his property. This much involved tale incidentally conveys the idea that the Baas was himself getting too rich on his farm. For the Native provides his own seed, his own cattle, his own labour for the ploughing, the weeding and the reaping, and after bagging his grain he calls in the landlord to receive his share, which is fifty per cent of the entire crop.

All had gone well till the previous week when the Baas came to the Native tenants with the story that a new law had been passed under which 'all my oxen and cows must belong to him, and my family to work for £2 a month, failing which he gave me four days to leave the farm.'

We passed several farmhouses along the road, where all appeared pretty tranquil as we went along, until the evening which we spent in the open country, somewhere near the boundaries of the Hoopstad and Boshof Districts; here a regular circus had gathered. By a 'circus' we mean the meeting of groups of families, moving to every point of the compass, and all bivouacked at this point in the open country where we were passing. It was heartrending to listen to the tales of their cruel experiences derived from the rigour of the Natives' Land Act. Some of their cattle had perished on the journey, from poverty and lack of fodder, and the Native owners ran a serious risk of imprisonment for travelling with dying stock. The experience of one of these evicted tenants is typical of the rest, and illustrates the cases of several we met in other parts of the country.

Kgobadi, for instance, had received a message describing the eviction of his father-in-law in the Transvaal Province, without notice, because he had refused to place his stock, his family, and his person at the disposal of his former landlord, who now refuses to let him remain on his farm except on these conditions. The father-in-law asked that Kgobadi should try and secure a place for him in the much dreaded 'Free' State as the Transvaal had suddenly become uninhabitable to Natives who cannot become servants; but 'greedy folk hae lang airms', and Kgobadi himself was proceeding with his family and his belongings in a wagon, to inform his people-in-law of his own eviction, without notice, in the 'Free' State, for a similar reason to that which sent his father-in-law adrift. The Baas had exacted from him the services of himself, his wife and his oxen, for wages of 30s. a month, whereas Kgobadi had been making over £100 a year, besides retaining the services of his wife and of his cattle to himself. When he refused the extortionate terms, the Baas retaliated with a Dutch note, dated the 30th day of June 1913, which ordered him to 'betake himself from the farm of the undersigned, by sunset of the same day, failing which his stock would be seized and impounded, and himself handed over to the authorities for trespassing on the farm.'

A drowning man catches at every straw, and so we were again and again appealed to for advice by these sorely afflicted people. To those who were not yet evicted we counselled patience and submission to the absurd terms, pending an appeal to a higher authority than the South African Parliament and finally to His Majesty the King who, we believed, would certainly disapprove of all that we saw on that day had it been brought to his notice. As for those who were already evicted, as a Bechuana we could not help thanking God that Bechuanaland (on the western boundary of this quasi-British Republic) was still entirely British. In the early days it was the base of David Livingstone's activities and peaceful mission against the Portuguese and Arab slave trade. We suggested that we might negotiate the numerous restrictions against the transfer of cattle from the western Transvaal and seek an asylum in Bechuanaland. We wondered what consolation we could give to these roving wanderers if the whole of Bechuanaland were under the jurisdiction of the relentless Union Parliament. It was cold that afternoon as we cycled into the 'Free' State of Transvaal, and towards evening the southern winds rose. A cutting blizzard raged during the night, and Native mothers evicted from their homes shivered with their babies by their sides. When we saw on that night the teeth of little children clattering through the cold, we thought of our own little ones in their Kimberley home of an evening after gambolling in their winter frocks with their schoolmates, and we wondered what these little mites had done that a home should suddenly become to them a thing of the past.

Kgobadi's goats had been to kid when he trekked from his farm; but the kids, which in halcyon times represented the interested on his capital, were now one by one dying as fast as they were born and left by the roadside for the jackals and vultures to feast upon.

This visitation was not confined to Kgobadi's stock. Mrs Kgobadi carried a sick baby when the eviction took place, and she had to transfer her darling from the cottage to the jolting ox-wagon in which they left the farm. Two days out the little one began to sink as the result of privation and exposure on the road, and the night before we met them its little soul was released from its earthly bonds. The death of the child added a fresh perplexity to the stricken parents. They had no right or title to the farmlands through which they trekked: the must keep to the public roads – the only places in the country open to the outcasts if they are possessed of travelling permit. The deceased child had to be buried, but where, when, and how?

This young wandering family decided to dig a grave under cover of the darkness of that night, when no one was looking, and in that crude manner the dead child was interred – and interred amid fear and trembling, as well as the throbs of a torturing anguish, in a stolen grave, lest the proprietor of the spot, or any of his servants, should surprise them in the act. Even criminals dropping straight from the gallows have an undisputed claim to six feet of ground on which to rest their criminal remains, but under the cruel operation of the Natives' Land Act little children, whose only crime is that God did not make them white, are sometimes denied that right in their ancestral home.

Numerous details narrated by these victims of an Act of Parliament kept us awake all that night, and by next morning we were glad enough to hear no more of the sickening procedure of extermination voluntarily instituted by the South African Parliament. We had spent a hideous night under a bitterly cold sky, conditions to which hundreds of our unfortunate countrymen and countrywomen in various parts of the country are condemned by the provisions of this Parliamentary land plague. At five o'clock in the morning the cold seemed to redouble its energies; and never before did we so fully appreciate the Master's saying: 'But pray ye that your flight be not in the winter.'

REPORT OF THE LANDS COMMISSION
An Analysis

The first section of this chapter, examining in detail the report of the Commission region by region, has been omitted.

General Hertzog's Scheme

It may interest the reader to know that General Hertzog is the father of the segregation controversy. The writer and other Natives interviewed him before Christmas 1912, at the Palace of Justice, Pretoria, when he was still in the Ministry. We had a two hours' discussion, in the course of which the General gave us a forecast of what he then regarded as possible Native areas, and drew rings on a large wall-map of the Union to indicate their locality. Included in these rings were several magistracies which he said would solve a knotty problem. He told us that white people objected to black men in Government offices and magistrates in those areas would have no difficulty in employing them.

General Hertzog was dismissed shortly after, and it has been said that in order to placate his angry admirers the Ministry passed the Natives' Land Act of which this Report is the outcome. Judging by the vigour with which the Union administration has been weeding Natives out of the public service and replacing them with Boers without waiting for the Commission's Report, it is clear that they did not share General Hertzog's intention as regards these magistracies. I cannot recall all the magistracies which General Hertzog mentioned as likely to fall in Native areas; but I distinctly remember that Pietersburg and Thaba Nchu were among them; while Alice and Peddie (and possibly a neighbouring district) were to be included in a southern reserve into which the Natives round East London and Grahamstown would have to move, the land vacated by them to be gradually occupied by the white settlers now scattered over the would-be Native block. He went on to forecast a vast dependency of the Union in which the energies and aspirations of black professional men would find their outlet with no danger of competition with Europeans; where a new educational and representative system could be evolved for Natives to live their own lives, and work out their salvation in a separate sphere. But the Lands Commission's Report places this plausible scheme beyond the region of possibility, for no Native area, recommended by this Commission, includes any of the magistracies mentioned.

General Hertzog's plan at least offered a fair ground for discussion, but the Commission's Report is a travesty of his scheme. It intensifies every Native difficulty and goes much further than the wild demands of the 'Free' State extremists. Thus, even if it be thrown out, as it deserves to be, future exploiters will always cite it as an excuse for measures subversive of Native well-being. In fact, that such legislation should be mooted is nothing short of a national calamity.

How They 'Doubled' a Native Area

Near the northern boundaries of Transvaal there lies a stretch of malaria country in which nothing can live unless born there. Men and beasts from other parts visit it only in winter and leave it again before the rains begin, when the atmosphere becomes almost too poisonous to inhale. Even the unfailing tax gatherers of the Native Affairs Department go there only in the winter every year and hurry back again with the money bags before the malaria period sets in. A Boer general describes how when harassed by the Imperial forces during the South African War, he was once compelled to march through it; and how his men and horses – many of them natives of the Transvaal – contracted enough malaria during the march to cause the illness of many and the death of several burghers and animals. Of the Native inhabitants of this delectable area the Dutch General says: 'Their diminutive deformed stature was another proof of the miserable climate obtaining here'.[47] When the Land Commissioners contemplated this 'salubrious' region, their hearts must have melted with generosity, for whereas in our own healthy part of South Africa they have indicated possible Native areas by little dots or microscopical rings (as in Thaba Nchu for instance), here, in this malaria area, they marked off a reserve almost as wide as that described by General Hertzog himself at our Pretoria interview. It is possibly in this way, and in such impossible places, that the Commission is alleged to have 'doubled' the Native areas. In the rest of the country they ask Parliament to confiscate our birthright to the soil of our ancestry in favour of 600,000 Boers and aliens whose languages can show no synonym for home – the English equivalent of our *ikaya* and *legae*!

The Britishers' vocabulary includes that sacred word: and that, perhaps, is the reason why their colonizing schemes have always allowed some tracts of country for Native family life, with reasonable opportunities for their future existence and progress, in the vast South African expanses which God in His providence had created for His Children of the Sun. The Englishman, moreover, found us speaking the word *legae*, and taught us how to write it. In 1910, much against our will, the British Government surrendered its immediate sovereignty over our land to Colonials and cosmopolitan aliens who know little about a Home, because their dictionaries contain no such loving term: and the recommendations of this Commission would seem to express their limited conception of the word and its beautiful significance.

Ignorant of the Coming Servitude

All too little (if anything at all) is known of the services rendered to the common weal by the Native leaders in South Africa. In every crisis of the past four years – and the one-sided policy of the Union has produced many of these – the Native leaders have taken upon themselves the thankless and expensive task of restraining the Natives from resorting to violence. The seeming lack of appreciation with which the Government has met their success in that direction has been the cause of some comment among Natives. On more than one occasion they have asked whether the authorities were disappointed because, by their successful avoidance of bloodshed, the Native leaders had forestalled the machine-guns. But, be the reason what it may, this apparent ingratitude has not cooled their ardour in the cause of peace.

Today the Native Affairs Department has handed over £7,000 from Native taxes to defray the cost of the Land Commission, consisting of five white commissioners, their white clerks and secretaries – the printing alone swallowed up nearly £1,000 with further payments to white translators for a

Dutch edition of the Report. But not a penny could be spared for the enlightenment of the Natives at whose expense the inquiry had been carried through. They have been officially told and had every reason to believe that the Commission was going about to mark out reservations for them to occupy and live emancipated from the prejudicial conditions that would spring from contiguity with the white race. For any information as to the real character of the contents of the Dutch and English Report of this Commission, they would have to depend on what they could gather from the unsalaried efforts of the Native leaders who, owing to the vastness of the sub-continent, the lack of travelling facilities and their own limited resources, can only reach a few localities and groups.

It may be said with some reason that English leaders of thought in South Africa have had a task of like difficulty: that they worked just as hard to get the English colonists to co-operate loyally with a vanquished foe in whose hands the Union constitution has placed the destiny of South Africa. It could also be said with equal justice that the Boer leaders' task has been not less difficult, but it required their greatest tact to get the Boer majority – now in power – to deal justly with the English who had been responsible for the elimination of the two Boer flags from among the emblems of the family of nations.

But the difficulty of their task is not comparable to that of the Native leaders. English and Dutch Colonial leaders are members of Parliament, each in receipt of £400 a year, with a free first-class ticket over all systems of the South African Railways. They enjoy, besides, the co-operation of an army of well-paid white civil servants, without whom they could scarcely have managed their own people. The Native leader on the other hand, in addition to other impediments, has to contend with the difficulty of financing his own tours in a country whose settled policy is to see that Natives do not make any money. His position in his own country approximates to that of an Englishman, grappling single-handed, with complicated problems, on foreign soil, without the aid of a British Consul.

Bullyragging the Natives

For upwards of three years the government of the Union of South Africa has harassed and maltreated the rural Native taxpayers as no heathen monarch, since the time of the Zulu King Chaka, ever ill-used a tributary people. For the greater part of our period of suffering the Empire was engaged in a titanic struggle, which for ghastliness is without precedent. I can think of no people in the Eastern Hemisphere who are absolutely unaffected by it; but the members of the Empire can find consolation in the fact that almost all creation is in sympathy with them. Constant disturbance has brought a realization to the entire universe that nature, like the times, is out of joint. The birds of the air and the fishes, like other denizens of the deep, are frequently drawn into the whirlpool of misery; and a mutual suffering has identified them as it were with some of the vicissitudes of an Empire at war. And they too have in their peculiar way felt impelled to offer their condolence to the dependents of those who have fallen in the combat on land, in the air, on sea, and under the sea. And while all creation stands aghast beside the gaping graves, by rivers of blood, mourning with us the loss of some of the greatest Englishmen that ever lived, South Africa, having constituted herself the only vandal State, possesses sufficient in compassion to celebrate the protection conferred on her by the British Fleet and devote her God-given security to an orgy of tyranny over those hapless coloured subjects of the King, whom the Union constitution has placed in the hollow of her hands.

Is there anybody left on earth who is just enough to call on South Africa to put an end to this cowardly abuse of power?

We appeal to the Colonists of Natal, who have declared themselves against the persecution of their Natives; and would draw their attention to the fact that in spite of their disapproval, expressed to the Lands Commission, the Union Government, at the behest of a prisoner, is still tyrannizing over the Zulus.

We appeal to the Churches. We would remind them that in the past the Christian voice has been our only shield against legislative excesses of the kind now in full swing in the Union. But in the new ascendancy of self and pelf over justice and tolerance, that voice will be altogether ignored, unless strongly reinforced by the Christian world at large. We appeal for deliverance from the operation of a cunningly conceived and a most draconian law whose administration has been marked by the closing down of Native churches and chapels in rural South Africa.

We appeal to the Jews, God's chosen people, who know what suffering means. We would remind them that if after 1913 there was no repetition of a Russian pogrom it was largely because the Native leaders (including the author) have spared neither pains nor pence in visiting the scattered tribes and exhorting them to obey all the demands of the South African Government under the Grobler[48] law pending a peaceful intercession from the outside world. But for this self-imposed duty on the part of the Native leaders, I am satisfied that numbers of the Native peasantry would have been mown down early in 1914, and humanity would have been told that they were justly punished for disobedience to constituted authority.

We appeal to the leaders of the Empire – that Empire for which my own relatives have sacrificed life and property in order to aid its extension along the Cape to Cairo route, entirely out of love for her late Majesty Queen Victoria and with no expectation of material reward. We ask these leaders to honour the plighted word of their noble predecessors who collectively and severally assured us a future of peace and happiness as our membership privilege in the Empire for which we bled. They were among the noblest Englishmen that ever left their Native shores to create a prestige for their nation abroad. They included heroes and empire-builders, too many to mention, who all told us that they spoke in the name of Queen Victoria and on behalf of her heirs and successors. What has suddenly become of the Briton's word – his bond – that solemn obligations of such Imperialists should cease to count? And if it is decided that the Victorian Englishman and the twentieth-century Englishman are creatures of different clay (and that with the latter honour is binding only when both parties to the undertaking are white), surely this could hardly be the moment to inaugurate a change the reaction of which cannot fail to desecrate the memories of your just and upright forebears.

We would draw the attention of the British people to the fact that the most painful part of the present ordeal to the loyal black millions, who are now doing all they can, or are allowed to do, to help the Empire to win the war, is that they suffer this consummate oppression at the bidding of a gentleman now serving his term for participating in a rebellion during this war. We feel that it must be a source of intense satisfaction to Mr Piet Grobler in his cell, that the most loyal section of the King's South African subjects are suffering persecution under his law – a fact which, looked at from whatever standpoint, is equal to an official jus-tification of the ideals for which he rose in rebellion. And if there is to be a return to the contented South Africa of other days, both the Natives' Land Act – his law – and the Report of the Lands Commission – its climax – should be torn up.

Courting Retribution

For three years and more the South African Government have persecuted my kinsmen and kinswomen for no other crime than that they have meekly paid their taxes. I had come to the conclusion, after meeting colonials from all quarters of the globe and weighing the information obtained from them, that in no colony are the Native inhabitants treated with greater injustice than in South Africa.[49] Yet in spite of all I had seen and heard, I must say that, until this

Report reached me, I never would have believed my white fellow-countrymen capable of conceiving the all but diabolical schemes propounded between the covers of Volume 1 of the Report of the South African Lands Commission, 1916, and clothing them in such plausible form as to mislead even sincere and well-informed friends of Natives. There are pages upon pages of columns of figures running into four, five or six noughts. They will dazzle the eye until the reader imagines himself witnessing the redistribution of the whole subcontinent and its transfer to the Native tribes. But two things he will never find in that mass of figures; these are (a) the grand total of the land so 'awarded' to Natives; and (b) how much is left for other people. To arrive at these he has to do his own additions and subtractions, and call in the aid of statistics such as the census figures, the annual Blue Books etc., before the truth begins to dawn on him. They talk of having 'doubled' the Native areas. They found us in occupation of 143 million morgen and propose to squeeze us into 18 million. If this means doubling it, then our teachers must have taught us the wrong arithmetic. Is it any wonder that it is becoming increasingly difficult for us to continue to love and respect the great white race as we truly loved it at the beginning of the century?

We would submit a few problems in this Report for the British people and their Parliamentary representatives to solve:

Firstly: Who are to become the occupants of the lands from which the Commission recommends the removal of the Native proletariat?

Secondly: In view of certain upheavals which we have seen not very long ago, and others which might take place in the future, it is pertinent to ask, concerning the 'very small minority of the inhabitants' – the whites – alluded to by Mr Schreiner at the head of this chapter,[50] (a) what proportion is in full sympathy with the ideals of the British Empire; (b) what proportion remains indifferent; and (c) what proportion may be termed hostile?

Thirdly: Does the autonomy granted to this 'small minority' amount to complete independence, or does it not?

Fourthly: Would it not be advisable also to inquire of 'the vast majority of the inhabitants', the King's black subjects, doomed by this Report to forfeit their homes and all they value in their own country, (a) how many of these are loyal, and (b) how many are not?

Finally and solemnly we would put it to all concerned for the honour and perpetuity of British dominion in South Africa, can the Empire afford to tamper with and alienate their affections?

As stated already, this 'very vast majority of the inhabitants' of South Africa has been strafed by the 'very small minority' for over three years. And when the burden loaded on our bent backs becomes absolutely unbearable we are at times inclined to blame ourselves; for, when some us fought hard – and often against British diplomacy – to extend the sphere of British influence, it never occurred to us that the spread of British dominion in South Africa would culminate in consigning us to our present intolerable position, namely, a helotage under a Boer oligarchy. But when an official Commission asks Parliament to herd us into concentration camps, with the additional recommendation that besides breeding slaves for our masters, we should be made to pay for the upkeep of the camps: in other words, that we should turn the colonials into slave-raiders and slave-drivers (but save them the expense of buying the slaves), the only thing that stands between us and despair is the thought that Heaven has never yet failed us. We remember how African women have at times shed tears under similar injustices; and how when they have been made to leave their fields with their hoes on their shoulders, their tears on evaporation have drawn fire and brimstone from the skies. But such blind retribution has a way of punishing the innocent alike with the guilty, and it is in the interests of both that we plead for some outside intervention to assist South Africa in recovering her lost senses.

The ready sympathy expressed by those British people among whom I have lived and laboured during the past two years inspires the confidence that a consensus of British opinion will, in the Union's interest, stay the hand of the South African Government, veto this iniquity and avert the nemesis that would surely follow its perpetration.

Her mind must have been riveted on South Africa when, quite recently, Ida Luckie sang:

> Alas, My Country! Thou wilt have no need
> Of enemy to bring thee to they doom ...
> For not alone by war a nation falls.
> Though she be fair, serene as radiant morn,
> Though girt by seas, secure in armament,
> Let her but spurn the vision of the Cross;
> Tread with contemptuous feet on its command
> Of Mercy, Love and Human Brotherhood,
> And she, some fateful day, shall have no need
> Of enemy to bring her to the dust.
>
> Some day, though distant it may be – with God
> A thousand years are but as yesterday -
> The germs of hate, injustice, violence,

Like an insidious canker in the blood,
Shall eat that nation's vitals. She shall see
Break forth the blood-red tide of anarchy,
Sweeping her plains, laying her cities low,
And bearing on its seething, crimson flood
The wreck of Government, of home, and all
 The nation's pride, its splendour and its power.
On with relentless flow, into the seas
Of God's eternal vengeance wide and deep.
But, for God's grace! Oh may it hold thee fast,
My Country, until justice shall prevail
O'er wrong and o'er oppression's cruel power,
And all that makes humanity to mourn.

53

'A South African's Homage', in A *Book of Homage to Shakespeare* (1916)[51]

A Book of Homage to Shakespeare was published in celebration of the three hundredth anniversary of Shakespeare's death. Plaatje had been invited to contribute by Israel Gollancz, the editor of the book and a professor of literature at King's College, London, whom he had probably met through his friend, Alice Werner, a lecturer at the same college. Plaatje subsequently visited Shakespeare's birthplace, Stratford-upon-Avon, later in 1916, where he was introduced at a Brotherhood meeting as 'a well-known Shakespeare scholar'.

I had but a vague idea of Shakespeare until about 1896 when, at the age of 18, I was attracted by the Press remarks in the Kimberley paper, and went to see *Hamlet* in the Kimberley Theatre.[52] The performance made me curious to know more about Shakespeare and his works. Intelligence in Africa is still carried from mouth to mouth by means of conversations after working hours, and, reading a number of Shakespeare's works, I always had a fresh story to tell.

I first read *The Merchant of Venice*. The characters were so realistic that I was asked more than once to which of certain speculators, then operating round Kimberley, Shakespeare referred as Shylock. All this gave me an appetite for more Shakespeare, and I found that many of the current quotations used by educated Natives to embellish their speeches, which I had always taken for English proverbs, were culled from Shakespeare's works.

While reading *Cymbeline*, I met the girl who afterwards became my wife. I was not then as well acquainted with her language – the Xhosa – as I am now; and although she had a better grip of mine – the Sechuana – I was doubtful whether I could make her understand my innermost feelings in it, so in coming to an understanding we both used the language of educated people – the language which Shakespeare wrote – which happened to be the only official language of our country at the time. Some of the daily epistles were rather lengthy, for I usually started with the bare intention of expressing the affections of my heart but generally finished up by completely unburdening my soul. For command of language and giving expression to abstract ideas, the success of my efforts was second only to that of my wife's, and it is easy to divine that Shakespeare's poems fed our thoughts.

It may be depended upon that we both read *Romeo and Juliet*. My people resented the idea of my marrying a girl who spoke a language which, like the Hottentot language, had clicks in it; while her people likewise abominated the idea of giving their daughter in marriage to a fellow who spoke a language so imperfect as to be without any clicks. But the civilized laws of Cape Colony saved us from a double tragedy in a cemetery, and our erstwhile objecting relatives have lived to award their benediction to the growth of our Chuana-M'Bo family which is bilingual both in the vernaculars and in European languages.

In the beginning of this century I became a journalist, and when called on to comment on things social, political, or military, I always found inspiration in one of other of Shakespeare's sayings. For instance, in 1910, when Halley's Comet illumined the Southern skies, King Edward VII and two great Bechuana Chiefs – Sebele and Bathoeng – died. I commenced each obituary with Shakespeare's quotation:

> When beggars die there are no comets seen;
> The heavens themselves blaze forth the death of princes.

Besides being natural story-tellers, the Bechuana are good listeners, and legendary stories seldom fail to impress them. Thus, one morning, I visited the Chief's court at Mafeking and was asked for the name of 'the white man who spoke so well'. An educated Chieftain promptly replied for me; he said: William Tsikinya-Chaka (William Shake-the-Sword). The translation, though perhaps more free than literal, is happy in its way considering how many of Shakespeare's characters met their death. Tsikinya-Chaka became noted among some of my readers as a reliable white oracle.

It is just possible that selfish patriotism is at the bottom of my admiration for Shakespeare. To illustrate my meaning let me take a case showing how feelings of an opposite kind were roused in me.

I once went to see a cinematograph showing of the Crucifixion. All the characters in the play, including Pilate, the priests, and Simon of Cyrene, were white men. According to the pictures, the only black man in the mob was Judas Iscariot. I have since become suspicious of the veracity of the cinema and acquired a scepticism which is not diminished by a gorgeous one now exhibited in London which shows, side by side with the nobility of the white race, a highly coloured exaggeration of the depravity of the blacks.[53]

Shakespeare's dramas, on the other hand, show that nobility and valour, like depravity and cowardice, are not the monopoly of any colour.

Shakespeare lived over 300 years ago, but he appears to have had a keen grasp of human character. His description of things seems so inwardly correct that (in spite of our rapid means of communication and facilities for travelling) we of the present age have not yet equalled his acumen.

It is to be hoped that with the maturity of African literature, now still in its infancy, writers and translators will consider the matter of giving to Africans the benefit of some at least of Shakespeare's works. That this could be done is suggested by the probability that some of the stories on which his dramas are based find equivalents in African folk-lore.

54

Sechuana Proverbs with Literal Translations and their European Equivalents (1916)

Sechuana Proverbs with Literal Translations and their European Equivalents was published during the course of 1916 by Kegan Paul, Trench, Trubner and Co Ltd, of London. It ran to 98 pages, and included 732 Tswana proverbs with both literal translations and their closest European equivalents, set out in three columns. The Preface and Introduction to the book are reproduced here, omitting only some of the lists of examples of proverbs given.

PREFACE

Much of the oral native philosophy is too plain and therefore too frank for civilised ears. This is particularly true in regard to some of the proverbs relating to the relation between men and women. In this collection, sayings of that class are carefully omitted. This omission is not inconsistent with primitive Sechuana custom. Old people never mentioned such sayings in the presence of youth or of uncircumcised adults, whom they always classed with the children.

It is the author's belief that had these aphorisms been collected thirty years ago, this book could have been enlarged to nearly three times its size. With the spread of European speech and thought in South Africa, these primitive saws are fast being forgotten, and in order to arrest this process, the author appeals to all authors of Sechuana to:

(a) communicate to him any Sechuana proverbs known to them which are not included in this book;

(b) point out errors (if any) in the translations, or wrong readings in the originals; and

(c) draw his attention to any European proverbs which would be better equivalents to the corresponding Sechuana proverbs in this book.

When it is borne in mind that I wrote the book in England, where there was no one versed in the language to whom I could go for advice, this request will I hope be found reasonable.

That there are many more unrecorded proverbs I have no doubt. For it will be observed that many of the maxims in this collection are of pastoral origin and refer to all kinds of game; yet (with the exception of the occasional reference to the buffalo in no. 490) I cannot recall any proverbs referring to the *nare* (buffalo),the *phofu* (eland), the *kukama* (oryx) and the *tshepe* (springbok). The meat of these animals in the early days was a 'feast of the gods' among the Bechuana, who had various ingenious ways of preparing it.

The skin of the last-named antelope was used for carrying babies on the backs of their mothers or their nurse-maids, and also as mats or as grain bags. The hides of the other three beasts were applied to several domestic uses, including mats, milk-sacks, sandals, whips, shields, ropes, etc., so that they were indispensable in the indoor and outdoor activities of the Bechuana.

The *phofu*, in addition, has a huge lump of kidney fat for which Bechuana herbalists paid a very high price, using the suet for mixing medicine.

These proverbs pay much attention to less useful game (*vide* nos. 71-77, also 580-590 and 643-651, etc.) and it seems incredible that such useful animals as the above-named four could have entirely escaped proverbial notice.

Any information on the subject will be gratefully received by the author ... The result will I hope serve the additional purpose of placing a polyglot collection in the hands of native readers in South Africa.

INTRODUCTION
The Bechuana

The object of this book is to save from oblivion, as far as this can still be done, the proverbial expressions of the Bechuana people, who inhabit the Bechuanaland Protectorate, Southern Rhodesia, the northern division of Cape Colony, including Griqualand West, the whole of the Orange Free State and the Western half of the Transvaal.

According to traditions, the Bechuana migrated from the far interior during the fifteenth century. Some Central African places, hundreds of miles north of Bechuanaland, now occupied by tribes speaking entirely different languages, bear such Sechuana names as *Naka-tsa-Pudi* (goats' horns) and *Mosi-oa-Thunya* (the smoke explodes).

Their Disposition and Habits

Historians describe the Bechuana as the most peace-loving and timid section of the Bantu. Their statements, however, do not seem to be quite in accord with the facts; for, fighting their way south, from the Central African lakes, some of the Bechuana tribes became known as 'The people with the sharp spear'. And if I am not much mistaken they were the only Natives who indignantly, though vainly, protested against the South African Defence Act which debars Native citizens from joining the Citizen Volunteer Force.

Before the annexation of Bechuanaland to the Empire, a British Commissioner reported as follows to the War Office concerning one Bechuana tribe – the Barolong:

> They are by nature far from being bellicose. They only desire to be left alone to tend their stock and hunt in the Kalahari desert. A great proportion of them have assumed garments of European cut, missionary work has been actively prosecuted amongst the Bechuana and numbers are now professing Christians. They are represented as apt scholars, and generally as being morally and intellectually superior to the Native tribes of the coast. (G.B. and I. War Office.)

As if to modify his information regarding the peaceful habits of the Bechuana, the same officer further says: 'The Chief Montshiwa was said in 1880 to be able to put in the field 800 well equipped horsemen.'

But the proverbial phrases in this book do seem to support the view that 'they are by nature far from bellicose'; for whereas many of the aphorisms have reference to peace, it will be observed that there are very few war proverbs amongst them.

The Bahurutse of the Western Transvaal are said to be descended from the senior Bechuana clan; another tribe from the same stock would be the Batlharo of Kuruman, amongst whom Dr Moffat established the base of his missionary work; but it is not clear whether these two tribes are senior to the Kahlahari. This, however, is by the way, as we are concerned, for the purposes of this work, with their language rather than their history.

Their Language

As far as the writer is aware, the first person who put this language on paper was Robert Moffat,[54] the Apostle to the Bechuana, in the first quarter of the nineteenth century. He began by printing a spelling book and a few detached portions of Scripture, etc., and in 1829 set to work at the first Sechuana version of the Holy Bible. To realize what this means, it must be remembered that, being first in the field, he had, so as to speak, to create the language from a literary point of view – to use it, that is, not only as a written medium of thought, but for the expression of entirely new ideas, and that without the help of educated Natives, or of Europeans more familiar with the vernacular than himself. Both these forces are now at the disposal of his successors in the same field. His letters, and those of his wife, show the heroic tenacity of will with which this work was carried out through countless difficulties and interruptions, often on the part of the people he sought to benefit. It was finished at last in 1857. His Bible has served the Bechuana Churches for upwards of fifty years and the Native demand for it is more insistent since the issue of the Revised Version.

Their Newspapers

One of the author's most valued treasures is a file of *Molekudi ua Bechuana (The Bechuana Visitor)*, the first newspaper published in the Sechuana language, from 1856 to 1857. It was a partly religious, partly political and social monthly issued by the Rev. Mr Ludorf of the Wesleyan Mission, from the Mission Press at Thaba Nchu. To compare it with the Native weeklies of today is like comparing the diminutive *Daily News* (5 ¹/₂d.) of 1848 (a copy of which I saw in 1914, at the Anglo-American Exposition at the White City, London) with the ¹/₂d. *Daily News and Leader* of today.

The next Sechuana paper was *Mahoko a Becwana (The Bechuana News)*, a monthly review of current news and religious comments. It was issued by the mission press at the Kuruman Moffat Institute and ran successfully for a number of years. The Revs. A.J. Gould, R. Price, John Brown and various other agents of the London Missionary Society each succeeded to the editorship, and the little sheet increased in size and popularity until it became a fair-sized periodical with a very smart cover. During the first week of each month the Native peasants in Bechuanaland, and elsewhere, used to look forward to its arrival as eagerly as the white up-country farmers now await the arrival of the daily papers. How little did the writer dream, when frequently called upon as a boy to read the news to groups of men sewing karosses under the shady trees outside the cattle fold, that journalism would afterwards mean his bread and cheese.

The Lutherans subsequently started a monthly which ran under the editorship of Revs. W. Behrens, L. Meyer and other missionaries at Bethanie (Transvaal). Its title is *Moshupa-tsela (The Guide)*, and I believe that the Rev. T. Tonsing, a young missionary who grew up among the Bechuana, is the present editor.

The first Native-owned paper was *Koranta ea Becoana (The Bechuana Gazette)*, founded by Chief Silas Molema in 1901. It appeared weekly, was printed partly in English and ran for seven years at Mafeking.

Chief Molema has the distinction of being the first Mochuana who started a day-school in Bechuanaland, teaching Natives to read and write English. He opened his school in 1878 and conducted it alone in the Native chapel, started by his father, until the Wesleyan mission took it over, ten years later, and installed him as principal.[55] This post he held there till there were qualified Native teachers, when he was succeeded in the principalship by the Rev. M.J. Moshuela.

At present there are three Sechuana, or partly Sechuana, papers issued in South Africa, viz., the *Tsala*, edited by the author, *Molomo*, by Mr. L. T. Mvabaza and *Batho*, by Mr D. Letanka.

Compared with Other Nations

Archdeacon Crisp, in *The Bechuana of South Africa*, says:

> It is said that an English peasant uses a vocabulary of from 300 to 400 words. A Bechuana shepherd uses at least 4,000. His language possesses a fecundity of terms and acuteness of idiom

which will enable those who learn it to explain any problem
and to convey any message upon matters which affect mankind
in common.

The comparison here is perhaps not quite fair to the European. For it must be
remembered that the breeding and tending of cattle is the occupation most
honoured among the Bechuana, and that those who follow it command a large
vocabulary, not merely because they are shepherds (though, as such, they are
familiar with an enormous number of technical terms), but because they are
likely to be the most intelligent and the best-informed members of the
community, rather than the reverse. In the days when neither schools nor
books existed in the country, they would acquire this vocabulary – and learn
to use it with purity and correctness, from their parents, and especially from
their mothers.

The best Sechuana-speakers known to me owe their knowledge to the
teachings of a grandmother, or a mother, or both, just as I myself, as a pioneer
Sechuana journalist and translator, am indebted to the teachings of my
mother and two aunts. Again, most of the prominent Bechuana have, like
myself, been shepherds for some period of their lives, if not the whole.

A reference to the following pages will show that most of the proverbs
originated on the pastures or the hunting-field, and the wealth of the
Sechuana vocabulary lies in the same direction. For instance, one can easily
translate into Sechuana such outdoor phrases as 'a group of boys', 'a band of
harvesters', 'a herd of cattle', 'a flock of sheep and goats', 'a flock of springbok',
'a troop of hartebeest', and 'a herd of wildebeest'. In addition to the regular
translation of these phrases, they are ordinarily referred to in such short nouns
of multitude as *thakana, letsema, matlape, marele, serapa, lotlaka* and *bodumo*
respectively. But the moment we leave these concrete objects on the veld and
seek to express abstract ideas, the elasticity is at an end, and the poverty of the
language comes painfully into prominence. But it is a fact that
notwithstanding its shortcomings, Sechuana is not only fully equipped for the
expression of thought, but that it also includes proverbial sayings that find
close parallel even in European folk-lore [...]

Further Comparisons

The similarity between all pastoral nations is such that some passages in the
history of the Jews read uncommonly like a description of the Bechuana
during the nineteenth century. In the Psalms the similarity is so emphasized

that it seems difficult to persuade oneself that the writer was not a Mochuana,
e.g. Psalm 144, 11-14 and numerous other passages. The same thing may be
said of the stories of the Patriarchs contained in the Pentateuch. The late
Bishop Colenso once wrote as follows in reference to his translation of the
Bible into Zulu:

> Some of these difficulties would only occur to one in the same
> position as myself, engaged as a missionary in translating the
> Scriptures and therefore compelled to discuss all the minutest
> details with intelligent *Natives, whose mode of life and habits and
> even the nature of their country so nearly correspond to those of the
> ancient Israelites*, that the very scenes are brought continually,
> as it were, before their eyes and vividly realized *in a way in
> which an English student would scarcely think of looking at them* ...

Sechuana Orthography

One difficult point in regard to this language is presented by its different
systems of orthography. These are five. We have firstly an Anglican spelling of
Sechuana; secondly, a Congregational; thirdly, a Lutheran, and fourthly, a
Wesleyan, besides the fifth spelling of Sechuana used by the Natives in their
own newspapers. The Natives cannot understand why the missionaries who
have perfected the orthography of the Zulu, Xhosa, Suto and Pedi – other
Bantu languages in the same subcontinent – cannot agree upon the
orthography of this particular one. They all seem unanimous on one point
only, that it should be written with twenty letters of the alphabet, using some
of these twenty letters to represent more than one sound. The confusion is not
diminished by the action of some missionaries in Bechuanaland who are, it
seems, trying to ignore the Native press, including Sechuana papers which are
not only encouraged but also found helpful by missionaries in Zululand,
Kaffraria and Basutoland.

It is hard to see how the Bechuanas, who do not number more than a
quarter of a million, can be benefited by learning to write their language in
five different ways. In fact we have more than five, for the Lutherans on the
south bank of the Vaal use Berlin Sechuana books, and those on the north
bank use Hermannsburg Sechuana books. On crossing the Vaal, a Lutheran
Mochuana finds his hymn-book utterly useless; and as translations of the same
well known hymns differ not only in spelling but also in the wording, a good
memory is not of much help to him.

How different from the European churches in the same country, whose visitors are not only provided with free hymn-books, but have the added satisfaction of singing their own familiar hymns in an Anglican, Baptist, Congregational or Methodist church in the same metre, the same rendering, the same orthography and the same number of verses.

It is comforting to know that this anomaly is confined to Sechuana and that Zulu, Xhosa and Basuto worshippers have no such worry. That beautiful and elastic language – the Xhosa – is the result of a blending together of various dialects, co-ordinated by means of one common orthography. The work was carried out by missionary writers with Native assistance. Sesuto literature also owes its present state of perfection to Native co-operation with the missionary bodies working in Basutoland.

It means that the confusion in Sechuana is going to be a lasting one. A few years ago some missionaries gathered to take the initial steps towards co-ordination and co-operation in the output of Sechuana literature, beginning with a common orthography. This was a praiseworthy act, as the present confusion, by dissipating energy, is apt to hamper missionary enterprise among Sechuana-speaking Natives. They invited the author to attend their conference and give his advice; but when the fact was announced, a sharp letter came from London regretting that the missionary agents had invited the author to have a say in the deliberations over the method of writing his own language.

This ignoring of intelligent Natives in a discussion concerned with their language is responsible for the deplorable fact that Sechuana is systematically 'murdered' in those day schools where the vernacular is taught. The headteacher is usually the white missionary, who, even if a good linguist, must, except in rare cases, have the accent and use the idiom of a foreigner, and the pupils invariably drop their mothers' accent and speak the language 'as the teacher speaks it'. In the course of time, when it is decided to impart the language through Native tutors, the latter will all be speaking a kind of 'School Sechuana' with accents varying according to their tuition, but all equally alien to native speech.

Basuto and the Letter 'R'

This is well exemplified in the case of the Sesuto language. The Basuto, who have benefited morally and intellectually from Continental missionary enterprise, have now adopted the uvular 'r' instead of the lingual 'r'. They have caught this pronunciation from the French and Swiss missionaries of the

Paris Evangelical Mission. This change of pronunciation has spread so rapidly that at the present time – less than 80 years after this mission commenced work in Basutoland – the majority of Basuto (quite half the older generation and nearly all the younger Basuto) have adopted it.

After considerable hesitation over the five systems mentioned above, I have decided to adopt in this book the language and orthography used by the Sechuana newspapers.

It is my pleasure in conclusion to express my gratitude to Mr W.C. Cross,[56] of Hanwell, London, and Miss A. Werner,[57] Lecturer in Swahili at Newnham College, Cambridge, for practical assistance received while compiling these proverbs.

55
D. Jones and S.T. Plaatje, A *Sechuana Reader* (1916)[58]

The Sechuana Reader *was written jointly by Daniel Jones and Plaatje, and consisted of a collection of readings, mostly Tswana fables and folk-tales, reproduced in Setswana (using the International Phonetic Alphabet) and with both literal and free translations into English. These are supplemented by linguistic information about the structure and features of the Tswana language, and set out the case for using the International Phonetic Alphabet as a means of representing the Tswana language.*

In the Introduction to the book Jones and Plaatje set out the threefold objectives they had in writing it: to provide 'a collection of reading matter suitable either for native Bechuanas or for foreign learners of the Sechuana language'; 'a guide to the pronunciation of the language'; and to demonstrate the desirability and feasibility of writing African languages on the 'one sound one letter' basis.

Plaatje and Jones both wrote Prefaces for the book. Plaatje's is reproduced below. In his Preface Jones referred to the 'constant meetings' he had with Plaatje between May 1915 and September 1916, to the 'unusual linguistic ability' he believed him to possess, and to the further published work they expected to result from their collaboration.

PREFACE
By S. Plaatje

I had but a vague acquaintance with phonetics until early in 1915, when Miss Mary Werner[59] took me one day to the Phonetics Department of University College, London, where Mr Daniel Jones[60] was conducting a class. After some

Daniel Jones of University College, London, with whom Plaatje collaborated on their Sechuana Reader.

exercises I gave the students a few Sechuana sentences, which Mr Jones wrote phonetically on the blackboard. The result was to me astonishing. I saw some English ladies, who knew nothing of Sechuana, look at the blackboard and read those phrases aloud without the trace of European accent. The sentences included the familiar question, 'leɪnɑ ɟɑ̄-xɑ̄xo ɪ̄mɑ̄ŋ?' ('What is your name?'), and it was as if I had heard the question put by Bahurutse women on the banks of the Marico River. I felt at once what a blessing it would be if missionaries were acquainted with phonetics. They would then be able to reproduce not only the sounds of the language, but also the tones, with accuracy. Their congregations would be spared the infliction, only too frequent at the present time, of listening to wrong words, some of them obscene, proceeding from the mouth of the preacher in place of those which he has in mind (which have similar conventional spellings but different tones).

The frequency of such errors will be understood when I mention that there are at present not more than about half-a-dozen missionaries who can really speak the Sechuana language with fluency. Yet I have heard some of them say ŋːkwē (Mr Nose) for ŋːkwɛ̰ (tiger), bṵːɑ̄ (to skin) for bùːɑ̰(to speak), nɔ̀ːtɔ (a note) for nɔ̰ːtɔ (a hammer), etc.

If phonetics were studied by everyone who wished to learn the language, we should soon hear no more of such errors; moreover, authors of books would no longer be constrained to make such statements as 'the difference in sound in this word can be distinguished by a Native, but not written'.[61]

Since my first introduction to phonetics it has been my pleasure on many occasions to sit and listen to Mr Jones reading aloud (from phonetic texts) long and difficult Sechuana passages, of which he did not know the meaning, with a purity of sound and tone more perfect than I have ever heard from Englishmen in Africa who did know the meaning of the words they were uttering.

It is not the foreigner alone who would benefit by a study of the phonetics of Sechuana. The younger generation of Bechuana are to some extent losing the original Sechuana tones. This is particularly the case in the south of Bechuanaland, where the children now generally say, e.g. kĕɑ-xo-Fɨ̀ːtɑ instead of kĕɑ-xo-Fɨ̰ːtɑ (I am taller than you).

It is my hope that Sechuana readers of this little book will induce their friends to acquaint themselves with the use of phonetics, if only to retain a correct pronunciation of their mother-tongue. No elaborate course of study is necessary for mastering the principles of phonetic writing. I was myself able to write phonetically soon after I had tried. Had the subject been a difficult one, this book would never have been written, as my exacting duties in London would not have permitted me to follow an elaborate course of instruction.

Sol T. Plaatje

Box 143, Kimberley, South Africa

56

'Publication of the *Mendi* casualty list', letter to the editor, the *Friend* (Bloemfontein), 10 March 1917

The Mendi *was a troopship which sank, following a collision with another ship off the Isle of Wight on 17 February 1917, with the loss of over 600 lives of the South African Native Labour Contingent, en route to France as a labour battalion in* support of the allied war effort.[62] Since his return to South Africa earlier in 1917 Plaatje had played an active part in supporting recruitment for the battalion.

Native Complaints

Sir, I hope that your sympathy will be extended to the Native people, especially to the relatives of the passengers on the ill-fated transport *Mendi*, in the tenterhooks on which they are hoisted by the authorities. For the past fortnight and more, personal inquirers after relations have been worrying the life out of me, and I am inundated with written inquiries from different parts of the Union. But my repeated appeals to the Native Affairs Department for information have thus far only elicited the assurance that the press and relatives are being communicated with.

I have before me some unofficial information, received in the last mail, direct from one of the survivors, who gave particulars of two certain and two presumed drowned, but the bereaved relations have received no official information, while the local branch of the Native Affairs Department has 'no news' from headquarters to convey to the anxious families.

Yesterday's papers contain a Reuter's message conveying what purports to be an official list of those rescued; yet the name of the surviving correspondent above referred to does not figure in the list. I am sure you will agree with me, Sir, that such departmental aberrations give the Natives very little encouragement to rely on the veracity of official lists.

The fault lies with the Union Government, who have initiated the policy of converting all public offices into white men's jobs, regardless of the harm resulting from such one-sided methods. The consequent effects, though prominent at all times, have seldom been so painfully in evidence as with the disaster to the *Mendi*. It is hardly necessary to add that (let alone our indirect taxes) the Native Affairs Department collects annually from Natives, by way of direct taxation, more than enough money to enable it to afford the employment at headquarters of at least one intelligent Zulu, one intelligent Xhosa, and one intelligent Chuana, Sotho or Pedi, to ensure the correct and expeditious entry of Native recruits.

This course, which was advantageously followed by the Cape government, would have averted the present haphazard methods of relying on white 'experts', who in turn depend on their less-lettered office-boys for the spelling of Native names. Besides, the old Cape system would have proved of immense value to European clerks who would be saved the ordeal of mutilating Native names beyond recognition, as has apparently been done with some of the names in this official list. And some of us would be saved the unnecessary and painful labour of comforting bereaved families – a duty that clearly belongs to a department we are taxed to maintain.

One cannot help thinking that if some department, other than the Department of Native Affairs, had the handling of this important matter, the Natives would long since have been told of the fate of their relatives.

I have a photograph of one unofficial survivor taken with my brother-in-law in the same battalion. Telegraphic inquiries by the latter's wife (or widow?) have proved to no avail. And after our people's admitted 'splendid sacrifices' it seems a pity that they should be rewarded with the agony and uncertainty of an official 'roll of Natives saved' which does not include the names of proved survivors. The suspense is not only saddling some of us with much unsalaried labour, but it also has the effect of not stimulating recruiting.

I am, Sir, etc.,
Sol T. Plaatje,
Editor of *Tsala ea Batho*

Kimberley,
10th March 1917

57
Letter to Mrs Cobden Unwin, 18 May 1917[63]

Jane Cobden Unwin (1851-1949), wife of the publisher T. Fisher Unwin, was a member of the executive committee of the Anti-Slavery and Aborigines' Protection Society, and had supported Plaatje's campaign against the Natives' Land Act while he was in England.

Box 143
Kimberley, S. Africa
May 18, 1917

Dear Mrs Unwin,

Please do not take me for a hopeless ingrate. On landing at Cape Town I found, besides other difficulties, that a horrible bill was before Parliament to confirm all the horrors of the Land Act.[64] This meant hard work just from the moment of landing. We are given twelve months to show good cause why these difficulties should not be confirmed and I am hard at work to enlighten the innocent and unsuspecting Natives and to work up a good case for presentation to our English friends to enlist their co-operation in our uneven struggles against the Boers.

In the ship I noticed that my book would receive a cordial reception. Last month a Boer member – Colonel Mentz, Minister of Lands – referred to it as a 'scurrilous attack on the Boers'. A chorus of English members promptly defended it so vehemently that even in the subsequent days when the book was quoted by English members during the debates not one had the nerve to attack it again. I will not be surprised if the redoubtable Mr H.[65] makes capital out of the fact that a Boer member – a cabinet minister – attacked my book, and says nothing about the unanimous defence of the English members including Mr James Henderson of Durban (who called it 'a triumph of Native education') and Mr Van Riet, K.C., of Grahamstown, the only Dutch member who is a Unionist.

The debates have brought forth orders from all over South Africa. We have been waiting and waiting for a fresh shipment of the book but we get not a word from England.

Still, I am glad to have found my family in good health. Mrs Plaatje turned her house into a workshop, it has no appearance of a home. In fact she shoved the machinery on one side and is doing ironing on my counter in the office also until I can make a start with the paper.

I saw Mr and Mrs Msane. They were well though the former had been ailing. Mr Dube has left his brother in charge of his school and is busy with an insurance company at Johannesburg. The Congress will meet at Bloemfontein at the end of May when and where I hope to meet the others. My kindest regards to you and Mr Unwin. Please excuse this hasty scrawl.

From yours gratefully
Sol T. Plaatje

58
Letter to Mrs Cobden Unwin, 10 July 1917[66]

Box 143
Kimberley, S. Africa
10th July, 1917

Dear Mrs Unwin,

I am not certain that you received my intimation regarding my arrival at home last March because the sea pirates are playing pranks with out mails. For instance at the end of May, after a silence of 8 weeks, I received English letters written in May – they having taken just over three weeks to reach me. And during the second week in June I received letters written during March and April, some of them having taken just over three months to reach here. I have already heard twice from Mrs Solomon[67] but not once from you yet. I am at ease, however, for they say 'no news is good news'. Mr Cross is trying to keep me posted with the trend of events; but he too complains of being 'worked to death'.

I am sending you an Indian paper printed in Durban which will give you an insight into the 'ever-increasing spirit of justice' (?) which Mr Harris tells people is taking possession of the Union of South Africa. Harris by the way has almost succeeded in unwittingly smashing the Native Congress. A letter was read from him applauding the Congress for 'adhering to the principle of separation since Mr Plaatje has certainly left the impression here that you were opposed to it'. His letter purported to be an acknowledgement of the Pietermaritzburg resolution of October 1916 *against the Lands Commission's Report*.[68] That resolution you will remember I gave you in a newspaper cutting before I left London and of which I have since sent Mr Cross a copy.

In forwarding the resolution to the Anti-Slavery and Aborigines' Protection Society the Congress Secretary said in his covering letter somewhat like this: 'While the Bantu people *would gladly welcome the principle of (segregation/separation)* if (properly/justly) carried out there is no denying the fact that the commission's report is bad.'[69]

On receipt of this communication, Harris, it would seem, promptly threw aside the resolution of Congress condemning the whole policy and also the whole of the secretary's letter, and fastened upon the words I have underlined which he is exploiting with the energy of a politician in the interests of our opponents.

The reading of Harris' letter created an outburst of indignation. Delegates wanted to know when, where and under what circumstances Congress 'adhered' to the policy of separation.

I tried to point out that the whole thing could be rectified by writing a letter to the society. I pointed out further that the secretary of the Congress made the same mistake as I did, that is, mistaking Harris for a friend and thus becoming less guarded in his expressions he relied on the sympathy of a real sympathizer with the Boer policy – but Congress would not be appeased. They denounced Mr Dube for laxity in his management, which made possible the sending out of clumsy correspondence calculated to compromise the cause.

The result was that both Mr Dube and secretary resigned on June 3rd and until June 23rd Congress had neither head nor scribe. They asked me to assume its leadership but I pointed out that the deterioration of my business during my enforced absence in England made the idea utterly impossible.

At length Mr Makgatho[70] was on the 23rd *ultimo* appointed president. I have been much about telling Natives about the coming trouble. They know nothing about it. It has been put back, thanks to the English opposition (not till the end of the war as stated in some quarters) but for 12 months commencing last April. In other words, till NEXT SESSION.

I was arrested in Johannesburg last month and charged with infringing half-a-dozen of the multifarious regulations by which Natives are surrounded in this country, which constitute Mr Harris's 'growing spirit of justice'. I deposited a £5 bail, asked for a postponement till the 5th instant and prepared an elaborate defence that was likely to bring before the courts these official outrages upon Natives. The authorities presumably discovered the publicity in store for their numerous pinpricking rules and regulations for when I appeared on July 5th to answer their peccadilloes, they failed to put in an appearance and the case was dismissed. I am now proceeding against them for wrongful arrest.

I reached Pretoria last week to find a letter from Mr Cross stating that the third edition of my book, for which I have been waiting since March, was now on its way. Hoping that with their elaborate forwarding agencies between this and London, the Central News Agency might have a consignment to hand I telephoned to Johannesburg only to discover that I was too late to get any copies out of their consignment. They had received 100 copies by the same mail that brought Mr Cross's letter and while the letter was being redirected from home the whole consignment was sold out at Johannesburg in two days. I have since met Mr Burns who said he saw half-a-dozen copies on their window on the Friday afternoon. Having no money he went home for some and on returning next morning not a copy was to be had and the Central News provincial branches are, like myself, still clamouring for copies.

It seems a pity that we have an Aborigines' Protection Society in England who seem to be concerned with the welfare of only those Natives who are well cared for, like the labourers in France. They have collected £10,000 for these while unfortunate wretches like the daily increasing number of victims of the Natives' Land Act are left to shift for themselves. Thirty-seven families in the Pretoria district will be evicted this month, 21 families in Potchefstroom district and more round Heidelberg. I am only referring to those I have met. Of course some of them will become servants, others will give up country life and flock to the cities where this law is not in force while others will leave the Union altogether; but nobody cares for them.

Another matter which cries to heaven for justice is the case of the dependents of the units of the labour contingent who die in France. As Natives they have no relief from the various war funds, towards which Natives have contributed nearly 100,000 pounds – principally the Prince of Wales'. When the *Mendi* sank with 600 war labourers off the Isle of Wight, their deferred pay to families ceased and beyond the bare intimation regarding the disaster they have not received a penny's worth of relief. In my travels I have met with several war widows with two, three or more children badly in need of relief; and it seems such cases are beneath the dignity of the benevolence of the aristocratic A.P.S.

If my former letter has not arrived please let me thank you once again for the generous hospitality you were good enough to extend to me during my stay in London. My wife and I send our best regards to you and Mr Unwin and also to Mrs Saul Solomon and other friends. I am spending the weekend with my family before going off to see to the troubles of our poor people under the tender mercies of the Boers. Natives are keenly interested in General Smuts's statement to the British public regarding Boer Christian morals.[71] Some members of the Dutch Reformed Church (coloured) with the labour contingent in France appealed for a Native Chaplain. General Botha could not get one throughout South Africa and the Wesleyans had to lend him one.

Sol Plaatje

59
Letter to the editor, 'Native bill: A leader's reply', *Imvo*, 12 February 1918

This letter was a response to an article written by Mr William Hay, entitled 'Native Affairs Bill', which appeared in Imvo *in its issue of 25 December 1917. 'Those of us Europeans who are interested in the welfare of the Natives,' the article began, 'are much concerned about the measure in regard to which the Natives appear to be "as sheep without a shepherd"'; and it went on to bemoan the shortcomings of 'Natives who pose as the leaders of their people' and 'Native organisations which claim to be the proper organ for expressing Native opinion', and their failure (in his view) to respond effectively to the Native Administration bill.*

Sir , I saw in a recent issue of your paper an article, over the signature of Mr William Hay[72] of Cape Town, complaining that no Native has thus far offered 'any intelligent constructive criticisms' on the Native Administration Bill.

Mr Hay must have missed a good many issues of *Imvo* (to say nothing of other news organs) wherein it was repeatedly pointed out how the provisions of this bill were 'less liberal than those of the 1913 Act'. *Imvo* has also urged the appointment of a white and black conference, under the chairmanship of a Supreme Court judge, at which the difficulties could be aired; and if that was no 'intelligent constructive criticism' I want a fresh definition of the phrase.

Mr Hay is right in saying that the Natives practically gave no evidence before the Lands Commission of 1913-1916. Other Natives could, I think, explain why they refrained from giving evidence and the following is my reason. The Commission – or rather two members of it – stole into Kimberley almost unannounced. They sat on a day that I was due to leave for Pretoria. I managed to give evidence, before the departure of my train, and promised them fuller facts and figures later on. On my return to Kimberley I found that they had posted to me for correction, not my evidence but an abridgement of it. I may here add that this was not my first experience of commissions, and, seeing the uselessness of tendering evidence for someone else to condense, I dropped the matter.

Last February a Native conference met at Pretoria and selected eight witnesses to lay the Native view before the select committee. When this was made known the government announced that they wanted no witness who comes to give evidence against the principle of the bill as that had already been accepted by Parliament. Congress thereupon decided that it was useless to send to Cape Town eight gagged men who are not to say a word against our four years' persecution under certain provisions of the 1913 Act which the bill is designed to take over and perpetuate, and they told the government so. For if they were not to criticise these pernicious principles of the usury and exploitation, what were they going to fetch at Cape Town?

Mr Hay says: 'There are now quite a number of Natives who pose as the leaders of their people and there are Native organisations which claim to be the proper organs for expressing Native opinion. Naturally, under these circumstances their European friends *stand aside*.'

But pray why should they 'stand aside' when the 'leaders' and 'organisations' would appeal to the government through them? If, instead of standing 'aside', Mr Hay had stood up 'for' the Natives alongside of Bishop Furze,[73] Rev. Amos Burnet[74] and other friends he would know that four years ago the backveld

Natives acted as joyfully as he expected they should have done and when, two years later, the Lands Commission showed in a voluminous report that the 'gift' was a sham – the revelation being further demonstrated by the attitude of the government at subsequent interviews – they were disillusioned. In fact they were astounded, after what the government told them, to find Mr Hay writing to *Imvo* as late as last month repeating their timeworn misconception in these words: 'All the land at present occupied by Natives it is proposed to give (?) to them. I should have thought that every Native would have jumped for joy at hearing that.'

The effect of his standing aside is that Mr Hay is not aware of the series of conferences that took place and are still taking place in different parts of the country since three months ago, between the government or its representatives on the one side and Native chiefs and people on the other side. At nearly all these meetings definite questions were put to the government by the Natives but were never satisfactorily answered.

I may add that the government's failure in that direction has placed enormous difficulties in the way of those of us, who, in answer to the King's call, took upon ourselves the task of recruiting Natives for the Labour Contingent in France. But if Mr Hay can do so he would facilitate our 'jumping' feats by answering each of these Native questions: 'How can "*all* the land .... occupied by Natives" be given to them when the commission proposed no Native areas in the thickly inhabited Native districts lying between Peddie and the eastern province?' And nothing at all from Kimberley in the north-west, to Carolina on the Portuguese boundary in the north-east. That vast territory in the centre of the Union is in parts congested with black mealie planters, some of them owning their own farms which are also declared European areas. When they asked what is to become of them the government referred them to the malarial areas in northern Transvaal where they could both 'buy and hire' land – not a word about 'give' – or otherwise, stay where they are as servants.

Now the Natives ask:

'Why must the white man remain where he is in his own way while the independent Native farmer can only remain where he is by becoming a servant?' And seeing that he has to 'buy' land thus 'given' to him why can't he buy or hire it near to where his ancestors had been in occupation? 'If this is a *gift* from "their friend Mr Sauer", why should the Free State whites give up nothing in the Free State while the Free State Natives (who up till 1913 could rent land wherever they pleased) go and hire it only in the fever areas of

Sekukuniland or remain in the Free State as serfs?' Again, 'Why should the Grahamstown and Knysna Natives be obliged to squeeze into the already overcrowded Transkei after and while the Transkeian whites are not disturbed?'

According to the last census, more than one third of the horned cattle of the Union were in the Transkei, so, how could it possibly accommodate more cattle from the midlands?

I have spent the last two months in that part of the Free State where the barbarities of the provisions of this Act operate with draconian severity. Space will forbid the mention of more than one or two phases.

I have seen men who prior to 1913 rented land or ploughed on shares and gained from 500 to 1,600 bags of grain each year. Under the tender mercies of 'the gift bestowed upon them by their friend Mr Sauer' they have been reduced to servants and limited to the production of only a dozen (sometimes less) bags for themselves and the remainder for the landowner and, in addition, they have to render unpaid labour to the landowner for the right to stay on part of the land they formerly occupied by ploughing on shares.

Taking advantage of the same law other landowners have likewise changed the status of their former Native tenants who used to pay 33 $1/_3$ per cent of the produce in lieu of wages. They are now permitted to cultivate small patches on condition that they plough for the master during four or five days in the week before ploughing one or two days (in some instances only half a day) in the week for themselves. The Natives have besides to render unpaid labour with their families and oxen all the year round for the privilege of grazing a few cows.

Last week I saw a Native lad with a swollen head conveyed to the doctor. His parents gave me strict injunctions not to mention that the serious injuries were inflicted by the farmer. A prosecution of the baas would surely result in the eviction of the whole family and, under the 1913 Act, they will at once be homeless unless they give up country life and go into a town location.

It is possible that the Natives' failure to 'give clear answers which all can understand' is due to our deficiency in English, for it must be allowed that the effort to expound our numerous difficulties under such an unprecedented measure is stupendous.

I will therefore refer Mr Hay to the great debates on the second reading of the Native Administration Bill, towards the end of April and beginning of

May last year. (Writing away from my library I cannot give exact dates.) He need not waste valuable time reading the argument of extremists on both sides. Let him just read the lucid disquisition of a moderate critic – like the learned member for Albany – one of His Majesty's counsel whose command of English is beyond all doubt. For an answer to Mr Van der Riet let him refer to the vicarious generalities and declaration of his conversion by the Prime Minister – or arguments of the northern ministers (who supported the bill just because it is the first step towards segregation) of those of the Cape ministers (who supported it simply because it contains *no suggestion* of segregation). Having read these conflicting justifications of the measure let him then oblige by telling us the exact nature of this 'gift' or at least so much of it that ought to cause every Native to 'jump for joy'.

Suppose the Cape provincial administration passed an ordinance making it a criminal offence for shopkeepers to charge 33 per cent or 5 per cent profit, making it lawful for them to charge from 80 per cent to 90 per cent *plus the unrequited labour of the customer*: in the light of my recent experiences under the Act of 1913, I would be very sorry to see Mr Hay 'jump for joy' at such slavery and usury.

I am, Sir,
Sol. T. Plaatje

Frankfort, O.F.S. 3rd January, 1918.

60
Letter to the General Manager, De Beers, 22 March 1918[75]

Tsala ea Batho/The People's Friend
Cor. Shannon and Selby Sts.,
Kimberley, 22 March 1918

A. Williams,[76] Esqre,
General Manager, De Beers Co.
Stockdale Street Kimberley

My Dear Sir,
    I have the honour to request that you be good enough to bring your kind influence to bear upon the tramway department of the De Beers Consolidated Mines Ltd., to kindly donate the old Malay Camp tram shed, on the

Alexanderfontein track (now partly dismantled) so that we may fit it out as a meeting and concert hall for the Natives of the Diamond Fields. I saw Mr Grimmer[77] before his departure last week. He was very sympathetic and advised me to make representations to you soon after your arrival, before the shed is further dismantled. I also pointed out to him the serious need of such a place for the Natives, and I have since noticed three charity concerts that had to be abandoned after several postponements because the singers, having completed their rehearsals and being assured of patronage, could not get a hall for the performances.

In 1914 I mentioned this difficulty to Sir David Harris[78] and Mr E. Oppenheimer,[79] then mayor of Kimberley. They both promised to render us every assistance when we come to them with a workable scheme which was delayed, however, by the outbreak of the war.

The shed occupies a peculiar position. Half-way between Green Point and no. 2 Location, and within easy reach of no. 3 Location. It is in the same row as the Malay Camp Native churches and schools, in the same street as the Malay mosque and priest's house and almost opposite the Arabian school, towards the erection of which De Beers Company made a liberal contribution; and its construction is so singularly suitable for the purpose that a donation of its kind would go much further than any big sum of money with which the company might assist us to build another after the war.

As you have worked with tens of thousands of Natives and studied their nature from your youth, so to say, it is hardly necessary to point out to you that an appeal for contributions out of their scant income, in aid of some scheme beyond the horizon – something that they do not actually see – (however deserving) will always meet with a limited response, thus falling heavily on the shoulders of the few who undertook it. But the striking appearance of this shed, and the knowledge that it is already theirs, would stimulate 'all the (Native) world and his wife' to give so readily towards its equipment that it will not be necessary to ask individuals for large amounts in these hard times, or much less run the building committee into debt; so that apart from the intrinsic value of the shed, and having regard to its peculiar and exceptional character, its potential value as a gift to the Natives cannot be appraised in pounds, shillings and pence.

Let me add, sir, at the risk of being too personal, that there is a belief among some of the Native population here that I am in the pay of De Beers – employed to keep them quiet. The only base of this erroneous impression is that they have asked me on three or four occasions to write or head a deputation to De Beers to appeal for financial support in favour of this and that scheme, as other sections of the community had received similar help. My answer in each instance was that the thing was too insignificant for the company's notice and, having offered my contribution if they would put their hands in their pockets and raise the money among themselves, I have advised them to leave De Beers Company alone until we had a national object in view. This I submit is just such an object, and I would respectfully appeal to the sympathy of your company to take the same view of it, for the hall, if granted, will become the property of members of any church or no church.

Some years back, while I was working at Mafeking, the Kimberley Natives bought a little hall. After paying down a sum of money, they could not keep up the instalments, with the result that they eventually lost everything; and should the company feel pleased to entertain this application, you would be requested to safeguard the place by stipulating in the grant that the trustees cannot borrow money on it; and should the Natives be removed from the Malay Camp, the removing authorities should build for them another hall of the same quality elsewhere.

A donation of this kind from the Company to the Natives will, I feel certain, enhance their loyalty to De Beers as a generous employer of labour; for these and many other reasons I sincerely trust that you will feel pleased to endorse this request in the name of the Natives of the Diamond Fields and adjacent districts and territories which supply the mines and the city with labour. Your company has made some generous donations during the past quarter of a century, but for the most epoch-making because of its high value for the purposes of the recipients, and the consequent measure of their gratitude this request, if granted, will constitute the gift of the century.

Yours very respectfully
Sol Plaatje

Plaatje wrote similar letters to Sir David Harris and Mr William Pickering, the former securing a recommendation that it would be 'good policy to help the natives in the direction suggested by Plaatje'. De Beers considered Plaatje's request at its Board meeting on 2 April, and agreed to lease the building to Plaatje at a nominal rent of 1/- per annum. Plaatje was informed of this when he visited Mr Grimmer at De Beers offices on 4 May.

61
Letter to W. Pickering, General Secretary, De Beers, 13 May 1918[80]

P.O. Box 143
Kimberley,
May 13th 1918

W. Pickering Esq. D.S.O.
The Lodge, Kimberley

My Dear Sir,

I beg to thank you for so kindly urging your co-directors on the board of De Beers Company to provide the Natives of Kimberley with a meeting place. I am calling meetings to inform the Natives about it and their thanks will be officially communicated to the Company together with some telegrams I have received from friends in appreciation of the action by De Beers. I do not propose to make anything public in the press. I will leave that over until the Natives have got together a decent little sum towards improvements showing (in the words of one congratulatory telegram) 'that De Beers' generosity has not been wasted on us'.

Please let me add that in moving the company in this direction you have incidentally conferred an honour upon me personally for nobody can ever rob me of the distinction that when De Beers Company extended its well known generosity for the first to the Native community, they used me as their medium. On the other hand I feel the great responsibility and shall request you and your co-directors to keep an eye on this scheme of the hall so that whatever use it is put to may be for the advantage not only of the Native population but of the community at large.

As a father you will, I feel certain, appreciate my solicitude for it would be more cruel than kind for any man to present his son with a motor car, put him on top and starting the machine off without first seeing that the son knows how to control it.

Thanking you again for your fatherly action and assuring you that as far as lies within my power your kindness will never be misplaced.

I beg to remain, Dear Mr Pickering,

Yours very respectfully,

Sol Plaatje

62
Letter to the General Secretary, De Beers, 3 August 1918[81]

In May and June Plaatje made progress in establishing his Brotherhood organisation in Kimberley, and in preparing for an official opening of the hall. When his request to the Governor-General of South Africa, Lord Buxton, via the local Civil Commissioner, to formally open the hall produced no response, Plaatje wrote directly to the Governor-General's Secretary. When this failed to produce a response, Plaatje telegraphed the Prime Minister, General Botha, who passed on the suggestion to Lord Buxton. The opening ceremony duly took place on 7 August.

The Diamond Fields Men's Own Brotherhood
PO Box 143
Brotherhood Hall
Lyndhurst Road
Kimberley
3rd August 1918

The Secretary,
De Beers Co.,

My Dear Sir,

I am in receipt of your letter of the 1st inst. and in reply I beg to state that no arrangements are yet definite, no tenders being accepted. The only preparations on foot being the arrangements for the laying of the foundation stone next Wednesday. And Mr Boyes[82] has instructed us to prepare the Natives to give a loyal reception to the King's representative. As soon after Wednesday as it convenient for you or the directors I shall be at your disposal. In the meanwhile I beg to draw your kind attention to your very courteous letter of June 11th in which it is stated that there was no intention to impose any stringent restrictions upon us, as long as the building could be handed back in good order. This you will please recall was in answer to my observation to the general manager that the terms of the previous letter would likely prevent us from turning a good tram shed into a better meeting and entertainment hall.

Further, I beg to explain the cause of my delay in answering your letter of the 1st inst. I had to attend the Native Congress at Bloemfontein to prevent the spread among our people of the Johannesburg Socialists' propaganda.[83] I think you are aware of our difficulties in that connection since Mr Pickering, writing to me on an entirely different matter, a few days ago, ended his letter thus: 'For God's sake keep them (Natives) off the labour agitators.' The ten Transvaal delegates came to Congress with a concord and determination that was perfectly astounding and foreign to our customary Native demeanour at conferences. They spoke almost in unison, in short sentences, nearly every one of which began and ended with the word 'strike'. It was not difficult to understand the source of their backing for they even preceded the Congress and endeavoured to poison the minds of delegates from other parts. It was only late on the second day that we succeeded in satisfying the delegates to report, on getting to their homes, that the Socialists' method of pitting up black against white will land our people in serious disaster, whilst the worst that could happen to the white man would be but a temporary inconvenience.

When they took the train for Johannesburg, at Bloemfontein station, I am told that one of them remarked that they would have 'converted the Congress had not De Beers given Plaatje a hall'. This seems intensely reassuring as indicating that Kimberley will be about the last place that these black Bolsheviks of Johannesburg will pay attention to, thus leaving us free to combat their activities in other parts of the Union. Only those who saw the tension at this Congress can realize that the building discussion of this hall of ours came just at the opportune time for South Africa.

The Congress has sent Mr Meshach Pelem,[84] a most respected Native in business at Queenstown and Glen Grey, to represent it when our foundation stone is laid. He is to hand the enclosed message[85] to the Governor-General and Mrs Pickering. I sincerely trust that a Native envoy, on such a mission at such a time, will be received with the same kindness and courtesy for which De Beers is noted. With that hope I will with your kind permission take him to the head office on Tuesday morning, to pay his respects to the general manager and thence to the magistrate.

Yours very respectfully
Sol Plaatje

63

Letter to the President, Kimberley Chamber of Commerce, 18 November 1918[86]

Sir,

I beg leave to draw the kind attention of your Chamber to the economic restlessness among the Native population. It could be safely said that up till last month our committee, which includes the local leaders of Native thought, had succeeded in preventing the trouble spreading to Kimberley, and it is equally certain that this success was mainly due to the general satisfaction evoked by the timely generosity of De Beers Co., who recently gave a hall to the local Natives.

The movement may be said to have begun last year. Then Natives in different parts of the Union complained that although the cost of living had increased, some employers were making this an excuse for reducing the wages of Natives, the force of the complaint being that they were expected to face the high cost of living with lower wages than before the war. The unrest reached its climax in June of this year, when the Native population of Johannesburg threatened to strike at the beginning of July unless every employee, male or female, received forthwith an increase of 1s. per diem. This outbreak had various results:

(a) Some persons, European and Native, were arrested and tried, it was alleged, for inciting the Natives;

(b) The rapid spread of the outbreaks to Cape Town, Port Elizabeth, Kingwilliamstown and other places, particularly in Natal where the unrest assumed features that were very disquieting;

(c) Some merchants in Pretoria and Johannesburg promptly acceded to the demand, and raised the wages of their Native employees;

(d) General Botha appointed a Commission to enquire into the causes of the outbreak on the Rand (The report of this Commission appeared in yesterday's *Government Gazette*.)[87]

The discontent is now manifesting itself in our midst, and after doing everything to maintain the desirable relations that have always existed between master and servant in Kimberley and district, our committee[88] has decided to appeal for the help of your Chamber, as representing the leading section of European employers in Kimberley. It is suggested that the Chamber of Commerce could assist by kindly requesting local employers to consider that the Native labourer has to bring up his family under circumstances created by the enhanced cost of the bare necessities of life, in a such an expensive place as Kimberley, without war bonuses of any kind, that families who have lost their breadwinners at the various fronts are not in receipt of Government assistance, but are a burden to their own relatives, and if employers could be persuaded to appreciate the labourer's point of view and grant an increase in wages wherever possible, it is urged that this will strengthen the hands of our committee in preventing a possible movement to organise the existing discontent, thus creating a friction "twixt master and man' with all its attendant inconvenience, dislocation and bad feeling.

In conclusion I would beg to assure you that there are no politics behind these representations; our only object is to keep Kimberley free from the ugly features that characterised the movement in other towns, and our one desire to perpetuate the healthy equilibrium that subsisted hitherto between the several sections of the community of this city.

(sgd) Sol T. Plaatje

The letter was discussed at the meeting of the Kimberley Chamber of Commerce, and in debate considerable sympathy was expressed for the hardships suffered by the African population. The meeting agreed that Plaatje should be invited to discuss the matter further with the President of the Chamber of Commerce, and to defer further consideration of the letter till then. Judging from the minutes of the Chamber of Commerce it seems that no immediate action was taken.

The issue of wages to Kimberley's African population arose again, however, in July 1919, and the following month a resolution was passed recommending to members of the Chamber that, 'in view of the increased cost of living the mercantile community be recommended to meet the Natives by dealing with their demands in a generous spirit and by granting them higher wages if possible'.

64
Letter to W.Z Fenyang, 2 August 1919[89]

At a special meeting of the SANNC in Johannesburg in December 1918 Congress resolved to send a second deputation to England. Plaatje was elected as leader of the deputation, and – after many delays – sailed from Cape Town on 11 June 1919.

Fairly Grange
Longfield, Kent
2 Aug 1919

My Dear Fen,

I am sending you the report of our case in Parliament.[90] It confirms what I wrote in my last letter namely that the English people this time are more amenable to reason than they were the last time.

South African Native National Congress delegation to England, 1919. Top row, left to right: R.V. Selope Thema, J.T. Gumede, L.T. Mvabaza. Bottom row, left to right: S.T. Plaatje, Rev. H.R. Ngcayiya.

For instance: the Government assured members that the colonial vote will not be taken for a week then they took it suddenly on Wednesday while they were unprepared for it and most of our supporters were away. Yet the few who were present made a bold stand.

But I am very unhappy on the score of finance. It will cripple the whole movement and bring it to nought. When I arrived here I found that I could not get freedom of movement unless I paid part of the old accounts.

So I disgorged £54 and at least £200 is wanted immediately. It meant that I handed over everything, pocket money included, and I am standing now between two fires – the old debts and my present expenses.

I have been to arrange two meetings at Reading where I had three days with Kgoatlhe's friends. Now I have come to address two meetings here in Kent to get further resolutions sent to Parliament. *Bo* Thema[91] and *le* Mvabaza[92] are doing good work. I sent them to places that are easy to manage (if I am engaged) but not out of London because there is no money. Our hope is in the country – not London – and this scarcity of money is helping the Boers, because we can't go out and strike out.

Mr Makgatho promised me £100 here in London and I laid my plans in anticipation of it. But now that I am here I hear nothing from him. As soon as English people find out that I have no money there will be a terrible setback because they will consider me a d —— fool if after what I endured in 1914-17 I came penniless again.

Life here is infinitely more costly than last time and if one shows any hesitation he loses his few friends and they are not so easily picked up again. The other delegates are disgusted for I brought no money; and they are losing all heart in the campaign. The fact that I (their so-called leader) am penniless drives them more desperate and I hope that something could be done to get say £300 partly for old debts and partly for the present campaign.

The position is really serious and I am beginning to tremble that the deputation will soon be disgraced – after which we will NEVER AGAIN manage the Boer. We have to strike out *now* or *never*.

Please help or we are undone. When I left S.A. I spoke with Mr Malan.[93] He promised to see into the question of Barolong money at Mafeking – since then I have not had a word from home tho' three mails came after me. All these things make me feel very desperate and I tremble that the fight will be lost through lack of funds just when we are thinking of holding the reins.

What do you think?

Please send me a line.

Kind regards,

Plaatje

Another thing – Makgatho and Pilane[94] promised to pay Ma-Sainty* £6 a month. Please find out if they are doing it and drive them to it as you have a more serious undertaking there.

65

Article, 'The late General Louis Botha, P.C., M.L.A.', *African World*, 6 September 1919

The African World *was a weekly news magazine, published in London, containing both general and commercial and financial news on African affairs. Plaatje had written several articles for it during his previous visit to England between 1914 and 1917.*

---

*   Plaatje's wife Elizabeth (mother of Sainty, or St Leger, their eldest son).

General Louis Botha, first Prime Minister of the Union of South Africa. In his obituary Plaatje wrote that 'General Botha may be said to have stood between the Natives and the overbearing section of colonial feeling that was for degrading him further'.

Only two months ago, Rt. Hon. W.P. Schreiner, High Commissioner for South Africa and ex-premier of the colony of the Cape of Good Hope, departed this life. Today a sorrowing empire is mourning the loss of General Botha. The report of his death came with tragic suddenness, as very few people had ever heard of his indisposition. To his Native friends – and he had a good many – the death of 'La Visa',* so tragic in its suddenness, came like a bolt from the blue. Its suddenness eclipses even the dramatic rise of the deceased General from the very common position of an ordinary Boer farmer to be the most important white man in Africa – the one Dutchman who sat at the same table and dined with Queen Victoria's son.

The South African Native occupies a position that is inferior to that allotted to black men in other parts of the same continent, and General Botha may be said to have stood between the Natives and the overbearing section of colonial feeling that was for degrading him further. As Prime Minister of the Transvaal he was also chairman of the then dominant party – Het Volk; and at annual meetings of this body he was often attacked for not introducing legislation to impose further restrictions on the Native population of the Transvaal. His excuse was always that it was useless to pass such a law, as His Majesty the King would never confirm it. The Imperial Government by passing the Union constitution, which vested the entire management of the Native people in the colonial government, deprived the premier of his old excuse, and thus was ushered in the beginning of General Botha's race difficulties, and also of the Native troubles. I read several alarming propositions in Dutch papers that were ministerial at the time, but subsequently joined forces with General Hertzog against the premier. Some such suggestions were very common: 'Now that we have full power over the Native population, what is Botha waiting for? We want a stringent pass law, stopping all movement of Natives; and we want absolute prohibition of Native farming.' General De Wet,[95] it will be remembered, confessed to have rebelled because the magistrate fined him 5s. for flogging a Native.

The Natives' Land Act

Some English papers were just as bad. And that made his position all but intolerable, for when he shunned Scylla (the Boer tyrant) he tumbled into Charybdis (the English colonial negrophobist). Some such contributed articles were very common in the English *Farmer's Weekly*, published in the Free State: 'It is true that we have restricted the movement of Natives so that

---

*   A Xhosa epithet, or nickname, meaning 'a likeable person'.

he cannot be seen abroad without a pass. But when he has a pass in his pocket he still has a right to the public roads. When will the government rectify this? The Native should be made to feel that unless he is a servant in the employ of a master, he has no place for the hollow of his foot.'

It was as a concession to this form of pressure that the Natives' Land Act was passed amid the bitter resentment of the Natives and the jubilation of the white farmers. When Natives found the conditions so intolerable that they left the Free State and Transvaal by the thousands, the white farmers turned round and blamed Botha's government for not providing them with Native labour.

At this time Hon. J.W. Sauer, then Minister of Native Affairs, and faithful colleague of the premier, died and bequeathed to General Botha the scabby heritage of a seething discontent among the Native millions, who, having despaired of colonial justice, were now going overseas for mercy. Just at that time the war broke out, and for five years it kept the Natives between the horns of the same dilemma: but General Botha's position was seriously complicated by the war and the Boer rebellion, led by General de Wet in conjunction with other Boer leaders of the Union defence force, who were till that time in the pay of the government. The Cape Dutch, like all English and coloured political opponents of the premier, rallied round him, and vied with each other to make him feel that as [long as] the war lasts he shall not have an enemy no matter what grievances. It is a pity that the Dutch Nationalists could not see things from that point of view.

Criticisms of the backveld press

In 1917, General Smuts, his faithful lieutenant, relinquished the African command, and came over to Europe. His extended absence provided the Nationalists with a bone of contention: repeatedly they attacked the Ministry for spending the taxpayers' money on a man in the service of foreign governments – the allies. Those who do not read the Dutch papers will never understand what kind of opponents the deceased premier had to face. In the backveld press, if there be a drought they blamed Botha for not looking after the Boers in distress; if there be destructive floods they blamed Botha for a lack of foresight, and said he should have been prepared for the weather; if a disease breaks out it was imported by Botha's wicked war policy; if in self-defence one Native struck back a blow at a Boer, the pluck was instilled by Botha, who cloaked the blacks in his 'pestilential khaki' from which they imbibed all sorts of notions.

In 1917 I addressed a meeting at Bloemfontein attended by the mayor and councillors of the city, with some of their friends, and declaimed against the inhuman laws of the Orange Free State, of which Bloemfontein is the capital. In Parliament the following week, the deceased premier was the object of a savage attack by a Boer leader, who said General Botha's policy was an insult to the whites since it permits a Kaffir to criticise their policy.

In 1918, the Native population became almost unmanageable. At public meetings they pestered General Botha with requests to order employers to grant them an increase of wages, as their old-time 2s. per day was helplessly inadequate to meet the soaring prices of necessaries. The whites, on the other hand, bombarded the premier with telegraphic resolutions urging drastic steps to keep the Natives 'in their proper place'.

General Botha called Mr Makgatho, the president of the Native Congress and said to him: 'You look after the Natives and I will look after the whites; but always bear in mind that if either of us neglects his duty, we will answer for it to a higher power.'

Changed views
Whenever I interviewed General Botha by myself the medium was always the 'Taal';* in company with other Natives the interview was conducted in Zulu or in the Transvaal Sesotho, with both of which (and their allied dialects) the deceased general was quite at home. More than once, after hearing a narrative of the wrongs and cruelties that Natives have to endure, he lamented with a deep sigh the fact that he did not possess the same powers as the late President Kruger.

In May 1917 General Botha added fuel to the Nationalists' fire by confessing from his seat in Parliament that as a young man he held certain views regarding the treatment of Natives; that he *now felt certain that those views were wrong, and that a policy of repression boded no good for the Union.*

On his entry into German South-West Africa, at the head of his victorious troops, General Botha, addressing his burghers, appealed to them not to ill-treat the Natives of German South-West. He reminded them that their task of conquering the country was rendered easy by the friendly attitude of the Herero Natives in the former German colony. After his return to the Union, he always paid high tributes to the splendid action of the 23,000 who accompanied him to German West and the striking loyalty of those who remained behind.

Perhaps the biggest testimony ever paid the Natives, even by himself, was delivered when he announced the loss of the transport *Mendi* off the Isle of

---

*   Afrikaans: literally, 'the language', signifying Afrikaans rather than Dutch.

Wight, when it went to the bottom with over 600 South African Natives bound for France; and he again reminded the whites of their indebtedness to the loyalty of the Natives.

Rigours of the pass laws

Fifteen years ago I read a speech delivered by him in Middelburg, Holland. In the course of it he mentioned the faithfulness of a Native young man, a playmate of the general's son, all though the desperate hardships of his two years' guerilla campaign. The women, too, were not always forgotten, as Mrs Manye-Maxeke,[96] president of the Native Women's League, might tell us.

In 1915 there was a reference in Parliament to the rigours of the pass laws as administered in the Free State, especially against women. Free State Boers always regard such a suggestion as a Botha-English onslaught on the walls of their sacred Jericho. But the premier said it was monstrous that anyone could defend a law that demanded Native daughters of sixteen and seventeen to leave the parental roof for the benefit of domestic service – at an age when daughters most needed parental care. The promise to introduce ameliorating legislation unfortunately required some votes as well as the wish, and that shall remain one of the unredeemed promises of the late statesman.

Last year De Beers Company gave me a tram station to turn into a meeting place for the Native Brotherhood. When I made application for the Governor-General to come and lay the foundation stone of the first Native Brotherhood meeting place in South Africa, the idea was, of course, opposed. However, a telegram to General Botha settled the thing, and Lord Buxton came and performed the ceremony under distinguished auspices.

A South African war echo

I wonder if it is generally known that the colonial's antipathy against colour contributed largely to General Botha's marvellous rise during the Anglo-Boer War. It happened in this way:

General Buller's troops were arranging to cross the Tugela, to penetrate the Boer trenches, and hurry to the relief of Ladysmith. After crossing the river they were to march across the open country up to the krantzes, in which the invisible Boers were presumed to be entrenched. Their Boer commander having been taken ill, Louis Botha was in command of the waiting Boers. On the eve of the great march General Buller's Mosuto groom warned his master that the scheme was the maddest exploit he had ever heard of, that it would lead the Queen's 'Johnnies' into the lion's mouth.

In fact, he accurately predicted every disaster that followed, and wound up by suggesting a better plan. General Buller was so favourably impressed that he laid Molife's plan before his war council. But like many other 'rooineks', General Buller made the fatal mistake of disclosing the source of his inspiration. The idea of a British general, on the eve of an important attack, wasting the precious time of his council with the opinion of a Kaffir was about the limit. The fact that Molife had engaged in mountain warfare all his life against the Matabele, against Bechuanas, against the Boers, against British troops, and against colonials and Boers combined, could not shake their colour prejudice; nor even the fact that the pages of South African history books contained records by Theal and other writers to the effect that in all their encounters against white and black warriors, Molife's side had never been beaten.

But his victorious career could not count in South Africa as long as his skin is black. Molife's advice was turned down, thanks to the foolhardy prejudices of his colonial guides, the original scheme was attempted, General Buller lost the fight and many precious lives from the rifles of Botha's numerous invisible Boers. He also sacrificed much of his own reputation; and Botha was a made man from that day.

I last saw the general alive at Mr Schreiner's funeral at Golders Green, surrounded by many of his Anglo-African friends. How little did we all dream that he was leaving on his last voyage, and that today there would be such an immense gap where 'La Visa' used to be. Even his Nationalist adversaries must feel at a loss to find some substitute for his broad shoulders as a billet for the hammer-blows of their republican propaganda. And I but voice the feelings of a large section of our vast community who will sorely miss him in the threatening rigorous enforcement of the colour bar, when, with them and on their behalf, I say, 'Peace be to thine ashes.'

Sol T. Plaatje

66

Letter to Travers Buxton, Organising Secretary of the Anti-Slavery and Aborigines' Protection Society, 29 October 1919

On 29 September four black South Africans – including two members of the SANNC deputation, Levi Mvabaza and Richard Selope Thema – were forcibly ejected from the Union Castle liner, Edinburgh Castle, docked at Southampton, shortly before it was due to sail for Cape Town – the result of protests from demobilised South African soldiers who objected to their occupying third-class cabin accommodation. The incident generated a great deal of publicity, questions were asked in the House of Commons, and further problems were caused by the action, taken jointly by the South African High Commission in London, and the Anti-Slavery and Aborigines' Protection Society, to divert £200 (authorised by the President of the SANNC, S.M. Makgatho) to support the men ejected from the Edinburgh Castle *rather than the work of the SANNC deputation.*

43 Tavistock Square
London, WC1
29th October 1919

Travers Buxton, Esq.,
Secretary, AS and AP Society
Denison House
Vauxhall Bridge Road, S.W.

Dear Mr Buxton,

I have not been able to communicate with you since our interview with the High Commissioner last Saturday. From the High Commissioner's Office, we went straight to Lambeth Palace,[97] from there I had to catch a train at Paddington to keep three week-end engagements. Since my return to town on Monday my programme had been further upset by the indisposition of Mr Thema, hence my delay in calling on you.

On Saturday morning we found Mr Blankenberg[98] as courteous as usual. He informed us that he had received his long expected cablegram, from the South African Government, but I am sorry to say, the contents of the message are very disquieting. Thus: you will remember that when my friends returned from Southampton, after their ejectment from the *Edinburgh Castle* on the night of the 29th *ultimo*, I took them over to your office. My hands being more than full with propaganda work, I could not possibly spare the time to go into their grievance or into the matter of their maintenance, pending a settlement of their complaint. You were kind enough to undertake both duties, and it was understood that you would eventually recover the amounts thus disbursed from whoever is responsible for the Southampton outrage. The question of locating responsibility was to come up afterwards.

But the High Commissioner sets the matter at rest, by means of this cable, which authorizes him to pay maintenance allowance up to £200 for and on behalf of the South African Native National Congress, so that the whole thing comes down to this, that the Native Congress is to repair the damages caused by white soldiers at Southampton![99]

But, Sir, the funds in possession of the Congress have been raised out of the scant income so hardly earned by the poorly paid, downtrodden Natives of South Africa – (voluntary sacrifices on their part without the menaces and threats of imprisonment that usually accompany other levies from them) – with the specific object of enlightening the British public on the South African legislative excesses that are making the Union well nigh uninhabitable for its aboriginal inhabitants. And as I pointed out to the High Commissioner on Saturday, I do not believe that the South African Government (whatever our grievances against it) would wilfully be party to such an immoral transaction as withdrawing money from such a propaganda and misapplying same to defray the cost of military excesses; and I cannot but feel that there is a misunderstanding somewhere at either end of these long-distance cablegrams. I feel certain that none of the Congress leaders would vote away propaganda money to cover up the Southampton outrage. How could they? Let us suppose for the sake of argument that the unfortunate occurrence at Southampton was the work of civilian hooligans and not of soldiers in Government uniform; how could the Congress be made to pay?

The Rev. H.R. Ngcayiya[100] was sent here, I am informed, by the Rhodesian Natives and not by Congress. The Congress was not consulted when he was elected, so how could it be forced to maintain him here?

Mr Xaba, a theological student returning from Edinburgh University, is not even known to the Congress, so how could the Congress be held responsible for any damages sustained by passengers on the *Edinburgh Castle*, or any other Union Castle Liner?

As regards the two Congress delegates, Messrs Thema and Mvabaza, we received word that they should go home as there was not enough money to keep the lot of us here. Congress financed them right down to Southampton and into the ship. Their passages were duly paid and the money is in the hands of the Union Castle Co., and they were supposed to reach their homes on or about October 21st, when all Congress expenditure on their account and the maintenance of their wives would terminate. The reason why they are not now in Africa is well known to you, so how could Congress be saddled with their further expense?

In the name of the Native people of South Africa whom I represent in this country, I shall protest as I hereby do, in the strongest possible language, against the Native Congress being made to pay for any damages caused by the demoniacal prejudices of white soldiers in uniform. Even tyranny has its boundaries and I think it is more than sufficient that the already oppressed

Natives are taxed to pay the pensions of white soldiers and for the free
education of white children in Transvaal while Native war widows and Native
orphans are left to shift for themselves; but the imposition of a fine of £200
upon the Native Congress (for that is practically what the High
Commissioner's instructions amount to) for crimes committed by white
soldiers at Southampton is really carrying the South African tyrannies beyond
all earthly bounds. The money was collected for a definite purpose and I hope
you will not be a party to the proposed irregularity.

As appointed head of the Congress Delegation here, I beg to claim the
whole of this £200 for deputation work and not for any damages incurred at
Southampton or elsewhere.

Yours Very Respectfully

Sol T. Plaatje

First Vice-president, S. A. Native National Congress

And Chairman of the South African Native Delegation

*Plaatje's letter was part of a long-running correspondence involving the Congress
delegates, the South African government and the South African High Commission in
London, and the Anti-Slavery and Aborigines' Protection Society. The original
misunderstanding stemmed from the failure of S.M.Makgatho, President of the
SANNC, to point out that Xaba and Ngcayiya were not official SANNC delegates,
and the South African authorities' subsequent unwillingness to accept that this was
so. Litigation followed, but eventually (in 1926) the South African authorities
decided to write off the funds advanced to support the Congress delegates since it was
'considered inadvisable in the interests of the administration to take legal action
against the Native Congress'.*

67

**Pamphlet, *Some of the Legal Disabilities Suffered by the Native
Population of the Union of South Africa and Imperial Responsibility*
(London, 1919)**

*This pamphlet was written by Plaatje as part of his work as leader of the SANNC
deputation to England in 1919-20. A second edition was printed and sold by Plaatje
while he was in North America in 1921 and 1922.*

The root of the evil involved in the legislative tendencies of the Union
Parliament lies in the Act of Union which excluded coloured taxpayers from

the exercise of the franchise. The result is that no matter how loudly they protest against an accumulation of wrongs, the legislature is not obliged to take any notice of their protests. A dozen of sympathetic members of Parliament have now and again delivered weighty protests against the anti-colour excesses of the Union Parliament; but, in a house of 130 members, their protests had about the same effect as a drop in a bucket of water.

The following are among the prohibitions imposed by Parliament since the accomplishment of Union:

(a) In Cape Colony (where Natives have exercised the franchise for sixty years) coloured voters may not now elect a man of colour to represent them in the legislative assembly. No Native taxpayer is entitled to a vote in Transvaal, Orange Free State or Natal (The South Africa Act, 1909).

(b) Coloured persons are excluded by act of Parliament from membership rights in the Dutch Reformed Church outside Cape Colony (1911).

(c) Coloured mechanics are precluded from working as skilled labourers in the industrial centres (Mining Regulations, 1911).

(d) Coloured citizens are excluded from military training in the citizens' defence force of the Union (Act 13 of 1912).

(e) The settlement of Europeans on crown land and the establishment of a land bank to advance state funds to white farmers is limited to Europeans to the exclusion of Native taxpayers (Acts 15 and 18 of 1912).

(f) Native miners are not allowed to benefit by the pensions and other advantages provided by law for miners who contract miners' phthisis (Act 19 of 1912).

(g) Natives are prohibited from buying fixed property in the Union except in tribal locations, that are already overcrowded and where tribal lands, being legally inalienable, cannot be bought or sold (Act 27 of 1913).

(h) The lease of landed property to Natives is forbidden in the Union under a penalty of £100 or six months' imprisonment. They may only acquire interest in land from other Natives and this means nothing as Natives never had any land to let (practically the whole of the land being in the hands of Europeans).

(i) Native passengers holding tickets are not allowed to travel in any train other than in a Native compartment. The effect hereof is that when a crotchety conductor refuses to carry Natives in his train, even though there be plenty of room in the carriages, it is lawful for him to leave them stranded in the veld, with their tickets in their pockets, if his excuse be that he had no compartment available for Natives. This hardship was imposed under sub-sections 4-6, section 4, of Act 22 of 1916.

(j) Natives, whatever their qualification may be, are not employed in the public service except as 'casual' menial labourers (Public Service Regulations, 1912).

(k) Native interpreters have been dismissed in the law courts and their places filled by white men, some of them with the most imperfect knowledge of the vernacular, this reducing to a farce the administration of justice as far as Native litigants are concerned.

OLD RESTRICTIONS HAVE BEEN DRAWN TIGHTER BY RECENT PROCLAMATIONS AND EXTEND THROUGHOUT THE UNION, DURING AND SINCE THE GREAT WAR.

1. No Natives can get licenses to search for precious stones even in proclaimed diggings outside Cape Colony. In the Cape Province men of colour exercised this right along the Vaal River diggings for forty years before the Union. But now, committees of white diggers are empowered to examine all applicants and to refuse or recommend their applications for digger's licenses. These committees consistently refuse all coloured applications in Cape Colony and recommend white ones only.

2. After the British occupation of the Orange River Colony, the crown colony government made it lawful for Natives to hire land and graze their cattle in the Orange River Colony – now Orange 'Free' State. This right was abolished by the Union Parliament in 1913 and Natives can only live in the Orange 'Free' State as serfs in the employ of Europeans.

3. The Pass Laws on Farms. A Native employed on a farm must have a service pass. He cannot visit his brother on an adjoining farm without a 'special' pass in addition to his service pass: and if he finds it necessary to continue such a visit, from the adjoining farm to the next (his master not being there to give him a third pass), the service pass and the 'special' will not avail him anything.

4. If a Native earns say £1 per month, under one white farmer, and another white farmer offers him £3 per month, it is a crime under the pass law to take the better job without a consenting pass signed by his master – the one-pounder.

5. Urban pass laws vary in different towns and municipalities but their rigorous operation is not dissimilar in the several districts. A Native

arriving in an industrial town from the territories, obtains a free pass which gives him one week in which to look for work. Failure to find work in the week gets him into trouble. He thus takes on anything that offers. Before commencing to work he must be contracted to his employer for a number of months and pay the government a fee of two shillings per month for that service contract. This contract entitles him to stay on the mining property or in the particular part of the town where he works. He requires a 'special' pass to visit his brother in the same town. If when he obtains leave to see his brother he finds him away in another part of the town, and attempts to follow him up, the monthly pass and the 'special' pass will not save him from imprisonment.

6. Natives residing in the town and holding all their passes and permits are not allowed outside their own houses after 9 p.m. without a special pass signed by their employer.

7. In some of the towns married women are not allowed to stay in their husband's houses without paying the town clerk one shilling each per month for the privilege of enjoying their conjugal rights. Failure to keep up this payment involves a fine of £1 or 30 days' imprisonment.

8. Daughters are not permitted to stay under the parental roof unless they:
   (a) Work for a white person; and
   (b) Pay the town clerk a fee of one shilling per month. The girls so taxed often earn only 10/- to 15/- per month.

9. The multifarious pass enactments in force in the different districts of the several provinces of the Union, are embodied in acts of Parliament, in ordinances and in a thousand proclamations, and government notices, and regulations, each of them having the force of law the moment a new issue of the *Government Gazette* containing one or more fresh ones leaves the government printing works.

   These curfew regulations and pass laws are now extended to the Cape Colony, where they never existed before the date of the Union.

10. In the northern provinces, Natives pay over and above the ordinary taxes (which are also paid by white men), special Native taxes that are not leviable against the whites. From the proceeds of the special Native tax, the Transvaal Provincial Council gets £340,000 per year for the maintenance of educational institutions for the free and compulsory education of white children – institutions to which the children of Native taxpayers are not admitted. If there were no missionaries, the children of Native taxpayers would get absolutely no education.

11. Latterly we have had to pay taxes in order to provide pensions for white war widows and white orphans, while our own war widows and orphans whose breadwinners fell in the recent great war are not cared for.

The Land Act (g) & (h)

Of all the anti-Native laws conceived by white men in the history of European colonization in South Africa, no single measure has ever created so much misery and distress among the Natives as did the Natives' Land Act of 1913. It has cut off the very roots of Native life by depriving us of nature's richest gift – our ancient occupation of breeding cattle and cultivating the soil. Natives may only carry on their ancestral occupation as servants in the employ of, and for the profit and benefit of, white men; and any European permitting Native cattle to graze on his farm is liable to a fine of £100 or six months' imprisonment. This means that Natives who formerly earned a decent livelihood by hiring pieces of land from white men, cultivating the same and sharing the produce with the landowner, have since been evicted and replaced largely by ill-requited labour.

Thousands of former farm tenants, finding their lifelong occupation suddenly made illegal, have been forced to sell their cattle for what they would fetch, and have drifted into the cities where, among strange surroundings and incomprehensible restrictions, their lot has become unbearable. Others, after trekking round with their emaciated stock in search of a place to graze them, and losing many head by starvation on the trek, have left Union territory altogether to seek places of abode in the protectorates or in Portuguese East Africa. Many of such evicted tenants – men, women and children – perished through privations or succumbed to malarial fever or other climatic diseases in strange regions. Hundreds of such victims now lie buried in Madiloje, Southern Rhodesia, etc.

Others have got rid of their stock, accepted the new conditions and become serfs, so that men who formerly earned up to £200 per year as farm tenants, with plenty of spare time for their improvement, had perforce to submit themselves and their families to complete indenture at £20 or £30 per annum per family, and their time is never their own.

These prohibitions operate nowhere so harshly as in the Orange Free State, where even the tribal locations, which have in a measure mitigated the severity of the operation of the Land Act in other parts, do not exist. Two men in the O.F.S., each of whom had a farm left to him under their uncle's will, were debarred from taking transfer as it was unlawful to pass landed property to persons of colour. And whatever may be said of other restrictions, those involved in the Land Act certainly call for instant abrogation. When first passed it was said to be only temporary – 'for a period of two years'. But this is the seventh year of our suffering, and the end is not yet in sight.

The Native Administration Bill passed the second reading in 1917, the further stages being postponed apparently till after the general election in 1920. Among other drastic designs it proposes to confirm and make permanent all the temporary hardships of the Land Act of 1913 and to introduce prohibitions that are not now in existence. The judges, for instance, are to be deprived of all jurisdiction over Natives, so that the provincial divisions of the Supreme Court may exist solely for the benefit of white litigants, thus abolishing Magna Charta as far as it concerns the Natives, who are left to the caprices of the officials of the department that taxes and rules them. The appellate division of the Supreme Court – a court too high for the scanty means of the Native population – alone will be open to them.

It further proposes to divide the Union into white and black areas, allotting over 87 per cent of South Africa to the one million whites, leaving $12^1/_2$ per cent of South Africa to the five million blacks, much of the $12^1/_2$ per cent being awarded to the blacks by reason of its unsuitability for cultivation and its unhealthy climate.

A curious part of this unjust segregation proposal is that the bulk of the 12 per cent awarded to Natives is in the English province of Natal. No allotment is made in favour of the tribes in the Cape midlands. There is practically no place in the Orange Free State where Natives could pasture their stock, and no provision for the black mealie planters of Transvaal, except the uninhabitable malarial districts of the north, which, plus the tribal locations, make up the 12 per cent in the entire Union.

The Natives Urban Areas Bill[101]

It has been found that some Natives, evicted from the rural districts under the Natives' Land Act, have become partly free by migrating to urban areas and complying with the numerous pass regulations. So this bill provides for a fine of £100 or six months' imprisonment on any one attempting to sell or lease a house to a Native in any town or village of the Union.

Native men and women may only work if they obtain passes and pay a shilling a month each for the privilege. These new restrictions and prohibitions are to operate even in towns and villages at present free from the pass laws.

IMPERIAL RESPONSIBILITY

In official quarters it is sometimes said that, the Union of South Africa being a self-governing dominion, the empire cannot interfere. But if the Union Parliament is permitted to make South Africa absolutely uninhabitable to the Native population because of their loyalty to the empire, has Britain got room enough in her little island to accommodate the black millions thus hounded out of their own homes? Many of these hardships are imposed to placate the overbearing section of the Boer population, who refer to the Union Jack as 'the rag', and oppose the government because of its imperialistic leanings.

The statement that autonomous government cannot be interfered with is not supported by precedents. But for British and American public opinion, the Belgian atrocities would still be flourishing in the Congo.

Lord Hardinge, as Viceroy of India, has successfully interceded against a Union act of Parliament passed in 1913, aimed at the few thousand Indian residents in South Africa. The result of his intercession was the Indian Relief Act 22 of 1914.[102]

Equally ironic is it to say the Natives 'must fight their case against their own government in their own country'. The Natives have protested by written and telegraphic resolutions and by personal deputations to the South African government ever since 1911, and the only response has been a multiplication of the draconian prohibitions, because the only means of talking to a constitutional government is the ballot, which the Natives have not got. And it sounds sarcastic in the sufferers' ears to hear of references to 'their own country', especially in those parts of South Africa where a Native cannot even buy or hire a house.

On February the 28th, 1906, the following resolution was proposed by Sir William Byles and accepted by the House of Commons without division:

> That in any settlement of South African affairs this house desires a recognition of imperial responsibility for the protection of all races excluded from equal political rights, the safeguarding of all immigrants against servile conditions of labour, and the guarantee to the Native population of at least their existing status, with the unbroken possession of their liberties in Basutoland, Bechuanaland and other tribal countries and reservations.

The Imperial Government of the day, through the Colonial Under-Secretary, Mr Winston Churchill, accepted the resolution in language which left nothing to be desired, for he said:

His Majesty's government will not resist the motion of my hon. friend, but, on the contrary, we shall gladly further his wish to inscribe it in the journals of the house.

We accept fully the proposition that there is an imperial responsibility for the protection of Native races not represented in legislative assemblies, and I have in former times, not so long ago, joined with my hon. and gallant friend, Major Seely, in asserting, as I hope it may always be in my power to assert, the right of any British subject of any race or any colour, however humble may be his position, and however distant the land in which he dwells, to the sympathy and respect of the House of Commons ... A self-governing colony is not entitled to say one day, 'hands off: no dictation in our internal affairs', and the next day to telegraph for the protection of a brigade of British infantry.

The South African abominations mentioned above are aimed principally at 'Native races not represented in legislative assemblies'; and if such a resolution, by the Imperial parliament, is to be trampled under foot it will be difficult to make the suffering Natives believe that the allies have not lost the great war, in which they participated, in the hope that it was waged for the amelioration of the condition of oppressed people.

And today, those Native races who had been impelled by what they believed to be Britain's love of justice and fair play, to make enormous sacrifices for the spread of British dominion in South Africa, are bitterly disappointed to find that, if things are left as they are, a British dominion will be the first to be called to order when the League of Nations meets.

68

Extracts from interview of South African Native National Congress delegation with the British Prime Minister, David Lloyd George, House of Commons, London, 21 November 1919[103]

Plaatje was accompanied in this interview by three other members of the SANNC deputation, and also by a group of prominent supporters from London's African community. The Colonial Office was concerned that the Prime Minister should be 'very carefully advised as to what his reply should be [and] the less said to this

Deputation by the Prime Minister the better'. Before Plaatje spoke, Levi Mvabaza made an opening statement listing various grievances and disabilities (detailing pass laws in particular) suffered by the African people of South Africa, and emphasised the loyalty of the African people of South Africa to the British Imperial Government. Lloyd George's verbal response to the representations is also reproduced in this extract.

MR SOL PLAATJE: I am very sorry we have to weary you with our African difficulties, but if we were to speak till tomorrow morning we would never succeed to enumerate them all. As a matter of fact we have been to the Colonial Office with these troubles, and they told us we had better go and settle our affairs in our own country. But what footing have we got in a country where we cannot even buy or hire a house? They could more logically advise us to go and fight our case in Scotland or in Wales for there at any rate nobody will prevent us from hiring or buying a house if we have the money.

We may point out that we foresaw all the troubles that my friend has been trying to explain, at the time the Union constitution was passed limiting the franchise to white people only. The basis and the circumstances are not clearly understandable to people on this side of the Atlantic. But we clearly foresaw everything at the time so our people sent a deputation over which was supported by some of the brainiest white people in South Africa. Two of them were former Prime Ministers of Cape Colony, another is Mr Justice Gardiner who has since been elected to the bench. Mr Schreiner actually accompanied our deputation at his own expense, and they tried to point out that it was going to be a very dangerous business for the five million blacks if the constitution was passed exactly as it came from South Africa. In that contention we were supported by some eminent colonial statesmen.

MR LLOYD GEORGE: Does General Hertzog support you?

MR PLAATJE: No, Sir. We were not against passing the constitution. What we wanted was some sort of safeguard so that when the legislature passes hard laws against us we may have some means where to appeal to. The imperial government of the day gave our deputation the assurance that if we trusted the South African statesmen they would keep an eye on the South African government, who have promised to do the right thing by us. And my friend has been trying to show you how they discharged that trust. Things have been growing from bad to worse with the result that there are towns in South Africa

where married women are not allowed to live in their husband's houses
without the consent of the town clerk and unless they pay a shilling a month.
But when they passed a law that Natives shall neither buy nor hire land in
South Africa, our people felt that it was impossible to believe that the people
of Great Britain who loved us so much that they sent missionaries to teach us
a hundred years ago when they did not know us, could be aware of what is
going on. So they sent a deputation to come and enlighten the British public
on what is taking place.

Under this law, a Native formerly living as a tenant farm is not allowed to
stay there unless he is a servant in the employ of the landowner. That is to say
if my friend has a farm – and what we call a farm is a stretch of territory
extending right away from here to Uxbridge – and I come to him and say,
'Will you allow my 50 head of cattle to graze on our farm?' the legislature steps
in and says, 'As long as these cows belong to that black man, they shall not be
allowed to eat the wild grass on your farm, but if he agrees to sell them to a
white man it shall be lawful for the same cows to graze there.' If the white man
allows cattle of a black man to graze on his property he is liable to a penalty of
£100, or six months' imprisonment. And for every day in addition as long as
the cattle remain on his property, there is an extra fine of £5. Now what is the
crime we have committed? We pay taxes on equal terms with the white people
and over and above that, we pay special Native taxes, I presume on the colour
of our skin, for people of another colour have not got to pay it.

With this money the government builds schools – some of the most
beautiful schools you have seen anywhere – and from which our own children
are excluded. They dare not go to these schools, schools built with our money.
We are not entitled to any of the benefits of the Workman's Compensation
Act passed by the Union Parliament. Why do they do these things? Because
being voteless we are absolutely helpless. Sir Thomas Smartt and other
members like the Right Honourable J.X. Merriman have protested against
these things again and again but their arguments take no effect. Great Britain,
with whom our fathers bargained in the earliest days to come and take our
country under her protection, has thrown us away. The people who rule South
Africa are the followers of General Hertzog and all Great Britain tells us is
that she has nothing to do with it. And our object in coming over is to let the
facts be known to the British public and to enlist the sympathy of the Prime
Minister in these matters.

We don't expect the Prime Minister to go over there and catch General
Smuts by the scruff of his neck and say, 'You must relieve these people or I will

David Lloyd George, the British Prime Minister, who received Plaatje and his colleagues at the House of Commons in November 1919. He told them they had presented their case 'with very great power', and that he had 'listened with some distress to the story you have told of the restrictions which are imposed upon you in your native land'.

knock you down!' What we want done is simply in a constitutional manner. It is useless to go and tell our people that the home government is absolutely powerless – even when we are oppressed. It would be useless to tell them that since they know that when the Natives of the Belgian Congo were oppressed the people in England raised their voices against it, and the Foreign Office in this country communicated with the Belgian Government with the result that the Native's condition in the Belgian Congo was so ameliorated that white men from our part of Africa who have been to the Belgian Congo, have returned and said it was impossible for them to make money in the Belgian Congo because the Belgians did not allow the white man to exploit the labour of the Native as they are allowed to do in British South Africa.

You did that for Natives under a foreign flag. It is rather hard lines on the millions of Native people whose only crime is that they are not loyal to the local rulers of their country, but that they are loyal to the British flag which out there is called a foreign flag. If in these circumstances you leave these people to the mercy of their oppressors their lot is going to be difficult indeed, and it would be difficult to convince them that the allies have not lost the war because they heard that the allies were fighting for the protection of oppressed nations. If ever there was a case which called for protection it is the case of the Natives of South Africa who are told that they have no right to buy or lease land in their own country.

The land on which I first saw the light is now the property of a German named Wolff whose movements were restricted during the war, and if he offered it to me – the land where I was born[104] – he would be liable to a fine of £100 or six months' imprisonment. It has become unlawful for a man to poke his nose outside his own house after 9 o'clock at night. Even in Cape Colony, where no such restrictions existed before the Union, he is not allowed to go outside his house without a written permit. There is the Railway Act which provides for the separation of Natives and whites. If a black man is found on the railway platform, and there happen to be white people there, he is liable to arrest.

The country is becoming intolerable for us to live in. In Cape Colony where I started my career, in the post office at Kimberley, my son cannot now go and work there, not even as a messenger, because he is coloured. In Cape Colony we have some hot springs at a town called Aliwal North. Years ago I used to go and swim there for pure pleasure and not out of necessity. After the recent influenza epidemic my little daughter, who had overworked herself while ministering to patients, got literally shrivelled up by rheumatism. We were advised to send her to Aliwal North, but we found on her arrival there that because of her colour she was not allowed to take the water, not even to save her life.

These things are not confined to particular provinces of the Union, but are spreading all over and it is becoming unbearable for Natives to live in some parts of the country. Our only request is, in view of the fact that you have ameliorated the lot of the Belgian Natives under a foreign flag, and at the instance of Lord Harding you successfully intervened in favour of Indians who appealed against the operation of an act passed by the Union Parliament in 1913, you should consider us in the land of our fathers. The Native has no other place to go to. Our one crime is not that we want to be equals of the Dutch but that we are loyal to a foreign flag, the Union Jack. If it offers us no protection then our case is indeed hopeless.

MR LLOYD GEORGE: When I heard in Paris that your deputation was coming over to this country with a view to presenting their case to the British government I heard at the same time that there was a deputation from General Hertzog and his associates. He also wanted to present a case of a totally different character to the British government. His claim was presented in the name of self-determination that the whole of South Africa should be independent of any connection to the British empire at all. He told me, however, that he did not think the coloured population of South Africa agreed with him, who numbered about 5,000,000, and that he only spoke on behalf of a third of the white population. You now confirm that he did not speak on behalf of the coloured population.

Well let me say at once that I fully recognise, and recognise with gratitude the loyalty which your people have shown to the flag when we appealed for recruits to help in a very great struggle for freedom and liberty throughout the world. The response that came from your population was a very gratifying one and it was to us a very welcome testimony of the fidelity of your people to the British throne.

I have listened with some distress to the story you have told of restrictions which are imposed upon you in your Native land. It is very difficult for a British statesmen to express an opinion upon matters which do not come within his cognisance and, of course, I have not heard what is to be said on the other side. You know exactly what the constitutional position is. The dominions of the crown are practically independent in all legislative and administrative matters pertaining to their own areas. The British ministry never interferes with the internal affairs of Canada, New Zealand, Australia or South Africa. It has become the established practice of the constitution and therefore we could not, whatever view the British ministry might take of these very drastic and severe regulations – we could not directly interfere with the government of South Africa.

I shall take full note of all you have said. Any further particulars you may have I should like you very much to put my secretary in possession of. I have a shorthand note of the very clear and able and temperate speeches which you have delivered here. You have presented your case with very great power and I shall feel it to be my duty to communicate directly with the Prime Minister of the Cape [sic] and to inform him of the character of the deputation and the way you have presented your case and all the facts which you have brought before me.

I saw General Smuts when I was in Paris and I receive this deputation with his full approbation and consent and I have no doubt at all that General Botha takes exactly the same view. Having received the deputation with their knowledge and with their full approbation it will certainly be my duty to communicate the pith and purport of what you have said to me at the earliest opportunity. You know perfectly well from your experience and from your observations the general attitude which Great Britain has taken with regard to the dominions. If South Africa were under the control of the British Parliament, well, I should know exactly what to do. I should certainly take all your grievances into immediate consideration and examine them very carefully and give due weight to all you have said with the feeling that we were dealing with a population which has been very loyal to the flag and who have rendered service when it was required by the British empire. But when you deal with a self-governing dominion I must follow the fixed practice of the constitution and all I can do on behalf of the Imperial Government is to communicate with the Prime Minister of the Cape [sic] the whole of the facts as they have been presented to me.

I am very glad to have this opportunity of meeting you and of hearing from you of your case. Without expressing an opinion, which I have no right certainly even to form until I have heard the other side, I can only say that at the present moment you have said enough to convince me that it is certainly a case which ought to be taken into the consideration of the South African government and I shall certainly take the earliest opportunity of presenting the whole of the facts to General Smuts.

The deputation withdrew.

Lloyd George was clearly impressed by the deputation and the representations they made to him, and he fulfilled his promise to communicate with General Smuts – in letters dated 7 January and 3 March 1920. In reply, Smuts denied the points which had been put to him, accused the delegates of 'distortion and exaggeration', and claimed that 'improved machinery was in any case under preparation': this was to emerge as the Native Affairs Act of 1920.

69
Address to Pan-African Congress, Paris, 1921[105]

The second Pan-African Congress was convened by Dr W.E. B. Du Bois, the prominent black American leader and President of the NAACP (National Association for the Advancement of Colored People), and held in London, Brussels and Paris in August and September 1921. Its aim was to provide a forum for the expression and discussion of the grievances of black people across the world, and to strengthen their demands for justice from colonial and other governmental authorities. Plaatje (by this time in America) was invited to attend by Du Bois, was unable for financial reasons to do so, but prepared a paper which was read for him by Du Bois. Du Bois announced the paper as having come from 'a South African Native propagandist now touring the States, but deciding to remain anonymous for the present'.

Mr President and members of the Pan-African Congress,

I bring to you the greetings of six million British subjects, aboriginal Natives of the Dominion of South Africa. I know that some of our friends question the utility of a Pan-African Congress; but if the European nations, with all their economic and political power; if the white races, with all their aeroplanes, their anti-aircraft, their battleships and submarines, find it necessary to form a League of Nations to protect their interests surely the circumstances governing the African races who lie so helplessly at the mercy of their exploiters should impel them towards a closer union if only to counsel one another how best to face the appalling difficulties by which they are surrounded. For instance, our friends from British West Africa and the British West Indies have access to the councils of the British Empire under facilities which probably we of South Africa will never know; how then could we profit by their advantages or where could they deliberate and assist us to mitigate the rigours of white rule in another part of the same empire if not through such an assembly?

South African Natives

Everybody knows that the negro races throughout the world occupy an inferior position to that of other sections of the human race; but it is not so generally known that the Natives of British South Africa are assigned to a far lower level than that occupied by negro races in the rest of the civilized world or even in Africa itself. Up to the end of the last century, we had in South Africa two British colonies (the Cape and Natal) and two Boer Republics (the Orange Free State and Transvaal). Then we had the South African war during which the success of British arms 'cleaned up' the whole subcontinent and hoisted the British flag all over. One of the objects of this 'clean up', it was alleged, was to free the coloured races from the Dutchman's yoke. The Natives then were as intensely loyal to Queen Victoria as their descendants are to her memory today, and had every reason to be. But Queen Victoria died in 1901 and the Natives have since been made to feel that, in South Africa at any rate, British justice is the prerogative of a people of another race and colour, whether or not they owe allegiance to the British flag.

The Union Parliament

In 1909 an imperial act of Parliament federated the four colonies into one British dominion. Under the constitution of the Union, black people have no votes except in the Cape Province; and even there they may not elect a man of their colour to represent them in the Union Parliament. From then on the new parliament became notorious for the most barbarous legislation that ever characterized white man's rule in South Africa; the effect of it being that the South African Native today finds himself an exile and a helot in the land of his ancestors.

Fresh restrictions and discrimination

Natives are by law debarred from membership rights in the Dutch Reformed Church, the leading Protestant church in South Africa. That this feeling is not peculiar to the Boer church only may be gathered from the constitution of the South African Missionary Conference. Membership of this Conference is open to '(a) All Protestant European missionaries, whether acting or retired; (b) Officials of mission boards of all churches and societies south of the Zambesi and Cunene rivers; and (c) Ordained Native ministers sent by churches represented at the Conference by European missionaries. Ministers of European congregations may be enrolled as associate members.' So that coloured church organisations and coloured missions cannot have representation at the general missionary conference of South Africa.

In 1912, citizens of colour were by law debarred from participating in the citizen's defence force; and a new enactment debarred them from doing skilled work in the industrial centres. God almighty, maker of heaven and earth, has decreed that 'in the sweat of thy brow shalt thou eat bread', that (if the labourer's skin be black) is unlawful in British South Africa.

All that the Native is allowed to do is the ill-requited 'unskilled' work. Occupations that call for the highest skill and which are too hard for the snow-white hands or the cultured brains of the aristocratic whites (such as, for instance, scientific cooking by women, expert mining by men, and the spelling and deciphering of the difficult African names of the Native labourers) are classed as 'unskilled' and remunerated at half-a-dollar per day, *or less*.

Before 1916, no railway conductor could eject a Native passenger from any train because of his colour; under the Railway Act of that year, however, the conductor of a half-empty train may leave a Native passenger stranded in the veld with his ticket in his pocket on the plea that he had no Jim Crow compartment on his train. And crotchety conductors take advantage of this law to punish or torment Native travellers in a country with very limited train services.

Draconian prohibitions

By far the most outrageous of the monstrous crimes that characterised the South African Parliament's crusade against law-abiding Natives was the passage and enforcement of Law No. 27 of 1913. Under this enactment the Native is not only ostracised but outlawed from the land of his fathers.

Outside the Cape Province this law imposes drastic penalties (six months' imprisonment or a $500 fine) on any white landowner who attempts to sell or lease land to a Native. The only condition under which a Native may stay on a farm is as a serf in the employ of the white man; and the latter must certify that the Native has worked at least three months in the year for the right to stay on the farm. Since Europeans took possession of the subcontinent Native peasants made a living by renting portions of farms and sharing the produce with the land owner. Since 1913, when the act came into operation, thousands of these unfortunates have been evicted from their farms. Many of them flocked to the slums of the cities where amid appalling squalor they eke out a painful existence in congested quarters under new and unknown urban restrictions. Many more travelled from farm to farm seeking vainly for a place to abide and, having lost all, they had perforce to return to the farms and settle down to the peonage proscribed for them by law. It was during this period of roaming and wandering that I heard Natives of the former British colonies lament the death of Queen Victoria and the passing away of a royal sympathy that they once knew.

I have also met with Native women in the Transvaal weeping beneath the ruins of the Kruger regime now past and gone, under which they told me that their right to raise grain was never challenged. The homes that once were a heaven to the families of Native peasants are now monuments of shattered hopes, leaving them perplexed by the relentless vicissitudes of a civilized tyranny. Thousands of them left the dominion and fled to the Native protectorates, to Rhodesia and to Portuguese East Africa. Many of their children died of exposure on the trek while their attenuated flocks and herds perished by the roadsides through lack of fodder. I cannot think of a single legislative enactment in all the history of the scramble for Africa that has pauperized the Natives as that fell measure has done.

The farm on which I was born is the property of a German who was confined to his farm while I did unsalaried recruiting work for war service in Europe; if that good German attempted to sell or lease to me a piece of the land on which I first saw the light he would be liable to a fine of $500, or six months' imprisonment under Chapter XXXIV of the laws of my Native province, the Orange Free State; if I had ten cows and he allowed them to graze on his farm he would be liable to similar penalties for infringing the dominion law No. 27 of 1913, which prohibits farmers from allowing any interest in land to aboriginal Natives.

And what have we done to deserve this rude unsettlement and persecution? We have faithfully borne more than our share in the spread of British dominion in South Africa; for a mere pittance, we have built the beautiful railroads and magnificent cities and towns of the subcontinent; in return for a scant subsistence allowance and at frightful loss of life we have during the past quarter of a century produced for our masters more gold and diamonds than the rest of the world; we have paid all the government's taxes both fair and unfair, in addition to which we have given our sons and daughters in service to the most thankless taskmasters that ever controlled forced labour.

Constitutional appeals futile without votes

We have appealed to the authorities against the abominations arising from the multiplicity of the anti-Native legislation of our several governments within other governments, only to learn that civilized administrations have no time to waste on voteless complaints. The municipal authorities replied to all our petitions by passing the buck to the Union government; the general result has been to convince the Natives that the ruling Englishman of today is but a successor to the Englishmen of Queen Victoria's day and there the connection ends.

Victims of peonage in other lands can appeal to law against their oppression; but in British South Africa a mild peonage is legalized by the pass law which, under penalties of $25 or a month's imprisonment, indentures Native labourers to their employers for three, six, nine or more months at a stretch; and under the above penalties the labourer has to pay the government monthly registration fees of 25 cents to 50 cents.

Legalized serfdom

If, after working hours, the labourer desires to go to church or to visit his mother on adjoining farm, or a nearby suburb, he goes to prison with hard labour if he went without the written permission of his master. If during the period of his indenture a new master offered him three times his present wages and he gave notice to leave and take the better job, he goes to prison unless he can produce the written consent of his master, the bad payer.

Starvation wages

In the Orange Free State this peonage applies to both men and women. Their scanty wages, limited by acts of Parliament amount to a little more than a subsistence allowance; and when the high cost of commodities throttles them, and they ask their employers for redress, the government proceeds against them for infringing the Pass law.

During 1918, and up to recently, several chambers of commerce conceded that Native wages were too low; but the government stepped in each time and coerced the Natives by means of armed forces to go to work on the old wages. In the Cape province, where the pass law does not apply, and where the request for a living wage is not in conflict with any statute, Native workers recently assembled at Port Elizabeth and resolved to approach their employers and demand a better wage. I am informed, and verily believe, that many of the employers were actually engaged in considering the justice of their claim; but as soon as the intentions of the meeting were made known, the government intervened by arresting and incarcerating their spokesmen, shot and killed a score of the unarmed Natives, and wounded many more, and scattered the crowd.[106]

Government intervention

The Government's activities in keeping down Native wages, coupled with their exile of the Natives from the farms, has not only impoverished the people but it is steadily undermining the health and proverbial virility of the South African Natives. South Africa, formerly a refuge for tubercular sufferers from other lands, is now the hot-bed of that fell disease.

Gold mining is accompanied by miners' phthisis; Native miners who contract it return to their squalid homes where, with nothing to show for their terms of ill-requited labour, and having no money to combat filth and disease, their phthisis develops into tuberculosis and they become purveyors of lung disease and syphilis and so spread infection among their relations.

Hygienic lectures

To lend some irony to the tragedy we now and then hear of a visit paid to a Native settlement by well-paid scientists lecturing to these paupers on the laws of hygiene – scientists whose learning should convince them of the futility of preaching the laws of health to a proletariat who earn not enough money for food and raiment, let alone soap. How could anybody's ten fingers, however black, protect an unpaid community against contagious disease or usher in a penniless hygienic millennium? I think such lectures would do more good on the minds of employers and municipalities who profit by the pain and sweat of the Natives, but they are wasted on their pauper serfs.

I wish these lecturers would after each discourse inspect the horrible centres of infection planted in several Native locations by some rich South African municipalities and called 'public latrines'; some 'for men' others 'for women'. Some old Native women own their own W.C.'s and keep them cleaner than the foul structures owned by the municipalities. I have travelled in many lands and have seen the homes of toilers but have NEVER seen anything as horrible as the housing conditions of the Native workers in the towns and the farms of British South Africa.

Natives hopelessly insolvent

At Bloemfontein in 1919 when the cup of Native misery, accentuated by the high cost of living was filled to the brim, the Native workers voiced their troubles. In response to their representations the chamber of commerce met and decided that the lowest figure on which a Native could subsist very sparingly was 18/- (about $4^1/_2$ dollars) per week. This figure was manifestly absurd but, basing their action on that figure, the members of the chamber of commerce very generously agreed to raise the wages of their Native employees to a minimum of 16/- (exactly \$4) per week. It will thus be seen that white exploiters of Native labour are determined that the South African Native as a class shall remain perpetually insolvent.

With the Natives' Land Act of 1913 and the multifarious pass laws limiting the wages of Native labourers there seems no way out of these appalling conditions. But the tax-gatherers of the provincial and municipal authorities, like the dominion treasury, continue to levy their pound of flesh from the scanty Native earnings; and when they are through with them, they give way to the officials of the Native Affairs Department who collect a special direct Native tax; failure to pay the latter involves the delinquent in a fine or imprisonment. In the Transvaal, part of this Native tax is handed to the provincial authorities for the financing of public schools for the free compulsory education of the children of well-paid white people, schools in which the children of black taxpayers are not admitted. I have made diligent enquiries but have not heard of any place where peons are compelled to pay a direct annual tax for the education of the children of their taskmasters. And I have seen communities who would have been infinitely better off as out and out slaves, for then they would exist tax-free and their housing, feeding and medical care would be the concern of those who profit by their toil.

The saving grace

But for missionary activities, directed and financed from abroad, the South African Natives would be all still engulfed in ignorance and superstition; notwithstanding the persistent efforts of such foreign civilizing agencies, however, South Africa's determination to keep the Natives in ignorance and barbarism is attended with a considerable measure of success. Most of the partly educated Natives of our dominion have acquired their knowledge without much school. I for one never saw the inside of a high school until I went as author and lecturer to Europe and North America, where I visited universities as guest of college professors and instructors. At Great Britain's most famous universities I found representatives of nearly all the coloured races of the world, British subjects as well as foreigners. Basutoland is also represented, but there is at this moment not a single Native of the Union of South Africa in any of the universities of Great Britain. Economic stress due to the limitation of Native wages by means of the pass laws has been the most effective weapon in the hands of the enemies of our educational progress. Thus, the intellectual suffocation of the Natives and the systematic withholding of wages due to them, have contrived to render the Native so inarticulate that these administrative wrongs and cruelties have never received the publicity they deserved.

The Labour Party

One noteworthy paradox is that while workers the world over are combining against capitalists, in South Africa on the contrary it is the capitalists' press that occasionally raises its voice against the systematic ill-treatment of Natives. Our grievances therefore are mainly against the government who legislate at the behests of a relentless white league of white lawyers, overseers, mechanics and what not, who style themselves 'the Labour Party of South

Africa'. They will not see a Native painting a house or cleaning a motor car and they are now organising to boycott any garage that mends or parks a car driven by a Native.

A few years back a Native farmer invested $4,500 in agricultural machinery. But when the benefits of its use stimulated progressive agriculture among his Native neighbours, he was forbidden under the Machinery Act of 1912 to use his own plant unless it be operated by a white man. The real motive actuating this inhibition was that that 'Native was making money'.

In 1918, the white employees of the Johannesburg municipality struck work; they held up the city government for a time until their wages were increased from $27 to $40 per week. A week later the Native labourers at the sewerage works of the same municipality refused to go to work until the council deemed an outstanding promise to raise their wages from $3 to $3¹/₂ per week. They were all arrested under the pass law and sentenced to a month's labour *without pay* at the very work at which they struck. Our petition to His Excellency the Governor-General to intercede on their behalf was vigorously supported by the capitalist press which pointed out the justice of their claim, the importance of their work, the smallness of their pay and the unprecedented nature of their sentence; on the other hand, the labour organ, which so recently supported all the extravagant claims of the white strikers in the same service, related gleefully how the magistrate had taught those Natives 'a stout lesson'.

Only a couple of months back Sir Lionel Phillips, one of the South African mining kings, again flayed the arguments of the government and the 'white Labour Party' and complained that the country will never prosper as long as experienced Native workers are prevented by the government regulations from doing skilled work.

Now, I cannot weary the conference with a narrative of the whole chapter of our misfortunes, but I think I have said enough to convince the delegates that the South African Native, unlike his kinsmen from other climes, is not clamouring for the fuller life which is often sneeringly referred to as a claim for 'social equality with the white man'; his is but a cry for the bare living rights which every creature born into the world is entitled. A cry that every lover of freedom is bound to heed.

British Indians

Attempts have been made repeatedly to extend these abominations to the few thousand Hindus resident in South Africa; but each time a new law was passed against them the government of India took up their cause and compelled the South African Parliament to withdraw its fangs from the Indian sojourners.

But the Native millions have no such outside influence to fall back upon; and one result of our numerous petitions of the past decade has been the conviction that John Bull jr. is a 'new Pharaoh who knew not Joseph'. He is too busy turning his world into a white man's paradise and will not be bothered with the worries of black folks who, having helped to spread British dominion in South Africa, are still sacrificing life and limb in the bowels of the Witwatersrand mines for the financial might of the British empire.

Representation

One possible remedy against these iniquities would be the extension of a reasonable franchise to all taxpayers irrespective of colour. Against that we have the hackneyed lie that the blacks outnumber the whites by 5 to 1 and would vote Europeans out of the country. Now, the blacks in the same proportion have exercised the franchise in the Cape Province for 60 years and, while their limited franchise has protected them from the onslaughts of aggressive racialists of the white race in Cape Colony, they don't look like controlling the vote for 600 years to come. If instead of rushing to arms every time Native labourers want their pay, the government would adopt a neutral attitude (or mind its own business) and allow Native workers to confer with their employers, we might some day succeed to bargain for some profit and dignity out of the present chaos and indignities of profitless and unceasing toil.

Fresh demands

The farmers of Transvaal are now circulating for signatures a petition demanding a new law to indenture small kaffirs from the age of 12, and forcing all Native peasants to work, for the right to live on farms, nine months in the year; then go to the mines for the remaining three months to earn the government Native tax (e.g. for the education of the children of well-to-do landowners). Since there are only twelve months in the year, and these are to be fully claimed by the landowner and the government's tax-gatherers, the Native would welcome some advice on how to procure a calendar with extra months during which he could earn some food and raiment for himself and his children.

There is some little hope, however slender, that this petition may not be granted in full. This hope is founded on the result of the recent reorganization of parties in South Africa. There is a fresh administration at the helm and, unlike its predecessors of the previous nine years, it has not during the last two sessions introduced fresh humiliations on the helpless Natives.[107] But the forgotten truth is that the restoration of peace and contentment among the tribes is not possible without scrapping the experimental Native legislation enacted during the first nine years of the Union.

Native loyalty

Our tormentors also attest that the Natives, when decently treated, are intensely loyal to all lawfully constituted authorities. But when we see how men of another race and colour, who hate the British flag, are accorded British protection and allowed to revel in plenty at the expense of the loyal black millions, we sometimes wonder whether our loyalty has not been the means of our undoing. I might remind the congress that soon after the outbreak of the war all but one of the German colonies dropped into the lap of the allies like so many ripe apples. But in East Africa, where the Germans treated the Natives like human beings, the Askaris* fought and kept at bay the combined forces of the allies from the French and Belgian colonies, with thousands of Indian warriors from the far east, contingents from British West Africa and the West Indian islands to say nothing of expeditionary forces from South Africa, efficiently officered and equipped with all the modern weapons at the command of the allies; but, in defiance of them all, the Askaris fought doggedly and kept the German flag flying in East Africa until the armistice was signed and peace declared over Europe.

This brings me to the question of the mandates.

The former German colonies

During the past century there ensued, as is well known, a wild scramble for Africa. In the scramble the South African Natives, having regard to the benevolent spirit then manifested by Queen Victoria's advisers, bore more than their fair share. They shot down their own brothers in the hope of extending a partnership in a world empire in which all men would be equals. But to their consternation they now find themselves in a different empire, under the harsh rule of new Englishmen, and their gallantry on the South African battlefields is rewarded by acts of parliament making them permanent hewers of wood and drawers of water for another race; and they are asking whether the problem of the mandates over the German colonies was not a providential intervention opening the door afresh for a reconsideration of that scramble. Your conference could claim a say on the question of those mandates and ask the League of Nations (or whoever is in charge) to curb the greed of powers who have created a hell for other groups where they held sway. The Native Congress of the Union, the African Political Organization of the Union of South Africa and the chiefs and tribes of the adjoining protectorates

---

*   African soldiers (some 13,000 in total) recruited by the German Defence Force in German East Africa, under the command of Colonel Lettow-Vorbeck.

have all pointed out to the Imperial Government, and to the peace conference, South Africa's unfitness for a mandate over subject races.[108]

If European and Asiatic races can decide on all the mandates, surely those Africans who fought for civilization and received not even a pension for the children of their dead warriors in the great war should be entitled to some say at least in the question of the disposal of Germany's former African possessions; so that African exiles like those I have described may have some place they could resort to to lay their banished heads and grow their own vine and fig tree. If your conference would rise to a question such as this I think nobody would doubt its usefulness.

Mr President and members of the Pan-African Congress, in the name of the toiling black millions of British South Africa, I wish every success to your deliberations.

70

Pamphlet, *The Mote and the Beam: An Epic on Sex-Relationship 'twixt White and Black in British South Africa* (1921)

The Mote and the Beam was published by Plaatje when he was in the United States, and sold at 25 cents a copy. By the time he left there in 1922 Plaatje claimed to have sold 18,000 copies.

By 'Black Peril' the South African whites mean 'assaults by black men upon white women'. It is an unsavoury subject. I do not wish to write about it, but the importance attached to it by white contributors to the daily press, who usually give only one side, impel me to give the other side of the same picture. It is such a painful subject to deal with that, through fear of wounding the susceptibilities of the more sensitive of my readers, I will refrain from telling all I know about it.

Sanctimonious White South Africans

History does not condemn Christianity because some of its adherents were criminals, nor the Puritans because some of them burned witches. But white writers on this subject are apt to condemn us all for the sins of a few; and, in doing so, they forget that before the European invasion there were no prostitutes in South Africa. Again, they forget that members of their own favoured race whom white juries refused to convict, have saddled hundreds of Native women with nameless babies and we do not blame clean-living white men for the sins of the erring few. Moreover, they are too apt to overlook the fact that fancy salaries, free education and preferential treatment have not succeeded in keeping white people's fingers off other people's goods.

I do not for a moment deny the existence of a criminal class among Natives, especially along the Witwatersrand gold reef. Every race in the world has its criminals, and no human effort has yet succeeded in ridding society of crime; but, in South Africa, thousands of Natives have been sent to prison with hard labour for such innocuous peccadilloes as 'walking on the pavement', 'visiting their parents for longer than forty-eight hours' while on a month's leave of absence, 'looking at the shop windows', 'riding in the ordinary railway carriages' instead of in the Native compartment – which is not always found in the train. All these are artificial crimes manufactured by the authorities, with the result of herding innocent Natives into prison, and bringing them in contact with real criminals.

It is a miracle that in the circumstances the bulk of the Native population has managed to keep out of gaol. I know my white fellow-countrymen as well as I know my black kinsmen, and that knowledge leads me to say without fear of contradiction that if the laws and by-laws at present applicable to Natives were applied to white men, for only six months, ninety per cent of the white population would at the end of that period be gaol-birds. But 'they bind heavy burdens and grievous to be borne, and lay them on men's shoulders; but they themselves will not move them with one of their fingers'.

Twentieth-Century Pharisees

In regard to the sexual relations that exist between white and black people in South Africa, there are some white men who are never so happy as when descanting upon the moral decadence of the South African Natives; that is to say, they demand for the Native a higher ethical standard than they themselves practise. Their habit of domineering over Natives in South Africa is now leading them to dogmatize on a subject upon which they might well keep silence whenever they cross the seas. I will refer to one such instance, by no means isolated but one of the most recent and fairly typical.

A colonial girl, not long ago, landed in Great Britain and heralded her presence by airing the following extraordinary views in the columns of an evening paper: 'I was amazed when I came to England and saw for the first time in my life white girls courting black men.' The action of these girls, she complained, created 'an impression of equality between the whites and the blacks,' and when they return 'to the kraals of the Transvaal,' these black men will 'become discontented and make the other Natives dissatisfied' by telling them 'stories of the good time they had with English girls in Europe'.

Now, when I read this article, I had been travelling for seven months in Great Britain, and I can confidently say that, with the exception of a few dozen Natives returning home from war service in Europe, there were no Transvaal Natives for English girls to pay court to. The hundreds of black men that I have spoken to at different centres in England came from other parts of the globe, and had no desire to go and share our serfdom in 'the kraals of Transvaal'.

Profiting on the Labour of Others

The trouble about many of my white fellow-countrymen and countrywomen is that they think the whole world is within the boundaries of Transvaal, wherein, they presume, their domination is unquestioned. Their self-esteem may perhaps be attributable to the fact that during the great war they exploited all the benefits , but did for the cause of empire proportionately less than, for instance, the little island of Jamaica or that of Trinidad, who, by means of annual levies, are still helping the mother country to bear the cost of the great war. But it is consistent with the South African paradox to which we are accustomed that, whereas Trinidad and Bermuda got nothing for their pains, South Africa alone has annexed the diamond fields and cattle ranches of German South West Africa. It was done under a different name, of course, but the fact remains that it is annexation pure and simple.

Grown wealthy on the proceeds of ill-requited black labour, by profiteering on wool and other commodities, also the product of black-sweated labour, white South Africans now cast aspersions on their fellow-whites in other lands, and boast of visionary virtues 'in Transvaal where,' the same writer said (with a pen whose facility seemed to have been untrammelled by such trifles as facts), 'black and white unions are prohibited'. One wonders if she always closed her eyes when she passed through such places as Doornfontein, Roodepoort and Maraisburg? For white and black unions are not only prevalent in the above Transvaal city slums and suburbs, but also in such country places as Korsten, Magatespruit and Mara, up in the Zoutpansbergen of the Transvaal, where white and black parents cohabit and procreate children that are neither white nor black.

Where do Mulattos Come From?

The 'impression of equality' is written in ineffaceable blood on the foreheads of hundreds of thousands of half-caste children all over South Africa. They are to be found in the streets of urban centres, around water-furrows in the rural areas, and carried on washerwomen's backs, all over the Transvaal; and it is not necessary for anyone to travel six thousand miles to get that impression 'for the first time in England'.

While referring with marked approbation to the parody on law which prohibits 'black and white unions in the Transvaal', the same writer refrained from explaining that the Transvaal law only prohibits the unlawful cohabitation of white women and black men. She conveniently forgot to mention that the same travesty of law allows a white man to cohabit with as many black or coloured women as he chooses, so long as he does not marry any in Transvaal. The result is that some white men take advantage of this one-sided law to flood the country with illegitimate half-castes. I have known white men who (encouraged by this devilish law) have spent the flower of their manhood in procreating illegitimate children with coloured concubines in Transvaal and who years afterwards deserted their offspring and moved to another part of the country; where, in the evening of their days they settled down with lawful white wives, and thought no more of the past.

Yet people from such a lecherous country dare to hold up their abode as an example of racial purity to be followed by English girls in Europe! I have seen them scowl and blush with simulated fury – one of them nearly created a scene one evening – because they found that 'The Bird of Paradise' on Shaftesbury Avenue was a real Hawaiian beauty and not a painted white actress. I have since wondered if they had really forgotten the attractions of other birds of paradise, not of the Lyric Theatre, but of a paradise extending all the way from Witwatersrandfontein in the Transvaal to the dark forests of the Congo basin. A paradise with pools of lovely waters so attractive to some white men who find them 'not too cold, not too warm, just beautiful – with summer all the year round – where everything comes for the asking'.

Of course, the continental libertine in Africa is more honest. For instance, the Belgian will drive side-by-side with his Congolese consort along the streets of Elizabethville in the broad light of day. But the British colonial specimen of the same brood, on the other hand, will leave his swarthy concubine to mind his suburban cottage after supper while he proceeds to Johannesburg to join the white man's chorus, perhaps in declaiming against the employment of Native labour and the presence 'in our midst of these millions of unsophisticated savages'. Having done his 'duty' in that connection he will take a seat in a suburban tramcar (which clean-living black taxpayers are not allowed to use) and return for the night to share a concupiscent bed with the black companion of his liaison. And while we are sweated and fleeced to maintain the pomp of this modern Babylon, we are denied a voice in its government, because of the colour of our skin; this moral leper, however, because he is white, enjoys manhood franchise and holds the destiny of our unfortunate country in the hollow of his unholy hands.

Not All Tarred with the Same Brush

It may be explained that those Transvaal Natives who are enamoured of white girls almost invariably take their white lovers across the border and marry them there, then return the next day to live with their white wives in Transvaal without the interference of the law. In justice to the whites (and lest it be supposed that all the children of mixed blood are illegitimate) I must add that some white men who are allowed by the Transvaal laws to cohabit illegally with black women, and who are debarred by the same law from marrying them in Transvaal, have nevertheless taken similar steps to legalize their unions beyond the provincial boundaries, and have returned to live in the Transvaal with their lawfully wedded black wives; so that only a Pharisee and a hypocrite could, after spending a lifetime in Transvaal, declare to have seen such unions 'for the first time in England'.

The Natives' Shining Ethical Standard

It is not at all necessary for me to dwell upon the moral code of the South African Natives before the advent of the whites, for white pioneers have written about it sufficiently. Under it there were no mothers of unwanted babies, no orphanages because there were no stray children. The Natives had little or no insanity; they had neither cancer nor syphilis and no venereal disease because they had no prostitutes. It differed entirely from that of the Christian dispensation, but it was seraphic compared with the diabolical white man's law of Transvaal which prevents men from marrying their wives and forces them – sometimes against their wish – to make harlots of good mothers, adulteresses of potential housewives and bastards of children born of true parental love. And the white race – capable of enacting and enforcing such a law – the white race which, by the aid of regular and irregular alliances with black women, have become progenitors of the three-quarters of a million mulattos in South Africa, a race that has introduced lung-sickness and venereal disease into South Africa, should have been the very last to talk of racial purity.

It is just possible that we are hopelessly blind; but it must be confessed that we cannot see the disgrace in a white family and a black living a mile apart on the same farm, while it is apparently no disgrace for a white man to sleep in the same house or share a railway compartment with a black man, if the latter be a servant, as laid down by the South African laws.

If it be a disgrace for a white man and a black to live in the same street or a European to ride in the same tram with a black passenger (as laid down in the South African municipal and traffic regulations) our myopic reasoning cannot see the propriety of his sharing the same blanket with, and sleeping in the same bed as, and in the bare arms of, a black woman.

Here the reader may justly ask: 'Your book claims to be a record of your own personal observations. Did you personally see these mixed couples in bed?' My answer to that would be: 'Certainly not. But I have seen black mothers nursing half-caste babies; I have seen the white fathers of some of these babies; and some of them know that I know them.'

There was a time when it was an abomination for Basuto to have social intercourse with Shangaans, and when Bechuana custom forbade intermarriage with Matebele. They carried their prejudice to its logical conclusion and allowed no exceptions in favour of illegitimate unions with Shangaan or Matebele girls. But a white South African apparently finds no paradox in procreating illegitimate half-castes with the girls of a race he looks down upon.

I think white people from the Transvaal would create a better impression, if they made an effort to preach and practise at home the standards of morality they preach to white girls of other countries. Under present circumstances the English girls so severely criticised could justifiably say to their lecturer, 'Physician, heal thyself'.

Where Law Abets Immorality

Those of us who are simple 'Natives' of this country, and who cannot claim the arrogant designation of 'white South Africans', must surely be very ignorant, for we simply cannot understand how the squint-eyed policy embodied in the marriage laws of the Transvaal is anything to feel proud of.

Again, the partiality of the Transvaal laws keep the white men perpetually between blinkers, and makes it difficult even for government commissions to arrive at accurate statistics. Take, for instance, the commission appointed in 1912, to enquire into cases of criminal assaults on women, both white and black. It found in effect that whereas the white woman is legally protected from such onslaughts, the black woman is left a victim both to the men of her own race and to those of the numerous other nationalities who congregate round the industrial centres of South Africa. Still that commission only arrived at half the truth, for while it dealt fully with cases brought before the law courts, or reported to the police, on the complaint of white women, it could only have touched a mere fraction of the complaints relating to black women. The police court records register fully the cases of guilty Natives; but they also include the convictions of a number of innocent Josephs condemned to penal servitude on the specious testimonies of the guilty mesdames Potiphar; they, cannot however, claim an extensive record of white men who have raped Native women although there are numbers of such instances.

The partiality of the law makes it almost impossible for an outraged Native to prove an ugly charge against a white man; and so white men who rape Native women are almost invariably allowed to go unpunished. I was present in court one day when a white youth was tried for a criminal assault upon a respectable married Native woman. Of course he was acquitted. After the trial I heard a shopkeeper accost a juryman and enquire about the result. The juryman said: 'He —d the poor woman right enough, but it would have been a shame to send him to prison for that.' 'Good!' exclaimed the shopkeeper, 'Shake hands.' I have since made inquiries and found that both this shopkeeper and juryman take holy communion.

It is not the white rapist alone who goes scot-free – thanks to the double standard of justice – but also the white man who commits adultery with a Native woman by her consent. It was in Transvaal where, one evening in 1912, a young black husband returning home, found a white policeman, who was supposed to be on duty, in bed with his wife. Instead of seeking legal redress, the injured husband was himself kept busily engaged preparing his defence, for the policeman (in order to cover up his own misconduct) had trumped up a false charge against him. The Native was exonerated, but another charge was promptly brought against him by the same policeman; and by the time he succeeded in clearing himself a second time, he was so heavily involved in legal fees that (thankful to escape with his skin) he was glad to make himself scarce and leave the seducer of his wife to a higher fate. Many similar cases could be cited of Transvaal Natives who suffered persecution because it was their misfortune to find white men stealing their black wives, and the injustice of the law makes such outrages possible. White Transvaalers may pride themselves on the excellence of such forms of 'purity', but it is as well they should understand that serious-minded Transvaal Natives do not envy them their one-sided virtue.

White Men of Real Virtue

But there are some white people even in Transvaal who do not arrogate to themselves the privilege of lecturing foreign whites on the subject of miscegenation. These admit that in many of these 'black peril' cases the Natives are not the only ones to blame.

I once read an article in a Johannesburg newspaper in which an European upbraided white women for the temptations to which they subject their Native houseboys. Let me say again at the risk of repetition that this was in Johannesburg, Transvaal, and not in England.

'No white man,' he said, 'would keep straight if it was part of his duty to bring the early morning coffee into the bedrooms of ladies in various stages of undress. Yet thousands of houseboys in Johannesburg are constantly made to perform such duties as if their ... .'

He might have gone further and explained the existence of white women in Johannesburg of the character of Potiphar's wife, and just as many Natives of the character of Joseph. I could fill a book on such first-hand information – about the vicissitudes of houseboys – but from these I select only one story illustrative of the unenviable lot of this class of worker, especially in Johannesburg.

The Modern Mrs Potiphar

A young Zulu obtained employment on a few months contract at a suburban residence. It was his duty to make himself generally useful inside and outside the house. His duties included the taking in of the inevitable early morning coffee to the bedroom of the lady of the house.

Other details being immaterial, I will just mention that every afternoon after lunch he had to fill the bath in one of the rooms for the mistress's after-dinner ablutions. During the first week he only had to fill the bath, and empty it afterwards. Later, however, his worries began with an order from the mistress saying, 'Come and sponge my back'. His first objection to this command was dissipated by the happy assurance that there was no harm meant. His objections were renewed later on when he was requested to 'sponge' a good deal more than her back. Orders succeeded further orders until eventually he was ordered to perform duties of an unmentionable character. We have his word that he resisted the most serious of all these temptations.

But matters reached a climax one afternoon, when, after stoic resistance, the houseboy thought the mistress's insistence was assuming a dangerous form; so he put on his hat, followed the baas to his office, and there and then demanded his discharge and the cancellation of the remainder of his contract, as he said 'he had an urgent summons from home'. The baas was at first inclined to ignore the request, but he started in amazement when the boy said he would rather face a prosecution for breach of contract than return to work another day. The mistress, so the baas told him, had pronounced him the best boy they had ever had, and his immediate discharge was therefore unthinkable. At first, the boy would on no account betray the mistress, but as the baas persistently demanded an explanation, the boy, after a variety of evasions which failed to satisfy the curiosity of his master, at length laid bare the whole story. On this, the master prepared a plan to verify the facts related, and next day, after lunch, he pretended to return to work, but quietly took up a place of vantage in an ante-room whence he personally witnessed an exact performance of what the boy had told him. He saw and heard the persuasions of his wife, and the stoic resistance of the boy, until he thought he had seen enough, when he emerged from his hiding-place.

At sight of her husband the woman gave a low scream, which attracted the attention of white men walking in the street. 'The boy! The boy!' she screamed, 'The boy! The boy!'

A Typical 'Black Peril' Case

The boy said he could scarcely tell where the white men came from who rushed into the house; but in as short a time as it takes to tell, they seemed to come through the windows and from the walls, and even from the roof, and before his astonished master could explain the facts, these would-be rescuers of outraged womanhood had jostled him out into the street and down to the police station. His master followed him to the charge office, and there explained the case to the officer in charge. His release secured, the master accompanied him to the pass office, where he cancelled his contract, presented him with five pounds and repeatedly stroked his shoulder saying, 'Good boy, good boy!'

A case of this character is usually presented to readers of the South African daily papers in flaring headlines, such for instance as: 'Another black peril case', 'Outrageous attack on a white lady', 'The brute caught in the nick of time', 'Providential rescue of victim in a fainting condition'. These headlines would be repeated every time the adjournment of the case was reported, until the offender finally came up for trial before a judge and jury. The names of the parties are seldom given in such cases, and the papers refer to the accused in such comprehensive descriptions as 'the brute', 'the black monster', 'the black devil', etc., so that, by the time he receives his sentence, readers are under the impression that they have read five or six different assaults upon so many white ladies, instead of only one.

Needless to say, the Zulu case I refer to entirely escaped the customary and unusually vigilant attention of Reuter's faithful correspondent. I know of several cases where the 'mistake' was not discovered until the streets of nearly every South African town were littered with the dreadful placards. Even then, when the editors found that there was no case against the Native, they had not the decency to tell their readers that it had been found necessary, in the interests of the white man's prestige, to drop the prosecution.

Now it is certain that just as the majority of white women are not like Potiphar's wife, so too the bulk of the Rand houseboys cannot all be like Joseph; but it is equally certain that just as some black peril convicts are justly punished, there are others who should really have been tried side by side with the mistresses instead of the latter appearing as complainants.

Is it a 'Black' or a 'White' Peril?

When Lord Harcourt, in the opinion of the South African Natives the weakest Colonial Secretary that ever succeeded Joseph Chamberlain at Downing Street, was questioned about the Natives' Land Act, he justified it as a means of stopping 'black peril' cases. Now the 'black peril' reports are as rare on the farms as they are rife in Johannesburg – and that act specifically says it shall not operate in urban districts. How then could the act be expected to stop the black peril where it does not operate? But when Mr Harcourt – he was not a noble lord then – allows colonials to use him as their tool in proclaiming the sins of black folks from his seat in the House of Commons, a Native Bechuana like myself cannot help remembering that one of the first white women born in Bechuanaland grew up unmolested by the thousands of Natives surrounding her until, when already married, she was outraged by a white travelling trader.

When the lady's husband followed and remonstrated with the offender, he ignited the gunpowder which formed part of his merchandise, with the result that there was an explosion in which he himself, the husband, and a crowd of Native onlookers were blown to pieces. And as it is true that white men brought Christianity and civilization to Bechuanaland, it is also true that the first authenticated cases of rape, murder and suicide in Bechuanaland were the work of a white man.

71

'Mr Sol T. Plaatje explains his mission', letter to the editor, Negro World, 18 June 1921

In its issue of 23 April 1921 the Negro World, *the organ of Marcus Garvey's Universal Negro Improvement Association, carried a review of* The Mote and the

Beam *by Hubert H. Harrison, the paper's contributing editor. He considered* The
Mote and the Beam *to be 'a nifty little pamphlet', but felt that 25 cents for eleven
pages was rather too expensive, and 'not a regular business proposition'. Plaatje's
reply, reproduced below, was published in the* Negro World *on 18 June.*

To the Editor of the *Negro World*:

Mr H.H. Harrison,[109] a few issues back, made some kindly references to my
books. Having an unsalaried job and having to work 'in between times' for the
maintenance of my family, I have not the time to always return such personal
compliments; but I am constraint to trouble you for space to correct one
remark made by H.H.H. which might adversely affect my mission to this
country. Thus H.H.H.: 'On the whole *The Mote and the Beam* is a nifty little
pamphlet. But we think it a neighbourly act to remind Mr Plaatje that people
in America will hardly pay 25 cents for a pamphlet of eleven pages, however
good. They may do it as charity in church or at Liberty Hall, but not as a
regular business proposition.'

The fact is I hardly know whether to thank 'H.H.H.' for the 'write-up' or
the *Negro World*, which, he says, paid him $15 to write it; but the trouble is
that Negro leaders of the calibre of H.H.H., who constantly speak to tens of
thousands of our people all over the world, through the columns of the *Negro
World* and other media, fail to grasp the true inwardness of my mission here.
They treat it like 'a business proposition'.

Let me say again, sir, that I am not here on business. I have travelled 9,000
miles purely in aid of the most oppressed Negroes of the world. I would gladly
have stayed at home and earned $15 per week, like H.H.H., although I would
have had to work all the week and a good deal harder for it; but the Natives I
represent are so oppressed they could not, even if they would, pay me $15 or
any other sum – worked they ever so hard. But, if somewhere, at one time,
somebody had not left home and hearthstones and travelled to the Southern
slave plantations, in the face of the bitterest hostility on the part of the slave
owners; or if, a hundred years ago, someone had not travelled to the South
African wilds and made incredible sacrifices on our behalf, neither H.H.H.
nor I would be able to write. Somebody did it for us, so why not I for the black
millions who lie so helplessly at the mercy of the South African Boers?

If we were any other race but Negroes, the heavens would long since have
resounded with a diapason of war for our deliverance; but, because we are
Negroes, clever penmen of our complexion stigmatize the efforts on our behalf
as 'a business proposition'. Other races do things differently. Whenever they

learn of a cause that needs assistance, the editors appoint themselves collectors and appeal to their readers to send money. In that manner starving Poles, and oppressed Jews, like the Belgians when their cities were overrun by Germans, get speedy relief. The Chinese starvation is a case in point; not only newspapers but the movies screened their appeals for bread and thousands of American dollars from the cities of Canada and the United States, and millions of bushels of corn from the prairie and southern plantations have been despatched to the east and saved millions of Chinese from starvation.

When Madame Curie was on her way here from Europe, the newspapers called for a subscription to a $100,000 fund. A few days later they had to appeal to their readers to stop sending more money as the fund had been over-subscribed. Why don't they rally to a cause like ours? Because, sir, they are waiting on the editors of our race to write up a purely Negro hardship; and while the whites are waiting for a lead that will never come from Negro journals, Negro editors are themselves waiting on the waiting whites to put their stamp of approval on our Negro cause. Therefore, as long as H.H.H. and his $15 column colleagues ignore our cry of pain because it does not bear a white man's O.K., a few of us must continue to bear the unsalaried burden of a thankless cause.

Fortunately the editor of the *Negro World* is of a different mental composition. He did not wait for a white man's stamp and readers of the *Negro World* up and down the country are alive to the sorrows of South Africans of colour. Some of them have encouraged me by boarding and lodging me free gratis. Others cheerfully pay 25 cents for *The Mote and the Beam* as a means of promoting the cause of their downtrodden brethren across the ditch.

I attended a meeting the other day at New Bedford, Mass., where I was a total stranger; yet three members of the audience knew the contents of *The Mote and the Beam* almost by heart. A Bedford man had seen it at Connecticut and ordered it from New York. He showed it to some friends who also ordered copies.

Last month Mrs Cuny Hare introduced me to a New England gathering where I displayed copies of all my works. A number of people secured copies of my books and booklets which range in price from a dime to $2.50. A week after this meeting I received the following letter: 'Enclosed, please find $3 for twelve more copies of *The Mote and the Beam*. It is of absorbing interest and should be widely circulated.'

From this it will be seen that members of the other race pay 25 cents for *The Mote and the Beam* as cheerfully as my Negro readers. The prices of all my other works apparently have the approval of H.H.H. All of them were bought

COME AND HEAR

Mr. SOL

PLAATJE

Of Kimberley, South Africa

Gives thrilling account of the condition of the Colored Folk in British South Africa.

A Touching Message well and lucidly told

The story has gripped nearly a thousand audiences in England, Scotland, Canada & U.S.A.

IT WILL THRILL YOU

Bethel A. M. E. Church

West 132nd Street, bet. Lenox and 5th Aves.

Sunday, March 13, 11 a. m.

THE BLACK MAN'S BURDEN IN SOUTH AFRICA

Friday, March 18th, 8 p. m.

THE BLACK WOMAN'S BURDEN IN SO. AFRICA

Interspersed with Quaint African Music sung in his own native tongue

Free Will Offering for Brotherhood Work among the South African Tribes

ADMISSION FREE

COME EARLY AND AVOID THE CRUSH ! !

Dr. MONTROSE W. THORNTON, Pastor

'Come and hear Mr Sol Plaatje': Campaign poster from Plaatje's American tour, New York, March 1921.

on that occasion, but I have not heard again from their buyers. I am inclined to think that H.H.H. misjudged the price of the 'nifty little pamphlet' as easily as he miscounted its pages.

I should add that every dollar and every nickel raised at a meeting where I speak, and every freewill offering lifted at any church service where I preach, goes towards the Native Brotherhood building fund to which I give my services entirely free. I earn my own living and that of my family by the sale of my works, including *The Mote and the Beam*.

I am, sir, yours for Africa

Sol. T. Plaatje

72
Letter to Mrs Sophie Colenso, 31 March 1922[110]

243 West 128th St.,
New York, N.Y.,
March 31, 1922

Mrs. F. Colenso,[111]
'Elangeni',
Amersham, Bucks.
England.

Dear Mrs Colenso,

I must apologize for my long silence. It is all due to sickness and overwork.

I have not had much success financially but have almost recovered my health at the hands of a very good German-American doctor.[112] It is such a pity that I couldn't stop with him a long time. I had always to go away to earn money to pay board, lodging and travelling expenses; which are very high in this country. Had I had the chance to remain in New York under his treatment for three months at a stretch, I could by now have been a new man, physically; but circumstances are always beyond our control.

Besides my health, the trip has been a very great educational value and I have stored up an immense amount of knowledge which ought to be very beneficial to my work at home in South Africa.

It is dazzling to see the extent of freedom, industrial advantages, and costly educational facilities, provided for Negroes in this country by the union government, the government of the several states, by municipalities and by

wealthy philanthropists. Those who die and those who remain alive
continually pour their millions of money towards the cause of Negro
education; and it is touching to see the grasping manner in which Negroes
reach out to take the fullest advantage of the several educational facilities.
And oh, the women! They are progressive educationally, socially, politically,
as well as in church work, they lead the men.

It is very inspiring to get into their midst, but it is also distressing at times
and I can hardly suppress a tear when I think of the wretched backwardness
between them and our part of the empire, as compared with other parts. I
cannot understand why South Africa should be so God-forsaken, as far as her
political and industrial morality is concerned. No wonder they are always
flying at each other's throats; and what a terrible amount of blood they shed
during this month. It seems to me that the whites in South Africa are yearly
becoming more savage than the Natives.

When I last wrote to England, I congratulated her on the Irish settlement[113]
and here they are still fighting just like Kilkenny cats. Really, Mrs Colenso, I
am getting tired of this world and its everlasting squabbles.

Miss Lottie Gee is in a new gorgeous company that 'struck oil', so to say.
They have held the attention of the Broadway crowd for thirteen months –
afternoon and evening, often with midnight shows – and they are still in high
favour. Mrs Asquith and all prominent visitors flock to their theatre. No
coloured company has stayed so long in one place. They have now formed a
second troupe which is touring the American provinces.

I have definitely decided to leave the United States next May for Canada
and hope to sail, D.V., from Halifax, Nova Scotia, in June.

I continue to hear from Mrs Plaatje. She seems to have borne her
bereavement since our daughter Olive's death much better than I do. They are
only worried by my continued absence from home.

I do hope you are keeping well and that God will be with us until we meet
again this summer.

Yours respectfully
Sol T Plaatje

P.S. Please see Olive's obituary in the magazine, under separate cover.[114] Only
one mail will catch me in this country. Let me hope that I will find Gebuza's*
family in fine form. My best regards to them all. S.T.P.

---

* The Zulu name for Bishop Colenso.

Our church at Philadelphia gave me a moving picture projecting machine costing $420.[115] But films of coloured people are *too dear* and no church body of persons could donate any.

73

Account of North American tour [typescript], late 1922[116]

In a letter to one of his supporters in November 1922 Plaatje had this to say about the account he had written of his experiences in Canada and the United States of America: 'When I returned from North America I drew up a rather lengthy description of my experiences and mailed it to Miss Molteno. I was so sorry to inflict on her 30 pages of typewriting, but I felt she was entitled to some particulars of my trip if only as a memento of something that cost her and her niece a lot of money.'

Of the 30-page account only pages 6 to 24, reproduced here, have survived. No part of the account ever appeared in published form, and Plaatje evidently wrote it very much for the private interest and enjoyment of his sponsors and supporters. This provenance helps to explain its nature – selective in its coverage, making no mention of the contact Plaatje had with the radical Garvey movement, emphasising the educational benefits Plaatje derived from his visit to North America, and presenting something of a rose-tinted view of 'race relations' in the United States in comparison with the situation in South Africa.

... gatherings, including theatrical performances, begin and end with the playing of the National Anthem.

Jet-black West Indian girls come from Jamaica, Trinidad, etc., to Canada for work. They earn up to 10/- and 12/- per day at domestic service. Some of them attend night schools and the Academy of Music and practice their home lessons on the mistresses' pianos. I also visited some of the Negro farms. Many descendants of freedmen and old fugitive slaves from the South still live and farm round Buxton and Dresden in the counties of Essex and Kent in the Province of Ontario. Here, too, as in the towns, everybody must send his children to the public schools or go to gaol. I was rather apprehensive of the Canadian winter, but the weather throughout was wonderfully congenial. Beautiful sunny days and starry nights, especially after the rain, made the chill very agreeable and bracing. A phenomenal fall of snow between Christmas and New Year made the sky all the clearer and the sunshine more beautiful on the mounds and mounds of whiteness that covered the earth.

Newspapers said Canada never had such a mild winter since 1863. I had but one experience of zero weather in the middle of January 1921. At 5 a.m. it was 12 below zero, at 9 a.m. it as 8 below; and 2 above at noon.

I left Canada for America on Monday morning, January 31st, carrying the well wishes of the Canadians who warned me to be very cautious in America where they said colour prejudice is still rampant. White Canadians said: 'They are not like us, you know.' Black Canadians, on the other hand, said: 'Now you are going to God's own country where you will find some real white people.' Amid such conflicting advices I had naturally to make my own judgement.

I crossed the border about noon and reached Buffalo. My first stop in the United States, where I was advertised to speak the same evening. The intention was to spend Tuesday till Thursday in sight-seeing and leave for New York on Friday morning. My first American meeting was crowded and it was painful to see for the first time in my life people turned away by the hundreds unable to hear me for lack of standing room. The pastor told me he never saw his church so crowded since 1915 when Booker T. Washington spoke there. I finished up by speaking not once, but every evening up to Friday night when I went direct from the meeting to the midnight train for New York.

During my stay at Buffalo I visited the magnificent Niagara Falls – that wonder of North America – surrounded by gigantic hydraulic engineering works which distribute light and power from both banks of the Niagara River to distant cities and factories in the United States and Canada. I was driven along the fashionable Delaware Road and was shown the house in which President McKinlay died, and down to Delaware Square and the spot where he was shot. All this time I had not seen a trace of the notorious colour prejudice of Americans.

Travelling in the Pullman car may be described as 'ultra de luxe'. It certainly has a better bed than a second-class cabin of an up-to-date ocean liner. I woke up at daylight on February 5th just as the train was leaving Albany, the capital of New York State. Opening the blind and looking out straight from the bed I found our train gliding at 50 miles an hour along the edge of the Hudson River which was frozen like a rock. Habitual traveller that I am, this nevertheless is the most fascinating railway journey in my long experience. The early morning sunshine on the snow; the gathering clouds and unsettled sky in the hazy distance; the icy scenery on the far side of the river, all gliding rapidly yet gracefully by; it was a poetical panorama and a wonderful treat to the eye that rolled into view through the carriage window behind which I lay.

Now and again we would pass a rocky island standing almost like an iceberg but more solid because the congealed river water around it, and people walking to and from it dry-shod, gave it the appearance of a lonely kopje on the veld. Then a train would issue from the ice-bound scenery on the far side of the river, run parallel with us or in the opposite direction. The picturesque and unforgettable sight was a veritable anthology on a foreign theme.

I got up and went to the beautiful and spacious lavatories of our carriage where a number of fine-looking Americans were washing. Then back to the dining-car for breakfast.

The inside of a Pullman diner is more like a dining-hall than a dining-saloon on wheels. A number of clean- and trim-looking Negro butlers were waiting on the very nice people at the different tables just as they do in hotels. The late Dr Pullman, the designer and first owner of the Pullman cars, made this specially a Negro job. He arranged for Negro scholars, when schools break up for the summer, to come and wait on the Pullman diners and Pullman sleepers and also on his day-coaches called 'parlor cars', and so earn their college fees, by wages from his company and tips from the rush of summer tourists – and summer holidays in America are a veritable stampede. The arrangement has been adopted by nearly all the railways systems of the United States and Canada.

From the breakfast-table I studied further the thrilling panorama through the carriage-window as the train sped along. For three hours we had been hugging the east bank of the Hudson River. Men in furry coats were busy chopping up blocks of ice in the middle of the river and big horses dragged away loads of ice on skis on top of the hardened water. It looked so strange and unbelievable.

When I returned to my carriage I could scarcely recognise it. The beds and the partitions had disappeared and I could see now who were my travelling companions of the night. The upper berths had been tilted up and now formed part of the carriage roof. The lower berths, including my bed, had been transformed into cosy little settees and the New York morning papers were available. Should South Africa ever get some Pullman carriages of this type, the Jim Crow Act, No. 22 of 1916, would prohibit a Native from looking into one, except perhaps as a cleaner in the sheds where the carriages are parked with all the passengers out. How different can people be in different hemispheres! Americans and their wives in front of me; Americans back of me; Americans to the left of me – all lounging away, studying alternately their morning papers or the beautiful scenery outside.

Now and again one of them would speak to me precisely as if the world had no such thing as colour. All down the bank of the Hudson River we glided till ten o'clock when this happy reverie was interrupted by the sight of the lofty sky-scrapers; and so on to the terminal station on 42nd Street, where friends were waiting to welcome me into New York. Chinese and Negro passengers came out of the different carriages of the same train. Coloured passengers were not bunched together. Each had boarded the nearest carriage and selected his own most convenient seat and Americans did not seem to be the worse for it.

By this time my heart-trouble was so distressing that I felt as though I was saying good-bye to this world. Indeed I hardly believed that I would live through that winter, for the Canadian doctors told me that my heart leaked so badly that they could do nothing for it as there was no way to mend or operate on a heart. However, on arrival at New York, an old coloured journalist,[117] with whom I had been corresponding for years, gave me a list of five doctors – two coloured and three white. He said they were very clever men and if either of them could not help me nothing else would. More for his name than anything else, I selected one – Dr. George Sauer, a German-American – and he did me a world of good.[118] I don't know if it will come back later but I have not been troubled by it since the end of last year. Even when I broke down and was laid up with rheumatism and neuritis for six weeks during the following winter, I never felt the pains in the heart that were such a handicap in my work and made life almost intolerable.

The stupendous activities of Americans can never be adequately told. They have to be seen to be appreciated. At times it seemed difficult to believe that one is in this old world of ours, or that Americans are flesh and blood the same as we are. Among the middle classes, old women and young girls work much harder than the men and get very good pay. The upper classes, it naturally follows, are 'coining money' asleep or awake; and while their menfolks are at offices and businesses, raking in the dollars, the women devote their God-given leisure to more practical things than football and races. They hand out money for welfare associations, found this or that reform club, endow schools and improve their churches. Cleanliness in the homes of their poorer neighbours occupy a prominent place in the programmes of the 'idle rich' and the development of literature and art run side-by-side with their pursuit of happiness. Not a single item on this useful programme is considered too good for the Negroes.

Nearly everybody is educated. The Negro population is 80% literate; and when the long-lived ex-slaves die out a hundred per cent literacy will be a certainty. In the north the percentage among Negroes is 93% literate and only 6% illiterate. This about a people who 60 years ago were slaves is a shining contrast to India's ages old civilisation whose native population is 95% unlettered and only 5% literate.

With 150,000 people in the centre of New York, Harlem is easily the biggest African city on earth. They own magnificent churches with gorgeous pipe-organs and beautiful choirs and a number of glittering chemists and barber shops and prosperous real-estate agencies all operated by Negroes. They have many splendid and well-furnished homes, with musical instruments (which the members of the family manipulate with remarkable skill), and commodious bathrooms replete with hot and cold water taps. Some of the tenements are crowded but many of the homes, especially the private houses, are good and comfortable; fitted with electric lights and telephones, with more than one line in some houses. A marked feature of this Negro city is the absence of the squalor which may be observed in the white foreigners' tenements to the east of Harlem.

The main trunk line to the metropolitan railway terminus runs through Harlem and has a station at 125th Street. There is a network of cross-town tram lines, one bus line along Seventh Avenue, two underground and two overhead railway lines along the other streets of Harlem. It was amazing to see the crowds of clean and well-dressed black men and women, issuing from the underground stations in the blare of the electric lights at night, and pouring through the streets of Harlem like Londoners in Oxford Street. The excellent housing conditions there are second only to Chicago's. Harlem's only trouble seems to be that house rent is too high, much higher even than white people pay for houses of the same standard in the white sections of the town.

Citizenship of the United States is open to all Americans from Canada to the Argentine and all foreigners of European or African descent, so that Australians could only join by virtue of their European blood. This completely bars the Maoris and all Asiatics. But a voteless Chinaman, Hindu or Japanese enjoys the protection of the law and freedom to trade like any Irishman or Pole; moreover, his children born in the States, are Americans by right of birth and therefore entitled to full citizenship.

The 15th Amendment to the Constitution of the United States specifically protects the Negro from exploitation by the sharks of the superior race.[119] In South Africa no such protection is possible, for there the Government is the chief shark with an unquenchable thirst for Native lands; and the Union Parliament can always be depended on to indemnify the Government's every act of cruelty to Natives, and to pass new laws to legalize future crimes.

Many phases of American life fascinated me; perhaps the most touching of all was the harmony between black and white. Even in the southern states where they have segregation; where black and white children do not attend the same schools, cleavage between the races is not acrimonious. It is true that in the south one sometimes hears of keeping the Negro in 'his proper place'. The same thing is said daily in South Africa; but if you ask for the whereabouts of this 'place' no one in South African can tell you. And if there be such a place in existence, it is clear that it is not in the Union of South Africa; still he must be kept in this imaginary 'proper place'.

In the southern states, this 'place' is clearly defined. Unlike the Yankees of the north, the southerner will not have a Negro in his hotel; but he has no objection to the Negro building his own hotel and eating there with his friends. He won't have Negro children in the same school as his own; yet many southerners are as keen as missionaries in the promotion of Negro education – though in separate schools. I always thought that all the big Negroes of the United States were graduates of northern colleges. But I found that Atlanta University, Shaw University and similar southern institutions have been responsible for the training of the most well-known Negro doctors, lawyers, preachers and politicians, including those holding high positions in the north.

On the river boats and southern lakes and bays, the Negro's 'proper' place is on the front decks, if the whites keep to the back, and *vice versa*. In the railway stations, his waiting-room is on the left, or just next door to the white waiting-room – no such place in South Africa. In the refreshment rooms the Negro's 'place' is downstairs, but he is served with the same food from the same kitchen, at the same price as the white passengers. No such arrangement in South Africa. In the trams his 'place' is the rear seats of the same car, if the whites sit in front, or the other way round. And if the trams are crowded the strap-hangers meet in the middle, and hang together, if separately, without any friction or ill-feeling. From Washington, the capital, and all the way east, west and north, these discriminations do not exist.

Of course, Americans commercialize everything; money-making is not the monopoly of the white race, so Negroes in the south make good money out of segregation.

Feeling that they are not wanted among the whites, except as workers, they take their wages (which, compared with ours, are astoundingly high) to their own part of the town. There they support their own grocery shops, their own barbers, chemists and pastry cooks, their own theatres, parks, beauty parlours and what not; and always the ubiquitous cinema. With so much money in circulation (which northern Negroes would spend in white people's places) they soon build their own banks and insurance offices, give lucrative jobs to Negro typists and clerks, make loans to themselves to purchase large farms and build magnificent churches and recreation places (towards the upkeep of which the whites contribute liberally), ride around in expensive motor cars and grow wealthier than the unsegregated Negroes of the north.

In Cape Colony we would never get licenses to do some of these things. In the Transvaal anyone can buy a trading license at the post-office, but a Native with a license will not get permission to build a shop in the town; and we have not the schools to equip men and women for commercial undertakings of that kind. And if we did have them, our working people are too poorly paid to support such enterprises.

If the American relations between white and black are human, those between master and man, and between mistress and maid are perfectly divine. The cordial relations of the races politically, like the commercial and educational development of the Negroes, are largely due to the liberality of white philanthropists, the speeches of Booker Washington and his associates, and partly due to the activities of Negro societies like Dr. Du Bois' National Association for the Advancement of Colored People, the Urban League, Negro Business League etc; but the human touch between masters and servants date from the time of slavery. White bankers and politicians have told me with pride about their black nurses and one lady referred to her old coloured maid as ' the noble soul who is keeping my children out of mischief and teaching them how to do right'. Dr Biglow at New York told of a proud Southern girl who, coming North to attend a Girls' High School, resented the presence of black girls in her class. Three days later the same girl was dancing and prancing in the seventh heaven of delight because she had that day 'received the best letter of her life' – it was from her black mammy in the South.

Early this year I read of two maiden ladies who lived together. The one sister died and left her estate to the surviving sister, except 1,500 dollars which she left to her coloured maid. During the spring the second sister also died and left the whole caboodle (the title deeds of a country house and 20,000 dollars in cash) to the maid. There was another such case and my inquiries disclose the fact that some of the well-to-do coloured families inherited their fortunes from white masters.

The Labour League in Atlanta, Georgia, is three-quarters white, yet their president is a Negro. Two months before I visited the city they struck against a wage cut. Employers offered to take the white man back on the old rates if they would consent to leave the Negroes out of their union. But those white men flatly refused to treat with employers except through their black leader. Of course, cases like this are the exception but they are an accurate register of the growing tendencies relating to the feeling between white and black in the southern states.

When it comes to public institutions American generosity with money is perfectly dazzling, especially educational institutions. Only this year the will of one American bequeathed the staggering sum of 400,000 dollars to Hampton Institute, where Booker Washington was educated – a further 400,000 to Tuskegee, Booker Washington's own school, and 800,000 dollars to a new school founded by one of Mr Washington's students. And a month before I sailed a Mr Mitchell of New Jersey died and left a cool million to Tuskegee. I could fill pages on similar benefactions announced while I was in the States. And while big sums are reported in the papers sums of 2,000 to 20,000 are constantly given to Negro institutes and welfare associations of which nobody ever hears a word.

I saw the books in the accounting department of Tuskegee.

Their budget for 1921 was a million and a half.They exceeded their estimates by 30,000 dollars and this huge deficit was covered by unexpected bequests and donations that reached their coffers during the year.

Another society, under the leadership of Carter Woodson of Richmond, Virginia, is tracing Negro history down and back to Adam. They publish one of the best quarterly magazines in existence.[120] I attended their annual conference at Washington between Christmas and New Year and found it very instructive. Last May, they received simultaneously two sums of 25,000 dollars each to add to their investigations.

At Chicago there is a Jew by the name of Julius Rosenwald. Whenever Negroes want to erect a YMCA or YWCA – they call them the 'Y' over there – they draw up their plans, tell him how much they have collected and he responds with a cheque for 25,000 dollars. Magnificent institutions in many of their towns owe their existence to Mr Rosenwald. And when you study his donations to Negro schools down south the story of such benefactions by one man who is still alive sounds like a fairy tale. The Lord only knows where and how they get the money.

There are other philanthropic foundations that only attend to what one may call wholesale transactions. They pay no heed to requests for ten to twenty thousand. They hand out their dollars only to imposing schemes involving expenditure by the hundreds of thousands, such as the building and furnishing of an educational institution or medical college from the foundation up, replete with outhouses and dormitories, and an endowment fund to ensure the salaries of the faculty. And if they are so liberal with Negroes it is easy to understand that they are more so with white institutions. I don't think there is a single Canadian or American hospital in debt.

During my stay a young lady told a newspaper reporter that she was willing to marry any respectable man who would consent to pay $2,000 for a necessary operation on her mother. In the midst of the numerous offers of marriage that rained upon her through the post, there came a cheque for $2,000, without any conditions, and a promise to send more if necessary to save her mother. An afternoon paper once contained a news item about an old pastor who was about to sell his horse. He had used it in his ministerial work for 40 years. He hated to part with the animal but his limited means since his retirement from active service forced the decision upon him; and he hoped the buyer would be kind to his old charger. Next morning's papers contained portraits of the old pastor and his horse, and an involved discussion on the longevity of horses. A few days later it was announced that the old gentleman is not selling his horse any more as a lover of animals has pensioned him for life.

When Madame Curie went to America the newspapers announced that she was in need of a gramme of radium costing a hundred thousand dollars and asked the readers to provide this before she landed on the other side. Cheques flowed into the newspaper offices in such profusion that before the end of the week the editors had to call a halt as all the money had been subscribed.

Efforts have been made to get Mr Rosenwald and other philanthropists to help institutions in Africa, but in each instance they refused to help any Negroes outside America. But I think that some Americans could be induced to consider the case of Africa, for their churches are doing wonderful work in Central Africa, West Africa, especially in Liberia, and the Far East. Unfortunately they don't operate in the Union of South Africa, except to a very limited extent on the Rand.

For instance, the Phelps Stokes Committee promised to pay part of the printing cost of my Native translation of the Fellowship Hymn Book and its tonic solfa tunes if I could get some one in England to finance it.

When they learned that through lack of cash I was likely to return without visiting the southern states they contributed without being asked $100 towards my trip south on condition that I visit Tuskegee, which was just what I was anxious to do.[121]

Ready as they are to finance a Negro who genuinely aspires to help his people, Americans whose pockets are too limited to endow schools and welfare institutes have helped individual Negroes through college and sometimes set him up in business as they do with their own sons. I know of ladies who each spend 100 dollars a month on the education and maintenance of two Negro boys. All this being excellent examples for Negroes to help one another and they do so.

Where the Americans rise superior to their South African cousins is that they are often ready to reward merit even if it involves the recognition of the black skin. The late Mr Rhodes, the most generous of all South African magnates, left his millions to British and foreign nations in scholarships at Oxford; in South Africa the Rhodes Scholarships are more elaborate and open to everybody except the Natives who piled up his wealth. In the United States the Rhodes Scholarships have no colour bar. Professor Alain Leroy Locke of Howard University, Washington, was the first black man who went to Oxford as a Rhodes Scholar.

When a Negro is appointed to an office previously held by a white man he gets exactly the same pay as his predecessor, whether as Registrar of Deeds, Postmaster or Judge. If there be more than one department of equal rank each with a separate head, such as Assistant State Attorney, Assistant Officer of Health or Assistant Superintendent-General of Education, and one of these happens to be coloured, he gets the same pay and exercises the same executive authority in his department as the white assistant heads in theirs.

The American Embassy and the United States Shipping Board in London have coloured clerks, and their treatment and pay is on the same scale as their white colleagues. Of course, South Africa cannot boast a black office-holder.

Three years ago one of the shining lights of the cinema world at Los Angeles observed some outstanding talents in a Negro child of eight. He took him over, licked him into shape, gave him parts, first at 50 dollars and afterwards at 200 dollars per week, and sent him to school in his spare time.

This little boy, now only 12 years of age, has already set up his father in business as a prosperous grocer. He is the favourite of cinema goers (or 'movie fans', as they call them over there) throughout the United States and Canada, and plays under the screen name of 'Sunshine Sammy'. Last year he became a 'star' at 10,000 dollars a year.

The great Methodist Episcopal Church consecrated two coloured bishops for the first time last year and their pay is $7,000 plus travelling expenses just like the white bishops. In the missionary churches of South Africa where the white ordained minister gets £300 per year or more his coloured colleague gets from £60 to £80 per year. That is South Africa all over.

I visited America at a very ugly time. They all say I came two years too late. In 1919, they say, you could as easily have got a hundred dollars as 10 or 15 today, and I believe them for where I got 40 or 50 dollars in 1921 I could hardly get 8 or 10 this year, and where I previously sold books like ice-cream in August I could now scarcely sell a pamphlet.

Thousands of Negroes were earning as much as £4 per day in munition factories during the war. Thousands of men and women came from the South and from the West India Islands after these high wages. The effect was a marvellous increase in the membership and income of Negro churches in the Northern States.

PART THREE
1924-1932

'A pioneer in literature'

Introduction and Commentary

Plaatje finally returned to South Africa in November 1923, re-united with his family after a period of nearly four and a half years' absence. South Africa was much changed. If Plaatje had left South Africa in 1919 in a period of unresolved industrial and political ferment he returned now to a country where black and white alike were making their adjustments to the new structures that had been created. So far as African politics was concerned, the South African Native National Congress (which had changed its name to African National Congress in 1923), was a shadow of its former self, its position challenged now by the Industrial and Commercial Workers Union, the first mass African trade union in South Africa; and many of the former leaders of the SANNC had found a niche in the variety of new institutions and organisations sponsored by the churches and industry (the mining industry in particular), designed to channel African aspirations into more moderate outlets. How an independent-minded African spokesman like Plaatje would find a role remained to be seen.

Plaatje's initial observations about what he saw around him, and the changes he noticed since he left the country in the middle of 1919, were expressed in three articles he wrote for the *Diamond Fields Advertiser* late in January 1924 (Doc. 74, pp.313-20). Overall he was far from impressed by what he saw: whilst he welcomed the evidence of increased attention being given to African social problems, on the Witwatersrand particularly, he was at the same time struck by what he perceived as the deterioration in African political life, the virtual demise of an independent African press, and the lack of initiative being shown by Africans themselves to address the problems they faced – a theme to which he was to return on a number of occasions throughout the 1920s.

Things had also changed greatly so far as the white political parties were concerned. General Smuts had replaced General Botha as leader of the South African Party, and his party now incorporated the former Unionist Party with which it had found common cause to meet the growing strength of the Afrikaner Nationalists, led by General Hertzog. In these circumstances Plaatje was now, in political terms, considerably better disposed towards General Smuts than he had

been in 1919 – evident both in the letter Plaatje wrote to the General early in
1925 (Doc. 79, pp.340-343), and in the campaign in support of the South
African Party during the general election of 1924 (Doc. 76, pp.323-29).

For Plaatje now saw in General Smuts and the South African Party (SAP)
the only effective means of resisting the political influence of the two groups
of people he believed to be most opposed to the interests of the African
people: the Afrikaner Nationalists, to whom he attributed the most oppressive
pieces of legislation since Union, and who were now the most fervent
advocates of segregation; and the white working class, seeking the protection
of the colour bar in employment, and a guaranteed place for their labour, at
the expense of African workers, in the mining industry. Both groups were now
united in an electoral pact.

Such an analysis underlay much of Plaatje's political writings throughout the
1920s, and his belief that African political interests were best served by
mobilising the African vote in the Cape province on behalf of the SAP (e.g. Doc.
76 pp.323-29). In return Plaatje sought to extract political concessions (such as
the Barolong land bill to which he returned in late 1923 – Doc. 75, pp.320-23);
he sought without success to secure financial support for resuscitating *Tsala ea
Batho*, which remained a continuing ambition throughout this period; and he
sought a role for himself in the counsels of the white politicians of the day.

Unable to re-start his own newspaper Plaatje earned a living in the 1920s as
a journalist. His writings appeared in the main English-language newspapers of
the day: the Johannesburg *Star*, the *Pretoria News*, the *Cape Times*, *Cape Argus*,
the East London *Daily Dispatch*, above all in his local *Diamond Fields Advertiser*.
Many of his pieces were in the form of political commentaries on the issues of
the day, seeking as ever to convey a distinctively African perspective,
particularly on issues that directly affected the African people. Hence Plaatje's
consistent criticism of the long-running threat to the African franchise as
General Hertzog's government sought to push through its segregationist
policies; his criticism of the government's failure to take seriously the
consultative machinery it had established under the provisions of the Native
Affairs Act of 1920 (Doc. 89, pp.366-68); his attacks on legislation introduced
to reserve jobs for highly paid white workers at the expense of blacks (Doc. 80,
pp.343-46); his criticism of the legislation which eventually took shape in the
Native Administration Act of 1927, seeking as it did to separate the
administration of justice of black and white (Doc. 83, pp.350-52); and on
numerous occasions, continued criticism of the Natives' Land Act of 1913 and
its effects on African social and economic life (e.g. Doc. 87, pp.361-63).

But not everything Plaatje wrote in the columns of these newspapers was political in nature or focus. There were several historical pieces as well (e.g. Doc. 82, pp.348-50), and as he travelled around the countryside, spending his time in the rural areas where he was more at home, he reported on what he saw going on around him – 'In Bechuanaland today' in April 1928, is just one example (Doc. 88, pp.363-66). And he wrote a number of obituaries, such as those of Silas Molema (Doc. 86, pp.359-61) and Sir William Solomon (Doc. 96, p385-90). In these a very clear sense is conveyed of the importance Plaatje attached to the role of individual character and leadership, for he recognised in the lives of these men an example for others to emulate – a conviction which had long guided his own actions. Throughout his life Plaatje was motivated by the belief that even the most severe disabilities and disadvantages could be overcome through sheer force of character and hard work.

In the articles Plaatje wrote for the newspaper *Umteteli wa Bantu/Mouthpiece of the People*, addressed to an African readership, a different emphasis is evident in Plaatje's thinking. In the white daily press Plaatje frequently criticised the government for its totally unsympathetic attitude towards African aspirations and representations, and on occasions he did the same in the columns of *Umteteli* as well. But more often than not, in addressing an African audience, he reserved his strongest criticism for the African people themselves: for their failure to unite, to support their own political leaders, to demonstrate that collective strength of character and integrity that he believed was so vital to their wellbeing – criticism evident in many of his public addresses (e.g. Doc. 78, pp.334-40) as well as in his writings in *Umteteli* (Doc. 92, pp.372-75).

One issue he frequently addressed was the question of leadership, much debated in the columns of *Umteteli* during the 1920s (Docs 81, pp.346-48; 92, pp.372-75). In Plaatje's writings on the subject, and his response to the criticisms made of him (particularly from those who thought him too closely associated with the cause of the South African Party) there is a recognition that his influence was no longer what it was, and it is clear that he strongly resented any aspersions being cast on his record in the service of his people. But implicit in these differences and debates was a wider issue, less to do with personal differences between African spokesmen, more a matter of the intense frustration felt by Plaatje and other prominent African spokesmen. Not only was the government deaf to their representations, and determined to implement its policies of segregation and retribalisation; now, increasingly, they found their roles being usurped by a new breed of white liberals and 'friends of the Natives' – the self-styled 'native experts', as Plaatje called them, who were so much involved in social and political affairs in the 1920s. And on the other side, their own relationship with the African people they still sought to represent was now rather more tenuous and ambiguous than had once been the case.

Plaatje was involved in a variety of other activities throughout the 1920s. He remained as concerned as ever about the administration of justice, which he monitored as best he could, drawing attention to injustices through private or public channels; he devoted a lot of effort to seeking to register African voters in the Cape, countering the efforts of National Party agents who were doing their best to remove them from the electoral roll; he attended the annual meetings of the government Native Conferences in 1925 and 1926, and made a significant contribution to the proceedings on each occasion; and, though little involved in the affairs of the increasingly moribund African National Congress, was always ready to attend other gatherings concerned to further African political and social life, such as the conference organised in Kimberley by his old friend Dr Abdurahman, at which he was again one of the leading spokesmen (Doc. 85, pp.357-59); and he was involved, too, in the affairs of the Cape Native Voters Association, of which he became president in 1931.

To many people Plaatje was also well known for his bioscope which features in several of the letters Plaatje wrote to R.R. Moton during the 1920s (Docs 77, pp.329-34; 85, pp.357-59). Generally the centrepiece of these shows were the films he had acquired in the United States, and his hope was that the scenes of black American life would provide an inspiration for those who saw them, particularly the children, a stimulus to individual effort to escape the restrictions that surrounded them. Perhaps not surprisingly, Plaatje's bioscope proved more popular amongst children than adults, to whom the message did not always appeal: not everybody had such faith as Plaatje in the efficacy of individual uplift in the difficult circumstances faced by most black South Africans.

Plaatje's involvement in the affairs of the Independent Order of True Templars (IOTT), which Plaatje also describes in these letters to Moton (Doc. 85, pp.357-59), sprang from this same belief in the need for moral regeneration, and an urge to address individual behaviour as a starting point for a wider process of political, social and economic advancement for the African people as whole. For Plaatje this work for the IOTT, in promoting the message of temperance, and in setting up new branches of the organisation, was to be a particular preoccupation during 1927 and 1928. And it enabled him at the same time to travel the countryside, reporting on what he saw around him, assuming the role of one-man advocate, addressing instances of injustice where he found them,

Early in 1929, as the next general election approached, Plaatje allowed himself to be drawn once again into the affairs of the African National Congress, and he was responsible for drafting the ANC's reply to General Hertzog's notorious 'Black Manifesto', which reiterated his determination to proceed with the abolition of the Cape franchise, so far blocked as a result of being entrenched within the Union constitution. In Kimberley he was involved once again in attempting to secure African votes for the local South African Party candidates, a task not made easier (as he explained in a letter to De Beers) by the activities locally of the 'enemies of native welfare', as he described them, supported by the South African Communist Party (Doc. 93, pp.375-77). In June 1929, however, to Plaatje's intense disappointment (Doc. 91, pp.370-72), the Pact Government was returned to power with an increased majority which now gave it overall control in the new Parliament. A renewed assault upon the Cape African franchise, whose survival Plaatje regarded as so crucial to his whole political strategy – for upon it depended his influence with white politicians – now looked inevitable.

In the late 1920s Plaatje returned with a new urgency to the task of writing in his native Setswana, seeking to preserve for posterity the riches of his language and culture which he believed to be under even greater threat now than in 1916 when his *Sechuana Reader* and *Sechuana Proverbs* had been published. Undeniably, written literature in Tswana was in a most unsatisfactory state. The language was still plagued by the lack of agreement on orthography to which Plaatje had drawn attention in 1916, little had been published beyond purely didactic religious works, and the one dictionary for the language was – certainly in Plaatje's view – wholly inadequate. In contrast, considerable progress was being made in creating written literatures in other African languages in South Africa, in particular Xhosa and Sotho: all points made forcibly by Plaatje in correspondence with the Bantu Research Committee of the University of the Witwatersrand, seeking financial support for his work (Docs 90, pp.368-70; 94, pp.377-81).

Plaatje's intense concern for the condition of Setswana was in part a product of his increasingly pessimistic observations of the effects of social and economic changes upon the lives of his people – the lawlessness, alcoholism, the breakdown in parental control, a disrespect for authority, the disintegration, in other words, in all spheres of African communal life about which Plaatje had written a great deal in the press. In the preservation of Tswana language and culture Plaatje saw a means of cultural regeneration, to enable the Tswana people at least to resist the consequences of what he perceived to be happening to them. Only then, as Plaatje saw it, could they feel pride in their customs and traditions, and only then could that process of moral regeneration, to which Plaatje was so committed in other spheres, be set in motion.

There was a more personal concern, too, in this renewed concern with Tswana literature and culture in the late 1920s. By now Plaatje was becoming frustrated at the scant opportunities that existed for him to exercise any meaningful leadership in the political arena in an increasingly segregated society, shunned by a government that saw no place for educated Africans, and irritated at the same time by the increasing numbers and influence of the 'so-called native experts'. In his work on the Tswana language and its literature, by contrast, there was a form of escape to the one area where his expertise was unchallenged.

Plaatje's efforts were concentrated in several directions. First of all, he had already completed translations of a number of Shakespeare's plays, but needed now to raise the funds to have them printed and published. It proved to be a long and difficult campaign, and in the end only his translations of *The Comedy of Errors* was printed and published in his lifetime: the Introduction Plaatje wrote for it (Doc. 95, pp.381-85) provides a revealing indication of the problems he faced in raising the money he needed to meet the cost of printing the book, of the difficulties inherent in the still unresolved orthography problem, and of his motives in embarking upon the task of translation in the face of local apathy and bewilderment.

Sadly, of the other three translations he had completed – mentioned both in the letter he wrote to De Beers in November 1929 in search of funds (Doc. 93, pp.375-77) and in his Introduction to *Diphosho-phosho (The Comedy of Errors)* (Doc. 95, pp.381-85) – only that of *Julius Caesar* was published (posthumously, in 1937), and the manuscripts of his translations of *Much Ado about Nothing* and *Merchant of Venice* have been lost.

Plaatje regarded this self-imposed task of translating Shakespeare into Setswana as not only a matter of the highest importance, but also as an entirely natural and appropriate thing to do. He was always struck by the parallels between the pre-industrial world about which Shakespeare wrote, and the themes he explored, and the Tswana stories and traditions which had been handed down to him from childhood. In his contribution to *A Book of Homage to Shakespeare* in 1916 (Doc. 53, pp.210-12) he had predicted that many of the stories on which Shakespeare drew would have equivalents in African folklore, and as he investigated this further so he found his predictions borne out. In this sense Plaatje saw the translation of Shakespeare as a natural and appropriate exercise, in no way contrived or artificial.

And there was another concern in this task of translating Shakespeare into Setswana: to demonstrate the capacity and capabilities of the Tswana language to render Shakespeare and his world into intelligible Setswana, and thus to vindicate the claims and status of Setswana as a language worthy of recognition and development – a point he had again made in his Introduction to his *Sechuana Proverbs* in 1916 (Doc. 54, pp.212-20). Judging by the comments of those qualified to judge *Diphosho-phosho* he certainly succeeded: Professor Clement Doke, of the University of the Witwatersrand, thought Plaatje's translation was 'remarkably good', while his friend and collaborator David Ramoshoana felt that Shakespeare 'has inspired Mr Plaatje to bring into bold relief the etymological beauties of his mother tongue', and that he had 'rendered the entire story in a language which to a Mochuana is as entertaining and amusing as the original is to an Englishman'.

Plaatje's other work in Setswana involved preparing a new, enlarged edition of his *Sechuana Proverbs*; compiling a dictionary to replace that by J.T. Brown, which he felt to be woefully inadequate and full of omissions and inaccuracies; and preparing what he variously described as a volume of 'Traditional Native Folk Tales and other Useful Knowledge', 'Bantu folk-tales and poems – traditional and original', and 'a volume of Native fables and traditional poems in the vernacular'. Neither the Dictionary nor the volume of 'Native Folk Tales' have survived, but they are clearly described, together with the many difficulties encountered in researching and compiling them, in several letters Plaatje wrote on this subject, all of them appealing for funds to support his work (Docs 90, pp.368-70; 93, pp.375-77; 94, pp.377-81). Fortuitously, two of the praise poems which must have formed part of Plaatje's collection are reproduced (in both Setswana and English) in the biographical sketch he wrote of Chief Montsioa, published in the *African Who's Who* in 1931 (Doc. 103, pp.413-19).

After his lack of funds, the greatest obstacle Plaatje faced in this work in Setswana was the still unresolved problem of orthography. His response was to go his own way, and to use some letters from the International Phonetic Alphabet in *Diphosho-phosho* – not an approach that commended itself to many other people with an interest in such linguistic matters, but for Plaatje at least it provided him with the satisfaction of rendering his translations in a form that distinguished all the sounds and tones of the spoken language (Doc. 95, pp.381-85).

In fact the issue of orthography had ramifications beyond Plaatje's choice of orthography in his own writings, and it became a central issue for him during the last few years of his life. Between 1928 and 1932 Plaatje found himself at odds with the moves being made, and sponsored by the government, in the direction of a standardised orthography for the major language groups in southern Africa, the ultimate goal being a single orthography for all of them. For Plaatje the direction these initiatives took amounted to an unacceptable threat to the integrity and the very survival of Setswana, and he applied himself energetically to resisting them: not only in his contributions to the press (Docs 99, p.397-403; 104, pp.419-21), but also in a great deal of behind-the-scenes activity and campaigning (e.g. Doc. 101, pp.404-406). Throughout the debate Plaatje made it very clear that he felt these issues should be decided in conjunction with Tswana-speakers and writers like himself, and not by the 'self-styled native experts', many of whom did not speak the language whose future they were deciding.

What was arguably the crowning achievement of Plaatje's literary career lay in another field: the publication of his English language historical novel, *Mhudi*, in 1930. Just as *Diphosho-phosho* was the first published African-language translation of a play by Shakespeare, so *Mhudi* was the first novel in English to have been written by a black South African. Set in the period of the *difaqane* in the 1830s, *Mhudi* reflects Plaatje's deep interest in the history of the Barolong people, about whom he wrote on a number of other occasions; and it provided an entirely characteristic synthesis of African and European literary forms, combining the style of a Western novel with the form and substance of African oral traditions. At the same time it provides both an exploration of the origins of South Africa's twentieth-century situation, and – in the thoughts and deeds of Mhudi, the heroine of the book – an indication of the ideals and behaviour that could enable South Africa to escape the conflict which continued oppression of the African people would inevitably generate.

Written in 1920, there is also much to link the book with *Native Life in South Africa* and the political campaigns Plaatje was involved in at the time.

But in his preface to *Mhudi* Plaatje expressed his concern, probably felt more strongly in 1930 than it had been in 1920, to indicate his purpose in writing it: firstly, 'to interpret to the reading public, one phase of "the back of the Native mind"', and secondly, 'with the readers' money to collect and print (for Bantu schools) Sechuana folk-tales, which with the spread of European ideas are fast being forgotten' (Doc. 98, pp.396-97). *Mhudi* thus gave expression to Plaatje's concern to preserve Tswana history and culture by recording aspects of it in the book, and using the proceeds from its sales towards the printing costs of the Tswana language folk-tales. It is one of the many tragedies of South African literature that these never saw the light of day.

Plaatje was very pleased to have seen *Mhudi* published, and he sent a number of copies to friends of his – including Robert Moton (Doc. 100, pp.403-404), whom he hoped might be able to help in publishing an American edition of the book (in vain, as it turned out).

Plaatje remained as active as ever during the last couple of years of his life, heavily involved in the IOTT as well as continuing to contribute to the daily and weekly press on the issues of the day. Further opportunities for him to convey his views were provided by the government's decision in 1930 to re-convene the Government Native Conference in Pretoria, the first time this had been held since 1926 – where Plaatje took the opportunity to air his views on the government's plans on the matter of African language orthography; and by the Native Economic Commission, to whom Plaatje provided both written and oral evidence when it visited Kimberley in February 1931 (Doc. 97, pp.390-96).

Several months later Plaatje became the editor of *Our Heritage*, a monthly periodical, in English and Setswana, which was supported by the IOTT. In fact *Our Heritage* was concerned not just with temperance matters, and Plaatje undoubtedly hoped it could be developed into the more general platform he had been seeking ever since his return to South Africa in 1923. In pursuit of this aim he attempted to persuade the Bechuanaland Protectorate administration to provide financial support for *Our Heritage* on the grounds that it was the only journal in existence which carried news about Bechuanaland in Setswana, but he was unable to persuade the Resident

Commissioner, Sir Charles Rey, to release funds for this purpose. *Our Heritage* ceased publication after only five issues, notable for two long articles it contained by Plaatje describing the trip he made to the Belgian Congo in 1931 to study race relationships on the copper belt.

Plaatje died of pneumonia in Johannesburg on 19 January 1932, on a visit in search of funds to print and publish his work in Setswana. At his funeral, and in the press in the days and weeks following his death, many tributes were paid to the unique contribution he had made to the life of his people, and of South Africa as a whole. G.A. Simpson, editor of the *Diamond Fields Advertiser*, summed up the essence of his achievement as follows: 'Mr Plaatje,' he said, had 'done a great service not only to the race from which he sprang, but to the whole community, both black and white, for he was a link between them, and enabled each to understand something of the natural feelings and interests of the other.'

From the African people and from the African press praise and respect were even more fulsome. The Reverend Zacharius Mahabane, a well-known Methodist minister, and until recently President-General of the African National Congress, who conducted the memorial service, considered Plaatje to have been 'a great patriot [who] devoted his great talents to the service of his people and country'. *Imvo Zabantsundu*, in one of many tributes from the African press, felt that 'the ranks of recognised Bantu leaders' had 'suffered a severe depletion in the deplorable demise of a staunch patriot and indefatigable toiler in the service of his fellow men ... His soul is departed but the memory of him and his work will live untarnished in the annals of Native history'.

Selected Writings

74
Article, 'Native Affairs: After four years', *Diamond Fields Advertiser*, 19, 22 and 23 January 1924

1

I spent the month of December in an effort to find and pick up the ribbons where I dropped them nearly five years ago; and so these lines were written in my Kimberley home, on the river diggings, partly in Bechuanaland and on the farms and locations of Transvaal, in some dorps and cities, and also in the long train journey from the north to the slopes of Table Mountain, whence I mail them after a long and weary tramp to the Cape Flats where I went to see the work of the municipality of the mother city, clearing and preparing the ground for a new Native township in the peninsula.

Most of the gatherings I addressed during this tour of observation were purely Native. Some of the urban meetings were mixed, white and black. My rural meetings were always too large for any church, and so had to be held in the open. One of my country meetings was attended by the magistrate of Potchefstroom in his capacity as Native Commissioner for the district.

I find the country under serious disadvantages. The suspended animation of De Beers' mines robs the population of a large portion of its means of livelihood, and the people's plight is accentuated by the continued drought. In my mind the depression is painfully marked, for whereas the fields abroad are fresh and green, here the scanty fodder is depleted by the ravages of swarms of locusts. To intensify the worries of the farmer, his emaciated cattle feed on dead insects, gorged with locust fungi, and die of the feed.

As if their cup of misery is not sufficiently full, the rural Native population is further worried by the operation of the Natives' Land Act of 1913, whose provisions still deny them the right to eke out their primitive existence on the farms. Investigating the effects of this unique enactment I find that no legislative measure conceived by the mind of man has ever impoverished a people to the extent the South African Natives have been pauperized during the past ten years by Act 27 of 1913. It is so peculiarly worded that no bands of policemen are necessary to enforce its provisions; unlike all other acts of parliament, its operation is automatic. Not only are its remorseless forays affecting urban Natives to a sinister degree, but its effects are now embracing white people too.

Urban Natives before the passage of this act had the means to defeat the effects of low wages in the several dorps. They could run livestock and get their rural brethren to plough for them. Obtaining free meat and free grain from the country a town Native's 12s. per week was partly available for white hawkers who had various devices of relieving Native housewives of their 'loose shillings'. Since their rural income is forbidden by the Land Act, town Natives must now feed and clothe their families entirely on the meagre wages and most Natives cannot do it on 12s. a week. Thanks to the law, none of them have any spare shillings for white hawkers; the latter now must whistle for their sustenance, and the result is a disquieting increase in the tribe of poor whites.

Municipalities too, I find, have a lot to thank this measure for; not only are town locations congested by the influx of Natives evicted from the farms, but the urban authorities have been compelled to extend their location areas to accommodate the overflow. Rural poor whites are moving townwards in the wake of their former Native customers and they also are thrown on the hands of municipalities. It is not clear what the authorities propose to do with the latter, but draconian regulations promulgated on December 7 explain fully how the government would deal with the Native refugees. With the prohibitions of the Land Act in the country and the harassing restrictions of the Urban Areas Act in the towns, providence alone knows where the Native peasant must go to!

It is, indeed, hard to be a Native of South Africa, outside the Cape Province, for perplexed and outlawed by acts of parliament in the land of his fathers, he has hardly a place on which to rest the hollow of his foot.

In all the foreign lands my wanderings have led me to, I have the freedom to own or occupy landed property anywhere. The only place where under a fine of £100 or six months' imprisonment, I may not even receive it as a free gift is my own Native province of the Orange Free (?) State, in the Union of South Africa.

The better-class people on the whole seem to feel that these restrictions have gone too far and they are looking for a way out of the dilemma. Native miners have in their compounds free bioscope shows at the expense of the Chamber of Mines; mine locations like the Robinson Deep, Ferreira Deep (to say nothing of the well-appointed and well-kept sporting grounds of the Crown Mines) own some splendid lawn tennis courts which many a European club would be happy to possess; and a magnificent structure with a large auditorium is about to be erected as a sort of civic club and social rendezvous for Rand Natives.[1]

Municipalities are also tackling the housing problem. I went to see the new location about seven miles from Johannesburg, and found rows of well built cottages; the thoroughfares between each two rows are rather narrow, but the little gardens in front of the houses are profuse with multi-colour dahlias, lilies, marigold, etc., with handy water-taps all over the location. Money that formerly went to auctioneers in exchange for discarded old zinc plates, as unsightly as they are unhygienic, is now invested in splendid pieces of furniture, with glittering glass-works over pretty sideboards. The place is a veritable picture of homely happiness, and a possible atonement for the twenty-years-old scandal which disgraced Johannesburg since 1904, when she bundled her Natives out of Vrededorp, dumped them on a sewerage deposit, and called it a location.[2]

The Pretoria housing scheme is an improvement on the old thing, and the old and new Randfontein locations are lit with electricity. In Mrs Charlotte Maxeke, the best-educated Native woman in the country, the Johannesburg courts have a sympathetic child welfare officer, who does for the wayward adolescents what no other court official could possibly do for Native delinquents in South Africa.

In the face of these improvements it is perhaps fair to hope that (when the Urban Areas Act is definitely launched) enlightened urban opinion will not tolerate, in the municipalities, a repetition of the horrors created in the country districts during the past ten years by the operation of the Natives' Land Act. But it is extremely doubtful if this new-born philanthropy will be competent to cope with a situation that throws on the hands of charity five-sixths of the entire population who should be left to fend for themselves as they did before Union.

2

One regrettable fact is that Natives are scarcely as well served by Native newspapers as they were formerly. Besides telling the news, Native papers used to give expression to Native opinion and act as interpreters of European thought and translators of government policy. It is not incorrect to say that, except to a limited extent in one or two instances, the Native press has almost ceased to function along these lines. Since my return I have attended many

Native meetings, found white journalists in some and missed Native reporters in all of them. Important meetings like Colonel Stallard's (to which I will refer later) and General Smuts' striking declaration on Native policy, delivered at the city hall, Johannesburg, on the eve of Dingaan's day,* found no room in either of the polyglot weeklies that Natives buy.[3] Purely Native news is sometimes clipped from the European press, by Native editors who should give it at first hand, and reproduced without translation as though Native journals were edited by scissors and paste.

Another regrettable feature of Native life is the alarming increase in drunkenness among Natives in most industrial centres. Half-a-dozen causes were given by way of explanation, but only two appear to be worth mentioning. Firstly, it is suggested that during the 'flu of 1918 the taps were turned loose and many an abstainer in fear of certain death took too strongly to alcohol. They never ceased to drink, and erstwhile moderate drinkers acquired the habit of drinking to excess.

Economic conditions due to the operation of repressive laws are cited as a second cause. Many depressed Natives, it is said, seek relief from desperation in strong drink. Be that as it may, but to a sympathetic student of the question the orgy of drunkenness is very disconcerting. Referring to this phase of things at one of my meetings a Native leader said: 'Here we are worrying the authorities for a relaxation of some of the stringent laws in force in the Transvaal; and, while the authorities are still considering such representations it does seem disheartening to find some of our people spending their weekends drinking, fighting and stabbing each other as if in proof that they are not fit for freedom.' Such conduct, said Mr Thema, disgraced all Natives in the eyes of other people. If the Brotherhood cannot reform such people the government will be bound, in the public interest, to build for them a zoo, as is generally done with all dangerous animals.

The Native Congress also seems to have fallen from grace. The Johannesburg branch especially, which did so much good a few years back, can no longer be complimented on the acumen and sobriety of its leaders. Tribal organisation has undergone a marked deterioration during the past five years, and nothing appears to have displaced the disintegration.

Apart from the Farmers' Association in the Eastern Province, composed largely of property owners united to safeguard their own little holdings, the

---

* Dingaan's day was 16 December, the anniversary of the defeat of Dingaan's Zulu army by a party of Boer trekkers at the battle of Blood River in Natal in 1838.

best Native association today appears to be the Industrial and Commercial Union of Africa, whose annual conference is now in session at East London. It is the only Native organisation in which politics are taboo, and the only one that has attracted coloured people and Malays in large numbers. With a burial benefit and a monthly newspaper organ it deals only with the affairs of that much despised fellow, the Native labourer of South Africa, who needs protection less from his employers than from the selfishness of the so-called Labour Party of South Africa. It is the only Native organisation whose headquarters will not screen any wrongdoers. Unfaithful officials are promptly handed over to the police to be summarily dealt with by the magistrates on the documentary evidence supplied by the head office. Officers are weeded out who succumb to the temptations of strong drink and kindred offences.

The conceiver and guiding spirit of this association is the son of a chieftain in the jungles of the far interior.[4] Coming to Cape Town at the age of 22 he saw the needs and got to work with the organisation of a black trade union in Cape Town, which has now extended to other parts of the Union. All his education was supplied by the limited curriculum of a Scottish mission school in Central Africa; yet some South African Natives continue to harbour suspicions against missions. They charge missionary pioneers with being mercenary harbingers of the present exploiters of Natives and Native lands. The Bible too is now sacrilegiously called the 'dope' which is administered before the actual work of dispossession. I find the Union laws as administered during the past eight or ten years have been responsible for a perfect wave of anti-religious feeling among Natives, especially in those parts where the disabilities are more severe. Religion is put down as one of the white man's methods of exploitation.

3

The people of Johannesburg constitute an absorbing sociological study. There was a time when Chicago and Montreal enjoyed an unenviable reputation. In some respects, however, Johannesburg as 'the university of crime' can give points to them both. White Randites, themselves an heterogeneous ethnological conglomeration, have, besides supplying the population with jobs, established a regular cave of Adullam, to which fugitive Natives flee from all sorts of obligations. Natives from everywhere are there. When the diamond mines closed down the labourers all flocked here to seek a fresh livelihood. Married Natives growing tired of their conjugal duties, like unfilial youths out of parental control in the territories, find an asylum there. With so many thousands of married people living and working apart from their spouses a distressing situation is growing up. An old Native, speaking at one of my meetings, said: 'Some people get angry when the whites talk of making a "white man's country" here; and yet that state of affairs is being created by people of our own race. Young Native girls come here to roam the length of the reef. Their conduct is so disreputable that they will never be good for anything. They will certainly never be mothers, live they ever so long. Where will the next generation come from?' Personal observation in the slums and in the residential quarters of the city would seem to show that the old man's remarks were justified.

But white people in Johannesburg as elsewhere are not all the same; and I think that a white census would disclose the fact that descendants of the old Cape and Natal settlers outnumber the speculators and the 'carpet-baggers', and they are to be found in every walk of life. In cosmopolitan Parktown I found, living side by side with aristocratic segregationists, some English and Dutch people, Jews and black but decidedly anti-white. It must be confessed that my enquiries have failed to elicit a satisfactory explanation of this curious phenomenon. The Johannesburg Natives also form a peculiar mixture. Some are anglicised and think imperially, while others are Dutchified, and many are democratised. Some will not forget the ancient glory of the rule of Mpande and Moshueshue and even the soviet can claim a few adherents. After the last revolution when the white ringleaders were sentenced for shooting Natives and other acts of terrorism, a number of Natives surrounded the home of General Smuts with a petition asking for the reprieve of the condemned white men.[5]

But the lot of them are being slowly Americanised. A white American missionary, the Rev. E. Ray Phillips,[6] has started a Greek letter club in one of the slums. While others go 'slumming' the friends of the Natives go there to discuss inter-racial problems with Natives and they do so in real Yankee style. I attended the last of these inter-racial gatherings when Colonel Stallard, K.C., spoke.[7] He took an hour painting a rosy picture of segregation and a most depressing view of present conditions in the Union. 'We are heading for disaster,' he said; 'no one is happy with things as they are, and we must call a halt. Complete territorial segregation is our safe alternative,' and so on up to the end, when he asked the Natives for their views.

Mr Stallard got huge lumps of Native views in response, and he got them straight if raw on occasion. He was told that segregation in one form or another had been the law of the land since Union; and, so far from being a possible remedy, it was the cause of the present Native misery. One speaker, referring to municipal segregation, said: 'Here in Johannesburg where there is segregation, we are taxed to maintain a tram service. Yet we are not allowed on the trams. Even our location car is not permitted to enter the town. In Kimberley', he continued, 'nobody is taxed to maintain the trams; when we alight from the train at Kimberley station we go and ride on the nearest tram. They never had any segregation law in Kimberley.'

Mr Richard Thema, who moved the vote of thanks in a very witty speech, said the best kind of segregation was voluntary. In London, where the law said nothing on the subject, he pointed out that most Jews were in Whitechapel and the Chinese at Limehouse; the English at Kensington and the Italians at Soho. Coming nearer home, he said at Kimberley, without segregation laws, the Natives lived in locations, mixed people in the Malay Camp, the Boers at Newton, and other Europeans at Belgravia, and nobody is in the other's way. In Johannesburg segregation by-laws had created discontent and distrust between white and black, yet Natives live in yards all over the town in spite of the law.

Mr Stallard at one stage admitted that the segregation of the Land Act was 'wicked'; and my personal observations certainly seem to support the view of the Natives. I should take two very extreme cases by way of illustration. The Union of South Africa, the only state on earth where segregation is enforced by fines of £100 or six months' imprisonment produces two-thirds of the world's gold supply, nine-tenths of all the diamonds, and grows the best fruit, cotton, etc., yet it has the raggedest and most illiterate people I have ever seen; and there is hardly any love lost between white and black.

New York State is the exact antithesis of South Africa. There segregation is prohibited by fines of 500 dollars or six months' imprisonment. If a cafe-owner ordered a coloured customer to another part of the dining-hall or a theatre manager offered them seats in the second row when they wanted front row seats in the same hall for the same play, they would go out and claim 800 dollars damages, and get the money. I asked why they paid so readily and was told that if the case were contested the defendant would be exposed to criminal proceedings for infringing the Civil Rights Act. Yet New York is the wealthiest state on earth; its population is the best housed, the best fed and best dressed; over 90 per cent of them are literate. The illiterate nine per cent is only made up of immigrants from the backward states of Europe and migrants from far south, where they have segregation, and I have never seen so much confidence between white and black as I found among the citizens of the empire state.

It certainly looks as though the prohibition of segregation were a sure cure for poverty, illiteracy and race hatred. Illinois and California have less drastic anti-segregation laws, and their wealth and prosperity are second only to New York's. Texas and Mississippi in the same United States have in operation pro-segregation laws on the same lines but somewhat milder than the segregation laws in the Union of South Africa. Curiously enough their ignorance, poverty, racial and class prejudices, like their squalor and disease, are about half as bad as ours. They even boast of a number of poor whites – something wholly unknown in the New England states.

75
Article, 'The case for the Barolongs: Tribe's relations with the voortrekkers', *Cape Argus*, 4 March 1924

Plaatje had pressed for the relaxation of restrictions on land inheritance for the Barolong since 1909, and finally achieved his aim with the passage of the Moroka Ward Land Relief Act, passed in September 1924. Plaatje's presentation of the historical background provided part of the moral justification for the measure. For earlier developments, see p.124.

In moving the second reading of the Barolong Land Relief Bill on Thursday, the Minister of Mines paid a glowing tribute to the Barolong friendliness to the early Boers. In doing so, however, Mr Malan[8] referred only to their relations since 1863. In this way he rendered a disservice to the Native cause. One parliamentary notist understood that the Barolongs were settled at Thaba Nchu 'as a reward for its service to the voortrekkers'. Please permit me, as a member of this tribe, to point out that the voortrekkers found us in permanent occupation of Thaba Nchu, duly acknowledged as owners by King Moshesh of Basuto, at that time the only authority in that neighbourhood.

Villiers was the first of the voortrekkers to visit our people in the early thirties and inquire the way north. He resumed his trek towards the Vaal River and camped for a time at Vechtkop. There he was attacked by King Mzilikazi's impis who left his camp in a perilous state.

The Boer leader appealed for succour, and in response, Chief Moroka sent draught animals and men to move the Boer laager with its women and children to a refugee camp in his own home at Thaba Nchu. The Matebele having relieved them of every beast, the chief also supplied them with milch cows and other animals, which the Boers used for ploughing purposes while recuperating at Thaba Nchu.

Attack on Matebele

In 1835 a larger company of voortrekkers, with the aid of the Barolong under chieftain Motshegare, besides Griquas and other Natives, attacked the Matebele stronghold at Choenyane (now western Transvaal) and forced King Mzilikazi to move farther north and settle in what is now called Southern Rhodesia.

Most of Cilliers' original party afterwards settled in the Transvaal, leaving the Barolong exactly where they found them. More immigrants arrived from the south, and a Boer government was subsequently established at Bloemfontein. A treaty between the Orange Free State and the Barolong recognised the sovereignty of Thaba Nchu and bound each contracting party to render military aid (apparently at its own expense) each time the other party was at war.

This treaty, which proved to be a one-sided bargain, practically made Thaba Nchu the buffer between the Boers and the Basuto. The Barolong alone bore the brunt of this agreement, for while their levies participated in the military campaigns that eventually drove the Basuto from their arable land along the Caledon valley back to the mountain tops, the Barolong, on their part, never had occasion to call on the Boers for aid.

In 1884 some Boer filibusters fomented a civil war among the Barolong and President Brand, for the first time in 50 years, called his burghers to the aid of their black allies. They arrived in time to learn that one of the freebooters had settled the row by shooting dead the chief of one of the contending factions; and so the sum total of the first Boer co-operation was to annex the Native state and proclaim it part of the Republic of the Orange Free State.

A questionable 'reward'

In 1802 the volksraad at Bloemfontein passed a law forbidding the sale of land to Natives, including the Barolong, whose unrequited military exploits had helped to push the Free State frontier into the heart of Basutoland. So, where is the reward? If systematic dispossession of a nation's allies amounts to a reward, then, indeed, the Barolong are to be congratulated on their friendship with white men.

To the abiding credit of President Brand and his successors in office, let me add that the Barolong never experienced any difficulty in acquiring landed property in territories that were formerly theirs; the presidents always issued certificates to exempt intending purchasers from the operation of that drastic law. For ploughing or grazing purposes nothing more than the owner's permission was necessary; and, if I understand the bill correctly, its object is to invest the Governor-General with the prerogatives of former presidents.

Unfortunately, the control of the Free State of President Brand and Chief Moroka has now passed into the hands of the Pharaohs who know not Joseph. They hail from all over the country. They listen to no reason. All they maintain is that it is a scandal for Natives to cultivate land except for white men. Their mentality stands revealed in the two speeches that followed Mr Malan's on Thursday. Their view of the Barolong is that they are 'as destructive as baboons ... they do not leave a mealie standing'. That is why in 1913 they were totally prohibited!

'Baboons'

But what are the facts? In 1911 some of the Barolong cultivated their lands to such good effect that they reaped as much as 3,000 bags of wheat in several places while their Boer neighbours reaped from 200 to 500 muid. That, in a nutshell, is the scandal from which the 1913 act saved the province of the Orange 'Free' State. One of the Barolong invested £900 in agricultural machinery. He was about to revolutionize Native farming in his district when the government forbade the use of his expensive machines under the Mines and Machinery Act (recently declared *ultra vires* by the Transvaal division of the Supreme Court).

If, as General Hertzog so forcibly pointed out, this be the character of baboons, political economists would retort that it were better to let baboons get to work and flood the Free State with food than have a lot of hungry poor whites groaning at the treasury gates for relief. But apparently the word 'economy' does not figure in some South African vocabularies, hence the tirade against Mr Malan's bill.

Not long ago the Prime Minister was wondering why the new Native was losing his respect for the white man and his Christianity. The Prime Minister was right. Numbers of Natives openly say that Christianity is a fraud. Self-styled Native experts, of whom South Africa has not a few, ought to have told the premier the question asked by nearly every Native. One of them is: 'When a body of Christians come together and pray to God for legislative powers to expel the aboriginals from their Native haunts and make it a crime for them to till the maiden soil, who can reconcile that with the biblical saying that "the earth is the Lord's and the fullness thereof"?'

This month, for the first time, I met Natives who totally disagreed with their tried and true friend, Senator Roberts.[9] That was on the question of responsibility for the existing depression. They generally agree with those up-country senators who attribute the prevailing drought, locusts and other plagues to the sins of the people.

Painful aftermaths

They admit that the Native sinned as heavily as the whites, but European sins, especially their ingratitude to the Natives, leave very painful aftermaths. They include repressive legislation which drives widows and orphans of another race out of their homes, and sends them wandering, to die of starvation and exposure in the wilderness with their belongings on their heads; and if cruelty to the fatherless will not anger the Almighty then, the Natives argue, He cannot be as just as Dr Roberts and other missionaries make him.

Look at the recent tragedy in the inland provinces. Natives driven from the farms by the 1913 Act always found an asylum in the urban areas. Last year an Urban Act was enacted.[10] Under its provision, Natives by the shoal were fined, last week and the weeks before, by the magistrates of Cape Town and Woodstock, and compelled to leave the city and go to Ndabeni to live. This week, the same Natives were arrested by the location authorities for overcrowding an already congested Native location. Thus inhumanities that were impossible under savage Native potentates have become the rule of Native life in civilized South Africa. Exiled from their Native environments in rural South Africa they flee into the cities only to find themselves between urban horns of the same dilemma. He would not be human if this did not exhaust his confidence in the integrity of the white man and the sincerity of his religion; and he contends that if senators believe the locust plague to be a divine punishment for the people's sins, the logical remedy is to stop sinning. So why quarrel with Mr Malan?

76

Article, 'Nationalists and Natives: A scathing indictment', *Cape Argus*, 29 April 1924

At the beginning of April 1924 the South African Party (SAP), led by General Smuts, suffered a series of by-election defeats at the hands of the Afrikaner National Party. As a result, Parliament was dissolved ('the recent political bolt from the blue') and a general election was announced for the following month, at which Smuts himself lost his seat. Plaatje campaigned on behalf of the South African Party, and this article was also published and distributed in leaflet form by the SAP during the election campaign in an attempt to help secure African votes in the Cape province.

Plaatje's article (described as a 'remarkable communication') was commended by the Argus to its readers in a lengthy editorial, supporting Plaatje's general view that the election of a Nationalist government, led by General Hertzog, would not be in the interests of the African people, and that they should therefore entrust their votes to General Smuts's SAP.

It is no exaggeration to say that the hopes of many a Native in this Union have been dashed to the ground by the recent political bolt from the blue. Of all the Native measures passed by Parliament since the inauguration of Union, the Natives can look back to only one that does not impose additional humiliations upon them. This was General Smuts's Native Affairs Act of 1920. Under this law the government calls once a year a conference of representative Natives presided over by the Minister, or his deputy, to discuss Native affairs. Two conferences have already met – the first one at Bloemfontein and another at Pretoria last year.

A commission appointed under the act consists of Senator Roberts (a great scholar and missionary, formerly of Lovedale, who enjoys the confidence of the Native masses and also of educated Natives), Dr C.T. Loram (an eminent philosopher, profoundly interested in Native welfare and education) and General Lemmer, of Marico, who is supposed to represent, more or less, the backveld view. Of course, the commission is not without defects. For instance, it is appointed purely for Native interests and is financed entirely out of Native taxes; yet it is a lily-white concern on which no Native may sit.

American visitors to England have often expressed disappointment when they called at the offices of the African Society and the Aborigines' Protection Society and found no Africans in the membership and on the staffs at either. They would mention the striking contrasts of their own urban leagues and the branches and headquarters of the National Association for the Advancement of Colored People, each staffed like a department of state, with pure black officials and a mixed directorate.

As illustrating their advanced method of ruling black people, one may mention a recent appointment by President Coolidge of a commission to investigate conditions on the Virgin Islands recently acquired from Denmark. The new commission is composed of six coloured men who, by virtue of the fact that they themselves are Negroes, are best suited to probe the minds of the Negro islanders.

Still, our Native Affairs Commission is groping along as best it can under South African conditions. They have already visited many centres in the Union and in South-West Africa, and the result of their work was embodied in bills that were pending when Parliament dissolved. They were at Cape Town during the recent session, investigating the origin and history of the numerous religious sects known collectively as the Ethiopian movement.[11]

Pass laws and taxation

Before the dissolution, the Natives were watching two measures with anxious expectation. One of these was the simplification of the numerous pass laws and regulations, and also the bill to equalize Native taxation throughout the Union. The effect hereof would be a reduction of the heavy direct taxes imposed on Transvaal Natives and, by a system of levelling up and levelling down, bring about uniformity in Native taxation throughout the Union.

It is a well-known fact that no single group in this Union is as badly treated by the central and local authorities as are the Natives of the Orange Free State, where the Nationalists hold unquestioned sway. Having next to no mission school grants, all their teachers go to the Cape and Basutoland after elementary training and many of their children are at present in Kimberley for schooling.

Even their womenfolk, including the wives and daughters of Native ministers and teachers, are compelled to carry passes entitling them to reside with their husbands or parents or go to gaol; not only have they the additional pleasure of paying monthly fees for these unnecessary documents, but the women are stopped at street corners and made to ransack their pockets and produce their passes at the behest of male policemen. They have practically no Native reserves or locations, and their tenure is purely one of sufferance.

In the Thaba Nchu district some Natives still hold some land awarded to the several families by the late Chief Moroka before the tribe came under Free State rule. If any Cape coloured person in this province has a footing on land, it is by grace of such Native landowners and in defiance of the policy of the burghers. Since their annexation, the bulk of these lands have passed from Native to white ownership, for while it is a crime to transfer fixed property from a Native to any non-European, it is no breach of the law to transfer Native property to Europeans. The urgent need of relief will be appreciated when I mention the case of two brothers who could not inherit lands left them in their uncle's will. The Registrar of Deeds was debarred from making a transfer in favour of Natives. Residents of the Cape could scarcely believe that such things are possible; yet it is the law of the province of the Orange 'Free' State, adjoining the Cape.

An act of justice

To remedy these evils, the government introduced a measure during the session just ended. It passed its second reading (not without Nationalist protests) and was referred to a select committee. When Mr Malan moved the second reading of this bill he was censured from the opposition benches for tampering with settled Free State principles.

General Hertzog argued that 'Natives are like baboons ... they do not leave a mealie standing', hence the objection to the removal of these draconian prohibitions. But the memories of some of us are not so short; we can recall why and how in 1913 the Natives' Land Act was forced upon the government by the backveld.

In the early days of Union some of the Natives ploughed and garnered from a thousand to three thousand bags of wheat; while their neighbours of another race and colour could only reap from 200 to 500 muid; and this 'scandal' the government was urged to stop by prohibiting Natives from farming in their own right.

But rational people would be inclined to say that if this be the character of baboons it were better to let baboons go to work and flood the Free State with food than have a lot of able-bodied poor whites knocking at the treasury gates as they are now doing, begging the government to feed their hungry children for them.

Dr Visser's views

I was present at Cape Town when another bill was before the House. Suddenly, Dr Visser, a Johannesburg Nationalist, rose and gave expression to some irrelevant and extraordinary views. He told a surprised assembly that the Natives enjoyed all (!) the advantages of good government and civilized life and paid only 3s. per annum towards its maintenance as against the tax of £16 (?) per white man; and he added, it was time the government stopped pampering the Natives.

I wrote to the *Argus* some facts and figures showing how the Natives were overtaxed and that they received precious little for their imposts. I sent a copy of this communication to the Johannesburg evening paper and the *Star* supplemented them with a leaderette in the following terms:

> It will come as a surprise to most people to learn that out of an adult white population of 140,000, nearly 8,000 persons claim to be unable to pay the poll tax of 30s. per year on the ground of indigency, and that out of this number 1,420 resided in the district of Pretoria ... It would be interesting to know how it is that in Pretoria over 1,400 Europeans could claim to be earning insufficient to pay 30s., and, in the American phrase, 'get away with it'.[12]

Transvaal poll tax

The Native adult male population of the Transvaal provides a poll tax revenue of approximately £400,000, exclusively of pass fees. When we consider the number of Natives who, after travelling long distances and paying train fares, are unable to obtain work in the towns, and the amount of wages paid on farms, it will be admitted that the £2 constitutes an appreciable proportion of their earnings.

If the plea of indigency or inability to pay were as successful in their case as in that of the 7,716 Europeans who are exempted from paying 10s., we fear that the government would derive considerably less revenue from this source than is the case. Moreover, the slightest infringement of the pass laws results in their being fined £1 or estreating bail to that amount; and yet Dr Visser thinks they are 'pampered'! We wonder how he or any other European would enjoy the process of being pampered in this way?

Needless to say, the *Star* is not a Nationalist organ; but it might have mentioned the tragedy that while the offspring of these heavy taxpayers have not a single government school to save them from the thraldom of ignorance, the children of the white tax-dodgers of the Transvaal can matriculate for nothing.

Coloured franchise

I have often heard General Hertzog speak; but frequently my limited intelligence finds it very difficult to follow his arguments. It would appear that this weakness is not peculiar to me alone, for an abler mind than mine, about whose political experience and educational experience there can be no doubt, recently passed the following judgement on the leader of his majesty's opposition: 'General Hertzog is in the position that whenever, wherever and however he speaks and is reported there is always some misunderstanding, and he is always misreported.'

Yet there are times when General Hertzog can be quite explicit and to the point. During the discussion of the Women's Franchise Bill[13] the general, with more relevancy than discretion, asserted that the old Cape government made a great mistake in ever granting the franchise to the coloured races of the colony. And truly if any Natives and coloured people vote for his followers after this statement, I will be the first to admit that, from the point of view of our best interest, it was a mistake to give us the franchise.

'Natives a menace'

Quite recently the general told a coloured gathering at Stellenbosch that the Natives were a menace to the coloured people and to the Europeans. How then could the coloureds have come into being supposing that there were no

Natives? Europeans are no relations of ours, but only the ingrates among them would deny that we are a golden asset to the economic life of this country.

Most people are aware that gold mining forms the backbone of this Union, and that there are mines in other parts of the world which cannot be worked except at a loss. Here, however, thanks to cheap Native labour, even low-graded mines can be worked and can circulate millions of pounds, without which this country would be very poor. Moreover, the opulence of some of our highly placed white farmers is based on the loyal docility of the sweated Native shepherds – the virtual wool-growers in the rural districts. Even in urban centres we support them. The work of the 200,000 Native miners on the Rand has enhanced the value of the large territories owned by prominent Nationalists; and anyone who contends that we are a menace to them is a romancer of the superlative degree.

Mr Tielman Roos

Mr Tielman Roos,[14] the arch-Nationalist in the Transvaal, alleges that he wants the segregation of the Natives and amalgamation of the white and coloured people. But sensible coloured men should understand that all that Mr Roos wants to amalgamate are the 40,000 coloured votes of the Cape, and after the election it will again be a mistake that the Cape ever enfranchised them. Let them only compare the wages paid to coloured men by Nationalist employers with those paid to others.

Lately General Hertzog informed a coloured audience that because of the existence of the Native vote, it was not possible to give the coloured people the education they were entitled to. There can be no misreporting here as my information is from the *Burger*, thus: 'Spreker sal nie sê dat die kleuring-onderwys is soos dit moet wees. Dit kan alleen hersteld word as die stemreg vir die naturel gesluit word.'*

With all due deference to his extensive knowledge of South African affairs and people, it must be allowed that I know the coloured people better than General Hertzog does. And I know that on the whole, no coloured community in South Africa is better educated than that of Kimberley, and I feel certain the secretary of the Kimberley school board would assure him that he never found it essential to disfranchise a single Native as a condition precedent to raising coloured people to their present stage of educational development.

---

* Afrikaans: 'The speaker should not say that the conditions of Coloured teaching are all that they could be. They can be improved, but only if the Native vote is terminated.'

Again, the Natives have no votes in the O.F.S., the mecca of nationalism, yet that province has the most unlettered coloured communities to be found anywhere in South Africa, if not in the world; and if the O.F.S. can boast a few educated coloured men, they all acquired it at the Cape where Natives have votes. So that the general's arguments are not borne out by facts. Neither General Hertzog nor Mr Advocate Roos has Native voters in his constituency. Why then are they not educating them there?

Can Nationalist leaders fondly hope that the coloured people are such fools as to be so easily gulled by fair promises of equal privileges with Europeans and ostracism of the Natives? In the backveld I have always heard them referred to by Nationalists at home as 'skepsels'.* The rude incivility to coloured passengers on the part of railway officials in country districts is in glaring contrast with the courtesy of their colleagues in other places. Unfortunately for the Nationalists those 'skepsels' are aspiring to higher things, and many are able to think for themselves.

Flowery promises

Coloured voters should sometimes read the Nationalist papers and understand the value of their flowery promises which are invented solely for the ballot box and not for the benefit of any non-European, no matter the percentage of white blood in his veins. Country visitors to the cities often write angry letters to the *Burger* and *Ons Vaderland* declaiming against the urban scandal of employing coloured messengers in municipal and government offices while many poor whites would gladly take their places, wear their smart uniform and draw their pay. That's the reason why Smuts must go.

The late General C.R. de Wet, in his lifetime high mogul of the Nationalist Party, gave as a reason for leading a rebellion against the crown, that the magistrate of Heilbron had fined him 5s. for flogging a Native. If the Nationalists are to attain power in the next election, let them get it by the votes of Europeans, but let no coloured person be responsible for the orgy of tyranny that is to follow their ascendancy.

77

Letter to R.R. Moton, 22 September 1924[15]

Plaatje had met Dr R.R.Moton, Principal of the Tuskegee Institute, Alabama, in May 1922 during his visit to the United States. The two men had formed a good

---

* Afrikaans: 'creatures' (derogatory).

Robert Russa Moton, Principal of the Tuskegee Institute, Alabama, whom Plaatje first met when he visited Tuskegee in May 1922: his portrait later adorned Plaatje's study at 32 Angel St., his home in Kimberley.

rapport, and were to correspond intermittently over the next nine years. Moton had given Plaatje some film footage of Tuskegee, which Plaatje showed once he was back home in South Africa.

Box 143
Kimberley
22nd Sept. '24

Dear Dr Moton,

I wish to congratulate you most heartily on winning the great hospital fight.[16] It was a great victory nobly won. I suffered two very great misfortunes lately. Dr Aggrey[17] passed through very wide off my area and I did not see him. Dr Jesse Jones[18] likewise. I heard of him at Bloemfontein then I hurried from Basutoland as fast as the train could carry me only to reach Bloemfontein two hours after he had gone south to Lovedale, en route for Cape Town, England and America. It was a bitter blow as I wished to enlist their material sympathy in the publication of our Native Fellowship hymnal still in the press through lack of a few hundred pounds.[19]

Their previous visit has done an immense amount of good to the Natives of Johannesburg. They have created in the universities there opinions of moral and social benefit to the Native, which in turn has generated a volume of material sympathy among certain merchants and mining kings. The Rev. Dr Bridgman[20] and his assistant Rev. Ray E. Phillips of the American Mission Board are the centre pillars of Johannesburg's social activities for Native welfare; they have created an incredible amount of active feeling for the Cause in that hostile centre. But Johannesburg is only a speck in British South Africa. Away from the beaten track and far from the reach of enlightened sentiment in these terrible times of drought, locusts and dwindling wages, the lot of the South African Native is not enviable.

Since 1883, statisticians claim, South Africa never knew a drought like the one we have endured during the past ten years. Sometimes you have to call on a poor family in order to offer some Christian sympathy only to hear such a tale of woe as would force you to part with your last half-a-crown even if your own family depended on it.

To the whites, the government not only offer relief but they are pressing public bodies to fire their Native labourers. If they are displaced by white men the treasury grants from 3/- to 5/- per day per white man for poor relief in order

COMMUNITY HALL, Bloemfontein

Friday, Saturday and Monday,
September 26th, 27th and 29th.

ROLL UP AND SEE
The Coloured American Bioscope

DIRECT FROM CHICAGO LLL., U.S.A.

First-Class Animated Pictures of England,
Japan, Coloured People in Brazil, America and
the West India Islands.

PRINCIPAL FEATURE.

Booker Washington's School, TUSKEGEE and her thousands of young
men and women students at Drill and Manœuvres.

The Immigration Department will not permit any Foreign Negroes not-even the Jubilee Singers—
beloved of our fathers—to land in the Union. You can only see Coloured Americans on the screen.

Don't Fail to see our FRESH FEATURES!

H.R.H. The Duke of York's Wedding at Westminster Abbey, King
George's First Daughter-in-Law; The Late Chief Khama and his
Bamangoato People at Serowe; Cricket and other Sports.

COME AND HEAR OUR RAG-TIME AND OTHER SONGS.

ADMISSION 1/-.   RESERVED SEATS 1/6.

Popular Children's Show, 5.30 p.m. Saturday and Monday,
Doors: Tickey per Child (3d.)

ORGANIZERS:
    Wasihoek, Mr. P. PAHLANE,
      (Sergeant at Arms).
CAPE STANDS:
    Mr. J. J. PETERSON.
BANTU LOCATION:
    Mr. MAKGOTHI.
BANDMASTER:
    J. G. NTLATSENG,

SOLOIST:
    Mr. F. Y. ST. L. PLAATJE.
PIANIST:
    Mr. CRAWFORD THOKA.
OPERATOR:
    Mr. GREYLING.
LECTURER:
    SOL T. PLAATJE.

*Leaflet advertising Plaatje's 'Coloured American Bioscope', September 1924. Plaatje described this
as 'a labour of love' in a letter to Robert Moton, Principle of the Tuskagee Institute, Alabama.*

that the latter should get 7/- or 8/- per day where his black predecessor (now thrown on the streets) got 2/- or 3/-.

I have been round a good deal with my films. With the poverty of the Native it is a profitless job; but when I see the joy, especially of the Native kiddies, at sight of the thrilling drills of Tuskegee and my explanatory remarks enabling them to enjoy that which I have witnessed and they cannot, it turns the whole thing into a labour of love. On three occasions I received a command from white folks to lecture and show them Tuskegee. Their fees, £10 in one instance, wiped off whatever losses I had had with the Natives. Unfortunately such white engagements are as scarce as diamonds; but believe me, Dr Moton, the moral effect of the Tuskegee films on white and black alike is incalculable.

At the risk of seeming importunate may I remind you of a promise to secure for us some such films from Hampton likewise showing the work of your Alma Mater? It would be a good thing to have Hampton before the novelty of my present programme wears off; and if you can add something showing advanced Negroes, like your recent Business League at Chicago, so much the better. I don't think that anything could be more inspiring. In any case please mail us the Hampton features, if available.

Every department of our work is tottering – thanks to the acute economic depression – except the children's day school, that is flourishing for, thank God, the Kimberley School Board pays the teachers. It is the only school board in South Africa which pays any attention to Natives.

The Natives had a shock of disappointment. I had had information that General Smuts made arrangements for your tour all over the South African railways. When I made enquiries recently I learnt that the new government began office by cancelling that arrangement.

Now, it is a pity that I am not aware of your arrangements and intentions; but I feel certain my Boer friends in the ministry could, on my representation, get General Hertzog to reconsider and rescind his own ban. Just as General Botha did on my representations in 1917 when he intervened after the immigration department had denied Rev. H. Payne and Mrs Payne a landing certificate.[21] I received the thanks of the Union Castle Company who had been commanded to carry them back to America.

The Boers are very mean in some things, for instance one of them may be as good as gold and a millionaire but yet never part with a shilling to a Native cause but he is very obliging with his accommodations to certain Natives if it costs him no money.

There are places so hostile to the English and their Imperial rule that even General Smuts as Prime Minister never visited them for fear of being hissed off the platform for his loyalty to England; but I always manage to get by, taking good care however to hold my hat in my hand all the time, even when, to the bewilderment of local custom, I am invited in by the front door. Our Boer 'crackers' are worse than southerners. Only yesterday – a son of a Boer senator and cousin of a crown minister (member of Gen. Hertzog's ministry), brother of a judge of the appellate division of the Supreme Court of South Africa, said to me: 'Man your politics are putrid: too full of Smuts. But we like you as you are the only kaffir who writes our language as beautifully as the other cheeky kaffirs write English.' The forgotten point, of course, is that when English missionaries were pushing their language into the bucolic mind of unlettered Natives, the Boer church was too bigoted to teach the cursed descendants of Ham.

I do sincerely trust that you are all right and that the great work at Tuskegee is still moving with the regularity of the Royal Mail.

My kindest regards to you and friends on the faculty.

Best regards from my family who had hoped to see you soon.

Yours very respectfully,

Sol. T. Plaatje

78

'The Treatment of Natives in Courts', address to the 1924 Joint Councils Conference, Pretoria[22]

Organised under the auspices of the Joint Councils, this conference took place shortly after the official Native Conference (set up under the provisions of the Native Affairs Act of 1920) in order 'to discuss the native question in all its bearings'. Plaatje's was the last paper read, and followed presentations by, amongst others, the Reverend Ray Phillips on sports facilities for Africans, Richard Selope Thema on the Joint Councils, Isaiah Bud-M'belle on the municipal representation of Africans, Advocate W.H. Ramsbottom on the administration of justice for Africans.

Mr Chairman:

The treatment of Natives in the courts of justice is a much simpler matter than, for instance, the rural land question dealt with last night. The courts are held mainly in the enlightened centres where magisterial vagaries frequently receive a speedy publicity, so that the Joint Council and other welfare associations are enabled to take such cases up. The wave of indignation over the recent cases in the Eastern Transvaal Circuit Courts is an instance.

I was in Pretoria on Monday, and heard the Minister of Justice address the official Native Conference. I also observed the manner in which Mr Tielman Roos impressed the Native delegates. I should like to point out that the minister came to the conference straight from an interview with a deputation from the Joint Council of Johannesburg, and if the minister appeared a different man to the delegates in the conference, it should be borne in mind that 'the first assegai that tamed the buffalo' was cast by Mr Advocate Ramsbottam and Mr Selope Thema on behalf of the Joint Council. They must have left him convinced that there were wider issues in the administration of justice than were dreamt of in the philosophy of Meintjes Kop.

But, Sir, there are remote places where things take place and injustices occur without ever reaching the light of publicity. My travels in the rural areas in connection with the evictions under the Land Act brought me face to face with cases that seemed hopelessly incredible even in this land of discriminations. There were cases such as one which occurred last month, in which the allegations were even more serious than the Standerton and Heidelberg cases in the same circuit. It seemed such a clear case for the hangman that, had the accused been convicted, a reprieve would have been out of the question. The jury, however, saved the accused by pronouncing him 'not guilty'. This, Sir, reminded me of a juryman in another town who had just returned from court. He entered a store and, on being asked about the result of a case on which he served, the juryman said, 'Oh, he raped the woman right enough but it would have been a shame to send him to prison for that!' 'Shake hands,' gloated the storekeeper, 'come and have a drink.' I was told that both the storekeeper and the juryman took communion.

There are other cases, especially in the outside districts, where clash of colour comes into prominence and when, having regard to previous experience in the courts, the parties consider it useless to set the law in motion. In the Klerksdorp district, for instance, I met a man conveying his son to the doctor and he would not tell how the son came by his wounds. I discovered later that the son had been severely punished (I wonder whether 'punishment' is a correct description, seeing that his face was badly mauled), by his master. The parents decided to screen the offender for fear of being turned off his property, in which case they had nowhere to go under the Natives' Land Act.

There is the case of little Annie Bekeur in the Heilbron district who was lifted bodily and drowned in a dam because she did not bring the ducks home quickly enough. The police seemed reluctant to take action, and because of personal experience in two other cases about that time, I also thought it useless to start criminal proceedings against the accused.

The conference, therefore, would have to consider what is to be done, firstly, in cases where it is inexpedient to take action and where the jury deliberately say a guilty white man is 'not guilty'. In the first set of instances, I should request the conference to evolve a plan of redress; but in the latter cases, my remedy would be abolition. I do not stand for the entire abolition of the jury system, but the act of 1917 should be so amended as to provide that (except where both parties prefer a jury) all indicted cases of violence between white and black should be tried by a court of judges, or by judges and assessors.

A prisoner in such cases may dispense with the jury and claim a fairer further trial. So why should a law-abiding Native with a just grievance against a white man, be forced to appear before a jury of his opponent's friends? It is a travesty of the jury system for white men are not his peers, and white juries in the rural districts may have a grudge against him because he owns too many cattle or reaps too much wheat. If a white man wants justice against a Native, why should he be afraid of the judge?

Definite steps must be taken to abolish a system which, I believe, obtains in this and an adjoining province, under which Natives are sometimes imprisoned without any trial. I have sometimes had to telephone Pretoria to secure the release of persons kept in prison for three or five days without any charge. I hope the Joint Council will pay attention to a disgrace which does not even obtain in the Orange Free State, bad as things are there.

As a boy I was tremendously fascinated by the work of the Supreme Court. Later, I became interested in the courts as an official in the Department of Justice, and there I developed a keen appreciation of the important role played by the court interpreter in Native cases. And when my public work expanded, I took a still wider interest; and one can appreciate my alarm when Union came into being and the new government began to segregate the races by dismissing the Native interpreters and engaging not white interpreters, but simply white men to interpret for Natives. There were no welfare Associations then; we had here, instead of a Joint Council, what was known as the 'University of Crime', and anyone interested in this kind of work had to finance it out of his own pocket like a hobby of his own. And you can appreciate my struggles at the time, and efforts to put things right.

The extent to which our judges are responsible for the marvellous loyalty of the Natives is not so generally known. Changes have taken place, and confidences have been transferred: but, for generations past, the judges of the Supreme Court – with one notorious and melancholy exception – have held the scales of justice as between man and man, as evenly as they are held at the Old Bailey. Anyone who does anything to bring about a change or affect the impartiality of the Supreme Court in any way is no friend of this country.

Sir, I remember a sentence delivered by Mr Justice (now Sir William) Solomon upon five white men charged with killing two Natives. Passing the death sentence, his lordship said: 'Perhaps when you were chasing these unfortunate Natives and shooting them down like springbok, you were not aware that you were committing as serious an offence as if you were shooting white men. But I would like you and other men who hold views like yours on this subject, to understand that the law makes no distinction between a man with a white skin and one with a black skin. The Natives you shot were just as much entitled to the protection of the law as yourselves.' Two of the prisoners were hanged, and three sentences were commuted to various terms of imprisonment.[23]

The late Lord de Villiers once, referring to the case of Chief Sigcau of Pondoland, said: 'When I ordered the release of the chief, imprisoned on the orders of the Prime Minister, it was stated that I had lowered the dignity of the white government in the eyes of the Native population. But I find the Natives more favourably impressed with the idea that they have the right of appeal against the actions of the white government.'[24]

Many here will remember that Lord de Villiers was the same judge who once had before him a sentence by the Aliwal magistrate, a woman charged with beating the chief constable. In quashing the sentence his lordship said: 'A Native woman in her hut should be just as secure as an Englishwoman in her castle', but today we are told by people who are qualified to speak that there should be no similarity of treatment between white and black in the courts of this country.

With all due deference to the high positions occupied by the present Minister of Justice and Professor Pittman,[25] they must pardon us for reminding them that their experience of South African law and practice is not superior to those of the present Prime Minister, who was at one time a judge in our courts, and Mr Advocate Henry Burton, the late Minister of Finance.

I once visited a town where there had been insistent complaints against the work of the circuit court interpreter. The court was sitting at the time and I attended in order to verify the facts. I took notes of a very short case, that is, what the judge said and what the interpreter said. Two different things indeed;

also the prisoner's answers and the interpreter's version: two different things again. On that faulty interpretation a man had got 12 months' hard labour. General Hertzog was Minister of Justice then and Mr Burton that of Native Affairs. When my letter reached Pretoria, General Hertzog promptly recommended the man's release, after he had served only one month of his sentence.

Again, I visited another town where some Natives complained against an assistant magistrate. They alleged that in his court a Native litigant stood no chance whatever of success in an action against a white man. Again I went to take notes, this time of two typical cases, secured a copy of the magistrate's own records, and forwarded them to Pretoria with a covering letter. Again General Hertzog, in his capacity as Minister of Justice, ordered an inquiry at the instance of Mr Burton. That assistant magistrate, to his credit, frankly admitted that it was quite possible for a magistrate to be influenced by the eloquence of clever attorneys with the result that innocent Natives suffered, if they are not legally represented.

Further, that magistrate promised to be more careful in the future, and so he was.

And, Sir, if the present minister is right and it is unlawful for the Minister of Justice to intervene when the courts go wrong, though grave miscarriage of justice take place, how did General Hertzog manage these things?

In 1919 a gang of Natives were sent to prison by a Johannesburg magistrate for going on strike. I drafted a petition to the Governor-General which was forwarded by the secretary of the Native Congress; white people also sent resolutions from Cape Town and other towns with the result that the Hon. N.J. De Wet promptly ordered the releases of the whole lot.[26]

I am glad to see so many Cape people present for in my tour in the old colony I have frequently found things that would not be tolerated in Bloemfontein or Johannesburg. The Cape should give us a lead in these matters because civilization came to us from there. Yet I have found in one old border town that Natives were not allowed to sit and listen to cases; at another place they could only squat but not sit on the empty benches which were reserved for Europeans. I also saw prisoners used as trek oxen (some of them imprisoned on insignificant peccadilloes); they were dragging wagons while donkeys were selling in the same town at one shilling a head.

We in the Cape and in Natal, Basutoland and elsewhere, who send out people here to work are indebted to the welfare associations and especially this Joint Council for the practical steps they always take in these matters. I wish that our folks in the rural areas and backveld dorps had similar bodies to safeguard their liberties as it is done in this city of strangers. I quite agree with what Dr Rubusana said this morning about interpreters. Their work deserves our attention as it is almost as important as that of location superintendents. One episode will illustrate what little interest our people take in Native life.

At the official Native Conference at Pretoria I met a group of men from a small northern village. I inquired after a friend of theirs and they were astonished to learn for the first time from me that he carried ineffaceable marks of slavery in the shape of his old master's initials, branded on his chest; yet they had lived with him for years in the same village.

Most white men are interested in us because they are after our goods. Other white men are interested in us because they want to save us from exploitation, but the best protection would be to stimulate the Native's own interest in Native life. Mr Mtimkulu[27] will remember that early this year I attended a meeting of the Cape Peninsula Native Welfare Association where they read an assurance from the government that the Native Urban Act is not being enforced. I was the only Native in the gathering who knew that and was worrying because, on that day 40 Natives were fined in a suburban police court and 12 more in the city magistrate's court and ordered to go and live in the location. The following week some of them were back again in court charged with overcrowding the location. Delicately and single-handed I pulled some strings and brought the chief magistrate and the town clerk together on their behalf. We shall never get better treatment in the courts or outside if we show so little concern in the misery of our fellow men.

Yet another instance, to illustrate Native indifference to Native needs. At the Pretoria conference I heard it officially stated that Natives pay about 2/- or 3/- per year indirect tax. I waited in vain for the Native view for, without taxing my brains, I could remember that the rawest Native I met this year was a Kalahari. He was engaged in buying, among a few other dutiable goods, one blanket on which customs duty was about 3/1d. At the other extreme, I remember meeting in Cape Town this year a Native who held a customs receipt for £26. This was in February. I did not see him again until this month (October) when in one week he had paid over £9 entertainment tax.

Now, the £26 was paid to the Union government and the £9 to the provincial authorities. Both sums are credited to white taxpayers in the government blue books. Native delegates in this Union are not interested in Kalaharis and so knew of no two extremes between which to strike an average in the vernacular; because they approached the subject, not through the

General Jan Christian Smuts, Prime Minister of South Africa 1919-1924, leader of the South African Party in opposition in the 1920s and early 1930s: Plaatje complimented him in 1925 'on the signal success as leader of His Majesty's opposition in Parliament and in the country'.

slender purse of the Native laundress who bears the brunt of the support of family life, but through the white men's spectacles as reflected in the government blue books.

I still remember the last days in this world of my little daughter. The post brought her a parcel which could have been of no earthly use to her; but she was not allowed to die until she had paid her last duty of 17/- on that parcel. That sum, like my own and her mother's taxes, was duly credited to white taxpayers. And if Natives leave white people to fight our battle for equal treatment and equal recognition inside or outside the courts I am afraid we shall continue to pay taxes and the treasury will keep on mailing the receipts to white people.

Finally, Sir, I wish to pay tribute to the judges of the Supreme Court and most Union magistrates for their fairness. Some of them have become unpopular among their people because they refuse to administer the law at the expense of Native rights. I have paid them similar tribute both here and abroad and I wish to repeat it, this morning, before you, Mr Chairman.

79

Letter to General J.C. Smuts, 19 January 1925[28]

General Smuts remained leader of the South African Party in opposition following its defeat by the Nationalist – Labour Pact in the general election of 1924. Plaatje had met Smuts in April 1924, shortly before his general election defeat, and it seems likely that the question of financial support for resuscitating his newspaper, referred to by Plaatje in this letter, was first raised on that occasion.

P.O. Box 143,
Kimberley,
19th Jan. 1925

General the Rt. Hon. J.C. Smuts, K.C., M.L.A.,
Irene,
Pretoria

Dear Sir,

I wish to write in the name of the Native people and compliment you on the signal success as leader of His Majesty's opposition both in Parliament and in the country. My personal duties and the troubles of the Natives gave me no chance to write earlier. I visited the Government Conference at Pretoria last year and was disappointed not to find either you or Mr Pilkington,[29] an old friend. It is disappointing that the government should gazette a number of revolutionary changes which were never mentioned at Pretoria last October.[30]

I am sorry to say that I have not been able to make any headway with the mining advertising requisite for the resuscitation of my paper. The Chamber of Mines seems willing; but such matters are controlled by their Native Affairs Department – the great Native Recruiting Corporation – and they are not disposed to advertise; but I think they only require some one to determine and express the advertising value and possible party gains. Sir E. Oppenheimer is sympathetic but advised me to wait till the beginning of the year when he will occupy a higher position in the Chamber.

It is a pity that a matter like this should be delayed while they have the money and need the labourers. Government agents are not losing any time informing the Natives of the visionary virtues of the Pact; while they broadcast the idea that the Natives owe their difficulties to the fact that in the last election they backed the wrong horse. Their uncontradicted statements are giving the Pact a good start. And our people are disappointed that the South African Party agents are not doing anything to counteract their propaganda among Natives, which should be reached regularly by a newspaper in the vernacular.

Some of them read in the American papers the perfect party organizations in the United States which leave no stone unturned regardless of the colour of the voters and it would have a bad effect if the matter is much longer delayed.

You should be doing a party stroke and incidentally benefiting the Natives if you took an early opportunity to remind Sir Ernest Oppenheimer to push the matter and strengthen his hands with any of the mining kings who have the authority to issue the word that would give us the annual financial vote.

The failure of the party to find seats for their tried and true friends, Advocate H. Burton, K.C., and Mr Malan,[31] is not very sweet on Native palates.

Again congratulating you on your leadership which, we trust, will bear fruit early, wishing you, on behalf of the Natives, greater success in the New Year.

I am, dear General,

Yours very respectfully

Sol Plaatje

Plaatje received a reply, dated 28 January 1925, from Smuts's private secretary, thanking him for 'the good wishes you express from yourself and the Native people', and indicating that the General 'will talk to Sir E. Oppenheimer about the matter you mention'. Whether he did so is unknown, and Plaatje ultimately failed in his attempts to resuscitate his paper.

80

Article, 'The Colour Bar', *Diamond Fields Advertiser*, 10 March 1925

'There is only one thing about which the pact is agreed,' said Sir David Harris during the last election, 'and that's the colour bar.' The Mines and Works Amendment Bill now before the house strikes at the very root of South African national existence. It is true that there was an intention on the part of the employers to use Natives as journeymen in this country; but in the absence of a legal bar some smart Natives have managed to acquire recognition even if they only received semi-skilled pay for highly skilled labour. Native labour has constructed our network of railways and created our deep level mines, and farmers unconsciously confessed in Parliament last week that farming is impossible without their kaffirs. They are still losing lives in the bowels of the earth in order that the Witwatersrand should yield nearly a million pounds' worth of fresh gold every week. I met an Australian engineer on board ship some years back who told me that until he saw the Zulus at work round Durban docks he 'never believed it possible for human beings to perform such heavy work', and similar praises were won by the Labour Contingent in France during the war.

And while the government is lavishly handing out state funds to boost, and pay premiums on, white manual labour, a most interesting sidelight comes from Johannesburg where, since October last, Europeans have displaced Natives as pointsmen at tram-crossings. The head of the tramway department reports that white men are bad time-keepers; that 'there were seven serious accidents in the few months that the white men were in charge of the points as against only one accident during all the previous years when Natives handled the points.' And for the safety of the travelling public he recommends that 'the white pointsmen be returned to relief gangs and that the Natives be put back on point work'.

The bill before the house proposes to exclude coloured men from the operation of the colour bar and make it applicable only to Natives and

Asiatics; but I am afraid skilled Natives will still find employment at unskilled pay on the mines, while an inexperienced European is appointed to supervise and learn the mining trade from them.

Mr Merriman once informed Parliament how he saw a European painting an electric standard. He was accompanied by an 'unskilled' Native who carried his bag. After painting the lower part of the post the painter and his Native 'hand' repaired to the next post. There he stood aside while the Native climbed the pole and cleverly painted the pole-top and other dangerous parts near the wires; and when the Native had painted more than half-way down the pole he stepped aside and allowed the 'baas' to paint the lower part of it. Should the bill become law, with the coloured man excluded from its operation, a Native will still scale and paint the top of the pole at unskilled pay while the white man smokes his pipe below. Then he will hand the brushes, not to a coloured man, but to the white smoker who incidentally draws the skilled pay. Ministers admit the dismissal of thousands of Natives, under orders from the Ministry of Labour, and their displacement by Europeans. Not an instance is reported of the appointment of a coloured man to a post previously held by Natives. The question is, if the principle of this bill is sound, why are the farms left out, seeing that machinery already plays an important role in farming operations?

Europeans who expect to benefit by thus robbing Peter to pay Paul are hoping to starve the Native out of existence, and so accomplish the establishment of a 'white South Africa'. Such a policy never answered anywhere, and here it only serves to belittle the European in Native eyes. They see in him an ingrate, for only an ingrate can possibly forget services so loyally rendered.

I have never heard of a Native war in which the ubiquitous Native did not participate on the white man's side. In the Native calendar, my birthdate is remembered by Sekukuni's war, the Bapedi of Chief Sekukuni having at that time driven the Boers down the mountainside and scattered them in every direction. In death and danger there is no colour bar, so the Transvaal government armed the Swazi hordes from the east and turned them loose on Sekukuni. Even the famous Dingaan was not crushed without the aid of Natives and Hottentots.

Today, however, there has arisen a number of new Pharaohs who know not Joseph, and the Bapedi and Swazi together must bow to a colour bar. What is true of the Transvaal is equally true in regard to the Free State, where the Barolong are today debarred from occupying land equally with the Basuto, against whom they fought to annex Basuto granaries and cattle stations in order to extend the Orange Free State frontier and reduce Basutoland to its present diminutive size.

In the beginning the popular cry was 'tax the Native and thus force him to come to work'; the next slogan was 'we should increase his wants and teach him the dignity of labour'. Now the Ministry of Labour only wants to teach him the indignities thereof; for when he wants work to satisfy his increased wants he is told that work is the monopoly of another race, and a colour bar should be used 'to force him back to his native environments'. But when he flees from the colour bar to those 'environments' he finds himself between horns of the same dilemma – the Natives' Land Act, which prohibits his stay there. In fact when a Native shuns Scylla he falls into Charybdis and hardly knows where he is.

The colour bar bill has one redeeming feature. The second reading speeches delivered by General Smuts and some opposition members and Mr Alexander[32] have shown that there is in South Africa a growing number of Europeans determined to do well by the Natives.

I still remember finding in the Congressional Library at Washington a collection of the world's greatest speeches with a sample of the gem-oratory of each. Right Hon. J.X. Merriman was among the number, and the speech selected to portray his style was his contribution to the debate on the Natives' Land Act of 1913. I think General Smuts' effort in similar vein last week, when the above bill was before the house, will rank equally with Mr Merriman's and with the great deliveries of the late Saul Solomon on cognate subjects in the early eighties. My correspondence shows that General Smuts' magnificent broadside has sent a thrill of satisfaction through the hearts of the Native people even beyond the Union boundaries where it is felt that the Union government cannot very well alienate the affections of the Native millions and expect to 'get away with it'.

It is an ill wind that blows nobody any good, and whatever the fate of this bill, we should thank Mr Beyers[33] for introducing it and thus drawing out the excellent sentiments expressed in Parliament last week; and should Parliament persuade the government to stay its hand, all loyalists should feel grateful. From an imperial point of view, it were a pity to enforce such a measure while the Prince of Wales is on his way to South Africa. And, if the bill be finally shelved, white people, for their own sakes (no less than through consideration for Native feeling) will have ample ground for satisfaction. Natives who have to endure the physical and mental agony of these perpetual legislative pin-pricks, and consequently were losing all confidence in the integrity of the white skin, will feel that the action of Europeans in high places is still animated by feelings of human justice.

Despite considerable protests both inside and outside Parliament, the Mines and Works Amendment Act (colloquially known by its opponents as the 'Colour Bar Act'), became law in 1926. Its central feature was to protect white workers by reserving for them the grant of certificates in competency in skilled trades.

81

Article, 'The leadership cult from another angle', Umteteli wa Bantu, 14 March 1925

I never really saw a copy of *Umteteli* until this paper was three years in circulation, and then only at long intervals. Launched while I was thousands of miles away, it is only since last year that I read it with anything approaching regularity.[34]

I have since followed with much interest a long series of well-written articles entitled 'Cult of race leadership' by an anonymous writer.[35] Much as one would dislike joining in a discussion with a 'cat in the bag' the articles are of absorbing interest and their continuation has almost given them the character of one of the gospels according to *Umteteli*.

Much is discussed concerning Native leadership but, unless this phase was touched upon before I knew the paper, I am afraid the trend of the present series of articles does not disclose the fact. Besides, it ignores one patent fact, that no man, whatever his qualifications, could possibly lead a community which is not disposed to follow him. Even Christ our Redeemer has found this hopelessly impossible.

My travels have revealed to me not only a measure of ability in different parts of the country but a distinct willingness on the part of some of our people to make every sacrifice on the altar of Native well-being. But the 'New Natives' of South Africa have evolved a distinct idea about the 'right' qualities of a leader, and no amount of oral or written preachments appear to affect their purpose. To the mind of the Native of today, the first and last qualities of the effective leader should be 'a well-dressed man with a lot of money'. If he did absolutely nothing for them they will elect him to any position he aspires to, and travel hundreds of miles at his bidding. I ought to know for I doubt if any other Native had the same opportunities of mixing with different tribes, in as many different localities, and studying their rural and urban lives, as extensively as I have had during the past quarter of a century.

At one extremity I have lived with Natives in the crowded slums around the shebeens of Cape Town and Port Elizabeth, and also among the wholesome if arid expanses of Bechuanaland, at the other extremity, with only the very distant horizons the limit of their outlook. I have spent months among the nude and congested Tembus in the rural districts of the Transkei, amid primitive conditions. I have sat at a sumptuous table in a Native home, described by the district surgeon as the finest in the whole district, and have spent a winter in the Kalahari.

The result of my varied observations and experiences north and south, east and west, could be summed up in these words: Natives recognized only one form of leadership – their hereditary chiefs – and no other. The multiplicity of the numerous clans and sub-tribes is due to the fact that a tribal chief was usually recognized only as long as he could enforce his authority. Failure in this respect very soon generated a hostile faction which in time broke away and settled elsewhere under a stronger petty chief who did not hesitate to proclaim his paramountcy. Now, with the passing of the age of hereditary chiefs and the advent of European authority and consequently disintegration of tribal rule, they will recognize only a well-to-do leader.

There are those who, never having tasted the bitter responsibilities frequently exacted from a national leader, are constantly scheming for prominence and power among their fellows, and they make frantic efforts to hinder the economic progress of likely rivals. They know that every contemporary who gets on in business or gets what looks like a sinecure from the municipal or the Union government is a potential barrier between themselves and what they imagine to be the joys of leadership. Hence they waste much energy and dissipate their strength in the unworthy task of preventing the social and economic advance of likely neighbours.

For instance, white people are worshipped by Natives because it is believed that most Europeans are millionaires. But let them discover that one white man is not rich then promptly he ceases to be an 'umlungu' he becomes at once a common 'igxagxa', or 'mampokoro'* whom it were a flagrant abuse of a borrowed word to call 'baas'. Outside the jurisdiction of hereditary chiefs only

---

* *Umlungu* (Nguni) means 'white man', while *igxagxa* (Xhosa) means 'a poor white', implying somebody who did not deserve respect; *mampokoro* is the Tswana equivalent of *igxagxa*.

a prosperous Native could do what he liked among his people. Such people having practically ceased to exist, detribalized Natives now have no recognized national leaders. They are groping about for one but cannot locate what they are after namely, a man of means. Other races usually relieve their leader of financial worries in order that his unfettered talents may be entirely at the disposal of the cause: our people, on the other hand, expect their leader not only to fend for himself and finance the cause but also to relieve them of their economic troubles: hence the attraction of the I.C.U.

I feel certain that if some of our lost leaders would consent to unfold the tale of their fall we would find that the decay of their fortunes synchronized with the loss of their former hold over their people; that since then, increased sacrifices on behalf of Natives only generated Native abuse and ingratitude where, formerly, a two-pence ha'penny sacrifice evoked a tremendous amount of enthusiasm.

So, if 'Resurgam' desires to see a successful Native leader in our midst he need only pick his man, endow him financially and watch the result.

82
Article, 'Descendants of the Koks', *Diamond Fields Advertiser*, 7 December 1926

According to a *Diamond Fields Advertiser* report, some Griquas are now taking possession of land acquired at a cost of £75,000 on the Fish River in the Cookhouse division. Some of these people for no apparent reason sold their farms in East Griqualand and migrated to the western province. They are descendants of an intrepid clan of warriors who may be said to have been the harbingers of civilization in the regions between the Orange and the Vaal rivers. They befriended the early missionaries, came to the rescue of the Bechuana in their disastrous encounters with the Matabele impis, supported early traders and European pioneers in their expeditions into the interior, and helped to move the flocks and herds of some of the voortrekkers from destruction by predatory wild beasts. In fact, some of them took part in nearly every war waged by Europeans against Native tribes. It is a standing complaint among educated Natives that in South African history books (except where Natives acted entirely under their own unaided initiative) tribal succour of Europeans is not even as much as mentioned, although tradition abounds with stories of battle after battle carried by Native legions in the cause of European colonization in South Africa.

The Griquas were not only fearless in war and the chase, but they were also immensely wealthy, many of them being great hunters and clever horse men. Most of the large Bechuana herds and flocks of our childhood days, we are told, were earned from Griqua cattle owners.

In 1862 the Griquas, under Chief Adam Kok who gave Kokstad its name, left Philippolis and migrated to East Griqualand, then known as Nomansland. They later acquired citizen rights in the old Cape Colony, became prosperous farmers, and their district now forms part of the Transkeian Territories. But early in the last decade, the Griquas were seized by one of those psychological aberrations which constituted a periodical visitation among aboriginal tribes. Beautiful farms were sold, many of them for a mere bagatelle, and the owners joined the trek out of East Griqualand. European advice and counsels of their saner men were incontinently spurned, and the tribesmen took their families west in the wake of Chief A. Le Fleur, who is credited by some with extraordinary prophetic and occult powers. In the past few years many erstwhile well-to-do Griqua families were to be found scattered over the western province from the Karoo to the Cape peninsula, combating privation and penury by resorting to 'street singing and passing round the hat'. It is difficult to conceive how these people can manage to raise £75,000, which the press report states is the purchase price of their new settlement.[36]

When the operation of the Natives' Land Act made itself felt in the Orange Free State, the Natives there likewise rejected every advice, and migrated north after an exiled Barolong chief,[37] who was said to have bargained with a concession company for a tract of land on the Rhodesian frontier. This was in 1916. The purchase price was said to be £88,000. When the agreement was signed and the first instalment paid over, the shares of the concession on the London stock market immediately soared from 5s. to £2. I am told that they never paid another instalment. Ten years have elapsed since their exodus from the Free State, and stories of fatal ravages by malaria among their ranks would form very gruesome reading.

Surviving members of their now attenuated families are scattered all the way north from Bulawayo as far us as Lake Tanganyika and the Belgian Congo. Those who returned to the Union are now threatening to sue the chief and his councillors for the recovery of the amounts contributed towards the initial payment. But the chief, unable to redeem his cash promises in terms of the agreement, is said to have lost the land and forfeited the instalments. Unlike the Tati forests, where the Barolong perished, the Fish River valley is one of the healthiest parts of this Union; but it is devoutly to be hoped that no such pecuniary disaster is in store for the new venture of the Griquas.

83

Letter to the Clerk of the House of Assembly, Cape Town, on the Native Administration Bill, 6 May 1927[38]

First gazetted in 1925, the Native Administration Bill was referred to a Select Committee to take evidence from interested parties and to refine its details. It was widely criticised by African political leaders for the arbitrary extension of the powers of the Governor-General over Africans, for its attempt to enforce a policy of 'retribalisation', and for the powers given to the government to act against people or organisations deemed to have acted in an inflammatory manner. It eventually became law as the Native Administration Act in 1927.

P.O. Box 143,
Kimberley,
6/5/27.

To the Clerk of the
House of Assembly.

Sir,

Native Affairs Administration Bill[39]

It is to be regretted in the name of the Native population of the Union that on referring the above bill to the Select Committee, the Prime Minister decided on calling only the officials of the Native Affairs Department (on whose recommendations its several provisions were drawn up) and no evidence from the Native people whose lot it will be to enjoy or endure the effects of its operation.

The Prime Minister has already shown some inclination to concede some points brought before his notice and that fact encourages me as a member of the last annual statutory conference at Pretoria, nominated thereto by unanimous decision of the rural Natives of Griqualand West on the invitation of the Prime Minister, and on behalf of the other tribal and detribalized Natives unofficially represented in various capacities by me, I beg to forward through you the following observations with the request that you will please do so kindly and lay them before the Select Committee.

The importance of this vital bill is that, unlike any other measure of its kind, it will, when enacted, effect some drastic changes in Native life not only politically but even socially. Its aim is to put all Natives under the same Native law. One could no more draw up a single code for all the tribes than fix the same speed limit for Adderley Street, Cape Town, and the highways of the Karoo; and one cannot but foresee trouble in any attempt to apply the same social code to the Bapedi (under whose tribal laws it is permissible for a Native to marry his first cousin) and the Tembus, under whose tribal laws it is an abomination, purged only by death, for a Native to marry a blood relation, however, distant.

The method favoured by the officials is to advise the Prime Minister to extend the Natal Native code and to make it the Native law of all the Natives of the Union. Now, it was always understood that the Natal code was based on the tribal law of the Zulus, but at the annual government conference members from other provinces learnt with surprise that this well-advertised code operates only in Natal, and not in Zululand. The Zulu representatives stated that it was the wish of their people that the code should be confined to Natal (where, they emphatically declared, it had done a lot of harm) and never be extended to Zululand where nobody wanted it.

In discussing the principles of the bill the members recalled the Prime Minister's repeated expressions of satisfaction at the conditions found in Transkei whence he returned just previously, and then regretted to find that conditions which so pleased the premier and satisfied Transkeian Natives were to be displaced by Natal conditions for which no Natives seem to care.

But to an observer it sounded rather anomalous that our government which not long before petitioned the King to stop creating any more South African barons and baronets should itself take power to create fresh tribes and fresh chiefs in the same country and invest them with new judicial and administrative powers.

HOLDING PUBLIC MEETINGS. Time and again divisions of the Supreme Court in Transvaal and elsewhere held that no charge could be laid against a Native, who calls a meeting of his fellows to discuss their mutual affairs.

And the government conference a year ago gave reasons showing the possible hardships if the holding of a meeting should be subject to the will of any chief or paramount chief. Some chiefs, it was urged, were against the education of their people. One of these may object to the opening of a school which the government would be willing to finance provided it is erected by the Natives. How is it to be obtained if the calling of the meeting against the wishes of the chief is to be made a criminal offence? And members urged that restriction and control of public meetings will only increase opportunities for secret meetings and so cause more trouble than it is thought to avoid.

I may mention that a similar attitude was adopted in connection with another subject which was down for control by Proclamation; and our people are glad to find the government has decided to drop that course. But it will put back the clock if public meetings which the Supreme Court has declared could not lawfully be restricted by regulation are now to be definitely controlled by Proclamation and placed in the power of local chiefs and government representatives. Finally, I should be guilty of a grave dereliction of duty if I failed to draw the attention of the Select Committee, and of Parliament through the Committee, to the dismay which overtook those Natives who saw or heard of some of the provisions of the schedule to this bill. Hitherto the Prime Minister showed commendable generosity in conceding to Native representation in connection with other provisions in the schedule; and it now remains for me to point out, on behalf of the Cape Natives, the serious light in which they regard the possible abolition of Act 39 of 1887, commonly known as the Hofmeyr Act – the Magna Charta of the Cape Natives.[40] Its abrogation will be a blow to the Natives who have enjoyed its protection for 40 years, for it is a mistake to suppose that it only helps 'registered voters'. At the government conference at which the bill was discussed this drastic change was not even mentioned.

Absolutely nothing can be said against this Act, except that it has created in the minds of Cape Natives an undying reverence for the memory of a much respected Cape patriot of Dutch descent, and Natives will feel that if anyone deserved punishment for disturbing the relations between white and black it is the person who suggests the repeal of such a useful measure which it is devoutly hoped the Prime Minister will see his way to leave intact, at least until the final settlement of his great scheme.

I am, sir,

Your obedient servant,

Sol. T. Plaatje

84

Article, 'Native doctors at hospitals: Problem for Provincial Council', *Cape Times*, 4 June 1927

According to a *Cape Times* interview,[41] his hon. the Cape administrator and the provincial council are about to settle an extremely knotty point. The question may take the form of an ordinance to prevent European nurses ministering to Native patients and provide for the training of Native nurses for the purpose.

This laudable object is likely to be permeated by a variety of intriguing cross-currents. Prominent among these will be the prohibition of European patients from consulting Native doctors, and the latter from carrying out operations in our hospitals. This highly important matter, however, was not mentioned in the administrator's speech at the opening of the council on Friday; but Natives have grown accustomed to having such disquieting race measures sprung upon the country by the Union Parliament without a preliminary notice in the speech from the throne.

It is true that our statute books contain laws that make progress illegal and Native industry a crime, but such hallmarks of the standard of backward nations are usually enacted by the Union Parliament with the combined responsibility of the entire cabinet and, as a rule, they do not emanate from this province. Again, men of average intelligence know that no self-respecting Native doctor would leave his surgery and go round touting for white patients, but the practice of Native doctors generally has a habit of spreading in unexpected directions.

Conditions in America

During my visit to the United States four years ago, studying race-relationships, I made it a point of investigating this aspect of it. I was not so keenly interested in the eastern, northern and western states (where all the people enjoy equal rights) as I was inquisitive about conditions in the south, where colour prejudice of a kind is sometimes rampant. I was particularly interested in the work of Native African doctors as distinct from the American Negro; and, to illustrate what follows, I may be permitted to relate the rise of one African Native doctor at Portsmouth, Virginia, because it is almost identical with that of Dr H. Gabashane (a Native of the Orange Free State, now practising in Mississippi), and not unlike the foundation of the practice of those Native doctors who have made good in this country.

Leaving a northern medical college, the young doctor went direct to the south, where the blacks preponderate. Knowing the racial spirit in the district, he had no idea of ever being consulted by Europeans. It happened, however, that his work in the Negro section was one morning interrupted by a telephone message from the aristocratic part of the town. Arriving there he was shown in through the back door by a lady whose 'help' (a coloured domestic servant) was ill; and she thought it proper to call in a black doctor in preference to the family physician. He prescribed some mixture with, in the opinion of the mistress, amazingly rapid results. It so happened that the lady had for years been afflicted by the same malady that had prostrated her 'help' but her relief was always of a temporary character. Envying the permanent riddance of her domestic, the lady at length decided to consult the Native (of course, without the knowledge and consent of her husband), with the same result.

Several months later, the seven-years-old daughter of the family took seriously ill. Notwithstanding the noble efforts of the family physician, the case so alarmed the mother that she explained to the father the means of her own recovery and persuaded him to try the black doctor. That case definitely established Dr France's reputation at Portsmouth. But one Native doctor at Mafeking is giving much trouble to certain Europeans by persistently curing sick white people, hence the proposed ordinance, and no one will envy the councillors the herculean job of drawing a line between black doctors and white patients.

A market colour barrier

I remember that at Johannesburg some years back the municipality enforced segregation between white and non-white patrons of the morning market. It may be surmised that the very best stalls were 'reserved for Europeans', so that loads of potatoes and other perishable produce were out of the reach of the Indian hawkers. The result proved both expensive and effective. One Boer farmer journeyed to the town to find out the cause of the hitch in the regularity of the market master's remittances. Ascertaining the reason, he loudly declaimed against colour barriers in general and municipal regulations in particular. Having declared his readiness to fight another Boer war for another three years if he could not sell his produce to the highest bidder, he ripped off the pailings and called the Indians to come over and buy. I believe they are still buying outside the colour line, for no prosecution followed, not even for malicious injury to municipal property.

It is still the law in the northern provinces (except in the city of Bloemfontein) that Natives may not use the side walk. I have no recollection of Natives ever organizing to resist it, and yet it is a dead letter because white people themselves prefer to honour it in the breach. It was at Benoni where a merchant saw a Native quietly comparing the prices of articles inside his shop window and a policeman came up and arrested the Native for violating the rule of the sidewalk. The Chamber of Commerce made the case their own, and so administered the first kick to the ban, leaving motor traffic to do the rest. The inexorable laws of nature, like commercial interest, show no respect for the tyrannies of the colour line. So, notwithstanding the law, the invincible motor gradually moved the Natives from the streets to the pavements because no respectable motorist has any ambition to make mincemeat of Native pedestrians.

Veritable scientists

Americans, who are veritable scientists in these matters, will go to any length with their colour distinctions, but they draw the line rigidly at the promotion of the public wealth and the maintenance of the public health. They have no trade restrictions against Negroes and, unlike us, they have no colour bar at their mineral springs, either north or south.

To a healthy man the policy of 'black doctors for Natives and white nurses for Europeans' is about as fantastically attractive as Marcus Garvey's slogan of 'Africa for the Africans and Europe for the Europeans', but it becomes biologically impossible in the face of stern realities, especially when a dear one is battling with death.

To the average Native, doctors are very much like other folks. They specialize in some things. They will swear by a local practitioner in cases of pneumonia, then travel 500 miles to consult a distant doctor known to them as a veritable wizard with neuritis; and yet again the medical profession is subject to psychic and biological rules that are unknown to other people's callings. In the southern states, for instance, where colour distinctions form part of the local creed, no European would dream of consulting a black solicitor, however able; yet they have no hesitation in attending the surgeries of black doctors and calling them in for consultation.

When I last visited Mafeking three months ago, I found many sick Natives besieging the surgeries of white doctors as eagerly as European patients crowded Dr Molema's;[42] and all the doctors seemed ready to treat them without any distinction of colour. This apparently meaningless right of choice is often dictated by dire necessity.

An outstanding experience

At the risk of seeming too precise I may be permitted to recall an outstanding personal experience. Thus, one of my penalties for constant attention to sufferers of the influenza epidemic was that I contracted an oppressive heart disease which was later pronounced incurable. For four years I tried in turn Native, coloured and eminent English doctors on both sides of the Atlantic without checking the progress of the attack. In the end a Canadian specialist, with characteristic North American bluntness, said to me: 'Your heart leaks so badly that we cannot help you. All we can do is prescribe something to ease the pain while matters take their course.' This seemingly brutal frankness was altogether superfluous, for I had already been convinced that the end was not far off. Three months later, however, when supposed to be at the last extremity, a German American took me in, and with permanent and really miraculous results. Consequently, I cannot be blamed for harbouring a grievous sense of injustice if, because of my race, I am debarred by a provincial ordinance from consulting a practitioner of German extraction. Or will the ordinance debar Europeans from consulting black doctors while permitting Natives to consult a white one or a black? The suggestion is impossible from the very nature of things.

How so? The indomitable white man (while claiming to exercise the right of wearing his hat in Parliament) feels insulted if a Native addresses him with his hat on. Is it seriously contended that he should watch a voteless kaffir choose his own doctor while every boss must seek medical aid within the four corners of an ordinance? Or are we to understand that a popular Native doctor, with unimpeachable bedside manners, should refuse to attend when called to see a dying European? Medical rules and questions of colour apart, the proposition opens up vistas in the region of inhumanity that are much better forgotten.

An unprecedented step

This unprecedented step is to be taken because a Native doctor in the northern outposts of the Union has got some white patients and that he operates on some of them in the Mafeking hospital. Because of this, the local hospital nurses last month went on strike, to the intense delight of Transvaal Nationalist members of Parliament, who telegraphed their congratulations to the nurses. But, unfortunately for the rest of us, no human effort has as yet succeeded to rid society of disease, and there are wider issues around the healing art than appear to be dreamt of in the philosophy of Transvaal Nationalists. The nurses have since been given two weeks to pay costs in connection with the action Dr Molema instituted against them and the hospital board for discriminating against his patients. Having regard to the limited income of nurses generally, it is devoutly to be hoped that Transvaal Nationalist members will see the importance of telegraphing a substantial contribution towards their defence fund, and not let these young ladies face a bill of costs incurred while 'upholding South African principles' in a manner that met with such spontaneous approval and invoked telegraphic plaudits from certain white circles.

It is to be hoped that when the Provincial Council discusses the questions all factors will receive due consideration, and that the councillors charged with such a difficult duty will discharge it to the credit of themselves and the prestige of the mother province of this unhappy dominion.

In the face of the legal action instituted against them the nurses agreed to work under Dr Molema, and to pay the costs incurred by him in the action he took against them. The local white community in Mafeking then set up a fund to help the nurses pay their costs.

85
Letter to R.R. Moton, Principal of Tuskegee Institute, Alabama, 29 June 1927[43]

P.O. Box 143,
Kimberley,
29/6/27

Dear Dr Moton

How are you? The struggle for life in South Africa is so grim that I could scarcely remember whether I owe you a letter or the other way round.

General Hertzog returned from the Imperial Conference[44] and was dined and wined by white people, especially the Boers who say that he returned holding in his hands a higher status for this dominion. Natives, on the other hand, saw no cause for rejoicing as they know only too well the true inwardness of the meaning of the much advertised 'dominion status'. This progressive elimination of the imperial factor only implies the ushering in of fresh fetters for the wrists and ankles of the darker races of this Union.

Parliament on its part did not leave us long in suspense as to what use they were going to make of their freshly obtained independence. There are now before Parliament bills to destroy the soul of the Native people by means of drastic laws, most barbarous in character. Some of them being more rigorous than the regulations that obtained in the southern states of America for the control of slaves before the emancipation proclamation of 1863. It will take a whole book to enumerate all of them and the import of each. For, while the discussion is raging, old restrictions are being tightened up. The opposition against Hertzog, numerically weaker, is always more innocuous with Native questions because the Boer followers of General Smuts can always be relied on to desert their leader and vote with Hertzog when a Native bill calls for a division.

As a consequence there is opening tomorrow in the city hall, Kimberley, a conference for all Natives, Coloured and Indian organisations in South Africa. Dr Abdurahman, member of the Cape provincial council, will preside; but it is like a vain hope for only a small minority in the Union Parliament care for the views of impotent resenters without a political blow behind it. The Indians are more fortunate because their protests are always backed and powerfully reinforced by the Viceroy of India and the united plea of over three hundred million swarthy British subjects of the Indian empire in the far east. But we Natives may commend our interests to the loving care of our heavenly father who in his kindness alone knows how to redress the sufferings of his erring black children, for David very truly says 'Lay not your trust on princes'.

But in the midst of the gloom there are indications of a silver lining along the dark horizon. Mr Mushet,[45] who succeeded the late Senator Schreiner as the Head of the Independent Order of True Templars (the coloured temperance alliance) has just appointed me his special deputy in the northern districts of the Union and thereby made me a high mogul of the order. During my stay at Cape Town I secured for my eldest son, St. Leger, the head clerkship in the office of the location superintendent near Maitland, Cape Town. He starts on the new job on the first of July. It is the first time that a South African municipality appoints a Native to such a position. It is devoutly to be hoped that the splendid example set by the mother city may be followed by East London, Port Elizabeth, Johannesburg and other South African municipalities in the near future.

Some time last year I wished to write to you but waited on hearing you were leaving with Mrs Moton for a round-the-world trip. It was to inform you of some of my experiences and the effect of the Hampton-Tuskegee films among the Natives. I had a letter from the principal of the higher mission school at Grahamstown telling the abiding impression made on his scholars by the Tuskegee drills and the 'Spiritual' ('It's me, it's me, O Lord') which I always make the Native children sing with me when I have a kiddies' matinee.

Another letter I wished to send you was from the superintendent of the Basutoland leper asylum, an M.D. in the Imperial service of Basutoland, acknowledging the peculiar joy I brought to the leper inmates by these pictures and wishing I would come again soon. I am so sorry I cannot lay hands on these documents at once. Anyway I hope that your health has derived much benefit from the tour and that Mrs Moton has been refreshed for the domestic and other duties awaiting her. My wife and I send best regards. Of

course you are now a familiar figure. Not only in the film but with the big
picture photograph in the house.

Yours very respectfully,

Sol T Plaatje

86

Article, 'The late Chief Silas Molema: Passing of a progressive Barolong chief', *Cape Times*, 13 September 1927

The death at Mafeking on Thursday last of Chief Silas Molema, at the age of
78, removes an outstanding character in the history of Bechuanaland and
recalls the work of the opening of the 'trade route to the north'.

The dead chief was the son of Molema, a Barolong chieftain, who
embraced Christianity and became a local preacher when things were still
very dark in the interior. In order to preach the gospel undisturbed, Molema
obtained the consent of his eldest brother, the supreme chief Montsioa, to
move with his followers and settle somewhere away from contact with
heathen rites and tribal ceremonies. Their settlement near Mafeking in 1870
subsequently proved the salvation of the whole tribe.

Turbulent days

In later years the Barolong suffered repeated attacks and were often hard pressed,
first by the Boers of Stellaland and Goschen (now Vryburg) and thereafter by
filibusters and hostile Natives from the Transvaal. The tribe found protection in
the thickets near Molema stadt, on the Molopo River, where the headquarters
of the tribe still are, among the wooded boulders of Mafikakgochoana, on both
sides of the river, from which the place derives its name – a corruption for
'Mafikeng' which means 'among the rocks'. Here they were besieged on six
occasions, as the frequent boundary disputes often culminated in military
campaigns, with loss of life and cattle on both sides. These troubles did not
terminate until the arrival of Sir Charles Warren's expedition in 1884, which
definitely terminated the wars by annexing Bechuanaland in the name of the
late Queen Victoria. Then there followed an era of peace and progress, which
was sorely strained by the rinderpest scourge. But the longest siege of Mafeking
was still to be successfully resisted under civilized conditions during the late Boer
war with General Baden-Powell in command.

As a teacher

Old Chief Molema's youngest son, Silas, whose funeral took place on Saturday
last, entered upon the scene in 1875. Returning from Healdtown Institution,

near Fort Beaufort, a well-educated youth, the son and brother of the most progressive and well-to-do chieftains among the Barolong petty chiefs, he could afford to open and conduct a day school where Bechuana children were taught English without paying anything. The school was often interrupted by the several quarrels with the Boers, as the teacher, being a sub-chief, always went on active service at the head of his regiment. Yet his educational work was so successful that when the Wesleyan mission took over his school in 1882 the tribe could already boast a number of educated men and women who could speak English fluently.

His fame as an educated Mochuana spread beyond the tribal boundaries. This made him interpreter and councillor to the great Montsioa and later to his sons Wessels, Badirile and Lekoko, who ruled after their father. Chief Lekoko, a nephew, was Montsioa's adopted son. He proved the wisest successor of the three; a friend to many Europeans, he received at the end of the siege one hundred heifers as a parting gift from General Baden-Powell.

Leader through three generations

It is not given to many public men to lead the political development of their communities through three successive generations, but Chief Silas began in 1875 and remained an active leader practically to the end of his days. The writer was at Mafeking last month and found him as energetic as ever with personal and tribal affairs and no sign of the approaching end.

Personally known to the High Commissioners and Sir Sidney Shippard, the Administrator, he took part in most of the national negotiations and boundary questions prior to and since the first annexation, and joined deputations to Cape Town, Pretoria and elsewhere, either as tribal spokesman or interpreter. Quite recently he headed a Bechuana delegation to Umtata to study the work of the Transkeian council system, and had since succeeded in forcing its adoption on his reluctant people. In April of this year he headed the last deputation of Bechuana chiefs to Cape Town in connection with the Native Administration Bill and, acting as their spokesman, Chief Silas so impressed General Hertzog by his eloquence that the Prime Minister acceded to their request and retained on our statutes the peculiar jurisdiction of Bechuana chiefs.

Dr Molema, a son

His political, religious and educational activities never diverted Chief Silas Molema from pursuing the tribal occupation of mealie planter and cattle breeder. He and his eldest brother, Israel Molema, were among the very first Natives of Bechuanaland to use a steam threshing-machine for their crops. Reputed at the time to be the best young man in the country, he married

Molalanyaha, the pretty daughter of Chief Chobe, of the Ratlou, at Wodehouse kraal. Together they raised a family of eight bright and well-educated young sons and daughters who, with their stepmother, now survive the dead chief. They include the renowned Dr Molema, who easily passed the Cape matric, and, proceeding to Glasgow, went through his medical course in the record time of three years and seven months.

A succession of missionaries, Imperial officers and civil commissioners stationed at Mafeking since 1886, always regarded him as their friend and Native adviser. The love of his people, who looked for his advice on every occasion, and his obliging disposition eminently suited him for the role of mediator between white and black, no less than the mouthpiece between Native strangers and the Barolong, for he was a thorough linguist.

Prominent among his administrative friends were the late Colonel C.G.H. Bell (the siege magistrate), Mr Geo. J. Boyes, who died at Cape Town, and Mr F. Graham Green, who lately retired from the Simonstown bench, and is at present a resident of the mother city.

Development of Mafeking

The late Mr Cecil Rhodes and Colonel Frank Rhodes were among his European friends. The Jameson Raid started from his farm, on which Pitsani siding now stands. He was to receive in exchange another farm much nearer Mafeking; but when the Raid ended in smoke he received £300 to cancel that provisional arrangement.

Mafeking, started by his father in 1870, has since developed into an important railway junction, and the market town of the surrounding farms and Native districts. The Protectorate government is also domiciled there. Other denominations are at work besides the original Wesleyan Methodists, and the Roman Catholics are now building a large training and educational centre. The many Natives who daily flock into the town for shopping and other purposes, who often came to him for help and advice, have really lost a guide, philosopher and friend, whom it will be hard to replace.

87

Article, 'Should the Nyandjas* be deported?', *Umteteli*, 3 March 1928

> I dunno what my mother want to stay here for
> 'Cause this ole world's no friend to her.

---

* Nyasas (from Nyasaland, now Malawi).

These lines occur in a thrilling Negro spiritual that I first heard abroad; and even today it never fails to touch me whenever I play it on the gramophone. I think if Native children understood the true inwardness of the position and outlook on Native life in this Union, they would tunefully and expressively sing something similar concerning their parents and their inhospitable native land. This brings me to my subject.

I have lately received four letters, each asking me to support a movement under the auspices of the African National Congress to compass the expulsion from the Union of all Blantyre[46] Natives. For public and personal reasons, I refuse to support the suggestion by either word or deed. For personal reasons I cannot entertain such a proposal. The time will come when more of my own relatives will find life intolerable in 'a white man's country' and migrate to Central Africa, where some of them are already; in that case, a Blantyre retaliation may prove very uncomfortable.

Thousands of my people, hounded out of this inhospitable Union by the rigorous application of the Natives' Land Act, trekked to the north ten years ago and soon became victims of malaria and other climatic diseases. The Wesleyan mission, with the aid of some Rhodesians, took a number to a Bulawayo hostel where they literally pulled them out of the jaws of death. Others got separated from their dying families, strayed like sheep without a shepherd and dispersing, their girls got married to Central African men; one went to Tanganyika and others to the Belgian Congo. They have forgotten their native Serolong and Dutch of the Orange 'Free' State, for living among new customs and strange surroundings they now raise children for unknown tribes of the far interior; they only speak French and Congolese, so who am I to suggest that black men should be expelled from a white man's Union?

There is an African saying, often forgotten by Natives of the present generation; it says, 'Mo-laea Kgosi oa ba a e italea.'*

Now for my public reason. It is the intention of certain people in this Union to rid South Africa of the Native population. How do we benefit the Natives if – wittingly or unwittingly – we play into the hands of such selfish people? Is there nothing better for our people to devote their time and energies to, than engineering a useless propaganda of this kind?

A few years ago the Union Government, for its own purposes, tried to deport only one Blantyre Native but could not succeed. Is it seriously considered that a government which tried and failed in the case of one, will

---

*   Tswana: 'Be careful about the kind of advice you give lest it backfire on you.'

deport a thousand Blantyre men to please the Natives? Natives cannot even get money out of the taxation and Native development fund to build a day school for their children so, in the event of deportation, who must foot the bill?

Greeks, Bulgarians and Poles in the cities of the Union are catering in a sphere which could be exploited by poor whites. Why not suggest to the government to expel such foreigners and install poor Boers in the city fruit shops? Instead of waiting to snatch jobs from Natives they could be better employed in the produce trade as middle men between farmer and consumer, and Natives would be more sure of their manual jobs. Supposing for a moment, which God forbid, we succeed in expelling Nyasalanders; does Congress fondly believe that it will end there? Will it not serve as a precedent for the expulsion of the Matebele and exclusion of the Swazis? Is Congress aware that school books are now being changed and that white and black children are being taught that the extinct Bushmen and Hottentots alone were indigenous to South Africa; that the Bantu are interlopers from across the Zambesi and that they only landed here at the same time as, if not later than, Van Riebeeck?

A few years back I was investigating some of those provocative and ruinous effects of the enforcement of the Natives' Land Act of this unfriendly Union. I got into argument with a Boer who said: 'We were all very happy when only Boers lived among the Barolong in Thaba Nchu. No one was hard up for land. This land scarcity began with the Fingo and Basuto invasion. Let the government drive the Basuto back to Basutoland and the Fingoes to their own haunts and no one will be hard up for land.' Mr Nyokong, who was present, intervened thus: 'You say we were happy with Boers and Barolongs only; how, then, did the Jews and Scotchmen get here? You drive out the Jews and the Englishmen and that will show us the way to drive out the Fingoes and Basuto.'

88

Article, 'In Bechuanaland today: Some recent travel notes', *Diamond Fields Advertiser*, 17 April 1928

Forty-three years ago Bechuanaland was annexed by the Imperial government, and 33 years ago was transferred to the Cape Colony. But in Bechuanaland today members of each tribe still 'gather in a circle, to hear crude justice administered by the head of the clan'. People in England often wonder at the severity of the sentences sometimes delivered in the courts of the Union, even as Cape lawyers are sometimes shocked by records of the weird judgements delivered by the Cape courts in the days of Van Riebeeck. As long as their decisions are not in conflict with civilized ideas Native chiefs in Bechuanaland exercise, in civil cases among their own tribes, unlimited jurisdiction within the four corners of the only surviving clause of a pre-annexation proclamation long since repealed by the old Cape Parliament; and the parallel institutions sometimes generate a clash of ideals even among units of the same community.

An experienced administrator attending what he knew as a 'big Native indaba' (in Bechuanaland called a 'pitso'), was surprised to see hundreds of Natives squatting on the ground or sitting on their haunches right through the proceedings. In the Transkei, he said, they would each bring a little stone and sit on it. In Bechuanaland again, they will seldom thank you for the gift of medicine till it has been used and done its work. Elsewhere Natives thank you, or not, the moment you hand them the parcel.

In the eastern districts of the Union over 70 per cent of Native cases have their origin in lobola disputes. Here in Bechuanaland such cases are unknown; but under the Native Administration Act of last year, lobola (hitherto the vice, or habit, of some tribes) has now become the law of the Union, so that any Native (whose mother, and whose mother's mothers were never bought) may now lawfully sell his daughter into wedlock at a price fixed by himself and enforce his demand with the authority of the law courts behind him.

Naturally, in the course of my itinerary I was often asked for the current news. At one place I related, inter alia, the newspaper controversy about Sunday observance, and the Bechuana also told me of a local difficulty. Their stock inspector is a Seventh Day Adventist, they say, and he insists on Natives dipping their stock on Sundays. Occasionally they want to dip on Saturdays, when he refuses to attend at his office. At other times he warns them to bring up their cattle on Sunday; when they refuse to do so it causes a row, calling for the intervention of the magistrate.

The Government has sent to the Batlhaping reserve a young Native as an agricultural demonstrator. The result was a big meeting of tribesmen, at which the principal chief was advised to tell the government that the need at the moment is a rain doctor and not a ploughman, unless indeed he could show them how to raise crops on arid soil. Judging by the tribal attitude the demonstrator seems to be in for an idle time, like a colleague of his who, having been sent to the Barolong out of season a year ago, departed after months without showing them how to plough a single acre.

It seems a pity that such useful people should be sent on blind alley missions among the Natives. If they got a few acres of land with a small plan, and invited the peasantry to their demonstrations, enough progressive Bechuana would attend the lessons, for seeing is believing. But the government which sends a school of agriculture with a wonderful array of implements in its own train to European farmers, who do not require much teaching, sends to the Natives a young man armed with nothing but his eight fingers and two thumbs, with no farming tools of any kind.

Booker Washington's methods are so different with Negro farmers. His moveable schools comprise a party of carpenters, ploughmen, and a nurse who quickly interest the womenfolk in indoor work till the Saturday afternoon, when they teach them games suitable for both old and young. On Sunday they will attend church and assume entire control of the singing. So that after the first weekend everybody is charmed by their work and converted to their innovations.

Mentioning the church reminds me that, in the southern states, the Negro church is either a Methodist or a Baptist: while here in Bechuanaland I had breakfast one morning with Congregationalists, lunched with Seventh Day Adventists, had afternoon tea with Roman Catholics, and supper with a Wesleyan family, while I spent the day mainly among Anglicans and adherents of the London Missionary Society – the original church of the Batlhaping – the church of Robert Moffat, who translated the Bible into the Sechuana language. Natives can appreciate the denominational cleavage between Roman Catholics and Seventh Day Adventists, but why the London Missionary Society and Congregationalists should conduct rival operations in the same tribe is a puzzle which will never be solved by the Native mind.

A real clash of ideals between the government and a Bechuana tribe occurred sometime back when a white man wanted to start a lime factory on a Native reserve. Adjoining the reserve is his own farm which he offered to the tribe in exchange. This was great news to the Natives, who figured that a lime dyke was of no tribal use compared with the arable lands and amount of grazing on the farm. But the exchange did not harmonize with the settled policy of the Union government. The government had no objection to a lease, as the money could be paid into the national fund for tribal development; but a transfer was not to be allowed. The objection roused a number of sleeping dogs. 'You raised our hut tax from 12s. to 30s. per annum,' they said to the Native Commissioner, 'and in the case of bachelors of 17 years, from nothing to £1 per annum. You then said the money was for Native development. Here are no government schools, unless they belong to white people, who pay no poll tax; no roads unless they lead to white people's farms; not one decent road to Kimberley (our labour and shopping centre) from the reserve, where vehicles move at tremendous risk.' The transaction was not sanctioned.

Economically the Bechuana, especially those in the south, are disintegrating. The Lichtenburg diggings which affected some centres very seriously proved to them a blessing during the recent lean harvests which synchronized with the sudden enforcement of the new Native tax. Without Lichtenburg a much larger proportion of the Bechuana would be in gaol for inability to pay the tax.

Everywhere I found general and genuine grief at the recent death of the Bishop of Kimberley and Kuruman who, in his lifetime, was not only the father of his church people, but a tried friend and adviser of all Natives regardless of tribe or denomination. He was expected in Bechuanaland during March when, failing to appear, news of his illness was closely followed by the announcement of his death. By his death the Bechuana lost a staunch friend who will not easily be forgotten, and almost everywhere the hope was expressed that, as his successor, the Church 'will give us another bishop and not merely a white man'.

89

Article, 'The Government Native Conference', *Umteteli*, 24 November 1928

Two years have passed since the last session of the annual Native Conference and some of us were wondering if it had been abolished. But if we are correctly informed the government is now about to convene a Native conference to meet members of the Select Committees on General Hertzog's four bills.[47] It is sincerely to be hoped that the Native Affairs Department will give our people ample notice to prepare for this the most important gathering since the institution of this consultative body.

When the Union Parliament or the provincial councils are about to consider important bills, Europeans who are interested in such legislation, make a point of travelling to the capital with the object of tendering their advice to members on the several provisions under consideration. The result is not only helpful to members but the lobbying they do is of inestimable value to the sections of the public affected by such bills.

The writer is one of the most recently appointed members of the annual Native Conference. Before I was asked to join, I made a point of always travelling to Pretoria when it met. We cannot depend on the daily press for faithful and extended reports of purely sectional debates. The public men among us should attend the coming conference to hear for themselves the modifications, mutual conciliations and compromises effected by the Select Committee and so warn members of any catch in the committee's recommendations.

On the opening day the Prime Minister takes the opportunity to talk to all the Natives on general topics. Pointed references to particular localities can best be met by residents from such areas using conference members to correct any misinterpretation of their peculiar needs. Their personal attendance and first-hand advice can save much correspondence and costly deputations to government. It is precisely for this reason that we find white people attending the Union Parliament even though one may find in the public gallery scores of reporters from all over the country.

Having regard to the importance of a gathering such as the coming conference it is to be regretted that the Native press on the whole appears to belittle the weight of the deliberations of past conferences. Editors merely gave their readers translations of abridgments of what appeared in the daily press. It should be remembered that European reporters perform their work with an eye on the public in general; they cannot always give prominence to specific topics of Native interest, of greatest benefit to the least lettered section of the constituency of the papers they represent. Such items fall within the province of the Native press.

I have sometimes heard the constitution of the Hertzog conference criticised for what is really a Smuts policy, and vice versa. I have also heard the conference blamed for things it never did, accused of not doing what it actually did, and sometimes let off from its own sins of omission and commission. I have likewise heard individual members criticised for neglecting the things they tackled and, at other times, denounced for not saying the things they actually said. I have also heard leading Natives who never attended this conference, upbraided for its decisions. Personal attendance by interested writers and thinkers will do away with much of this confusion. For as it is Europeans get second-hand information on deliberations of this conference while Natives are fed on third-hand information in the shape of retranslation of cuttings from the European press. It is just possible that this may account for the prevalent complaint about an alleged deterioration of the Native press.

Whether or not he be a member of the coming conference, it is the writer's intention to attend. Native leaders, friends of the Natives and others interested should try and be present, not only to learn at first-hand the fateful decisions under contemplation but also to advise members on the various aspects of the crucial proposals within the four corners of the four bills; for indeed, 'merogolos ia ea isatsing e hgonas ke go lela a lebagnie'.*

In fact the 'annual' Native Conference – established under the provisions of the Native Affairs Act of 1920 – did not meet again until December 1930.

90

Letter to the Registrar, University of the Witwatersrand, on 'Secuana language research', 3 July 1929[48]

Plaatje had first applied to the Bantu Research Committee, University of the Witwatersrand, in 1928, via Dr Clement Doke, a lecturer at the University's Department of Bantu Studies. Plaatje was awarded an initial grant of £25 in November 1928, and several further awards followed over the next three years.

P.O. Box 143
Kimberley
July 3rd 1929

The Registrar
University of the Witwatersrand
Johannesburg

Sir,

Sechuana Language Research

I beg to report the following progress made by me with the aid of a grant from the Research Department of the Witwatersrand University, more especially in connection with Bantu studies.

I should first of all mention the following reason why not more than 60 pages of manuscript is typed:

Last February, I was invited to an orthography committee in Pretoria where

---

*   Tswana: 'Those who have a dispute should be brought face to face to have their case (dispute) tried.'

some radical changes in the Sechuana spelling were recommended for adoption by a central body.[49] Should these recommendations be accepted, in full or in modified form, all my MSS will have to be retyped in accordance with the adopted orthography. For this reason I have since been adding to my notes without typing any manuscript, pending an official decision on the future method of spelling this language. I should also add that since May last, I was obliged to lay aside my research work as I had undertaken a temporary employ which kept me fully occupied until the 1st July,[50] so that I am now in a position to resume my Sechuana studies.

The research work completed thus far comprises:

I.   SOME FOLK-TALES, FABLES AND PRAISES OF BECHUANA CHIEFS[51]
     Some 60 pages of these and other stories are already in typewritten form but, as stated above, must in all probability be typed all over again. The remainder of my collection, still in rough notes, will be quite ready for the typewriter as soon as the Sechuana orthography committee have decided on the spelling. Meanwhile, I am continuing to gather more stories, etc.

II. OVER 300 UNPUBLISHED PROVERBS have been collected for my second edition of Sechuana Proverbs, with English Translations and Their European Equivalents.[52] As my first edition preserved as many as 730 Sechuana Proverbs with translations, etc., my second edition, now under preparation, will be half-as-large again. I am still collecting more rare maxims and proverbial sayings in hopes of rescuing from oblivion as many as possible of these primitive Native saws and preserving them for posterity. At the same time I am continuing my research for European equivalents to some of these old sayings.

III. During my research I have come across a good many SECHUANA WORDS NOT FOUND IN BROWN'S DICTIONARY of the Sechuana language – the only Sechuana vocabulary in circulation.[53] A serious study of this dictionary shows that in many cases it teems with solecisms and mistranslations. I have thus come to the conclusion that a useful purpose will be served if I added to my research work the recording of such omitted words and their translations besides a correction of the wrong reading in the printed dictionary.

For the latter, I was fortunate in securing the collaboration of Mr D.M. Ramoshoana,[54] an old Cape and OFS teacher, who is a keen student of Bantu lore with a wonderful command of English grammar.

With his aid and the advices of other interested Native friends (provided the necessary help is forthcoming) I hope to provide Sechuana readers with a more reliable Sechuana- English vocabulary. After filling the gaps with a number of unrecorded Sechuana words and their translation, I have further undertaken, with a degree of success, the correction of a large number of inaccuracies in the said Sechuana dictionary.[55]

Trusting that this brief outline is clear
I beg to be,
Dear sir,
Yours very respectfully
Sol T. Plaatje

91
Article, 'Another five years', *Umteleli*, 13 July 1929

In the general election of June 1929 the Nationalist-Labour Pact increased its overall majority, General Hertzog having emphasised throughout the election campaign his determination to abolish the Cape African franchise – eventually achieved in 1936.

The blow has fallen. We have lost the count and the Pact is to rule over us for another five years. Pact voters have struck a blow for intolerance and race-hatred; a knock-out blow for prejudice and repression.

In a sense it is perhaps better that the verdict was in General Hertzog's favour, for having got what he was after he may perhaps permit us to forget that in the winter of 1929, the Prime Minister – the 'father of the Natives' – risked the cold of the Stormbergen and the Snow mountains and proceeded from hilltop to hilltop, calling on all races to combine against Bantu people of the subcontinent, vowing that he and his would leave the country if he failed to succeed himself at the head of state affairs.

Thousands of voters who listened to this counterfeit election cry were thoroughly gulled, especially in the country districts where the god of colour prejudice rules without a rival. Thousands whose prosperity depends on the incessant toil of 200,000 black labourers in the mines, whose farming operations depend almost entirely on the loyalty of Native farm labour, professed to believe that their black benefactors were their menace and General Hertzog and his party their only mainstay. In the big towns, however, outside the Orange Free State white men are not so gullible; there the Afrikander fetish has to contend with the truth. The sermons of General Hertzog's missioners anent hordes of barbarians outvoting white people in 1950, were met with questions as to why this has not happened in 75 years; and their tales about more black children in school than white ones, were met with correct statistics issued by General Hertzog's and Mr Malan's own departments giving the lie direct to the scare sermons. We in the Cape and Natal have to qualify for our votes. In the Transvaal and Orange Free State a man need not own anything or know anything. He need only be white and 21 and the vote is automatic; and the ignorant voters of the platteland have carried the day against truth and goodwill for their Afrikander god.

In this orgy of misrepresentation one outstanding fact stands clearly demonstrated: the misnamed four Native bills, published four years ago, withdrawn, postponed, re-issued and put back and never really introduced till the eve of dissolution, were nothing but an election dodge. It was a cleverly conceived plan to give General Smuts and his followers an opportunity of voting for the constitution and of then going to the country with the cry that the South African Party had voted against the *ware Afrikander** fetish of colour prejudice and so secure a retaliation that will render Pact jobs safe for another five years. We may only hope that as they continue to collect their poll taxes and cotton blanket taxes they will leave Natives in peace.

In the eye of most Natives the Prime Minister's campaign of calumny, lumping us all as a barbarian menace to European civilization was nothing but colossal ingratitude. The first party of voortrekkers to cross the Orange River in the late twenties and early thirties of the last century, speedily felt the might of Mzilikazi, whose impis relieved the Boers of every head of livestock except their fowls and geese, leaving their women and children exposed to further attacks. It was a Native chief who raised enough men and draught animals among his tribe to rescue the stranded Boers and give them an asylum at Moroka's Hoek. Further, on the advice of an English missionary – a type of citizen much despised in Pact circles – these Natives made free gifts of milch cows and goats to keep the Boer families alive pending reinforcements from the Cape and Natal. In subsequent years the same Natives suffered heavily in life and property conquering large tracts of Basuto territories for the Free State. The Swazi and other tribes made similar sacrifices for the extension of Boer domination of Bapediland. Today the sons of the voortrekkers call them

* Afrikaans: 'true Afrikaner'.

a 'menace' and urge a combination of all white people in a campaign of repression against all Natives.

We have often heard (I wonder with how much truth) of some languages with no equivalents for the word gratitude; but we do know that the language of the Boers has a phrase called 'Stank vir dank'* and that is what we are in for.

General Hertzog has done one sensible thing and that was, immediately after this sordid campaign, to relinquish the portfolio of Native Affairs. After such a campaign of misrepresentation at the Native's expense, a sham 'father of the Natives' could not reasonably continue as the Union's head of Native affairs.

But even Natives could learn a lesson from the general election. The success of the Boers at the polls was due largely to a spirit of helpmekaar† and wholehearted co-operation. Nearly every Boer was prepared to risk anything to secure the return of Nationalist candidates. Afraid as they are of the gaol, some of them even risked that for the sake of Nationalist victory. Those of us who frequently came in contact with them in rural constituencies on polling day could not but admire their solidarity. Will the Native not learn a lesson here?

Our hats should be lifted to General Smuts for his defeat of Advocate Pirow,[56] the author of the four Native Bills and, next to Colonel Creswell,[57] the Natives' greatest enemy in the new Union cabinet.

92

Article, '"The Good New Times" and the "New Native"', *Umteteli*, 9 November 1929

General Hertzog's straight talk to the Free State Nationalists will give some breathing space to the South African thinkers who are concerned about the threatened abolition of the Cape Native vote. The Premier's intervention showed that during the life of the present Parliament at any rate we shall continue to have an English Governor-General and, at least for the next four years, Natives may still be enrolled as voters in the Cape province.

The fact is that Nationalists are not keen to represent the King at Government House any more than they are to represent Natives in

---

*   Afrikaans: 'small thanks' (lit. 'stinks for thanks').
†   Afrikaans: 'help one another', or 'mutual help'.

Parliament; but the Nationalists' scramble for jobs shows that some of them at least are not indifferent to jobs with high salaries. Some of them might offer to command a transatlantic liner, of which they know nothing, if the salary was sufficiently attractive and there were competent assistants to do the work. Nationalists ought not to be too anxious to upset a constitution drawn up with the co-operation of old republican presidents with the aid and advice of Generals De Wet, Hertzog and others; but they do feel that, in about a dozen cases, the Cape Native vote stands between as many Nationalists and £700 per annum plus a free first-class ticket over all systems of the South African Railways; and constitution or no constitution, they are making frantic efforts to browbeat the Native vote and annex these plums.

Even the stray scraps for the indigent, such as the old age pension and government doles, are not too mean for the envious eyes of some Nationalists. Professor Coulter of Ohio University, member of the Poor White Commission touring the country under the auspices of the Carnegie Corporation, states that their investigations 'revealed a lamentable dependence on the government for assistance'.[58] Correspondence in the daily papers shows that the old age pension in some localities is being drawn by well-to-do drivers of their own motor vehicles, including men who have houses to let; so that it is not only in the labour field where the Native is regarded as a menace to European pockets.

But while Native lethargy and wanton indifference is the order of the day in vital matters, it must be added that the inaction of our South African Party friends is not a bit reassuring. Beyond merely voting against General Hertzog, they make no effort to husband their fast-dwindling advantages outside the house. How different is the method of their opponents! The Nationalists are pigeonholing the Native Disfranchisement Bill, presumably for use as a bogey at the next general election; it is doubtful if the opposition leaders will do anything in the meanwhile to safeguard their own position, with or without the Native vote.

Is it possible to induce the lethargic Bantu to emulate the tactics of their opponents? The co-operation, unanimity and enterprise mobilized by Nationalists against the Native is so thorough as to excite our admiration. Cannot the Natives be persuaded to collaborate in getting more of their people on the register? There is a fresh registration every year, and at every registration and review of the old lists, Nationalists' agents manage to reduce the number of Native voters. Only one or two us worry ourselves over it, but for every five new names we put on the register here and there, ten are scratched off elsewhere; and at that rate there will be hardly enough Native voters left to scare the backveld at the next election.

We of the older generation took a special pride in showing our white benefactors that we were worthy of their help; but the psychology of the younger Native must often be perplexing to his friends. In the difficult task of registering fresh Native voters and counteracting Nationalist activities bent on scratching off old ones, we are often hampered by an insidious type of 'New Native' often found busily 'sowing thorns in our path'. Investigating the reasons why any persons, however black, should actively work against the enfranchisement of their own people and in favour of their political enemies, I found the motive to be sheer jealousy. It appears that from their point of view, our unsalaried efforts must be opposed lest the franchise thus acquired should gain for us the confidence of Natives and, possibly, recognition as useful leaders – something that someone else is after.

Personally I wish it to be known through *Umteteli* – and I hope that Native enemies of the Native franchise sometimes read this paper – that I have never in my life harboured any ambition to lead anyone. My record is purely that of loyal service to the Native cause; and he is needlessly dissipating his energies who feverishly tries to stop leadership coming my way. This, it should be added, is no new decision on my part. I made the position clear in 1917 when our people unanimously resolved to offer me the presidency of the Native National Congress – a much more virile and representative organisation than its copy today. In asking them to pass the honour to Mr Makgatho I told them then, and I repeat it today 12 years later, that I am content to serve as hitherto. There are only sixteen working hours in a day, and I could not possibly find the time to earn my own living while trying to lead unwieldy masses of another and more 'civilised' generation.

But the more I try to help the inarticulate masses that are hardly ever heard of, the greater the handicaps and the more gloomy appear the future. Besides the effects of the stranglehold of the liquor traffic on the throats of the 'New Native', many things break one's heart from day to day. For instance, busybodies are at present busy making overtures to Nationalists not to treat their people better; and some Natives are actually offering to go out on behalf of the Nationalists helping them to discover in certain constituencies exactly what Boer or Boers voted against the Pact during the last election, so as to ensure the victimization of Boers who voted against General Hertzog and his disfranchisement bill.

93
Letter to the Secretary, De Beers, on 'School readers in the vernacular', 19 November 1929[59]

The Diamond Fields Men's Own Brotherhood
and Women's Own Sisterhood
P.O. Box 143
Kimberley,
South Africa

November 19th 1929

The Secretary,
De Beers Consolidated Mines Ltd,
Stockdale Street,
Kimberley

Sir,

School readers in the vernacular

At the November meeting of the education committee of the Native Brotherhood, yesterday evening, it was resolved to ask you for an interview in order to make representations to the company regarding the above need in Native schools in this part of the Union. But in order to afford you an opportunity of judging whether an interview is necessary at all I made the suggestion, and the committee concurred, to submit the matter in writing, thus:

The Education Departments in all four provinces and also in Basutoland and Bechuanaland insist that, besides the official languages, there should be mother tongue instruction in all Native schools.[60] There is no difficulty as far as the Xhosa and Sesuto classes are concerned, because the Lovedale mission prints Xhosa books and the Paris mission in Basutoland prints Basuto books so that they have considerable literature in the vernacular.

In the Bechuana language, however (the language of Griqualand West, Orange Free State and Bechuanaland up to Southern Rhodesia), there is hardly anything available besides the Bible and the hymn books of the different denominations and our teachers are up against a quandary trying to comply with the new departmental demands. It is beyond the authority of the school boards and school committees to print books; they can only use books on sale to the public.

Mr Meadows[61] of the Perseverance School, and other teachers at Lyndhurst Road and in the north, consulted with our Brotherhood for the provision of school readers for the upper standards and the normal classes; and our education committee entrusted me with the work of compiling the necessary books in the Native language and they would help to raise the funds to meet the printing bills.

Now that some of the required books are ready, they need to be printed over the Yuletide vacation so as to have them available when schools reopen at the end of January. I have asked for quotations in South Africa and abroad and the cheapest proved to be the following:

(1) Translations of Shakespeare's *The Comedy of Errors, Julius Caesar* and *Much Ado About Nothing* £125.[62]

(2) Traditional Native Folk-tales and other Useful Knowledge £205.0.0.

(3) Sechuana Proverbs (with English equivalents) £57 18/-.

Quotations (1) and (2) being the cheapest were obtained from the Morija printing press of the French mission in Basutoland; the other (3) is from Kegan Paul, Treubner & Co., London, and they proved to be the cheapest in each line. Our committee is making efforts to avail itself of these three offers in hopes of meeting the immediate needs of the school requirements until better provision is made later.

It may perhaps be well to explain IN CONFIDENCE why our committee, which undertook the task last August, should thus far only have managed to raise £41 towards the printing of books that should be ready first thing after New Year. I may say in explanation that the officers of the Brotherhood are the leading social workers among Native communities in Kimberley and outside and since the elections last June and July our difficulties have been exceptional and varied. To mention a few, the Pact vendetta against Sir E. Oppenheimer was launched by enemies of Native welfare by sowing systematic dissensions among Natives in the surrounding locations. It taxed our resources physically, mentally and financially to defeat their aims and keep the Native vote intact. Again, besides our regular work we have had our hands full combating and trying to keep the Communist movement outside Kimberley; this has been a stupendous task since Mr Bunting came here last September and left his agents here to spread his communistic propaganda.[63] Just about that time our Brotherhood undertook to organize a farewell token of respect for Sir David Harris; this ambition is soon to fructify: it has already taken the shape of a Native hand-made kaross suitable for an old gentleman.

I mention these confidential incidents only to show that while I was proceeding with the work of compiling these books, the committee was not idling; and if outside meddlers had only left us undisturbed the raising of funds would have kept pace with the edition of the books.

Ten years ago, when the government definitely refused to build a school for Natives, De Beers Co. generously gave us the premises and contributed £100 in cash. The place is now being used by the Kimberley school board for the education of our children. The company, moreover, has each year contributed liberally towards our Christmas and New Year treat for the aged poor and infirm as well as for needy Native children; and should you feel pleased to give this appeal for help towards the printing bills your favourable recommendation for the sympathetic consideration of the directors, the advantage will be far more lasting and general than the ephemeral Christmas gift; the books will be a continuous benefit to future generations here and elsewhere and so merit the abiding gratitude of all respectable Natives.

Trusting that this earnest appeal will meet with the same generous sympathy that has always characterized the action of the De Beers directors where Native education is concerned.

I beg to be, Dear Mr Drake,

On behalf of the Native Brotherhood and Sisterhood

Yours very respectfully,

Sol. T. Plaatje

Plaatje's appeal to De Beers was not successful, and he was informed on 25 November that the board 'regret they are unable to accede to your request for a contribution towards the cost of the printing of these books'.

94

Letter to the Registrar, University of the Witwatersrand, on 'Sechuana Researches', 25 November 1929[64]

P.O. Box 143
Kimberley
25th November 1929

The Registrar
University of the Witwatersrand
Johannesburg

My dear Sir,

Sechuana researches

I have the honour to report that during October and November I went east
and spent some weeks trying to find intelligent old people between Thaba
Nchu and the conquered territory of the Orange Free State so as to get
information in order to sift and rearrange my collection of Native stories, etc.,
for my new Sechuana Reader. It was here I felt the value of your grant-in-aid,
however limited.

Nearly five years ago I communicated with old Maletisa[65] who lived in this
part of the country. I made an appointment with him to visit and obtain from
him praises of old Barolong chiefs and famous Bechuana hunters which few
people knew as well as he. Not only in their recital but also in explaining the
meaning of some cryptic passages and obscure Sechuana words, the old man
excelled. The keen struggle for bare existence forced me to postpone the trip
again and again; even when out that way, the time at my disposal allowed of
no opportunity to go out to his place. I kept on postponing my visit until two
years ago when I heard that the old man had died, and all that treasure of
Bantu folk-lore was buried with him. Had there been a grant, however small,
something like the one at my disposal in my present work, his store of Native
philosophy would have been recorded about a year before he died.

I reached Maseru while the Basuto parliament[66] was in session and had
some very instructive, if less helpful, talks with chiefs and other people from
different parts of the 'Switzerland of South Africa'. I went from there to
Matsieng and later journeyed to Mafeteng and district, getting valuable
information; the best part of my work was to find that my investigations
stimulated the Native peasants in the study of traditions and Bantu lore.

The best week of the trip was the one I spent at Morija comparing my notes
with some early Sechuana books of the Paris Evangelical Mission, writing known
thereabout as 'Sesotho-sa-kgale (old Sesuto).[67] It was my good fortune that my
visit to Morija synchronized with the celebration of Mokotla mission festival.[68]
The celebrations brought many interesting characters to Morija and I had some
very instructive chats with them, comparing information obtained from the
Leselinyana editor[69] with the knowledge of his brothers from the mountains.

I was agreeably surprised on finding that the plant at Morija includes type
for phonetic characters. I gave them one of my completed MSS to print –
Shakespeare's *Comedy of Errors* in Sechuana. I am using for the first time in a
Sechuana book the symbols ɛ and ŋ. They are not unlike the Roman letters

and so should not excite the ire of ultra-conservative missionaries who object to any innovation, however useful.

From the collection of old fables, overheard by us since early boyhood, it always appeared that the fox and the hare were the cleverest of animals. The stories collected during my present enquiries have changed some of my earliest impressions. From my latest systematic investigations (thanks to your grant) it now appears that for right down shrewdness – not merely the cunning of the jackal, but the acme of sagacity – according to old Sechuana folktales, the majority vote and the first prize must be awarded to the TORTOISE!

Research 'No. 2'
I have completed my collection of proverbs for the second edition of *Sechuana Proverbs and their European Equivalents* and am now busy at correcting and rearranging the translations, etc., which should be in the printers' hands at the end of this year (Kegan Paul, Trench, Trubner & Co., Publishers). The first edition, now out of print, came out in 1916 and had 730 Sechuana proverbs with translations and equivalents. They were written from memory while I worked alone in London. Your grant, I am grateful to add, helped me in collecting nearly 400 additional Native saws so that the edition now under preparation will certainly contain over 1,000 Sechuana proverbs.

I mentioned in a previous report that the typing of my new reader was held up by the choice of orthography. I had hoped that a conference called for the first time last February, under the auspices of the Native Affairs Department and the University of Witwatersrand to which I was invited, would ere long solve the spelling difficulty for this unfortunate language. A second conference took place in October to which I was not invited. Two Free State friends who were there tell me that they repeatedly inquired why I was excluded from the October conference and no one seemed to know who was responsible for my absence.[70] But I have learnt enough from them to realize that to wait for the orthography of the Pretoria conference will be like waiting on the Greek calends. Consequently I shall proceed with the typewriting of the remainder of my MSS as soon as I have disposed of and mailed the addenda for the second edition of my proverbs.

In doing so I shall let the future take care of itself and use the orthography I have employed hitherto. It is the same orthography I have employed in the proverbs; the same in use by Bapedi and Transvaal Basutos when writing to the two Johannesburg weeklies, *Umteteli* and *Abantu Batho*. It was never agreed upon by a conference of any kind. We just naturally found it more phonetically expressive of our mother tongues. There is hardly any confusion in our methods of spelling; we only experience confusion when we use the books of our several church denominations. One trouble of the missionary spelling is that it makes no distinction between the 'j' and 'y' sounds. Discarding the 'j' entirely missionaries used the 'y' to express both its own and the 'j' sounds. The resulting ambiguities are often awkward, as for instance 'njalela' (give me some seed) and 'nyalela' (marry my daughter). Missionaries write these words alike.

This disposes of two of my lines of research viz., the proverbs and the stories of the reader which I am typing as soon as I have posted the proverbs MS. There yet remains a third line mentioned in a former report – the collection and translation of Sechuana words that do not appear in any dictionary. The need for a revised and considerably enlarged Sechuana dictionary came into prominence in the course of my search for old stories and untranslated proverbs. It attracted the co-operation of Mr D.M. Ramoshoana, a studious English-Sechuana scholar. Between us we have rescued and translated over 400 words. With financial encouragement we can easily compile another 2,000 Sechuana words but it will require careful investigation in the interior of Bechuanaland where speech is less influenced by European ideas, so as to avoid the errors and omissions in Brown's dictionary.

In this connection, I may mention that Professor Jones of University College, London, has recently brought out a pamphlet illustrating 'The Tones of Sechuana Nouns'.[71] It may interest you to know that Professor Jones, writing alone in London, has in his little brochure 126 Sechuana nouns not included in Brown's big Sechuana dictionary (the official dictionary of that language) and he has rendered correctly 30 other nouns which appear but are mistranslated by Brown. One wonders how many untranslated words the professor would have given us, supposing he had dealt with all the nouns and perhaps the verbs too.

The pamphlet referred to was reviewed by Dr Doke in the *Journal of Bantu Studies*.[72] In that review the doctor credits me having collaborated with Professor Jones. This needs correction for I have not seen Mr Jones since I last left London in 1923. Moreover, I knew nothing about his work until a couple of months back when he sent me some copies. I have noticed only three words that are wrongly translated by the professor. This is creditable compared with the 'howlers' within the covers of the official dictionary, and the distance from which the professor wrote – in England, all by himself.

It may be justly asked why some missionaries working among Natives can make such glaring mistakes when writing the language of a people among whom they labour. The logical answer is that missionaries resemble other men in that they do not go to work the same way. While many ministers (especially in the south) usually look for the best Native to help them with his own language, others are so conservative that they will only accept help and co-operation from members of their own churches. But if none are capable they would rather produce inferior work than accept the aid of an outsider from a sister denomination, however capable, and the dictionary suffers from this policy.

One cannot very well quarrel with this conservatism where denominational books are concerned; but when it is imported into the revision of a universal book like the Bible (as has frequently happened in Bechuanaland) this line of action is I think indefensible.

I have enclosed a statement of disembursements for your kind attention and as it will more than exhaust my grant, I earnestly commend to you the remaining work – a better vocabulary in the language.[73] Should you feel pleased to recommend it for the favourable consideration of your committee on Bantu studies I can assure you that our investigations will not be confined to the mere collection and translation of words, but we shall follow up other branches as well.

I have the honour to be, Sir,

Yours very respectfully,

Sol T. Plaatje

Plaatje was asked by the Committee to complete an application form for a further research grant to enable him to continue his work during 1930, and he was awarded another £25 grant to help continue work on the Dictionary.

95

Introduction to *Diphosho-phosho* (translation of *The Comedy of Errors*)[74]

Diphosho-phosho, Plaatje's Tswana translation of The Comedy of Errors, *was published by the Morija Press in July 1930. The passage reproduced below is an English translation of Plaatje's Introduction.*

INTRODUCTION

The Setswana language has caused confusion amongst its native speakers because, unlike other languages we speak, it lacks a standard orthography.

MABOLELO A GA TSIKINYA-CHAKA

(The Sayings of William Shakespeare)

DIPHOSHO-PHOSHO

(Comedy of Errors)

A fetolecoe mo puong ea Secoana
ke
SOL. T. PLAATJE
Morulaganyi oa "Diane tsa Secoana le Maele a Sekgooa."
(Sechuana Proverbs and European Equivalents)
P.O. Box 143, Kimberley, South Africa.

MABOLELO a maŋoe a ga TSIKINYA-CHAKA
MASHOABI-SHOABI,
MATSAPA-TSAPA A LEFELA,
DINCHO-NCHO TSA BO JULIUS KESARA,
Le Buka tse diŋoe gape.

MORIJA PRINTING WORKS.

Title page of Diphosho-phosho (literally, 'Mistake upon Mistake'), *Plaatje's translation of*
Shakespeare's The Comedy of Errors, *published in July 1930.*

Most of the Setswana books we have, because they are religious literature, have been written in the following orthographies:

(a) That of the London Missionary Society and the Berlin Lutherans
(b) That used in literature from the Anglicans, Wesleyans and the Hermannsburg Lutherans.

Batswana authors find these orthographies useful in one way or the other. However, one common flaw with all these missionary orthographies is that they do not use the consonant 'j' in such words as *bojang* (grass), *mojaki* (migrant labourer), *dijana* (dishes).

In this book we have added the letter 'j' to the missionary alphabet, so that we can distinguish words such as *nyalela* (marry my daughter) and *njalela* (give me some seed). Had we not done this, readers would misunderstand Antifoluse when he said to his younger brother, *'U njetse tinare'* ('You have partaken of my dinner'), and would think he was using vulgar language, when in fact he was not.

Moreover, the 26 letters of the Roman alphabet used in all these books is insufficient for Setswana. That is why we have borrowed letters from the International Phonetic Alphabet, namely ɛ and ŋ .

As these letters are very similar to existing Roman ones we do not believe any readers will be taken aback when they see them. The first letter will be useful in distinguishing words such as *nche* (vo'elstruis) and *nchɛ* (soetriet – 'sugar-cane'); *serethe* (butter) and *serɛthɛ* (heel); *mme* (but) and *mmɛ* (mother); *tsenene* (rhino) and *tsɛtsɛnɛnɛ* (brilliance).

One other important letter or phonetic sign is ɔ. We were reluctant to use this as it is not very much like the 'o' with which we are all familiar. But if we had not used it we would not have been able to distinguish words like *botlhoko* (illness) and *botlhɔkɔ* (want); *segogo* (scarecrow) and *segɔgɔ* (sullen); *gololega* (be free) and *gɔlɔlɛga* (stretch); *selopo* (sheen) and *selɔpɔ* (sa tlou – 'elephant's trunk'); besides in borrowed terms such as *setomo* (steam) and *setɔmɔ* (ignoramus).

Moreover, in Setswana tone plays a very important role in that it conveys different meanings in words which look identical, such as *ditlhaka* (reeds) and *ditlhaka* (letters); *babadi* (readers) and *babadi* (killers); *buduloga* (be puffed up) and *buduloga* (open one's eyes); *maiphitlhɛlɔ* (hiding place) and *maiphitlhɛlɔ* (experience).

It has not been an easy task to write a book such as this in Setswana: it has been both difficult and intricate. But we are driven forward by the demands of the Batswana – the incessant and shrill cries of people exclaiming, 'Tau's Setswana will be of no use to us! It is becoming extinct because children are not taught Setswana! They are taught the missionary language! They will lose all trace of our language!' That is why we undertook to tackle this task.

After the translation and compilation of Shakepeare's play into a manuscript in Setswana, we found that we were short of £45 to pay for it to be printed. We sought assistance from well-to-do Batswana. We thought that when they heard that this was for a book in their own language they would stop simply asking for a book in Setswana and instead make it possible for it to be printed. We had asked that they meet us halfway and provide only £30, to be refunded in three months, but they would not lend us it to us, and we were only helped by a man of Indian origin.

Four Europeans then heard that certain Batswana were not willing to contribute any money for the printing of the Setswana book, even though they had it. And they were surprised to learn that a foreigner, who could not even speak Setswana, had contributed some money towards the printing of the manuscript. They then approached the author and told him that he should not bother to repay the Indian, and that they would repay him instead.

This lack of self-reliance on the part of Batswana is what is responsible for their backwardness. The Batswana have fewer printed books than the Basotho and the Ndebele, and these are read in their schools. The Batswana must try to be self-reliant and to compete with other nations in providing books for themselves.

The four Shakespearean plays printed in Setswana are:

Diphosho-phoso (The Comedy of Errors)
Mashoabi-shoabi (The Merchant of Venice)
Matsapa-tsapa a Lefala (Much Ado About Nothing)
Dinch-ncho tsa bo Julius Kesara (Julius Caesar)

In rendering complex sentences such as those of Shakespeare into the most difficult Setswana, we are indebted to Mr D.M. Ramoshoana, a teacher at the Wesleyan mission school at Hopetown, for his great assistance We are particularly thankful for his polished Sehurutse, and for his equally profound understanding of English. If it were not for his assistance, this play would not be of this quality.

We are also thankful to the following people for their financial assistance:
Rev. Francis Hill of the Anglican denomination in Johannesburg;
Bishop Meysing of the Roman Catholic Church here in Kimberley;

Mrs W Allan King[75] of Pretoria, together with her sister-in-law, Mrs King Botha, as well as Messrs M. Sammy and Son[76] (here).

Our thanks also go to the dedication of the supervisor of the Morija printing press and his assistants for the arduous task of printing in our language, which is unlike their own.

Once, in the company of Mr D.M. Ramoshoana, puzzled by a problem, we called out to a certain old man who was going past us, to assist us. The old man then said: 'What is it that you gain from your witchery, that after long and tedious journeys by train and lorry, you still spend sleepless nights with the lights on, working tirelessly on your books, when the rest of the people are asleep?'

The teacher replied thus: 'There are presently about 300 African languages which have their own printed books. If I were to die having translated one of Shakespeare's plays into Setswana I shall rest in peace, because I will have done something for you.'

Should someone still want to know what we benefit from our toil, that is our answer.

Solomon T. Plaatje
The Editor
P. O. Box 143
Kimberley, June 1930

96

Article, 'A friend of the Natives: The late Sir William Solomon', *Pretoria News*, 21 June 1930

Another great friend of the Natives departed this life when Sir William Solomon, former Chief Justice of the Union, breathed his last. The deceased judge descended from the Solomon line – a stock of sterling worth, and a family made famous in the last century by the political activities of his uncle, Mr Saul Solomon, father of the Cape constitution, and staunch champion of the rights of non-Europeans. The work of Saul Solomon and his associates secured for the Cape a constitution; so galling to the present-day rulers of this country because it made no distinction between man and man on the ground of race and colour. Sir Richard Solomon, brother of the late judge, was the first colonial-born statesman to occupy the post of Acting Governor-General. Deceased himself acted in a similar capacity after his appointment as Chief Justice. So that the 'friend of the Natives' never really suffered any disability on that account.

Sir William Solomon, Chief Justice of the Union of South Africa: 'I would like you and other men who think with you on these subjects,' he declared in a famous judgement in 1902, 'to understand that the law makes no distinction between a man with a white skin and a man with a black skin.'

When Kimberley had a three-judge court, and Mr Justice Solomon was puisne judge* under Sir Perceval Laurence (who predeceased him by about three months), Natives began to realise the true inwardness of the meaning of British justice as between man and man. After his transfer to Grahamstown, the war broke out, and the late judge came north again, as president of the Special Tribunals Court, with the late Sir John Lange and Mr Advocate Maasdorp, who later became Chief Justice of the Orange River Colony.

When the court visited Mafeking, Judge Solomon delivered a judgement which is still a byword among the Natives of Bechuanaland. Some white men were charged with killing a Native. In sentencing them, Judge Solomon said: 'Perhaps when you chased and shot down this unfortunate Native like a springbuck, you were not aware that you were committing as serious a crime as if you were shooting a white man. But I would like you, and other men who think with you on these subjects, to understand that the law makes no distinction between a man with a white skin and a man with a black skin. The Native you shot was just as much entitled to the protection of the law as you yourselves.' The death sentence was carried out in the case of two of the accused; the others, being reprieved by Sir Walter Hely-Hutchinson, served various terms of imprisonment.

Sir William's brother, Richard, once called 'the fanatical negrophilist', severed his connection with Kimberley when he became Attorney-General in the Schreiner ministry; and later died in London, where he was High Commissioner for the Union. When Natives see the high positions filled with distinction by statesmen of the old Cape Colony who, in their youth, sat in the same class with Natives – such as Chief Justice, High Commissioner, Acting Governor-General, or chairman of a huge mining corporation like De Beers Company – when they see the shining record of them all, and contrasting it with the present-day attitude against co-education, they, rightly or wrongly, are apt to draw only one conclusion; namely, a fear on the part of the authorities lest the South African whites should become as just and as tolerant as white men in Canada and New Zealand. But those were days of men,

> Patient, courageous, strong and true;
> With vision clear and mind equipped,
> All truth to love, all wrong to hate.

---

* A judge of a superior court, but inferior in rank to the chief justice.

On leaving Kimberley, for the sake of principle – something very cheap in these days – Sir Richard Solomon abandoned a retainership of four figures per annum, and all the perquisites and advantages appertaining to the legal adviser of Mr Rhodes and De Beers Company. How different from the statesmanship of today, when men can find from five to seven hundred golden reasons to chew up, and eat in public, their own views of yesterday!

One case in which the writer gave evidence before Judge Solomon created a great difference of opinion in legal circles. Some judges actually criticized the verdict. It happened in this way. Two rebel Boers were arraigned before the Treason Court and charged with shooting a Native under circumstances described by counsel for the defence as 'terrible'. Mr Justice Hutton appeared for the crown. The success of the defence depended entirely on the whereabouts of deceased's place of abode. The defence did not know it; and feeling against the rebels, very high at the time, was stimulated by memories of incidents connected with the recent bombardment of the place during the siege; and so loyalists were not disposed to assist the defence in finding a loophole. At the last minute of the 11th hour, Mr H. Burton, counsel for the defence, personally made the dramatic discovery that I held the key to the solution of the fateful riddle; and I was obliged to enter an appearance as witness for the defence.

My evidence relieved the defence, but outraged loyalist feelings. The two accused were acquitted on the murder charge, but later convicted and sentenced on other treasonable acts. The two Boers sent me through the jailer a verbal message of thanks. I never heard of them again, until 24 years later, when I read of one of them attending a Nationalist congress at Pretoria and offending the chairman (Mr Justice Tielman Roos) by threats to withdraw his sons from the defence force if the Pact Government did not immediately dismiss every defence officer appointed by the South African Party government!

One has neither time nor space to make here more than a passing reference to Sir William's concurring judgement (with Sir James Rose Innes and Sir Henry Juta, who died about a month ago) in the great land case which exempted the Cape province from the draconian tyrannies of the Natives' Land Act; nor the Native view of his interesting experiences on the Transvaal bench, and his disposal of Native Commissioners in northern Transvaal, and rural juries, who were apt to take sides with guilty white men against innocent Natives; nor his action against a Johannesburg attorney who received £15 from a Native client and refused to brief counsel because, he said, the fee was too small.

Almost the last case decided by Sir William Solomon, before retiring from office as Chief Justice of the Union, was a civil action by a Rand Native woman. Her husband was killed by a train at a Johannesburg crossing, and she sued the railway department for £400. The Rand high court dismissed her claim on the ground that her husband had been negligent when crossing the line. The woman appealed.

Before hearing the appeal, Sir William proceeded from Cape Town to Bloemfontein, via Johannesburg; the object being to make a personal examination of the scene of the tragedy. In giving judgement in the case, his lordship said he was satisfied that had the learned judge in the provincial court seen the dangerous character of the level crossing, he would have arrived at a different decision. Accordingly, the appellate court allowed the appeal, and awarded the widow £400, with costs in both courts.

Natives in the Union and beyond its boundaries will sympathize with the bereaved family in its loss. They would wish that his aged aunt Georgiana (Mrs Saul Solomon, senior), at Golders Green,[77] had been spared such a shock in the evening of her days. Still, it is hoped that she will take comfort in the fact that South Africa, irrespective of race, colour, creed or sex, is satisfied with the character of the noble career just ended. Natives, especially, would wish to assure her that her 'dear Willie', and other members of the Solomon family on this side of the water, continue to maintain their remarkable immunity from infection from the two local diseases which, they know, she dreads like the smallpox: the diseases of 'colourphobia' and 'ware Suidafrikan-itis'.*

The life and work of Sir William Solomon, on the contrary, shows that all 'friends of the Natives' are not overseas, and that it is possible to be born in South Africa and yet be just and upright with all people.

Here's hoping that timid South Africans who hesitate, through mistaken fear of public (?) opinion will in future see that in the long run it pays better to be just, and that they will take steps to rid their dominion of the unenviable stigma of being the only country in the whole of God's earth whose indigenous population is debarred from acquiring the fee simple to a square rood of their Native soil; the only country in the whole world where non-Europeans are debarred from joining the universal Scout movement – they may not even use the title 'Boy Scout' or 'Girl Guide' for their own separate race groups, however competent, through fear lest they should spread the Brotherhood

* 'True South African-itis'.

spirit during weekdays outside the churches. They can go to India or America to become Scouts, but not in this, the only country in the world in which a Native child, on account of colour, is debarred from attending a government school, maintained (sometimes exclusively) by the direct and indirect taxes levied on the child's own father and brothers.

The family is still represented on the Transvaal Bench by Mr Saul Solomon, who is making as great a reputation on the bench as he did at the bar. And in wishing peace to the soul of the departed man of law and equity Natives all over are singing, in the words of their traditional dirge:

> Raranyan oaga Rare!
> Godimo o go ileng a lale,
> A lale a robale.

> My father's little father!
> Up above where he is gone
> May he sleep and rest.

97
Further evidence to the Native Economic Commission, 1931[78]

The Native Economic Commission was appointed by the government in 1930 in order to investigate the socio-economic condition of Africans in urban areas, with a view to recommending 'measures, if any, to be adopted to deal with surplus Natives in, and to prevent the increasing migration to, such areas'. In the several reports the Commission tabled between 1930 and 1932 the main recommendation emphasised the seriousness of economic conditions in the 'reserves', and the steps which needed to be taken to make them viable. The Commission visited Kimberley in February 1931, having previously invited a number of individuals to submit written evidence on the economic position of the African population. Plaatje submitted two papers – one entitled 'Influx of Natives into Urban Areas: Some Remarks on General Economic Conditions'; the second simply entitled 'Further Evidence to the Native Economic Commission' (reproduced here). Plaatje then appeared before the Commission to give further verbal evidence, and to answer questions about his written evidence, on the morning of 26 February 1931.

There was a time when the Native was regarded merely as the manual labourer of the country. Today he is something very much more. Besides being the Union's cheap labourer, he serves as a buffer between political parties in

Parliament and, having regard to his meagre wage, he is also the chief taxpayer of the Union.

When looking at the country's revenue, we are too apt to imagine that every white man is a super-tax payer, forgetting that thousands of Europeans live on doles and government charities, and that Natives, besides paying their share of the country's taxation, must make up the deficiency.

All too often we forget that, while many Europeans farm with government stock for which they pay no hire, their Native servants, including those who earn 5/- per month, pay a direct tax of £1 per year, plus pass fees and indirect taxes; so that no male Native above the age of 18 (however poorly paid) escapes taxation. And while the government now levies from Natives taxes which 20 years ago would have caused a blush on nearly every white face, and give them NOTHING IN RETURN, thousands of white children attend schools, living in state hostels, absolutely board-free and rent-free.

Twenty years ago, it was roughly estimated by the late Mr Merriman, the greatest economic authority of his day, that the trade value of every European was equal to that of three Natives. The Native at that time was the hewer of wood and the drawer of water. He was taxed mainly on his Sunday dress. Now that he uses expensive furniture and gramophones and incurs heavy stamp duties, he has to pay additional poll taxes and pass fees. But taking Mr Merriman's figure of 20 years ago, which he put down at five million sterling (direct and indirect). It, however, did not include their entertainment taxes; it did not include their wheel taxes nor duties on petrol; it did not include their liquor fines – a growing source of revenue – nor their licence duties of one kind or another.

Whenever licences are considered, no one believes that a single Native contributes a shilling towards licence revenue. We are too ready to conclude that licences are bought by diamond merchants, auctioneers and representatives of foreign firms.

The Bloemfontein location, for instance, has 95 licensed hawkers. The severe restrictions on Free State Native hawkers compel the bulk of them to carry two licences each. These two licences at £10, however, do not confer on the Native holder anything like the trade facilities enjoyed by white general dealers, who only pay £5 for a licence. There are, in addition, scores of £3 licences held by Natives for the right to mend boots, take photographs, make bricks or perform any kind of manual labour, though the sale of his skilled labour does not cost the European labourer a penny. In addition, there are in the same location 19 motor owners and over two hundred licensed cyclists. I do not believe that many people are aware that a single Native community spends a thousand per year on licences only; yet the figures of Bloemfontein are but a flea-bite compared with the licence fees of Pretoria, Durban and Johannesburg.

Because they are represented by their own people in the councils of state, we have Europeans who pay income tax and others who are fed and housed by the state; we have, on the one hand, European adults with responsibilities to the state and, on the other, European minors with none. Among the inarticulate Natives on the other hand, tax-gatherers can see no distinction between adults and minors of eighteen years; a pauper Native, as long as he is outside a hospital must pay the same poll tax, the same pass fees and the same double duties on kaffir truck* as a Native who earns £5 per month; and both get next to nothing for their money. This is possible because the Native, without a voice in the councils of state, is treated like an alien in the land of his fathers. Even the Native Affairs Department is a European concern inside a white administration.

When the 1920 Act was passed there were faint hopes that this myopic vision was about to be remedied by the constitution of the new Native Affairs Commission. Hopes were expressed by friends of the Natives that the appointment of two or more aboriginal Native Affairs Commissioners would supply the administration with its missing second eye. Unfortunately this was not done; and the effect thereof is that, since 1920, we have had a European Native Affairs Commission to advise the government on Native interests. None of the commissioners sleep in the location; none of them travel in 'Jim Crow' cars; none of them are compelled to stand in the rain at wayside stations while empty waiting-rooms are reserved for Europeans who are not there; none of them (while travelling in strange areas) have perforce to spend their cold nights in the open veld, in the vicinity of hotels that will never admit them (this was the experience in this Union of Dr Aggrey, the black commissioner of the Phelps-Stokes Fund). In fact none of their children are excluded from public schools maintained by their taxes. All the members of the Native Affairs Commission being thus free from the legal disabilities of which Natives are the victims, what could they possibly tell the minister, or Parliament, which they do not know already, or which the Secretary for Native Affairs and his staff of white Native Commissioners and white sub-

---

*   Goods sold by traders to the African population – the term also had the connotation of cheap or tawdry.

Native Commissioners cannot tell them? The object of the 1920 Act was that the Commission should interpret the Native mind to the government; but, today, the Native belief is that in practice, the Commission regards itself as the mouthpiece of the government, appointed in the interest of the European population.

Next to the land trouble, the most burning grievance about which Natives and their ministers are constantly appealing to high heaven for retributive justice is the educational grants to Native schools and institutions in contradistinction with coloured, Indian and European school grants; and Native condemnation of the inequalities has been fully justified by the helpless mess in which the administration of Native education finds itself today; but the Native Affairs Commission has never been able to view the position as seen though Native eyes; how then, could they interpret Native feelings in this or any other matter?

Whenever Natives try to point out this partiality they are constantly met with suggestions of further taxation, as though Natives have not been paying 'further taxation' since 1925. What worries the Native is that he now pays further taxation for his miserably financed education; he pays, in addition, an undue share of the Union revenues. The more favoured coloureds and Europeans pay no personal tax unless they earn over £300 per annum; yet the incidence of this inequality cannot penetrate the civilized mind of the European Native Commissioner who himself is not subject to it.

Boiled down, it amounts to this that, despite the present multiple tax on Natives, they cannot boast a single government day-school, not even one to provide the exception that proves the rule; but other sections of the community who pay no 'further tax' have palatial education institutions and new ones are constantly going up. Native teachers in the Orange Free State have often to wait three months before they see the colour of their scant wages. Native teachers in the Transvaal and the Cape province have to incur heavy expense and sue the Government for the small pittance allowed them under the scale laid down by the Government itself. White, Coloured and Indian teachers, who pay no 'further tax' never have to sue for their much better salaries so, what guarantee is there that an addition to 'the further tax of 1925' will ameliorate any of these conditions?

Seven years ago I was investigating race relationships in the United States of America. At Washington I found the superintendent-general of education had four assistant superintendents-general of education. One of these four is a Negro. Thanks to his administration and invaluable advice to the department of education, parallels of the South Africa educational injustices are absolutely impossible among the several taxpayers of America. I found, further, that this mixed administration characterized nearly every department of state, including the treasury and network of intricate ramifications of their federal, their state and their municipal law departments. As far as my investigations went, Americans will never appoint a Negro economic commission or Negro statistical committee composed entirely of Europeans: because, they told me, hardly any white man can tell the president anything about the Negro which he does not know already, so that further information can only be supplied by the Negro himself because, they said, he is more competent to interpret the true feeling of his race than any European spokesman.

Even in Canada where, numerically speaking, the negro population is negligible, I found the assistant general manager of Toronto Street Railways – a huge municipal concern – was a Negro; and one of the four controllers who virtually form the mayor's cabinet was also a Negro and in their hands the interests of the Negro ratepayers, Negro employees and Negro passengers are safe. The United Charities also had a Negro department in charge of a Canadian Negress at forty-one dollars (about eight guineas) per week, organizing and dispensing relief amongst her own people.

In this country, such things are the prerogative of one race. No wonder that Natives in economic desperation have sometimes clandestinely sold their daughters and called the transaction *u-lobolo*,[*] or part of an ancient custom which their detribalized fathers never knew; and Parliament (acting presumably on the advice of the Native Affairs Commission) by passing a law recognising *lobolo* as a valid contract enforceable at law, has assisted the father in this process and thus practically removed the safeguards of old tribal customs.

Native economic conditions will hardly receive proper consideration because the administration of Native affairs, as the minister said at Pretoria last December, has to take into consideration first the interests of Europeans. Even the pass laws, said the minister, cannot be simplified without regard to the European view.

The Native population is inarticulate because it has no representation in the senate financed by their taxes; none in the Union assembly which spends their millions; none in the provincial executive, none in the divisional or

---

[*] Nguni, 'bride-price', usually in cattle, paid by an African man to the parents or guardians of his prospective wife.

municipal councils which receive their wheel-taxes, their dog-taxes, their entertainment taxes, their rates and a share of their poll tax – not even in the Native Affairs Department or among its welfare offices who, in the present state of race relations, cannot possibly see one more than one tenth of the sordid angles of Native life known to Jewish grocers and Indian hawkers.

Even the government railways, largely supported by Native traffic, cannot boast a single Native free pass-holder; in fact, it is their boast that they give no employment to Natives; where, then, can Natives find economic salvation if not in industries run largely by the aid of their earnings?

European taxes provide them automatically with an army of representatives who attend periodically the several councils of state, and ventilate at government expense European grievances before administrators of their own race.

Native taxes can purchase no such amenities. After paying taxes, they have to find further funds to send a fresh delegation each time they have a grievance to air; and, because they have no representatives at headquarters the subject is forgotten after each deputation leaves Cape Town or Pretoria.

Perhaps it may be argued that Dr Abdurahman's work on the provincial council and his municipal activities in the mother city had nothing whatever to do with the more liberal educational facilities enjoyed by Malays and coloured people in South Africa, or with the lighter taxes they pay; but facts are often more staggering than opinions.

It is admitted that without the Johannesburg mines not only farmers would be clamouring for a moratorium but the Union government, like other governments during the present depression, would also find it increasingly difficult to meet its financial obligations. No commission to my knowledge, ever reminded the Europeans that they owe their country's solvency to the labour of 200,000 Native miners who risk their life and limb toiling in the bowels of the earth for a mere pittance, in order that the Rand should yield nearly a million pounds worth of fresh gold every week; that other countries in the western hemisphere and in the antipodes have similar mines, but unlike South African mines they cannot be profitably worked through lack of cheap labour.

Natives have never seen a team of oxen, after pulling heavy loads over mountains, going to buy bread or peeling potatoes for their drivers; and they are beginning to ask why they must carry the broad end of the triangle and the apex as well. And, since Native muscle created the jobs for the other sections of the community, the Native Commissioner has still to be appointed who will remind the government of the justice of looking for 'further taxation' to those only who exploit the benefits of Native labour and Native taxes, and, insist on some consideration for the black bulwarks of the country's credit and a quid pro quo for their already heavy taxes.

FINALLY, the Native having been outlawed by acts of parliament from his natural environments in the rural districts, his influx into town locations is inevitable because even a Native cannot live in defiance of the law. Improved economic conditions in the urban centres, therefore, should be the aim of any scheme towards the betterment of Native social conditions. And whereas Native miners cannot continue to delve in old age, some reserve, near the towns, should be provided where the municipality may off-load its overworked labourers, where they could run their own goats and grow their own mealies.

98

Preface to Mhudi: An Epic of South African Native Life a Hundred Years Ago (Lovedale, 1930)

Plaatje wrote Mhudi *in England in 1920, but failed to secure a publisher for it until the Reverend R.H. Shepherd, chaplain at Lovedale and convenor of the Lovedale Press committee, accepted it for publication.* Mhudi *appeared in September 1930.*

South African literature has hitherto been almost exclusively European, so that a foreword seems necessary to give reasons for a Native venture.

In all the tales of battle I have read, or heard of, the cause of the war is invariably ascribed to the other side. Similarly, we have been taught almost from childhood, to fear the Matabele – a fierce nation – so unreasoning in its ferocity that it will attack any individual or tribe, at sight, without the slightest provocation. Their destruction of our people, we are told, had no justification in fact or in reason; they were actuated by sheer lust for human blood.

By the merest accident, while collecting stray scraps of tribal history, later in life, the writer incidentally heard of 'the day Mzilikazi's tax collectors were killed'. Tracing this bit of information further back, he elicited from the old people that the slaying of Bhoya and his companion, about the year 1830, constituted the *casus belli* which unleashed the war dogs and precipitated the Barolong nation headlong into the horrors described in these pages.

This book should have been published over ten years ago, but circumstances beyond the control of the writer delayed its appearance. If, however, the objects can be attained, it will have come not a moment too soon.

This book has been written with two objects in view, viz., *(a)* to interpret to the reading public, one phase of 'the back of the Native mind'; and *(b)*, with the readers' money, to collect and print (for Bantu Schools) Sechuana folktales, which, with the spread of European ideas, are fast being forgotten. It is thus hoped to arrest this process by cultivating a love for art and literature in the vernacular. The latter object interests not missionaries alone, but also eminent scholars like Dr C.T. Loram,[79] Dr C.M. Doke and other professors of the University of the Witwatersrand, not to mention commercial men of the stamp of Mr J.W. Mushet, Chairman of the Cape Town Chamber of Commerce.

The last time I wrote a booklet, it was to pay my way through the United States. It was a disquisition on a delicate social problem known to Europeans in South Africa as the *Black Peril* and to the Bantu as the *White Peril.* I called it *The Mote and the Beam.* It more than fulfilled its purpose for, by the time I left the States, over 18,000 copies had been sold and helped to pay my research journeys through several farms and cities of nineteen different states; and it is the author's sincere hope that the objects of this book will likewise be fulfilled.

In conclusion, I have to thank Rev. R.H. Shepherd, chaplain of Lovedale, and Mr M.R. van Reenen,[80] principal of the coloured public school, Beaconsfield, for helping to correct the proofs.

Sol T. Plaatje

32 Angel Street
Kimberley
August 1930

99

Article, 'Suggested new Bantu orthography', *South African Outlook,* 1 May 1931

The *Outlook* being a missionary organ, and its many readers largely interested in Native publications, I trust that for their information the editor will be good enough to spare some space for the following observations on the above subject.

The idea of the new spelling emanates from the International Institute of African Languages and Cultures (London), which aims at creating a uniform spelling for all the languages of the continent of Africa. In order to further the project from the southern end of the continent, a South African Orthography

Committee was appointed about two years ago under the auspices of the Native Affairs Department and the universities of South Africa.

Having examined the project in all its bearings, with the aid of my little knowledge of the Bantu languages, I must submit that, with the 26 letters of the alphabet, one could no more employ the same spelling for the languages of the whole of the continent than one could for say, English and Afrikaans. Some groups will have to be sacrificed for the benefit of others. In fact, this is happening already; because, far from hammering out a new spelling acceptable to all, the work of the Orthography Committee appears to have degenerated into efforts to dragoon the several provinces to exercise their authority in the direction of coercing the Basuto and Bechuana to drop their old missionary spelling and accept a new one adopted by the Zulu-Xhosa group, in collaboration with university professors.

It is to be regretted that at this end of the continent the scheme was attacked along real South African lines; i.e. the Natives know not what they need. So, let university professors lay down a scheme, in the light of science; and Native schools will have to adopt it or do without government grants!

This method had only one chance of success: namely, by keeping the people in ignorance so that their protests may come too late, when the proposition is already in permanent occupation of a prominent place in the curricula of our Native schools.

About two years ago, sub-committees were appointed for several South African languages; and their findings are now being considered, or adopted, by the education departments of the four provinces and the protectorates; but the bulk of the readers of these languages have hardly ever heard of a change.

I have seen the personnel of the Xhosa committee. It was composed of experienced European and Bantu authors – masters of their languages – some of whose Xhosa books are on my library shelves. They at any rate knew what to adopt and what to reject in the interest of their language.

The constitution of the Sechuana committee, on the other hand, was its exact antithesis. Ten Europeans and two Natives met at Pretoria over a year ago; most of the former knew nothing about Sechuana, while the two Natives appear to have been selected by virtue of two outstanding qualifications, viz., (a) none of them ever wrote a Sechuana book or pamphlet; and (b) neither of them ever lived in Bechuanaland or in districts where the unadulterated Sechuana is spoken. Two missionaries on the committee had done some work in the language and had translated its folklore for English and German magazines; but care seems to have been taken so to constitute the committee that, should they and the two Natives stand together and contend for any given point (as indeed they did more than once) the four of them would have to face a phalanx of eight Europeans whose sole purpose on the committee was to vote for the new spelling, regardless of consequences, whether or not they understood what they were voting upon. Is it to be wondered at that Sechuana writers and Bechuana missions will have nothing to do with their decisions?

The committee, however, did not worry over the views of the Natives or their missionary bodies, for, in the language of a leading protagonist of the new spelling, they could rely on the government grants to enforce their own decision through the Native schools.

The Transvaal province appears to have adopted the new spelling without any investigation. The Basutoland authorities placed it before a board of missionaries and Basuto authors who, after examining the scheme from every angle, came to the conclusion that it was wholly unacceptable.

The Free State director of education, we understand, first committed himself to an early enforcement of it in Native schools; but, on second thoughts, decided to convoke a meeting of his advisory board on Native education, which met at Bloemfontein at the end of January. The members and the churches represented on the board are as follows: Dr. T.B. Porteus, chairman (Presbyterian); Revs. F.P Roth and J. Weir (Wesleyan); Revs. J.G. Strydom, secretary, and H.A. Roux (Dutch Reformed); Rev. W. Illsley (Primitive Methodist); Archdeacon Hulme (Anglican); Rev. E. Muller (Berlin Mission); Mr. A.L. Barrett (Native Affairs Department); Rev. A.P. Pitso (Native Teachers' Association, O.F.S.) and Rev. C. Demas (African Methodist Episcopal Church). There were present also the director of education (Mr S.H. Pellisier), the Chief Inspector of Native Education (Mr H.F.G. Kuschke), and Mr Ross, Inspector of Native Schools.

The members of the advisory board who know the language are Revs. E. Muller of Bloemfontein and A.P. Pitso of Winburg; and they seem to have enlightened their attentive colleagues to good effect. Having heard Mr Franz of the orthography committee, who was also in attendance, the board, after considerable discussion, decided that the Education Department should obtain full information about the whole matter, 'ascertain Native opinion and circularize such knowledge through the synods of mission churches and Native Teachers' Association, with power to go into the whole matter; consult such Natives as they consider competent to give advice and report to the advisory board as to their findings'.

It is a question whether all the professors and men of letters who compose the South African Orthography Committee will quite like this open way of handling the subject. The Free State director of education, on the other hand, may yet live to thank providence for the gift of a most sensible board. In view of what I am about to quote, it is reasonable to assume that the timely intervention of the Free State advisory board, by preventing provincial authorities from enacting a serious injustice against the Native population (thus frustrating the creation of a first-class Native grievance) has also saved the face of the Education Department.

Dr Westermann, a director of the London body responsible for this movement, recently reviewed the work of the West African committees and his survey contains this significant passage: 'An orthography burdened with diacritical marks could hardly ever become popular.' This gentleman apparently is a wiser prophet than he knows, for the first offensive feature of the proposed new spelling is its numerous diacritics; and, almost invariably this question suggests itself to a Native: Why should the spelling of my language depend on unsightly diacritics, whilst other people spell theirs very neatly with only letters of the alphabet?

One has not the space to give samples of the confusing letter-juggling which we are asked to contrive in substitution of our own superior spelling. But one may be permitted to mention only one by way of illustration. For instance, we Bechuana are asked to dispense with the letter c in order that the Xhosa group may use it as a click. The far-reaching effect of this one omission is that words like *nca* (dog), *mocaca* (bitter), *cacanka* (be angry), etc., will be spelt so: *ntša, motšatša, tšatšanka.*

Should one forget to put a small ∨ on top of every *s*, then the words retain their old values, and they mean, not *dog*, etc. (as the writer intended) but, *a rift, flimsy* and *strut about* respectively. Hence our objection to the proposed ambiguities and our partiality for the missionary spelling whose consonants express our meaning definitely without the aid of diacritics.

I am not at all certain that the proposed spelling will be an improvement on the present Xhosa orthography; on the contrary I am afraid that the simplicity of Xhosa etymology will be weakened by the innovation. Only recently I was looking through the pages of Rev. J.W. Appleyard's 80 years-old *History of the Xhosa Language* and admiring his wonderful comparison, in three parallel columns, of English, Sechuana and Xhosa words. The very thought of displacing his lucid spelling by the incongruities under discussion made me shudder.

Let it be clearly understood, however, that I do not consider myself competent to express opinions on how adversely I think the proposed change will affect the Xhosa, the Herero and other tribes of whose languages I have a smattering. But, speaking for the Sechuana – a language in which, over 50 years ago, I first learned to articulate, and into which I have since translated some Shakespeare dramas, besides compiling its proverbs and finding European equivalents for most of them; and, speaking also from my knowledge of international phonetics, I have no hesitation in saying that, from the Sechuana viewpoint, the proposed changes are preposterous.

I once exercised on the typewriter the Sechuana Lord's Prayer in the new spelling. Having repeated it several times, I got myself timed, and it took me over six minutes to type it off. In addition, I required another three minutes to go over the copy, with pen and ink, and insert the necessary diacritics. In the present spelling it took me just under three minutes complete with punctuation marks.

In these enlightened days of rapid progress, of time and labour saving devices like linotypes, telephones and new Fords, how could anyone force upon our children (by threats to withdraw their government grants, the proceeds of poll taxes paid by their own parents) a cumbersome and retrogressive spelling that requires from 25 to 30 minutes to compose a letter which their grandmothers wrote very neatly, and with a better spelling, in eight or ten minutes? The proposition is hardly worth discussing.

On the question of consulting Natives I may be permitted to quote clause 5 of the memorandum of the London body already referred to, published in their official organ, *Africa*, of January 1928, p.16. Thus: 'It is obvious that in the composition of school books Native Africans must have a share; not only teachers and others occupied with education, but also leading members of the Native community should be consulted and their advice be given full weight. They, more than anyone else, are able to provide the necessary material: they represent the genuine indigenous point of view, and they can help to prevent serious mistakes.'

In the face of this, one may ask, could anyone imagine anything more pitiable than the fact of a director of education who (yielding to pressure from scientists and university professors) proceeded without proper investigation to force into his schools a new language scheme only to discover, later, that the scheme is rejected in London because it was found 'burdened with diacritical marks' and because it violated the principles of the originators in that it ignored 'the genuine indigenous point of view'?

Personally, I have nothing but the highest respect for the sound learning of university professors. I yield to no one in my admiration of their academic distinctions and high scholarship. The only trouble with the professors is that they don't know my language and, with all due deference, how could a string of letters behind a man's name enable him to deal correctly with something that he does not understand?

Simple knowledge is not enough. One has to be a musician to do justice to Sechuana idioms. Pioneer missionaries who first put this language on paper were great singers; and their musical ears were sensitive to the value of tones which play an important part in Sechuana prosody. It may be justly said that we shall never again have a Robert Moffat, a Roger Price or J.R. Cameron nor any of the missionaries of the late Victorian era, like Archdeacon Crisp, Canon Beavan, or Father Porte, who produced the earlier Sechuana books. The present missionary has not the same opportunities of arbitrating in Native disputes and of hearing the unspoilt Native speech. The *moruti** has ceased to be sole guide, philosopher and friend of the Natives. Under the changed conditions they go to the magistrate with their drought troubles, to the Native Commissioner with their land disputes, to the lawyers with their slanders and domestic differences and to the police when their property is lost, stolen or strayed. Only one man, therefore, is still capable of determining the spelling of this language. That man is the Native. And when the Bechuana themselves have decided upon an orthography more suited to the euphony of their idioms, language reformers may rest assured that it will not differ very materially from the missionary spelling which has served us so usefully for upwards of a century.

And then it would seem that the main object of the scheme is being overlooked, and that is uniformity. The Basuto, who speak a branch of the Sechuana, have rejected the proposition; so, why attempt to create a rift between branches of the same tongue by rounding off the Bechuana by themselves? In preliminaries to any steps towards uniformity of spelling, Sechuana will have to accord (not with the exotic Zulu or Xhosa) but with Sesuto which employs the same literary idioms.

Plaatje's article inspired a response form W. G. Bennie (Outlook, 1 July 1931), a well-known missionary and Xhosa linguist, and a member of the Xhosa sub-committee of the Central Orthography Committee, who argued that Plaatje's comments could not apply to the work of the Xhosa committee; and from W. L.

---

*   Sesotho: 'priest', 'minister'.

Thompson, another missionary from Mount Silinda in Rhodesia, who favoured a uniform orthography for all African languages. Plaatje's reply to Bennie, and Bennie's response to Plaatje's reply, then appeared in the Outlook of 1 August.

100

Letter to R.R. Moton, 16 July 1931[81]

Plaatje had sent Robert Moton three copies of Mhudi in late 1930, which Moton thanked him for in a letter dated 5 March 1931: the arrival of the books, he said, 'brought back very pleasant memories of your visit to Tuskegee and of our contact later in London'. The letter reproduced below is a response to this.

P.O. Box 143
Kimberley
16.7.31.

Dear Dr Moton

I was so pleased to hear from you again. I am wondering how it happened that I sent you a book without my autograph. I am wondering whether I did not perhaps send YOUR book to someone else, who should have received a blank one. One such case happened with six ordered by a Cape Town doctor. He returned, and exchanged, it for one with HIS name. Never mind: I am mailing you another by the next mail.

Can we not get a publisher over there to issue a SECOND edition? Any good publisher should successfully exploit the English and North American market with an overseas edition – 2nd print. Lovedale, not being commercial, have no agencies abroad and the field here is so limited that I am afraid, by the end of the year when this edition is exhausted, every South African reader will have a copy of Mhudi.

There is much that wants writing in the line of old Native research, but valuable data lies unprinted, of immense historic and anthropological value; I have no financial aid to visit such localities and the old people are fast dying out and being buried with the information which is thus being lost to posterity.

I frequently appealed to Dr Loram to use his influence in America for such financial aid. He would listen and question me so sympathetically – the net result was that after two years' raising false hopes, I read in the papers how he secured £250 from the government, and £900.0.0. from the Carnegie Trust for a white man to do in Zululand the kind of research that I have been explaining to him about my researches in Bechuanaland. I believe if a white man came along and stole my powder, he would have no difficulty in getting a £1,000 for half-cooked second-hand information (often distorted) about Natives. Yet a couple of hundred sterling could bring a Sechuana dictionary and a volume of Native fables and traditional poems in the vernacular to the printing press.

I do sincerely trust that you are enjoying good health and still making a success of your noble work.

With kindest regards to you and family from myself and wife and daughter
    Ever Yrs respectfully
    Sol T Plaatje

Kindly remember me to some of the faculty at Tuskegee who will still remember my visit.

Plaatje received a reply to his letter from G. Lake Innes, special assistant to Robert Moton, thanking him for the additional autographed copy of Mhudi, *but expressing doubt that* Mhudi *'would find the circulation in America all that you would hope to achieve for it'. Negro literature was indeed in vogue in the United States, he added, 'but not of the type your book represents'.*

101
Letter to Chief Tshekedi Khama, 11 August 1931[82]

Tshekedi Khama (1905-1959) became Regent (and effectively chief) of the Bamangwato, the largest Tswana tribe of the Bechuanaland Protectorate in 1925. Plaatje sought Tshekedi Khama's support in his campaign against the work of the Central Orthographic Committee's proposals, and wrote several letters to him on the subject between 1930 and 1932. Tshekedi Khama was by this time on a collision course with the new Resident Commissioner, Charles Rey, who sought to reduce the powers of the protectorate chiefs, Tshekedi in particular.

Box 143
Kimby
11.8.31.

My Dear Chief,
    I am not so sure of succeeding to go to Bechuanaland when the High Commissioner goes up next week. If I can find the fares, will you please

help me as you always do, to reach the meetings held so far from the railway line in Mangoatoland, so as to get some first-hand reports[83] between Mhalapye and Serowe – then back to Palapye to catch the train for Francistown?

When is your sister coming back? Regarding ORTHOGRAPHY, I shall be very sorry if you lose the confidence of the authorities. I should not like to see you categorically rejecting the government proposal to join hands with Basutoland,[84] gonne: kgetse ea tsie e kgonoa ke go choaraganeloa.*

Among whites, a point-blank refusal always creates the impression that one is obstinate. Therefore Chief, say: 'This is not merely a Ma-Ngwato language. I cannot decide alone. I must have plenty of time to confer with Bakgatla, Barolong, Ba-Hurutshe, etc., etc., u bale ba ba ko kgakal,† before agreeing to any fresh orthographic steps.' Fa ba kare 're potlakile.‡

Tell them this: 'I am not unwilling to be led. But, for goodness sake, don't rush me. If you drag my people along too fast we shall break our legs and necks; so what shall you do with the headless bodies?'

Say further: 'I found this language spoken when I was born; my fathers found it and left it here when they died. I can't help you to reform it in two months.'

They have told me that Prof. Dumbrell is anxious to print some *Dumbrell follies* next February; and he wants a hasty decision. I am sending you an extract from my reply.[85] Please don't let anyone know that I sent this to you. Fa ba ka itse gore kea tle ke itshebe ka maikaelelo a bone, mo-owetsana o ka kgla. Ka se ka ka tlhola ke utloela sape sa ko Mmushong. Kana fa e ne e se go utloana nabo. Nko ke se nke ke cose loderetlho lole loa ngogola go tsikinya dikgosi gore di loele puo ea cone. Le nna ke ne ke tla utloele go setse go atlhogile.

Ke rometse Mme, phuthelana ea dibanana Ke dilo tse di choenyan thata. Gongoe di fitlha di sale tala, gongoe di fitlhe di senyegele.

Thusa Phuyti, jaka gale, u romele mongoe a ee go tsela Mme dilamunu nyana tseo di e se di cheretlhege.

U di mo neele, u bolele le mashoabi ame ka go tshegedioa ke tiro ke tlhoka nako ea go nna mo marakeng ka metlha ke leta motlhango go tsileng tse di

---

* Tswana: 'because unity is strength'.
† Tswana: 'you should take into account people residing in the remote areas'.
‡ Tswana 'If they [government officials] say they are in a hurry'.

siameng. Ko shone se ke latlhang madi fela ka se se goafi, ka kea fitlhela ke
rakiloe ke ba ba gaufi.*

Best regards from my wife and daughter
And best wishes from
Your obedient servant
Sol T. Plaatje

*In fact the Bechuanaland Protectorate authorities did not go along with the proposals
of the Central Orthography Committee, and they were well aware of the opposition
to them in the Protectorate. A conference of education authorities from the Cape
Colony, Transvaal, and Orange Free State provinces, and the Bechuanaland
Protectorate, was held in November 1931, but no agreement could be reached.
Several further conferences were then convened within the Protectorate itself, and
plans to adopt the proposed new orthography were ultimately abandoned until a fresh
attempt was made in 1937.*

102
Article on Chief Moroka in T.D. Mweli Skota (ed.), *The African Yearly Register* (1931)[86]

*The African Yearly Register: Being an Illustrated National Biographical
Dictionary (Who's Who) of Black Folk in Africa, edited by T.D.Mweli Skota –
at that time General Secretary of the African National Congress – focused
particularly on black South Africans. Plaatje was one of the contributors to the book,
and his name was attached to the piece reproduced below.*

---

* Tswana: 'If they got to know that I at times gossip [reveal] their intentions, I would
never get any information about government from my source. Had it not been for my
cordial relations with them, I would not have been able to stir up chiefs into fighting for
their language. I would have heard about it belatedly (when the matter was already
over).

I have sent my mother [a respectful form of address, referring to the Chief's wife] a
package of bananas. Bananas are not easy to handle. They may still be fine when they
reach mother, or they may have perished.

Sir, duiker, help me as usual. Send someone to pick some oranges for my mother
before they rot.

Give them to her, and convey my apologies that I can't get fresh ones since I can't be
at the market to pick fresh ones when they arrive; I am pressed by work. This is why I
waste money buying rotten ones; customers who are close to the market get there before
I do.'

CHIEF MOROKA, of the Seleka Barolong, took charge of his people at Plaatberg when his father died in 1827.

Moroka was a young man in the early 'twenties of the last century when his people, the Seleka branch of the Barolong, were overtaken and harassed, first by the Manthatisi hordes, Sekonyela's people, and by Moletsane's Bataung, and later by the dreaded Matabele. It was during these trying times that, in January 1823, they met and made friends with the first white families they had ever seen. These were two Wesleyan missionaries – Broadbent and Hodgson – who found the Barolong in a disordered and excited state, having been rudely scattered by the raiders we have named from their peaceful environments between the Matlwase and Matlwasane valleys, along which flow the Schoonspruit and the Maquassi Rivers, tributaries of the Vaal, in the districts of Klerksdorp and Wolmaransstad in south-western Transvaal.

It was the intention of the Barolong to put as great a distance as possible between themselves and their enemies; accordingly, with great difficulty, they crossed the Vaal River and settled for a time at Motlhanapitse (the wild ass's jaw-bone) on the south bank of the Vaal, not far from Fourteen Streams. The place was so called because, in searching for a camping place, a chieftain unearthed the whitened jawbone of a zebra. The place, now one of the farms in the Boshof district, is in the Orange Free State; at present it enjoys the name of Plaatberg. It was here that the Barolong as a race really first opened their eyes, so to speak. Two Wesleyan missionaries had joined them as vanguards of the white population, now owning the Free State and Transvaal. It is clear that some Barolong had previously seen a white man from Portuguese East Africa, somewhere about the year 1780. His oxen were subjects of considerable interest. Women stared open-mouthed at the manner in which his bullocks submitted to the burden of heavy yokes on their necks. That, however, was a passing acquaintance.

The two missionaries, Broadbent and Hodgson with their families, were the first white people to permanently reside among the Barolong as sections of the same community. They astounded those Barolong who first saw a team of oxen 'dragging a moving white house'; some fled for all they were worth, mistaking the hairy occupants of the house on wheels for some unnameable monsters; and who can blame them? That was more than a century ago. Yet I can remember seeing, in the present century, civilized persons running like hunted foxes at the sight of an approaching motor car.

From these missionaries the Barolong learnt to dig for fresh water at places miles away from any fountain or running stream, and also learnt to train their

Chief Moroka of the Seleka Barolong: 'The life story of Moroka,' Plaatje wrote, 'is really the genesis of Barolong education as well as the history of their friendship with the Boers.'

tollies* to the yoke – a brand new enterprise. They saw their language put on paper, and were taught the art of reading and writing. They were definitely introduced to Christianity, under the influence of which the Barolong have now, a century later, produced three trained medical men, with two or three more about to qualify in Scotland; agricultural demonstrators; half-a-dozen authors, and not a few mechanics; with scores of trained teachers and ordained priests, many of whom can now construct their own schools and churches with burnt bricks or cut stones neatly pointed.

As long ago as the 'eighties of last century, about sixty years after his ancestors fled at the sight of a moving ox-wagon, a Native priest in charge of the Anglican mission at Bloemfontein, translated into Serolong, Shakespeare's *Twelfth Night*, and whose scholars performed it in the vernacular. All this development found its origin in Plaatberg, when Moroka as petty-chief took his instruction and wise guidance from the two white men who first came to live with his father's people. Motlhanapitse, however, proved not too healthy for a permanent settlement, and, on the advice of their missionaries, the Barolong evacuated the place in 1829 and moved to Thaba Nchu, one of the Basuto outposts, about 100 miles to the east. Here the Barolong, under the spiritual guidance of the successors of the pioneer missionaries already named, developed rapidly both materially and intellectually and, were there no such destructive forces as those imported by the liquor traffic, the present generation would most probably take a lead in every walk of Bantu life, including the spiritual life.

About 1834 the first party of emigrant Boers under Sarel Cilliers made acquaintance with the Barolong and passed on with their voortrekking expedition. They soon came into contact with Mzilikazi's vanguards at Vechtkop, in the Heilbron district. Here they had to resist a vigorous attack by the Matabele who relieved them of every head of their livestock. This fight marked the beginning of the tragic friendship of Moroka and the Boers. Word reached Moroka that the Boers, having lost all their cattle, were now exposed to starvation and further attacks. The chief nobly rose to the occasion. He sent teams of oxen to bring the Boers back to Thaba Nchu. On their arrival he levied from among his people gifts of milch cows and goats and also hides to make sandals and shoes for the tattered and footsore trekkers and their families, whom he settled in a place call Morokashoek. If South Africans were as romantic and appreciative as white people in Europe and America, Morokashoek would be a hallowed spot among the voortrekker descendants,

---

* Bullocks, or castrated bull calves (derived from the Xhosa, *ithole*, a calf).

and efforts would surely be made to keep the memory of the benefactors of their ancestors, as the Americans are doing with Crispus Attucks and the French with Alexandre Dumas.

In a couple of years the Boers had recuperated and, being reinforced by other Boer parties from the south and from Natal, the Barolong, combined with the Boers under Potgieter, drove the Matabele from Bechuanaland (now western Transvaal) to Rhodesia. Later other parties of Boers arrived from the south and occupied the Free State plains. These subsequently formed a Boer republic with Bloemfontein as the capital. Then there sprang up between them and Chief Moroka an alliance which cost the Barolong very dearly, and which involved sacrifices in men and materials for which history records absolutely no reciprocation on the part of the Boers.

In terms of their pact Chief Moroka with his men and with their own equipment helped the Boers to despoil the Basuto of what is now called the 'Conquered Territory'; they summarily erased the landmarks of King Moshoeshoe, forced the Basuto to the mountain tops, where, like rock rabbits they eked out a congested existence up on the plateaus; some of their chiefs today, who own their own automobiles, cannot go home in their cars.

I once met an old man who, in his youth, participated in those terrible sacrifices of men and material, exacted by the Boer-Barolong treaty, under which Barolong blood was spilled by the gallon in the wars against the Basuto in their own haunts. The ingratitude of the sons of their white allies made him feel bitter beyond expression. He could find no words to describe it, beyond the kaross-mender's maxim: '*Ga ba na phokojane oa morokagangoa nabo*',* for, across the colour bar, their perspective becomes so blurred that they can see no distinction between friend and foe.

Elsewhere I have written about the massacre of Plaatberg, where scores of Barolong warriors were hurled down a cliff by irate Basuto spearmen in a catastrophe that occasioned a re-grouping of the clans of widowed mothers and orphaned children, but voortrekker histories are silent about such awful sacrifices by black men in the interest of white civilization.[87]

A group of armed Basuto on one occasion raided the Bloemfontein fort, captured a big gun and made off with it (I presume a European writer would say 'stole' it). The Barolong intercepted the raiders at Brandsvlei and, after a brief engagement, recaptured the gun and restored it to the president.

---

* Tswana, lit. 'They don't even have a baby jackal-skin to enable them to sew together a kaross' (signifying complete ingratitude or lack of sympathy).

The sons of Moroka continued with this pact after the passing of their noble father and friend of refugees. Their quarrel over the chieftainship gave the Boers an excellent opportunity of reciprocating in some slight degree the sacrifices of their Native friends; but when the strife reached its climax, President Brand retaliated by annexing Moroka's territory, banishing his surviving son and confiscating all Barolong lands with the exception of the surveyed farms over which certain individuals held titles. Then they enacted Chapter XXXIV of the Law Book under which no coloured person could buy land – not even from another black. But the acme of the ingratitude of the sons of the voortrekkers came painfully into prominence in 1913 when, under draconian pains and penalties, Natives were debarred from even hiring the land for which their fathers bled (Act 27 of 1913).

It is mortifying to the descendants of the allies of the voortrekkers to find themselves ostracized and outlawed by the sons of their whilom friends, banished from lands for which they had helped to despoil the Basuto, forced to seek refuge in the attenuated holdings of the mountain folk, and the Basuto magnanimously offering them an asylum; now, too late, they rue the misplaced friendship of their fathers. How different was the action of his brother, Chief Montsioa, to the blind friendship of Moroka, some of them moan.

In the early 'fifties Commandant Paul Kruger sent a Boer messenger to Dithakong, the headquarters of the Ra-Tshidi, stating that he was leading an army against Sechele, the Chief of the Bakwena in the protectorate, and asking 'his friend Montsioa' to assist him with a couple of regiments, fully equipped. Montsioa sent word back to enquire for what offence Sechele was to be punished. The messenger returned with another message from Paul Kruger, 'Sechele is *parmantig*;* but if Montsioa did not feel disposed to expose his men to a fight, the commandant would be satisfied if he sent a troop of men to act as guides, as ox-wagon drivers and as herders to drive back to the Transvaal the looted Bakwena cattle, thus leaving the Boers to do the actual fighting.

The wily old hunter then sent back the following unmistakable reply, 'I shall at all times be ready to help my chief, Paul, with an army to proceed against anyone who has done wrong, but since the message does not disclose the exact point of the offence for which Sechele is to be punished, I shall find it difficult to persuade my people to provide a force to accompany an expedition against him.'

---

* Afrikaans: 'cheeky', 'impertinent'.

'All right,' said Commandant Kruger, 'I shall do without Montsioa and deal with him when I am through with Bakwena.' Chief Sechele, who suffered heavy loss of life, was despoiled and denuded of his cattle; his homes were destroyed including the mission house of Dr Livingstone, and many women and children were taken into the service of the victors.

When the expedition against Sechele returned with its gain, a fresh move was made against Montsioa whom the Boers found at Mosita. It is true they inflicted on him a heavy punishment in the course of a foray which is described by historians as 'the Blind War'. But if Montsioa lost men and material, he emerged from the affray with his character ennobled. He did not entirely lose his lands as Moroka did, and, as much of it was annexed to the Transvaal Republic was never placed out of bounds to his descendants.

To return to our subject, Chief Moroka was otherwise a wise ruler of his people, and other sections of the Barolong found the light of civilization through him. He led his people from barbarism into Christianity, from abject poverty into affluence; in fact, he died in 1880 leaving his country in a prosperous state, his people selling wheat by the wagon-load among Europeans away in Colesberg and Victoria West and trading at the newly discovered diamond mines of Kimberley, exchanging game hides, cattle and other produce for wagons, carriages, merino sheep and horses. He left them a regenerated tribe, quite different from their condition when he succeeded his father over fifty years before.

Chief Moroka's father, Sehunelo, lived just long enough to see and handle the first spelling-book printed in his language. It was shown to him on this death-bed. The first Bechuanaland boys to travel south in quest of education were the late Israel Molema and Stephen Lefenya, who, in the late 'fifties, like their successors after them, found their first mental equipment at Thaba Nchu under the wing of Chief Moroka. The aged Mr Lefenya, who is still alive, at the age of 96 years, was secretary to Chief Montsioa and two of his successors; he also served the Wesleyan Church for many years as evangelist. Mr Advocate Montsioa, of Johannesburg, who studied first at Zonnebloem and later at London, where he was called to the bar, owes much to Mr Lefenya. The first Bechuana newspaper was issued from the Wesleyan mission press, Thaba Nchu, during Chief Moroka's time – *Molekudi ua Bechuana*, May, 1856.

Chief Moroka was the first Native chief to survey portions of his territory and issue farms titles to individual members of his tribe; so that, after his death, when the Boers took over his lands they respected his title deeds. The bulk of these farms have since passed into other hands; but it is worthy of note that those granted to women have been better taken care of, and are still in the possession of their children. This sound precedent, however, was established too late to benefit many other tribes, as the country had by then been taken over by Europeans. It was followed by Chief Montsioa in Bechuanaland with beneficial results, and the safeguard became more noticeable when the Rhodesian railway line was built through the protectorate. The government awarded the railway company wide tracts of land traversed by the line, while the 'Barolong Farms' on which Chief Montsioa issued titles, not more than six yards on either side of the rails, were appropriated. Thus, the life-story of Moroka is really the genesis of Barolong education as well as the history of their friendship with the Boers.

103

Article on Chief Montsioa, in T.D. Mweli Skota (ed.), The African Yearly Register (1932)[88]

MONTSIOA, or Seja-Nkabo-a-Tauana. Among the best-known chiefs of the mid-Victorian days. The son of Tauana, the son of Thutlwa, the son of Tshidi, head of the second branch of the house of Tau, who was King of the Barolong about 1740. Montsioa was born soon after 1810, so that he was a young man in the late 'twenties of the last century when Mzilikazi, with his well-trained armies, trekked from the east, conquered the Bechuana tribes and proclaimed himself supreme ruler of central South Africa. He then commenced to levy taxes on the Bechuana tribes, including the Barolong along the Molopo River. In 1830, the Barolong sized King Mzilikazi's tax-collector, by name Bhoya, and killed him and his companion on cold blood. This seemingly isolated act brought down upon the Barolong the full force of Mzilikazi's wrath, and the Matabele impies swooped down upon them like an avalanche. The Barolong, who had fought their way down from the great lakes and were known among other tribes as baga Rungoana le bogale (the people with the sharp spear) witnessed, for the first time, a kind of warfare which made no distinction between man, woman or child; and for nearly three-quarters of a century thereafter, the Matabele and all tribes allied to them (e.g. Zulu, Xhosa, Swazi, Shangaan, etc.) were regarded with awe, and the Bechuana would have nothing in common with them. It speaks volumes for the magical force of Christianity if their descendants now inter-marry with members of such tribes.

Montsioa, as a young man just turned twenty, must have taken a prominent part in Bhoya's execution, for poets of the day immortalized the event with the following lines in his honour:

Montsioa (c. 1815-1896), Chief of the Tshidi Barolong: 'As a hunter in the chase, Chief Montsioa from youth was fearless as he was brave in war.'

Re kile ra ineelela dichaba,
Ra ineela, ka lecogo, merafe;
Seja-Nkabo a sale mmotlana,
A sale mo tharing eaga Sebodio.
Jaana ke mmonye a tlhatlosa motho lekgabana
A nale mmaba, a ea go bolaoa,
Seja-Nkabo-a-Tuana.

Too long we've bent the knee to foreigners,
Too long we've yielded the arm to strangers;
Montsioa, at that time, was still a baby
Astride the back of his mother, Sebodio.
Now have I seen him lead a man up hill,
Leading him up to the crest of Mount Kunana;
Conducting a foeman up to his kill,
Seja-Nkabo, the son of Tauana.

After their destruction by the Matabele, Tauana and his people found a shelter among Moroka's people – the Seleka branch of the tribe, at Thaba Nchu. The Barolong and the Boers were later reinforced by a contingent of Griqua horsemen, under an intrepid leader named Dout. The Barolong levies were led by Tauana's son, Motshegare; the combined forces being under the supreme command of Hendrik Potgieter – a friend of the Natives, if ever there was one. Together they defeated Mzilikazi's armies, and forced the Matabele to trek to the far north, now known as Southern Rhodesia.

After this overthrow and expulsion of Mzilikazi, Tauana and his people returned to the Molopo region, where he died and was succeeded by Montsioa as chief of the Ra-Tshidi section; but under him, they were not left long to enjoy their hard won peace. Soon after the voortrekker wave had spent itself by spreading out and settling land in the distant areas of northern Transvaal, the southern territories were overrun by stray whites, whose land-hunger vied with their utter disregard of the vested rights of those whose territories they invaded. Some bands of these were labelled filibusters (or freebooters), but the difference between the aspirations of such freelances and those of the newly established Transvaal Republic the Natives found it very hard to define. The similarity between them was particularly noticeable after the passing of the Potgieters, the Pretoriuses and others who, with their Native friends, bore the brunt of the pioneer work. Their places in the now settled country were taken by the new Pharaohs who knew not Joseph, and it was the bane of Montsioa's chequered life to have them as neighbours.

For instance, parties established the miniature republics of Stellaland and Goschen, with Vryburg as their capital; but, to their credit, let it be said that these settlers in their diminutive republic troubled the Bechuana very little. Much of the brigandage against Montsioa and the filibustering forays into Bechuanaland were usually organized on Transvaal soil and all captured cattle were promptly driven across the frontier into the South African Republic. Other Barolong tribes were cajoled and organized against Montsioa. The Ra-Tlou section, descended from the senior house of Tau, were assured that they alone should be at the head of all Barolong affairs including Montsioa's, and they were urged to join the Boers in their campaign against that usurper in order to bring about a desirable readjustment. Of course, white people were new in the country and it was not suspected that the solicitude of these intriguers for the regulation of the Barolong succession was stimulated by anything but a keen desire to place the house of Tau in its rightful position.

The tactics of the adventurers were remarkable. They first engineered a treaty between the British government and the Transvaal Republic. Under this treaty the English were to prevent the sale of arms to savages, so that white men alone could purchase firearms. The terms of this agreement were enforced by the British authorities with a firm hand, but some white men soon saw that the effect of the pact was to limit the spread of British dominion in the interior. Most 'savages' resisted the Boer expansion with no other object but to bring their own people under British protection; and many British pioneers sympathized with the violation of that treaty. Some actually came into Barolong territory and shared in the Native defence of their country against Boer encroachments. Among these may be mentioned the late Richard Rowland, Christopher Bethell and others. They not only procured arms for Montsioa but actually helped his warriors in battle. Bethell fell on the battlefield among the sons of Montsioa near the present Transvaal-Bechuanaland boundary.

The clashes between the Barolong and the Boers extended over several decades. These hostilities necessitated the removal of the headquarters of the tribe to the present site, where the natural formation of the rocks and the thickets in Montsioastad afforded some shelter to the defenders. Thus Baden-Powell's long defence of Mafeking was not the first; the place having been beleaguered more than once before the British annexation.

The High Commissioner, in a dispatch to the Colonial Office, about this time, points out the cruel anomaly whereby Her Majesty's colonial forces at the Cape were employed to prevent the delivery of arms and ammunition to Natives who were waging a grim struggle in the interests of British colonization; while the British colonial authorities, at the same time, were doing everything in their power to facilitate the delivery of arms to the Boers for use in subduing such loyal friends of the imperial government as Montsioa and his Barolong. (*War Dispatches*, 1877)

Dr J.E. Mackenzie, son of the famous missionary, writing on the development of Rhodesia, in a colonial magazine some years later, said, 'The British would never be able to repay the debt they owe to those two Bechuana chiefs, Montsioa and Mankuroane of the Bathlhaping, for the losses they have sustained in the wars they waged against the Boers in order to keep open for the British the trade route to the north, often in the face of British opposition.'

The history of these hostilities is unique in that Montsioa had among his praise names an Afrikaans ditty that was sung and played by Boers in the western Transvaal. I have forgotten the stanzas, but the refrain was:

> Hoe ry die pad, hoe ry die pad,
> Na Montsioa toe?
> Kanoonkop oor en die Molopo deur;
> Die Boer die skiet dat die stof so staan
> Maar die Kaffir op sy plek bly staan.*

It is not difficult to realize how these persistent raids and continuous losses of men and possessions which they involved were having a demoralizing effect upon Montsioa's tribe, and their plight eventually attracted the attention of friends of the Natives at the Cape. They strongly supported the Barolong's frantic appeals for British protection. The result of these petitions was the Warren expedition in 1885, which annexed Bechuanaland as far as the Ramatlhabama spruit, and proclaimed a protectorate over the territories of Bechuana tribes further north up to the Matabele borders. So that, after a most eventful life, the old warrior and hunter was able to spend the evening of his life in comparative peace.

---

* Afrikaans: 'How goes the road, how goes the road towards Montshiwa?/Over Kanonkop and across to Molopo,/The Boers' shooting kicks up the dust/But the Kafir remains at his place.'

This peace continued until 1896, shortly after the annexation of the Cape, when he was unsettled by the rinderpest scourge, which swept through Bechuanaland like a blizzard and denuded his territories of nearly every beast. Buffaloes and wildebeest in the forest perished like domestic kine and many flourishing cattle-posts were reduced to ruins. So that where formerly large herds of sleek fat oxen swarmed over the grasslands as a moving testimony of Barolong wealth, only heaps of whitened skeletons remained, the only vestige of the animal life that once throve there. It was a heart-breaking situation, the misery of his people being a thing terrible to contemplate. Hyenas and wild hounds gorged themselves to excess, while flocks of carrion birds and other scavengers of the woods were attracted by the stench of rotting carcasses.

As a hunter in the chase, Chief Montsioa from his youth was fearless as he was brave in war. He enjoyed a great reputation as a lion-killer – one of the Bechuana who would follow a wounded lion straight into a thicket. His character in that respect has also been put into irregular verse by the court jesters of his time, for they sang:

> Mogatsa Majang, tau ga di kalo!
> Tau ga di kalo, moroa Mhenyana.
> Ga di ke di bolaoa leroborobo,
> Di ba di etsa dipholofolo tsa gopo,
> Di ba di edioa pitse tsa gopo,
> Lekau ja Gontse-a-Tuana!
> Tau di bolaoa dile thataro,
> Lefa dile pedi dia bo di ntse.

> That's not the way to kill lions,
> O, husband of Majang!
> That's not the way, O, offspring of M'Henyana!
> Lions should not be butchered by the score
> Nor like hunted animals at the chase;
> Lions should not be slaughtered in such numbers,
> To litter the field like carcasses of.dead zebra,
> O, descendant of Gontse, son of Tauana!
> Six lions at a time are quite enough
> For, even two at a time are not too few!

And here is a rare coincidence: the name 'Montsioa' (he who is taken out) bears the same meaning as the Hebrew name 'Musheh' (Moses); and, as the Serolong expression has it – *ina lebe seromo* (an ill name is an evil omen).

Chief Montsioa survived the rinderpest catastrophe by barely one year. At the age of 86 he succumbed to pulmonary disorders aggravated by a fatty heart. He was buried by his people in his cattle-fold. Rev. Alfred S. Sharp, Wesleyan missionary, now in retirement in England, conducted the funeral service. Among the Europeans in attendance were Mr George J. Boyes, resident magistrate (who died at Cape Town, not long ago) and some Transvaal Boers, including his former military foes who, despite their proverbial weakness in the face of colour, could respect a brave man whenever they met one.

Among Chief Montsioa's Transvaal friends was included General Piet Cronje, a former adversary and the noblest Minister of Native Affairs that ever sat in a Kruger cabinet. He spoke the Barolong tongue almost like a Native and answered to the Native sobriquet of 'Ra-Ntho'akgale'.* After the peace of 1885, the old chief sometimes visited his Boer friends across the Transvaal border. On such occasions Dr Molema's father or the doctor's father-in-law (Rev. M.J. Moshoela, now of Klerksdorp) accompanied the old warrior as secretary, and sent back, during his absence, one bulletin after another to keep his people informed of the progress of their beloved chief and his reception among the Boers.

104
Article, 'A white man's Native language', *Umteteli*, 2 April 1932

European squabbles over the Native language have taken a new turn. It would appear that the gentlemen who control the Education Departments are definitely after a parody of the Native language to suit the tongues of Europeans and not of Natives. It is difficult to resist this presumption, for their aims and decisions are seldom reported in the Native newspapers. The Native language they regard as a plaything for the mental exercise of European students; hence, we have to rely on the European press for news of their activities against our language. Thus we learn from the daily papers that white men met near Rustenburg a week or two ago to standardize the Sechuana language; and for that purpose they will use the 'Sehurutshe dialect as their primary basis'.[89]

---

*   Tswana: a person of great knowledge and wisdom, commanding respect.

All this would be commendable but for the disquieting fact that the Bechuana tribes, whose language is said to be standardized by Europeans, are not taken into the white people's confidence. It is strange, but one is inclined to attach weight to the Native suspicion that these gentlemen have no intention of reaching finality in this European controversy over a Native tongue. By attempting to adopt Se-Hurutshe for all the Bechuana tribes (and doing so behind the backs of the people concerned) they are throwing an apple of discord between the Ba-Hurutshe and the rest, and so making sure of resentment. One wonders whether these gentlemen of the Education Departments have no better use for their time and money than to create dissension among Native tribes.

It is not improbable that the Ba-Hurutshe themselves will fail to identify their dialect when it emerges from the European conclave. The report contains hints of a departure 'from the original pronunciation of the Ba-Hurutse'; and so it was decided to invite – not a M'Hurutshe, but 'an authority from one of the universities' to tell them what Se-Hurutshe really is.

General Hertzog said, a week or two back, that 'half a truth was worse than a falsehood'. The would-be menders of Native languages very truthfully tell their public that for half-a-century there has been argument and controversy of the spelling of this language; but the learned gentlemen forget to mention that these differences and controversies raged mainly among Europeans, and that educated Natives – Bechuana, Bapedi and Basuto – never had a difference of opinion as to the direction in which to modify the missionary spelling so as to make it give the clearest and most effective expression to the idioms of their mother tongue; and that, while Natives, without conferences, without arguments and controversies, wrote these three languages in the same readable orthography, outsiders chose to influence the Education Departments to ignore the correct Sechuana spelling in favour of discordant Se-Ruti* versions so as to create an artificial problem – as a subject for a series of conferences.

One Native reader of the daily papers wrote to me angrily, thus: 'Since you are the first and, thus far, the only writer who ever suggested a standardization of our language, perhaps you will be good enough to explain how you went to Rustenburg and standardized our language without us.' It must be confessed, therefore, that I am in no way connected with the Rustenburg movement. By

---

* The language as spoken by (white) missionaries (from the Sotho *moruti*, meaning priest or missionary).

standardization, I had in mind a mutual understanding and the consent of representatives of the several groups who speak the three principal Sechuana dialects. I had no idea a new language conceived behind our people's backs, by a European 'from one of the universities'.

It should be added that I know several enlightened Bantu who have an intensive knowledge of a number of European languages. Such Bantu scholars have the advantage of reading the same authorities on European languages that lie at the disposal of, and are relied upon by, the Europeans themselves. They have the further advantage of a systematic contact with Europeans commercially, and also with European ideas through the daily newspaper – facilities which white students of Bantu languages of the future will never get; yet Europeans would resent the very idea of Natives, however qualified, laying down their standard of speech and writing. Then what right, it may be asked, has a European 'from one of the universities' to standardize a Native language?

Our language reformers say they depend on the poll tax returns to ram their stuff down our children's throats in schools. All of which goes to prove their superficial knowledge of the Natives whose poll taxes they propose to use so despotically. Over 61,000 Natives went to gaol during 1930 because they had no money to pay poll tax. The government may turn Native poverty into a crime punishable by fine and imprisonment to suit the aims of the Transvaal Education Department; but even the gentlemen of this department will learn from practical experience that if they incarcerated 600,000 Natives for refusing to speak the grafted language of a white man 'from one of the universities', they will find half a million of them preferring to speak their own mother-tongue even in durance vile.

We read further that textbooks in the new language are about to be prepared. Our educated friends may take it, from one who speaks not for Europeans but for the Bechuana tribes, that if their new books contain any of the hieroglyphics and diacritics so beloved of the Transvaal universities, they may be assured in advance of what they are asking for; namely, another half-century of controversy, this time not only among Europeans as hitherto, but among the Bechuana tribes as well.

Notes

Part One 1899-1910. 'All we claim is our just dues'

1.   Text and notes taken from Sol T. Plaatje, *Mafeking Diary: A Black Man's View of a White Man's War*, edited by John Comaroff with Brian Willan and Andrew Reed (Johannesburg/London/Athens, Ohio: 1990). This edition of the diary incorporates the results of research by Brian Willan and Andrew Reed into Plaatje's life and career since the publication of the original edition of Plaatje's diary, and includes a number of textual clarifications. The original edition of the diary, edited by John Comaroff, was published in 1973 under the title *The Boer War Diary of Sol T. Plaatje* (Cape Town: 1973). The two best modern accounts of the siege of Mafeking are to be found in Thomas Pakenham, *The Boer War* (London: 1979) and Tim Jeal, *Baden-Powell* (London: 1989).

2.   Kanya (now officially spelt 'Kanye') was the capital of the Bangwaketse chiefdom, and lies approximately sixty miles north-north-west of Mafeking, in what is now Botswana.

3.   A reference to the 'Staats Artillerie' who were responsible for the operation of the Boer artillery.

4.   David Phooko, a friend and distant relative of Plaatje's, employed as a constable attached to the staff of the Inspector of Native Reserves at Mafeking.

5.   A popular Australian musical group, who had performed in Kimberley in 1895 and 1896.

6.   A black American choir which toured Southern Africa on several occasions during the 1890s, making a considerable impact upon black audiences in particular. The choir visited Kimberley in 1890, 1895 and 1897. For further information, see Veit Erlmann, *African Stars* (Chicago: 1991).

7.   Philemon Moshoeshoe, warder at the Mafeking gaol, and a close friend of Plaatje's. Of Sotho origin, he had settled in Mafikeng (the original Barolong settlement next to which the 'European' town of Mafeking was situated) in 1894, and remained as gaol warder until 1912. In 1910 he became a naturalised member of the chiefdom.

8.   Barnabas Samson, a well known local teacher of Sotho origin who had moved to Mafikeng in the early 1890s.

9.   Mafikeng's Mfengu population ('Fingos') originated in the arrival in 1890 of Cecil Rhodes' Pioneer Column en route to lay claim to Rhodesia. The Mfengu members of the column decided to remain in Mafikeng, and settled close to the Barolong village.

10. As an interpreter and typist. Parslow was the war correspondent of the *Daily Chronicle*, shot through the head, during the course of an argument, by Lieutenant Murchison. Murchison was condemned to death by a court-martial, but his sentence was commuted to penal servitude for life and he eventually died in a mental asylum in England in 1917 (Jeal, *Baden-Powell*, pp.276-77).

11. 'Au Sanna' (elsewhere referred to simply as 'Sanna') was one of a number of familiar names applied by Plaatje and others in Mafeking to the Boers' 94-pounder Creusot siege-gun, one of four brought from France.

12. Bell papers (MS 7348), Cory Library, Rhodes University, Grahamstown. This was one of many reports Plaatje wrote for Charles Bell, the magistrate and civil commissioner, reporting the activities of the Barolong contingent and the intelligence they were able to gather about the activities and dispositions of the surrounding Boer forces.

13. A village situated approximately eighteen miles north-west of Mafeking. It was occupied by Barolong of the same tribe as those in the besieged town.

14. Ga-molimola (or Modimola) is also a Tshidi Barolong village, thirteen miles due west of Mafeking.

15. A reference to an incident relating to the arrival of the Warren expedition, occupying Bechuanaland for the British imperial government, early in 1885.

16. Stephen Lefenya, secretary to Chief Montsioa, and an important personality in local tribal affairs.

17. A small village with grazing-lands, some two miles to the west of the stadt.

18. Plaatje is referring here to 'Au Sanna', the Boers' 94-pounder Creusot siege gun (see note 11).

19. Petrus Viljoen ('Phil-june' was Plaatje's phonetic spelling) had been convicted and imprisoned for horse-theft before the siege, but was then released in exchange for Lady Sarah Wilson, captured by the Boers outside Mafeking. Lady Sarah was a daughter of the Duke of Marlborough, and married to Gordon Wilson, one of Baden-Powell's staff officers in the besieged town. For further details of Lady Sarah's exploits, see her *South African Memories* (London: 1909).

20. General Piet Cronje (1836-1911), commander of the Boer forces surrounding Mafeking.

21. About a mile from the centre of the stadt.

22. Vere Stent (1872-1941) was Reuters correspondent during the siege, and was one of the corespondents from whom Plaatje earned some money as typist and interpreter – the beginning of a long relationship with Plaatje. Stent subsequently became editor of the *Pretoria News*.

23. Cornelius Gaboutloeloe, a local headman and Wesleyan lay-preacher, and the man in charge of the Barolong cattle-guard during the siege.

24. Christmas Day was officially brought forward by a day by Baden-Powell because of his belief that the Boers celebrated New Year rather than Christmas Day, and that

they were likely to launch some sort of offensive. In fact there were no hostilities at all on 25 December.

25. Probably Mrs Lesoane, mother of Diamond Lesoane. In Tswana a married woman is referred to by the prefix *Mma* (literally 'mother'), followed by her husband's or son's name.

26. St. Leger was Plaatje's eldest (and at that time only) son, born on 14 November 1898, and named after the well known editor of the *Cape Times*, F.Y. St Leger, whose liberal views Plaatje much admired. Plaatje's wife Elizabeth had left Mafeking with St Leger in August 1898 for Burghersdorp and then Kimberley, and had not returned to Mafeking before the beginning of the siege.

27. The site of a Boer fort, some two and a half miles north-west of the centre of Mafeking.

28. Captain Charles FitzClarence (1865-1914), Royal Fusiliers, one of Colonel Baden-Powell's staff officers. He was subsequently awarded the Victoria Cross for his bravery during the siege.

29. Stories about Patrick Lenkoane, a man of Sotho origin whom Plaatje had known well in Kimberley several years earlier, and who later moved to Mafikeng.

30. Charles Bell, Resident Magistrate and Civil Commissioner.

31. Plaatje is referring here to *Nelson's Royal Reader III* (London, 1872), pp.26-28, which he had used while at school at the Pniel mission in the early 1890s. The series of readers was widely used throughout the English-speaking world. The story to which he refers was called 'The Wonderful Pudding', in which an uncle asks two boys for dinner, promising them a pudding, 'the materials of which had given work for more than a thousand men'. Expecting to find an enormous pudding when they arrived the two boys were disappointed to find a normal-sized plum pudding, and their uncle then explained how it was that so many people were involved in making it.

32. Sorghum, producing grain widely used by Africans for both porridge and beer (see 'kaffir beer' below). For Plaatje's use of the term 'Kaffir' elsewhere, and its connotations, see n.62.

33. Alfred Ngidi, a railwayman of Mfengu origin.

34. Plaatje's own label, it seems, for the protest by the Barolong women.

35. Ebenezer Plaatje, a cousin of Plaatje's, aged about six or seven.

36. A highly infectious cattle disease which swept through southern Africa in 1897, with devastating consequences for black and white alike. Cattle were affected for many years afterwards, and Plaatje's own father was amongst those who were impoverished as a result, having lost virtually his entire herd.

37. Properly, Mafikeng, a daughter of Molema, the founder of Mafikeng, and married to Lekoko Montsioa.

38. Patrick Sidzumo, a court messenger in Mafeking, whom Plaatje knew well.

39. Undated handwritten draft of letter inserted in original MS of Plaatje's Mafeking diary, in possession of Prof. J. Comaroff, Chicago University.

40. Probably Trooper Francis of the British South Africa Police, who had been put in charge of arrangements for distributing grain to the Barolong. He was subsequently shot and killed during the final Boer assault upon Mafeking in May 1900.
41. Probably Josiah Motshegare, a prominent Barolong headman.
42. Wessels Montsioa (1856-1903), chief of the Barolong. In fact during the siege Lekoko was recognised as the Barolong chief by the military authorities because of Wessels' general incapacity (very evident here) and unwillingness to co-operate (see Plaatje's obituary of Montsioa, pp.413-19).
43. Bell Papers (MS 7348), Cory Library, Rhodes University.
44. Ibid.
45. The 'attached paper' consisted of an exchange of comments between Lord Edward Cecil and Charles Bell, which ran as follows:
Cecil to Bell: 'Do you recommend this? What pay does Plaatje receive now?'
Bell to Cecil: 'I would suggest that this paper be returned to Plaatje and he be directed to communicate through the Head of his Department.'
Cecil to Plaatje: 'I naturally thought you had told Mr Bell before you wrote to me. Never write to me again about Service matters except through Mr Bell.'
46. Colonel Herbert Plumer (1857-1932) led the Rhodesian regiment, then engaged in harassing Boer forces to the north, and preparing to break the siege. The *Mafeking Mail* in its issue of 8 February reported an engagement at Crocodile Pools in which Plumer 'caused the enemy heavy losses' with his shellfire.
47. The first two diaries mentioned by Plaatje can be found in the archives of the Cory Library, Rhodes University, Grahamstown, and the Cape Archives Depot, Cape Town, respectively. The diary of Captain Greener, the paymaster, does not appear to have survived.
48. Thomas Monyapeng. He was Silas Molema's carriage-driver after the siege, and may have been engaged by Bell in a similar capacity during the siege.
49. This article reproduces one of the many reports Plaatje had written for Charles Bell and the military authorities, evidently with the permission of both Charles Bell and the military censors. It is probably Plaatje's first published article, significant also for underlining the extent of Barolong participation in raids across the Boer lines.
50. This is the draft of a letter inserted in the manuscript of Plaatje's diary. The name of the recipient is unclear, but it was evidently that of an African or coloured acquaintance of Plaatje's living in Kimberley. Although undated, from internal evidence – Plaatje's pony Whiskey is known to have been killed on 6 February 1900 – it must have been written at the end of February or the beginning of March 1900.
51. Plaatje's wife Elizabeth (nee M'belle) and their son St Leger who were both in Kimberley.
52. Plaatje was able to send money to Elizabeth via the runners used by Vere Stent,

the Reuters agent (Plaatje in fact organised this for him). The other 'agency' to which he referred was Ben Weil, the prominent local contractor, who had also agreed to convey a message and funds for Elizabeth, via Mr James Lawrence, member of Parliament for Kimberley.

53. A reference to the writer Samuel Cronwright Schreiner (1863-1936) and his wife, the novelist Olive Schreiner (1855-1920). Plaatje had known both of them when he was living in Kimberley a few years earlier. Cronwright Schreiner later encouraged Plaatje to take up a career as a journalist. Plaatje's reference to 'the effects of this maze' convey his concern that their pro-Boer sympathies were likely to make their position in wartime Cape Colony somewhat difficult – as indeed it did.

54. Philemon Moshoeshoe (see n.7).

55. A railway cottage, five miles from Mafeking on the line to the south, known as Five Mile Cottage.

56. A term for 'Cape Coloureds', signifying in this instance the Cape Boy Contingent. This was raised prior to the siege from the local coloured population, consisted of 67 men and was led by a white officer.

57. The 'Zulus and Zambesians' were among the several thousand black refugees, migrant workers from Johannesburg, who had been trapped in Mafeking at the beginning of the siege whilst trying to return to their homes. The 'Zambesians' were, very loosely, from the central African region around the Zambezi Valley, over a thousand miles to the north-east of Mafeking.

58. Tshipithata Motshegare, a younger brother of Josiah Motshegare.

59. Cape Archives (CA), AG 837, 3/1900, annexure A.

60. Plaatje's own mother, Martha Plaatje, who lived with other members of his family on the Pniel mission, near Kimberley. In 1898 she was in fact 65 years old. Plaatje's father, Johannes, had died in 1896.

61. Joseph Moss, interpreter to the Magistrate's Court in Kimberley. A handwritten comment in the relevant Civil Service file claimed that 'Moss speaks Dutch well and has to my knowledge interpreted in that language in the High Court'.

62. Derived from the Arabic term for 'infidel', in the nineteenth century the word 'Kafir' or 'Kaffir' came to be used by Europeans to denote a person of Xhosa origin, and also the language they spoke (the meaning here). The term was often used by whites to refer to Africans more generally in an offensive and derogatory manner. See J. Branford, *A Dictionary of South African English* (Cape Town: 1980) for further information on the usage of the word.

63. CA, AG 923, 106/1901, Annexure A.

64. Plaatje's letter had some handwritten ticks over the figures he mentions. They were obviously checked by a civil service official, whose only quibble was with the salary of the 'Native Interpreter' at Vryburg – who was on a salary of £96 p.a., not £100 p.a. as Plaatje stated.

65. Plaatje was involved in work relating to a number of 'treason trials', collecting evidence and information about the activities of 'suspected rebels', i.e. Boer subjects of the Cape Colony who had fought with their compatriots from the Transvaal and Orange River Colony against the Imperial Government. Notable amongst these cases was that of *R. v. Maritz and Lottering* in November 1901, in which Plaatje himself appeared as a witness (see his subsequent recollections of the case on pp.355-90). For further information on this case and its significance, see Brian Willan, *Sol Plaatje: A Biography* (London and Berkeley: 1984; henceforth, *Biography*), pp.96-98.

66. In 1899 Plaatje was the only candidate in Setswana and Sesotho, and was told by the Cape Civil Service Commissioner that it could not 'go to the expense of having papers prepared solely for one candidate'.

67. University of the Witwatersrand, Historical and Literary Papers, Molema/Plaatje papers, Db2. This manuscript, in the form of a foolscap-size bound notebook, was one of a number of documents formerly in the possession of the late Mrs Lucretia Molema, of Mafeking, and purchased by the University of the Witwatersrand in 1977, having been located by Professor Tim Couzens and Dr Brian Willan the previous year. For further information, see Marcelle Jacobson (comp.), *The Silas T. Molema and Solomon T. Plaatje Papers* (Johannesburg, 1978).

68. A reference to the dispute between Khama, chief of the Bamangwato, and his son Sekgoma in 1899. which thus dates the incident Plaatje describes. The Resident Commissioner being referred to here and above is Ralph Williams (see also n.116, p.433 for further details of Williams's career).

69. Dinuzulu (d. 1913), the Zulu king, was arrested in 1907 for sheltering tax resisters, and after a long trial was sentenced to four years' imprisonment. For the Bambatha Rebellion and its ramifications, see Shula Marks, *Reluctant Rebellion: The 1906-1908 Disturbances in Natal* (London: 1970).

70. See 'Sekgoma: The Black Dreyfus' (pp.104-19) for the context of this, and further information and references on the principal actors involved in this sorry episode.

71. Lord Selborne (1859-1942) was High Commissioner for Southern Africa from 1905 to 1910, and a central figure in the Sekgoma episode (see 'Sekgoma: The Black Dreyfus', pp.104-19).

72. The Native Territories of the eastern Cape (particularly the Transkei), the oldest areas of colonial settlement where there had developed by this time a tradition of knowledgeable and experienced magistrates, many of them the sons of pioneer missionaries.

73. Joseph Chamberlain, the British Colonial Secretary, toured southern Africa in 1902 and 1903. He visited Mafeking and addressed the Barolong on 28 January 1903, Plaatje acting as interpreter for him on the occasion (*Biography*, pp.112-15).

74. The British Bechuanaland Protectorate was established in 1885, but British Bechuanaland was then incorporated into the Cape Colony in 1895, despite the opposition of Chief Montsioa and his counsellors.

75.   Clause 8 of the Treaty of Vereeniging provided that no decision would be taken on extending the franchise to Africans until after the introduction of responsible government in the former Boer republics.

76.   Sir Godfrey Lagden (1851-1934), formerly Resident Commissioner in Basutoland and Swaziland, and at this time Governor-General of the Transvaal.

77.   The Barolong presented Joseph Chamberlain with a formal address of welcome on 28 January 1903, delivered by Chief Wessels Montsioa and then translated into English by Plaatje. It was accompanied by a more detailed petition drawing attention to various of their grievances, and requesting in particular that there should be no variation to the terms on which British Bechuanaland was annexed to the Cape in 1895. For further details, see *Bechuana Gazette*, 31 January 1903 and *Biography*, pp.113-15.

78.   A reference to the 'African Jubilee Singers', or 'South African Native Choir', formed in Kimberley in 1891 before travelling to both Britain and America. For further information, see Erlmann, *African Stars*, especially pp.46-47.

79.   Orange Free State archives, Bloemfontein, CO 161:2697/03.

80.   Sir Hamilton Goold-Adams (1858-1920) was Lieutenant-Governor of the Orange River Colony from 1901 to 1910. Previously he was Resident Commissioner for the Bechuanaland Protectorate, and served with Baden-Powell in the siege of Mafeking. Plaatje used to interpret for him in court cases over which he presided during the siege (see Plaatje's diary entry for 5 January 1900, pp.37-40).

81.   The pro-British party in the Cape, led at this time by Dr Leander Starr Jameson.

82.   The Transvaal Labour Commission was appointed in 1903 by Lord Milner, the High Commissioner for Southern Africa, in order to investigate means of providing the gold mines with an adequate supply of labour. Its chief recommendation was to import workers from China, which commenced in 1904.

83.   General Louis Botha (1862-1919) was one of the most prominent Boer wartime leaders, and in 1904, with General Smuts, formed a new political party – Het Volk – to represent and further Afrikaner interests. A large landowner and farmer, he became the first Prime Minister of the Transvaal in 1907, and in 1910 became the first Prime Minister of the Union of South Africa. (Plaatje wrote an obituary of General Botha, reproduced on pp.241-47).

84.   Russell Harding, a labour recruiter and a well known figure in Kimberley, was strongly opposed to the plan to import Chinese labour into South Africa (see 'Mr R. Harding on the labour burlesque', in the same issue of the *Bechuana Gazette*).

85.   A reference to the Witwatersrand Native Labour Association, created by the Chamber of Mines to give it a monopoly over labour recruiting across a wide region of Southern Africa.

86.   The Reverend Marshall Maxeke, speaking in Johannesburg, had complained that 'not a single Native has been asked to give evidence before the Labour Commission'

– originally reported by the *South African News*, and reproduced by Plaatje in this issue of the *Bechuana Gazette*.

87. *Imvo Zabantsundu*, the oldest African newspaper, was an English-Xhosa weekly, edited by Tengo Jabavu, and published in Kingwilliamstown.

88. The Afrikaner Bond was the political party in the Cape Colony which represented Afrikaner interests, in opposition to the pro-British Progressive Party. It was in office in the Cape between 1898 and 1900, and eventually merged with the South African Party under General Botha at the time of Union in 1910.

89. OFS Archives, CO 244:711/04.

90. Allan Kirkland Soga (d. 1938) was the youngest son of Tiyo Soga, the first African in South Africa to be ordained as a minister. The newspaper he edited, *Izwi la Bantu* ('The Voice of the People') existed from 1897 to 1909, and was notable for the support it extended to the Progressive Party (from which it also received financial support). For further information, see Les Switzer and Donna Switzer, *The Black Press in South Africa and Lesotho: A Descriptive Bibliographic Guide to African, Coloured and Indian Newspapers, Newsletters and Magazines, 1836-1976* (Boston: 1979).

91. Francis Zaccheus Santiago Peregrino (d. 1919) was of West African origin, and arrived in South Africa in 1900, having lived previously in both Britain and the USA. His newspaper, the *South African Spectator*, published in Cape Town, appeared intermittently from 1900 to around 1909. For further information, see Switzer and Switzer, *The Black Press*, and Christopher Saunders, 'F.Z.S. Peregrino and the *South African Spectator*', *Quarterly Review of the South African Public Library* 32, 3 (March 1978).

92. Alfred Milner (1854-1925) was High Commissioner for Southern Africa from 1897 to 1905, combining this post with that of governor of the Cape Colony (1897-1901) and governor of the Transvaal and Orange River Colonies (1901-1905). He had a major influence on British policy towards southern Africa before, during and in the aftermath of the Anglo-Boer war of 1899-1902.

93. Sir William Hoy (1868-1930) was Chief Traffic Manager of the Central South African Railways from 1902 to 1910, then appointed General Manager of the newly created South African Railways.

94. Many Cape Afrikaners were disfranchised before the general election of 1904, the result of having supported the Boer cause during the war: the narrow election victory of the Progressive Party was attributed largely to this factor.

95. The South African Party was a parliamentary organisation linking the Afrikaner Bond with a small group of liberal independents, later to develop into a Union-wide party in 1910. Tengo Jabavu and his newspaper *Imvo Zabantsundu* supported these independents, but was effectively countered by Progressive support for the rival *Izwi Zabantsundu*.

96. J.X. Merriman (1841-1926), long-time Cape parliamentarian, 'Cape liberal', and the last Prime Minister of the Cape Colony, 1908-1910. See Phyllis Lewsen, *John*

X. *Merriman: Paradoxical South African Statesman* (New Haven and London: 1982).

97. Details of the interview with Mr W.H. Barratt, Traffic Manager, Orange River Colony, Central South African Railways, were reproduced on the same page of the *Bechuana Gazette*. Mr Barratt promised a variety of improvements in conditions.

98. *Ilanga lase Natal (Natal Sun)*, edited by John L. Dube, published in Ohlange, Natal.

99. Or *Leihlo lo Babatsho*, published in Pietersburg, northern Transvaal, and edited by Levi Khomo.

100. Transvaal Archives Depot, Pretoria, AG 2288/04.

101. The Attorney-General of the Transvaal was Sir Richard Solomon (1850-1913), a member of a well known Cape liberal family. Plaatje may well have encountered Sir Richard in Kimberley in the 1890s when he was legal adviser to De Beers, and a member of parliament for the city. He was Attorney-General of the Transvaal from 1902 to 1906, and subsequently the Union of South Africa's first High Commissioner in London.

102. Plaatje had in mind Part 1, Clause 18 of the Cape Colony's Police Offences Act, no. 27 of 1882, which made the following, amongst various other minor misdemeanours, an offence (liable to carry a fine of £2 or 30 days' imprisonment, with or without hard labour): 'Swearing, or making use of obscene, abusive, insulting, or threatening language, or swearing, shouting, or screaming to the annoyance of the inhabitants in any street, road or public place.' Plaatje was probably very familiar with this piece of legislation as a result of his work as a court interpreter: many of those who appeared in court were charged with one or another of the offences covered by the Act.

103. In the Cape Colony the existence of the non-racial Cape franchise, enshrined in the constitution, protected those who qualified for it (males meeting literacy, income and property qualifications) from any laws or legislation otherwise specifically affecting the African population.

104. *Minutes of Evidence of South African Native Affairs Commission* (Cape Town: Government Printer, Cmd 2399, 1905), pp.264-70. For further background information and analysis of the Commission, see Ch. 2 of Adam Ashforth, *The Politics of Official Discourse in Twentieth-Century South Africa* (Oxford: 1990).

105. The African Methodist Episcopal Church (AMEC) was the largest black church in the USA, and in the 1890s it grew rapidly in South Africa as well, attracting many Africans from both the 'white' churches and the black separatist churches which had already broken away from white control. In the eyes of both black and white it was associated with a broader notion of 'Ethiopianism', implying in varying degrees rejection by Africans of white rule and authority; indeed the AMEC was often known colloquially as the 'Ethiopian Church' (see question 37

that was put to Plaatje by Captain Dickson, one of the SANAC commissioners). One of the prime concerns of the South African Native Affairs Commission, as it interviewed witnesses, was to establish whether there was any substance to the allegations, widespread amongst white opinion, that the AMEC fostered 'disloyalty' and encouraged a spirit of rebellion among the African population. On 'Ethiopianism' in southern Africa more generally, see J.M. Chirenje, *Ethiopianism and Afro-Americans in Southern Africa 1883-1916* (Baton Rouge: 1987).

106. It has not been possible to trace this reference in the *Bechuana Gazette* – some issues from this period have not survived.

107. Bishop Levi Coppin, head of the AMEC in South Africa, visited Mafeking in May 1903. Plaatje extended a warm welcome to him, but expressed reservations about the activities of several individual ministers whom he thought were damaging the reputation of the AMEC. On another occasion, in April 1904, the *Bechuana Gazette* had also carried an article criticising the activities of an elder of the AMEC, observing that 'some Ethiopian missionaries . . . will do a considerable amount of harm to humanity and the spread of Christianity' (*Bechuana Gazette*, 20 April 1904).

108. Chief Badirile Montsioa (d.1911) became Tshidi Barolong chief earlier in 1903, and had expressed the view, in his evidence to the Commission before Plaatje spoke, that there was no appeal against the decisions in court cases under 'Native law'. In fact the issue of whether the chief had exclusive right of jurisdiction in civil cases, or whether there existed a right of appeal to the magistrate, was a contentious one. When tested in the Cape Supreme Court in 1907 the judge did in fact rule that 'the chief still has original and exclusive jurisdiction in all civil cases' (*Mokaila vs Mokaila*, reported in *Mafeking Mail*, 24 April 1907).

109. F.R. Thompson (1857-1927), farmer, politician and one-time associate of Cecil Rhodes: he was known as 'Matebele' Thompson because of the part he had played in negotiating the charter of the British South Africa Company with the Ndebele king, Lobengula, in 1888.

110. The Brandfort Town Council regulations (published in their final form, confirmed and approved by the Lieutenant-Governor, in December 1903) were notable for the particularly stringent controls enacted over the African population. The section headed 'Native Regulations' imposed, amongst other controls, rigorous curfew regulations and (Article 137) a clause excluding all Africans from living within the municipal area 'unless in service'. (Orange River Colony, *Government Gazette*, 31 December 1903, Notice 751, 'By-laws and regulations for the Town of Brandfort').

111. Ewan Eustace Watkeys (1843-1911), Welsh-born businessman, Bloemfontein town councillor and Mayor of Bloemfontein for 1903-1904. He had a particular interest in educational and philanthropic causes, and had presented an address to

Joseph Chamberlain, the Colonial Secretary, on behalf of the citizens of Bloemfontein, when he visited the city early in 1903.

112. See pp.102-104, where Plaatje writes of just such a case.

113. The two leading secondary institutions for African students. Lovedale, near Alice in the Eastern Cape, was run by the Presbyterian Free Church of Scotland; Morija, in Basutoland, by the Paris Evangelical Missionary Society. For further information on Willoughby and Plaatje's relations with the London Missionary Society, see *Biography*, pp.129-30.

114. University of the Witwatersrand, Molema/Plaatje papers, Db2. Plaatje's allusion is to the Dreyfus affair of 1896, a famous case involving allegations of spying and betraying national secrets, against Captain Alfred Dreyfus, a French army officer, which divided French society and had enormous political implications. The central issue was whether, as the army and its supporters claimed, the honour and prestige of the army mattered more than injustice to any individual; and the Republican claim, that individual justice must triumph over all else. In the martyrdom of Captain Dreyfus Plaatje clearly saw parallels with the situation of Chief Sekgoma and his treatment by the British Bechuanaland Protectorate authorities.

Information about the Sekgoma case is to be found in the following published sources: Ralph Williams, *How I Became Governor* (London: 1913); Thomas Tlou, *A History of Ngamiland, 1750-1906* (Gaborone: 1985); J.M. Chirenje, 'Sekgoma Letsholathebe II: Twentieth-Century African Nationalist?', *Botswana Notes and Records*, 3 (1972); A.J.G.M. Sanders, *Bechuanaland and the Law in Politicians' Hands* (Gaborone: 1992). None of these sources provide a satisfactory account of the affair, however, and I am particularly grateful to Barry Morton, of Indiana University, for providing information and references resulting from research for his doctoral thesis on the subject.

115. While in Mafikeng Sekgoma stayed with Stephen Lefenya, long-time adviser and counsellor to the Tshidi Rolong royal family. Plaatje may well have obtained information directly from Sekgoma, having met him while he was staying there. Other sources are likely to include Lefenya, whom Plaatje knew well; and he may have had access subsequently to some legal documents and depositions relating to later legal proceedings, in particular Sekgoma's deposition dated 19 March 1909 (PRO, CO 417/480, pp.473-83). I am indebted to Barry Morton, Indiana University, for the information and references he has provided here.

116. Ralph Williams (1848-1927). Resident Commissioner of the Bechuanaland Protectorate from 1901 to 1906, he had first come to southern Africa as an intelligence officer in the Warren Expedition in 1885. He subsequently became Governor of the Windward Islands (1906-09), Newfoundland (1909 to 1913), and was rewarded with a knighthood. He describes the Sekgoma affair in his autobiography, *How I Became Governor* (London: Murray, 1913).

117. In fact 'Bechuana laws and customs' were extremely flexible on this point, and there were a number of examples where heirs to chiefdoms took office prior to the death of their regent.
118. No copies of the *Bechuana Gazette* have survived for this period.
119. Sekgoma II (not to be confused with Sekgoma Letsholathebe) was in fact estranged from his father, Khama III, but was eventually to become chief of the Bamangwato from 1923 to 1925.
120. Sekgoma received several letters from Lord Milner, Earl Selborne's predecessor as High Commissioner for Southern Africa; the reference to 'word of mouth' assurances relates to what took place at the meeting between a number of Tswana chiefs (including Sekgoma) and the British Secretary of State for the Colonies, Joseph Chamberlain, during his visit to Mafeking in January 1903.
121. From 'My visit to the Bechuanaland Protectorate', by Lord Selborne (reprinted from Imperial Whitebook), *Diamond Fields Advertiser,*, Christmas number, 1906, pp.4-5. Plaatje's reference was simply to 'DFA Xmas no', but the relevant passage from Selborne's two-page account of his visit has been added in to the text.
122. This is confirmed by Lord Selborne in his account (see note 121 above), where he relates that he had 'three days' shooting near Francistown' before returning to Johannesburg. However, there is no mention by Selborne of a further meeting with Sekgoma at Palapye Road station on his return journey.
123. The island of St Helena was a byword for a remote and inaccessible place of exile or imprisonment, particularly since the imprisonment there of Napoleon Bonaparte in the 1820s. More recently the island had housed Dinuzulu, the Zulu paramount chief, and Boer prisoners of war captured by the British during the Anglo-Boer War of 1899-1902.
124. Raditladi and Mphoeng were Khama's brothers, who broke away in 1894-95; Sekgoma was his son, who broke away in 1896-97.
125. Kgari, a pretender to the Bakwena chiefship, had broken away from his brother, Chief Sebele I; Pula, a pretender likewise to the Balete chiefship of Ramotswa, had broken away from his brother Ikaneng in 1891; Masoupa possibly refers to the village of Gobuamang, a Bangwatetse subject chief who was defying the Bangwaketse paramount, Bathoen I, at the time Plaatje was writing. I am indebted to Dr Neil Parsons for information on these points.
126. Proclamation no. 21 of 1906, *Official Gazette Extraordinary of the High Commissioner for South Africa,* Vol. XVI, No. 260, Johannesburg, 18 September 1906. Plaatje evidently did not have the text of the Proclamation to hand when he wrote his piece, but he clearly intended to include it, and for this reason it is reproduced here.
127. A reference to the application, made on behalf of Sekgoma Letsolathebe by Advocate H.H. Phear on 21 November 1906 for a writ of *habeus corpus* to secure

his release from detention (*Sekgoma Letsolathebe v. Panzera*, reported in the *Diamond Fields Advertiser* [weekly edition], 24 November 1906). Advocate Phear argued that the matter ought to come within the jurisdiction of the Griqualand West High Court on the grounds that Sekgoma was in effect arrested somewhere between Kimberley and Mafeking – both towns being within the jurisdiction of the Griqualand West High Court, despite Mafeking being the administrative capital of the Bechuanaland Protectorate. Mr Justice Lange did not accept this, however, and ruled that the Griqualand West High Court had no jurisdiction in the matter. He refused both leave to appeal and costs, and concluded his judgment by saying that it was open to Sekgoma to 'apply to the Courts in England' if an appeal to the High Commissioner proved unsuccessful.

128. A reference to Proclamation no. 21 of 1906 (see note 126 above).

129. A reference to Proclamation no. 46 of 1907, giving the High Commissioner similar powers of detention and expulsion in Basutoland as in the Bechuanaland Protectorate. A deputation of Basotho chiefs travelled to England in February 1909, requesting (unsuccessfully) the repeal of the proclamation, as well as the non-incorporation of Basutoland into the Union of South Africa, for which plans were then being made. For further information, see L.B.B.J. Machobane, *Government and Change in Lesotho 1800-1966* (Basingstoke: Macmillan, 1990), especially pp.114-23.

130. All former High Commissioners for Southern Africa.

131. Lord Selborne was appointed High Commissioner for South Africa and Governor of the Transvaal and Orange River colonies in April 1905. Plaatje is referring to the matter of land holding in the Transvaal during the period of British occupation and rule after the Anglo-Boer war. Ordinance 28 was disallowed in July 1905 by Alfred Lyttelton, Secretary of State for the Colonies from 1903 to 1905. See also Plaatje's article on the case of *Paulus Malaji vs. Kensington Township* syndicate (*Bechuana Gazette*, 9 November 1904), reproduced on pages 102-104 – an earlier case relating to the same issue.

132. That part of Bechuanaland which (since 1895) fell within the borders of the Cape Colony.

132. This is almost certainly a reference to Professor Courtenay Stanhope Kenny (1847-1930), Downing Professor of the Laws of England in the University of Cambridge. He was a leading authority on criminal law, and the author of the classic *Outlines of Criminal Law*, originally published in 1902. I have been unable, however, to trace the exact source of the words quoted by Plaatje.

133. Privately the British authorities recognised the weakness of their case when viewed in the context of British legal principles as opposed to the exigencies of colonial government and practice. Hearing about the case for the first time in October 1906, the new British Secretary of State for the Colonies noted that Sekgoma 'clearly has the law in its simplest aspects on his side. We cannot

imprison him or deport him without negation of every solid principle of British justice', and he continued: 'If we are going to take men who have committed no crime, and had no trial, and condemn them to lifetime imprisonment and exile, why stop there? Why not poison Sekgoma by some painless drug? Surely killing him will save money!' (PRO CO 417/434, minutes on file. I am indebted to Barry Morton for this reference and quotation).

Part Two 1899-1910. 'Champion for the cause of our peoples'

1. CAD, Pretoria, NTS 3139, 23/306. For further information and details about the history of land tenure in the Thaba Nchu district, see Colin Murray, *Black Mountain: Land, Power, and Class in the Eastern Orange Free State, 1880s to 1980s* (Edinburgh: Edinburgh University Press, 1991).
2. The recently formed Unionist Party, led by Sir Thomas Smartt, represented pro-British opinion. It survived for ten years before being merged with the South African Party (SAP).
3. A term, now considered derogatory, referring to the original inhabitants, of Khoi-San origin, of the coastal region of the south-west Cape Colony. Probably the sense and context here incorporates reference to people of Griqua origin, descended in part from Khoi-San (see Plaatje's article on the Griquas, pp.348-50).
4. South African Library, Cape Town, W.P. Schreiner collection, MSC 27, (1910) no. 1689.
5. William Philip Schreiner (1866-1919), former Prime Minister of the Cape Colony and leader of the Afrikaner Bond (1898-1900). Schreiner had a reputation as a leading 'Cape liberal', and in 1910 was an M.P. and 'Native Senator' (see note 6 below). Later he was South African High Commissioner in London from 1914 to 1919. See Eric Walker, *W.P. Schreiner: A South African* (London, 1937).
6. Under the provisions of the Act of Union four 'Native Senators' (in fact white politicians) were appointed in order to represent and protect African interests. The others were Colonel Walter Stanford, J.C. Krogh, and F.R. Moor.
7. Colonel W.E. Stanford, former Chief Magistrate of the Transkei, one of the South African Native Affairs Commissioners, and widely regarded as an expert on 'native affairs'.
8. This must date from 1893-95, when Hertzog practised as an attorney before becoming Judge of the Supreme Court of the Orange Free State. In 1910 he was Minister of Justice in General Botha's first Union cabinet.
9. Abraham Fischer, formerly Prime Minister of the Orange River Colony (1907-10).
10. A reference to the armed rebellion of the Zulu chief, Bambatha, protesting against the imposition of poll taxes in Natal in 1906. Plaatje's reference is to the subsequent release from imprisonment by the Union government of the Zulu chief Dinuzulu and others allegedly involved in the rebellion. See n.69, p.428.

11. King Edward VII died on 6 May 1910, having assented to the Act of Union in September 1909. In December 1909 he signed a royal proclamation declaring the date of the establishment of the Union of South Africa to be 31 May 1910, which duly took effect.

12. Plaatje's piece 'Sekgoma – The Black Dreyfus' provides a fuller account of this episode (see pp.104-19).

13. The schedule to the Act of Union set out the conditions that would need to be met if the Imperial government was to sanction the transfer of the protectorates of Basutoland, Bechuanaland and Swaziland to the Union of South Africa, widely expected to follow. The clauses quoted by Plaatje made specific reference to the protection of African interests in the event of the transfer of the protectorates to the Union – which never in fact happened.

14. Section 51 of the Act of Union required every senator and member of the House of Assembly, before taking his or her seat, to swear or affirm to 'be faithful and bear true allegiance' to the sovereign and his or her heirs or successors.

15. Reproduced from the *Transvaal Chronicle* [date unknown].

16. Rivers in the eastern Cape.

17. In fact this does not appear to have been published in the *Pretoria News*. I have been unable to trace this reference. The previous letter of Plaatje's to the *Pretoria News*, an obituary of the Bakwena chief Sebele, appeared in its issue of 10 February, and did not touch on this issue.

18. 'Jim Crow' was an American term used to refer to discriminatory and segregationist laws and practice, originating in the title of a minstrel song and dance show in the 1830s (see C. Vann Woodward, *The Strange Career of Jim Crow* [New York: 1957]). For further information about the experience of blacks on the railways in early twentieth-century South Africa, see Ronald Elsworth, '"The simplicity of the native mind": Black Passengers on the South African Railways in the Early Twentieth Century', in T. Lodge (ed.), *Resistance and Ideology in Settler Societies. Southern African Studies* 4 (Johannesburg: 1986).

19. The South African Native Convention, a precursor to the South African Native National Congress, was formed in 1909 and sought to amalgamate a range of provincial African political organisations already in existence. The particular meeting referred to was probably the second annual congress of the SANC, held in Johannesburg in March 1910. For further information see Andre Odendaal, *Vukani Bantu! the Beginnings of Black Protest Politics in South Africa to 1912* (Cape Town: 1984).

20. CAD, Pretoria, NTS 3139, 23/306.

21. In the cabinet reshuffle in June 1912 Henry Burton moved from Native Affairs to become Minister of Railways and Harbours; Hertzog became Minister of Native Affairs, retaining at the same time his portfolio as Minister of Justice; Abraham Fischer became Minister for the Interior. For information on the events and

circumstances surrounding the passage of the Natives' Land Act, see Harvey Feinberg, 'The 1913 Land Act in South Africa: Race and Segregation in the Early Twentieth Century', *International Journal of African Historical Studies*, 26, 1 (1993):65-110; and more generally, C.M. Tatz, *Shadow and Substance in South Africa* (Pietermaritzburg: 1962) and Tim Keegan, *Rural Transformations in Industrializing South Africa: The Southern Highveld to 1914* (London: 1987).

22. The South African Labour Party (SALP), formed in 1910, was modelled on the British Labour Party. Membership, however, was confined to whites, and the SALP claimed to be the first political party to have demanded total segregation This remained one of its central policies, making possible the formation of the Pact government (with the National Party) in 1924.

23. 'Act to make further provision as to the purchase and leasing of Land by Natives and other Persons in the several parts of the Union and for other purposes in connection with the ownership and occupation of Land by Natives and other Persons, known in abbreviated form as the Natives' Land Act, 1913.'

24. The Natives' Land Act was not in fact repealed until 1992.

25. Johannes Sauer (1850-1913), Cape politician and, from December 1912, Minister of Native Affairs with responsibility for piloting the Natives' Land Act through Parliament. He died on 24 July, 1913.

26. Sir Frederick Moor (1853-1927), former Prime Minister of Natal, and for a few months Minister of Commerce and Industries in the first Union government. He was forced to resign his position, however, after he lost his seat in the parliamentary elections of September 1910 – hence Plaatje's reference to his being 'punished … for joining the Boer Party'.

27. Marshall Campbell (1848-1917), Natal sugar industry pioneer and magnate, regarded as sympathetic to African interests, albeit from a segregationist perspective.

28. A reference to the clause excluding the Cape Province from the operation of the act on the grounds that the Cape franchise, which would be affected by the Land Act because of the effect on the landholding qualification for the franchise, was entrenched in the constitution.

29. Patrick Duncan (1870-1943), a former Private Secretary to Sir Alfred Milner and Colonial Secretary for the Transvaal, joined the Unionist Party after Union and was elected to Parliament in 1911. In the 1930s he became Governor-General of South Africa. The 'paper recently published by Mr Patrick Duncan' was entitled *Suggestions for a Native Policy* (1912), which argued in favour of economic 'integration' between white capital and black labour, and against 'total' segregation of the kind being put forward by Hertzog.

30. Dr Abdullah Abdurahman (1876-1940) was a well known coloured leader of Malay origin, member of the Cape Town City Council, and leader of the African Political Organisation (APO). The reference is to Dr Abdurahman's prophecy,

made at an APO meeting in Johannesburg in 1911, that white South Africans were about to embark upon a 'war of extermination' against the African and coloured people. The phrase was subsequently taken up and used by Plaatje.

31. De Beers archives, Kimberley, General Secretary's correspondence files.

32. A reference to the advertising placed by the De Beers Company with the *Bechuana Gazette*, the *Friend of the Bechuana* and the *Friend of the People*.

33. Electric trams were introduced in Kimberley by Gibson Brothers, long-established local transport contractors, in 1904-05.

34. School of Oriental and African Studies, University of London, Plaatje papers, MS 375. 495, STP2/2, bound notebook. Plaatje's handwritten notes appear to date from 1913 (derived from Plaatje's reference to the age of his daughter, Olive, born in December 1903), though much of the rest of the contents of the notebook dates from 1919-1920, when Plaatje was in England.

35. Isaiah Bud-M'belle (1870-1947), brother of Plaatje's wife Elizabeth, at that time interpreter to the Griqualand West High Court, based in Kimberley. On occasions the court went on circuit, and sessions were held at Mafeking.

36. Olive was in fact named after Olive Schreiner.

37. Alexander Jabavu was one of Tengo Jabavu's sons, and subsequently became editor of *Imvo* after his father's death in 1921. On Tengo Jabavu, see D.D.T. Jabavu, *The Life of J.T. Jabavu, Editor of Imvo Zabantsundu, 1885-1921* (Lovedale: n.d. [1921]).

38. Plaatje is probably quoting here from one of the works of Professor Henry van Dyke (1852-1933), American poet, Presbyterian minister, and Professor of English at Princeton University, best known for works of popular theology such as *The Gospel for an Age of Doubt* (1896) and *The Gospel for a World of Sin* (1899). I have been unable, however, to trace the source of this particular passage.

39. Rev. William Pescod was a well-known Methodist clergyman in Kimberley, closely associated with the interests of the coloured community.

40. Rev. John Dube (1871-1946), clergyman, educationalist, newspaper editor and first President (1912-17) of the South African Native National Congress. For further information on Dube, see Shula Marks, 'The Ambiguities of Dependence: John L. Dube of Natal', *Journal of Southern African Studies*, 1, 2 (April 1975), and *The Ambiguities of Dependence in South Africa: Class, Nationalism and the State in Twentieth-Century South Africa* (Johannesburg: 1986). On the foundation of the SANNC and its early years, see A.P. Walshe, *The Rise of African Nationalism in South Africa: The African National Congress 1912-1952* (London: 1970).

41. Plaatje in fact drafted a resolution opposing a strike by African workers ('Natives and Federation of Trades', letter from Plaatje to the editor, *Transvaal Leader*, 10 February 1914).

42. Thomas M. Mapikela (1869-1945), owner of a building business in Bloemfontein, President of the Orange Free State Native Congress, and (along with Plaatje, Rev.

Rubusana, Rev. Dube and Saul Msane) one of the members of the SANNC deputation to England.

43. Eventually published as *Native Life in South Africa* in 1916 (London: 1916).

44. Saul Msane (d.1919), well-known Zulu politician, employed as compound manager of the Jubilee and Salisbury gold mining company in Johannesburg, and prominent in the Transvaal branch of the SANNC.

45. Secretary of State for the Colonies, whom the deputation met at the end of June 1914.

46. 'A contemptuous South African term for British Indians' (Plaatje's original note). Asians had been banned from entering the Orange Free State in 1890, and this prohibition was entrenched after Union. Legislation designed to restrict Indian immigration into South Africa followed in the form of the Immigrants' Restriction Act of 1913 (referred to by Plaatje as the Immigration Law).

47. 'My *Reminiscences of the Anglo-Boer War* (General Ben Viljoen), p.122' (Plaatje's original note).

48. Piet Grobler (1873-1942) was member of parliament for Rustenburg (western Transvaal), and a strong supporter of J.B.M. Hertzog and his National Party. He had moved the resolution in parliament in favour of the Natives' Land Act of 1913, and two years later was imprisoned for having joined the Boer rebellion of 1914, opposing South Africa's invasion of German South West Africa. Chapter XXIV of *Native Life in South Africa*, reproducing a lecture Plaatje gave in London in February 1915, was devoted to Piet Grobler.

49. Plaatje's original note here read as follows: 'Some white South Africans in recent years have migrated to the Katanga region in the Belgian Congo. I have read in the South African daily papers, correspondence from some of them complaining of their inability to make money. They attributed this difficulty to the fact that the Belgian officials will not permit them to exploit the labour of the Congolese as freely as white men are accustomed to make use of the Natives in British South Africa.'

50. In the original edition of *Native Life in South Africa* Plaatje quoted at the head of this chapter part of W.P. Schreiner's evidence to the Natives Land Commission. 'Any policy,' Schreiner declared, 'that aims at setting off a very small proportion of the land of the country for the use and occupation of the very vast majority of the inhabitants, and reserving for the use and occupation of a very small minority of the inhabitants the great majority of the land of the country, is a policy that economically must break down somewhere. You can start and move in that direction to a certain extent, but you will be driven back by the exigencies of a law that operates outside the law of Parliament – the law of supply and demand.'

51. Plaatje's contribution to *A Book of Homage to Shakespeare*, edited by Israel Gollancz (London: 1916).

52. Hamlet was in fact performed at the Queen's Theatre in Kimberley in 1896, and again in December 1897, by the De Jong-Haviland travelling company.

53. A reference to the film 'The Birth of a Nation', based on *The Clansman*, which glorified the activities of the Ku Klux Klan in the American south. So horrified had Plaatje and several of his friends been that they registered their protest with the British Home Secretary, and succeeded in getting an undertaking that the film would not be shown in South Africa.

54. Robert Moffat (1795-1883), Scottish-born missionary based at the London Missionary Society's mission at Kuruman. He was the major figure in the development of Tswana as a written language, and his translation of St Luke's gospel was the first book of the Bible to be printed in any Bantu language translation. Lists of Tswana words and phrases, however, had appeared shortly before Moffat's arrival in southern Africa in the travel writings of Henry Lichtenstien, John Campbell, William Burchell and Henry Salt (for further information see M.A. Peters and M.M. Tabane, *Bibliography of the Tswana Language* [Pretoria:1982].

55. For further information on Silas Molema, see Plaatje's obituary of him (pp.359-61).

56. William Cross was H.M. Collector of Taxes in the London borough of Ealing, prominent in the affairs of the Brotherhood movement, and a friend and supporter of Plaatje's in his wider campaign in England. Plaatje's inscription in the copy of *Sechuana Proverbs* which he gave to William Cross referred to 'the helpful hours spent at 69 Shakespeare Road [Mr Cross's home] during 1915-16'.

57. Alice Werner (1859-1935) was another of Plaatje's supporters in his campaign in England. A close friend of the Colensos (see n. 111 p.446), she had assisted him with *Native Life in South Africa*, sought to raise funds to secure its publication, and was secretary of a committee set up to watch African interests in South Africa once Plaatje had returned to South Africa early in 1917. Subsequently reader and professor of Swahili and Bantu languages at the School of Oriental and African Studies, University of London, Alice Werner wrote extensively in her chosen field; her publications included *The Language Families of Africa*, a standard reference work on the subject.

58. D. Jones and S.T. Plaatje, *A Sechuana Reader in International Phonetic Orthography (with English translations)*, (London: 1916).

59. A younger sister of Alice Werner.

60. Daniel (later Professor) Jones (1881-1967) became one of the foremost academic linguists and phoneticians of his day. He spent his entire academic career at University College, London (in 1916 he held the position of Reader), and wrote and lectured extensively on his subject. He had collaborated with a young Chinese student in working on a phonetic transcription of Cantonese shortly before meeting Plaatje, and was already one of the leading figures in the International Phonetic Association and the leading authority on English pronunciation. For further information, see A.J. Bronstein, L.J. Raphael and C.J. Stephen (eds), *A Biographical Dictionary of the Phonetic Sciences* (New York: 1977).

442   *Sol Plaatje: Selected Writings*

61.   'Brown, *Sechuana Dictionary*, under *kgoba* (p.324). The distinction referred to is between kxȧbq̱ (to upbraid) and kxẋbā (to pound)' (Plaatje's original note).

62.   For further information on the *Mendi* and the South African Native Labour Contingent, see Norman Clothier, *Black Valour: The South African Native Labour Contingent, 1916-1918, and the Sinking of the Mendi* (Pietermaritzburg: 1987), and Albert Grundlingh, *Fighting Their Own War: South African Blacks and the First World War* (Johannesburg: 1987).

63.   University of Bristol, Cobden Unwin papers, APS file.

64.   Plaatje's reference is to the Native Administration Bill which was intended to confirm the recommendations of the Lands Commission (Beaumont Commission) in relation to the division of land into areas of African and European occupation, and to take the principle of segregation a stage further by separating the administration of the one from the other. The bill was eventually dropped after a Select Committee failed to resolve the details of land demarcation, but most of its provisions were eventually implemented in the Native Administration Act of 1927 (see Plaatje's letter on this subject on pp.00-00).

65.   J. H. Harris, Organising Secretary of the Anti-Slavery and Aborigines' Protection Society. Harris favoured the principle of segregation, and had expressed support on behalf of his society for the Natives' Land Act of 1913. He had also sought to undermine Plaatje's campaign against the legislation between 1914 and 1917. For further information on the Anti-Slavery and Aborigines' Protection Society's reaction to the Natives' Land Act of 1913, see B. P. Willan, 'The Anti-Slavery and Aborigines' Protection Society and the South African Natives' Land Act of 1913', *Journal of African History*, 20, 1 (1979):83-102.

66.   Cobden Unwin papers, APS file.

67.   Mrs Georgiana Solomon (1845-1933), widow of Saul Solomon, one of the great figures of the nineteenth-century Cape liberal tradition, was another of Plaatje's supporters in England. A member of the Anti-Slavery and Aborigines' Protection Society, she had strongly opposed John Harris's pro-segregationist policies. Plaatje had dedicated his *Sechuana Proverbs* to her. For further information, see W.E.G. Solomon, *Saul Solomon: The Member for Cape Town* (Cape Town: 1948), and on the Solomon family more generally, Richard A. Solomon, *The Solomons: The Genealogical Tree and Short History of the Solomon Family in South Africa* (Cape Town: 1989).

68.   The Congress resolution (at its meeting in Pietermaritzburg on 2 October 1916) condemned the Report of the Natives' Land Commission as 'disappointing and unsatisfactory, and [failing] to carry out the alleged principle of territorial separation of the races on an equitable basis', and backed this up with a list of more detailed objections to it.

69.   In fact the relevant passage in the letter (from R. V. Selope Thema, General Secretary of Congress, to Travers Buxton, Secretary of the Anti-Slavery and

Aborigines' Protection Society, undated [February 1917]), read as follows: 'While the Bantu people will gladly welcome the policy of territorial separation of the races if carried out on fair and equitable lines, they cannot bind themselves to support a Government which cannot carry out that principle with justice' (Rhodes House, Oxford, AS/APS S22 G205, Thema to Buxton [undated], enclosing SANNC resolution of 2 October, 1916).

70. S.M.Makgatho (1861-1951), a well-known Transvaal political leader, founder of the Transvaal African Teachers' Association and the Transvaal Native Political Union. He was to be President-General of the SANNC between 1917 and 1924.

71. This is probably a reference to a passage in Smuts's famous Savoy Hotel speech (delivered at the Savoy Hotel, London, on 22 May 1917), where he elaborated upon the need to build upon 'honesty, fair-play, justice, and the ordinary Christian virtues [as] the basis of all our relations with the natives.' The speech is reproduced in J.C. Smuts, *Jan Christian Smuts: A Biography of his Father* (London: 1952), pp.192-98.

72. William Hay (1845-1932), insurance manager, newspaper editor, former Cape member of Parliament (1892-98), and a leading member of the Cape liberal establishment.

73. Michael Furse (1870-1955) was Bishop of Pretoria.

74. Rev. Amos Burnet was a leading South African Methodist minister, sympathetic to African interests.

75. De Beers archives, Kimberley, General Secretary's correspondence.

76. Alpheus Williams (1874-1953), American-born General Manager of De Beers from 1905 to 1932, having succeeded his father Gardiner Williams in the same position. For further information on the 'tram-shed' episode and its broader context, see *Biography*, pp.218-24.

77. Irvine Grimmer (1862-1932) was the Assistant General Manager of De Beers from 1905 to 1932, and one of the pioneers in Kimberley's diamond industry.

78. Colonel Sir David Harris (1852-1942), member of Parliament for Kimberley, former soldier and diamond prospector, and a director of De Beers.

79. Ernest Oppenheimer (1880-1957) was mayor of Kimberley from 1912 to 1914, and a leading figure in the affairs of De Beers. Subsequently chairman of De Beers, and founder (in 1917) of the Anglo-American Corporation of South Africa.

80. De Beers archives, General Secretary's correspondence.

81. Ibid.

82. Geoffrey Boyes was the Kimberley Civil Commissioner.

83. The reference is to an executive committee meeting of the South African Native National Congress on 2 August. Amongst the resolutions passed was one (drafted by Plaatje) congratulating Africans in Kimberley 'on their good fortune and appreciation of the generosity of the De Beers Company which we feel certain will go far towards removing the causes of friction between White and Black in South Africa'.

84. Mesach Pelem (1859-1936), labour agent, businessman and former teacher from Queenstown in the eastern Cape, one of the founding vice-presidents of the SANNC, and also a former resident of Kimberley.

85. The text of the resolution of the executive committee of the SANNC (2 August 1918) expressed its appreciation of the generosity of the De Beers Company, and assured Lord Buxton of the 'unswerving loyalty of the South African Bantu races to his Majesty King George V and the British throne'.

86. Kimberley Public Library, Kimberley Chamber of Commerce Minute Books, Minutes of monthly general meetings, 18 November 1918.

87. For further background and information on this period of unrest, see Philip Bonner, 'The Transvaal Native Congress, 1917-1920: The Radicalisation of the Black Petty-bourgeoisie on the Rand', in Shula Marks and Richard Rathbone (eds), *Industrialisation and Social Change in South Africa* (London: 1982).

88. Plaatje is referring here to the committee of the Diamond Fields Men's Own Brotherhood, of which Plaatje himself was President, formed in July 1918.

89. University of the Witwatersrand, Molema/Plaatje papers, Da59; W.Z. Fenyang (1877-1957) was a wealthy Barolong landowner from Thaba Nchu, prominent member of the SANNC, and one of the syndicate which had financed Plaatje's newspaper, the *Bechuana Friend*, in 1910. For further biographical information, see Murray, *Black Mountain*; and for more on the SANNC's campaign in Great Britain, see *Biography*, pp.223-58.

90. The annual vote of Colonial Office funds provided the opportunity for sympathetic backbenchers (Mr Spoor, Henry Cavendish Bentinck, Captain Ormsby Gore, Colonel Wedgewood) to debate the general question of African rights in both South Africa and Rhodesia, and to urge the Colonial Office to use its influence to ameliorate matters (Hansard, *House of Commons Debates*, 30 July 1919, pp.2198-228). This particular report, probably from a newspaper, has not survived with Plaatje's letter.

91. R.V. Selope Thema (1886-1955), active in the early years of the SANNC, then its Secretary (1914-17) while Plaatje was in England, and by this time a member of the SANNC deputation of 1919.

92. Levi Mvabaza (d. 1955), one of the founders of the SANNC, formerly editor of *Abantu-Batho*, Congress's newspaper, and also a member of the SANNC deputation of 1919.

93. F.S. Malan (1871-1941) was the South African Minister for Native Affairs and Acting Prime Minister. In June 1919 Plaatje had sought unsuccessfully to persuade him to authorise the release of money from the Barolong National Fund (set up to promote the educational and economic development of the Barolong) to support the SANNC deputation on the grounds that this was representing, *inter alia*, Barolong interests.

94. President and Treasurer respectively of the SANNC.

95. General Christiaan De Wet (1854-1922), one of the founders of the Afrikaner National Party, was one of the leaders of the Boer rebellion of 1914, provoked by South Africa's invasion of German South West Africa.

96. Charlotte Manye Maxeke (1874-1939), social worker, educationalist and political leader, and founder of the African National Congress's Women's League in 1919; widow of Reverend Marshall Maxeke (see n.86, p.340).

97. The residence of the Archbishop of Canterbury, with whom Plaatje and Gumede had succeeded in securing an interview.

98. Reginald Blankenberg (1876-1960), was the Official Secretary, Office of the High Commissioner for the Union of South Africa, 1918-1925. He was knighted in 1920.

99. The £200 was advanced by the South African government (via their High Commission in London, who in turn involved the Anti-Slavery and Aborigines' Protection Society) to the Congress delegates, a promise having been received from S.M. Makgotho, President of the Congress, that his organisation would repay this, pending settlement of any action for damages which may have resulted from the incident.

100. Rev. Henry R. Ngcayiya (1860-1928), leader of the Ethiopian Church of South Africa which broke away from the south African branch of the African Methodist Episcopal Church early in the century (see also note 105, p.431). Ngcayiya was in the United Kingdom representing the interests of Africans from Rhodesia in connection with claims to land, and was not an elected member of the SANNC deputation.

101. 'This bill was accurately forecasted three years before on page 53 of my *Native Life in South Africa*; even its short title was correctly guessed' (Plaatje's original note).

102. The Indian Relief Act of 1914 relaxed some of the restrictions imposed upon Indians the previous year in relation to the immigration of children of families already living in South Africa, but did not remove restrictions on residence, land ownership or trading.

103. Public Record Office, CO 551/1137, 3473, 'Minutes of deputation'.

104. A farm called Doornfontein, near Boshof in the Orange Free State, an outstation of the Berlin Missionary Society mission at Pniel.

105. University of Massachusetts Library, Special Collections and Archives, Du Bois papers, r10 f65-73. For further information on this and other Pan-African Congresses, see Immanuel Geiss, *The Pan-African Movement* (London: 1974).

106. In October 1919 twenty-three Africans died when white civilians, assisting the police, opened fire on a mass demonstration in Port Elizabeth. Led by the Industrial and Commercial Workers Union (ICU), Africans in Port Elizabeth had been demanding a minimum wage of 10s a day to help offset the large increase in the cost of living over the previous few years.

107. Late in 1920 the Unionist Party was dissolved, its MPs joining General Smuts's South African Party. In the general election which followed, early in 1921, the

enlarged South African Party was returned to power with a large majority over Labour and Nationalist parties. White farmers' demands for greater controls over African labourers were eventually to find expression in the Native Service Contract Act of 1932, passed in the face of strong opposition from African political leaders, Plaatje included.

108. In 1915 the German colony of South West Africa was invaded by South African forces. At the end of the war, as part of the peace settlement, the victorious powers agreed to administer the former German colonies as mandates of the newly formed League of Nations. General Smuts negotiated a different form of mandate for South West Africa, leaving South Africa in effective control of the territory.

109. Hubert Henry Harrison (1883-1927), labour leader, author, journalist and former socialist, and one of the most prominent radical African-American leaders of his day. At this time he was a strong supporter of Marcus Garvey, but later parted company with him.

110. Natal Archives Depot (Pietermaritzburg), Colenso Papers, A204, Vol 57. For further information about Plaatje's visit to the USA, see *Biography*, pp.259-81.

111. Mrs Sophie Colenso was married to Frank Colenso, one of the sons of the famous Bishop William Colenso (1814-1883). She was a close friend of Plaatje's, and had been a strong supporter of his campaign in England.

112. See Plaatje's account of these experiences in his article 'Native doctors at hospitals', *Cape Times*, 4 June 1927 (pp.352-57).

113. A reference to the Anglo-Irish Treaty of 1921, which recognised the independence of the Irish Republic, excluding Ulster which remained part of the United Kingdom. 'Her' is probably a reference to Mrs Jane Cobden Unwin, who had a particular interest in Irish affairs, and supported the Irish Nationalist cause.

114. This obituary was not attached to Plaatje's letter. Olive died, however, in July 1921, at Bloemfontein railway station, after she was refused access to the 'whites only' waiting-room. Her health had been severely undermined by the influenza epidemic in 1918, when she contracted rheumatic fever. See also n. 34 p.439.

115. Presented to Plaatje by the Rt. Rev. J. A. Johnson, head of the AME Church.

116. University of the Witwatersrand, Molema/Plaatje papers, Db1, 'Account of visit to Canada and the USA, January 1921-October 1922', TS, incomplete, pp.6-24. The letter quoted below is from Plaatje to Mrs Lennox Murray, 17 November 1922 (University of Cape Town Archives, Molteno/Murray Brown collection, BC330 A81.2.3).

117. John E. Bruce (d.1925), a well-known Afro-American journalist, who was at this time one of the editors of the *Negro World*. Plaatje had exchanged newspapers with him while editor of the *Bechuana Gazette*, and the two men had then embarked upon what Bruce described as a 'desultory correspondence', during which they had come to know one another 'pretty tolerably well'(*Negro World*, 16 July 1921).

118. Plaatje's allusion is to J.W. Sauer, the Cape politician who died shortly after piloting the Natives' Land Act of 1913 through the South African Parliament (see n.25, p.438). Plaatje has more to say on his heart problems and the treatment he received in 'Native doctors at hospitals', *Cape Times*, 4 June 1927 (pp.352-57).

119. The 15th Amendment, ratified in 1870, reads: 'The right of citizens of the United States to vote shall not be denied or abridged by the United States or by any State on account of race, color or previous condition of servitude', and affirmed the power of Congress 'to enforce this article by appropriate legislation'.

120. Plaatje is referring to the Negro Society for Historical Research, founded in 1911 with the objective of 'collecting ... data, pamphlets [and] books bearing upon the history and achievements of the Negro race; [and] to establish a circulating library for its members, the special feature of which will be the published writings of the Negroes and the Negroes' friends upon subjects that enlighten and encourage the race in its struggles upwards'. The Society's quarterly journal was the *Journal of Negro History*. For further information, see Alfred A. Moss (jr.), *The American Negro Academy: Voice of the Talented Tenth* (Baton Rouge: 1981).

121. Plaatje visited the Tuskegee Institute in Alabama in May 1922, and was very impressed by what he saw. He met the Principal of Tuskegee, Dr Robert Russa Moton, and the two men commenced a correspondence which lasted until 1930 (see n.15, p.449, and Plaatje's letters to Moton reproduced in this collection – Docs 77, 85, 100).

Part Three 1924-1932. 'A pioneer in literature'

1. This was to be known as the Bantu Men's Social Centre, opened in 1924. Two American missionaries, Rev. F.R. Bridgeman and Ray Phillips, were particularly instrumental in its foundation, and it was to become an important focus for African social and cultural life on the Rand in the 1920s and 1930s (see also notes 6 and 20 below). For further information, see particularly Tim Couzens, *The New African: A Study of the Life and Works of H.I.E. Dhlomo* (Johannesburg: 1985).

2. See Plaatje's earlier comments on this episode in 'Segregation: idea ridiculed', pp.140-43.

3. In fact General Smuts's speech, delivered at the City Hall, Johannesburg, on 14 December, was devoted largely to the subject of Imperial preference, and appears to have had little to say on the question of 'native policy' (*Cape Times*, 15 December 1923).

4. Clements Kadalie (c.1896-1951), founder and leader of the ICU. Plaatje's favourable view of the ICU did not last long, particularly after the ICU came out in support of the Nationalist-Labour coalition in the general election of 1924. For further information on Kadalie and the ICU, see Peter Wickens, *The Industrial and*

Commercial Workers Union of South Africa (Cape Town: 1978) and Helen Bradford, *A Taste of Freedom: The ICU in Rural South Africa, 1924-1930* (Johannesburg: 1987).

5. A reference to the events of March 1922 on the Rand when a white miners' strike, sparked off by the attempt of the government and the mining industry to restrict the use and cost of using white labour on the mines, escalated into rebellion, and bitter fighting took place between miners and government forces.

6. Rev. Ray E. Phillips (1889-1961), American-born missionary of the American Board Mission on the Witwatersrand, author of *The Bantu are Coming : Phases of South Africa's Race Problem* (London: 1930), and *The Bantu in the City: A Study of Cultural Adjustment on the Witwatersrand* (Lovedale: 1938). Philips founded the Gamma Sigma Club in order to involve Africans in 'discussions and debate, essay-writing and extemporaneous speaking', and was later one of the founders of the South African Institute of Race Relations in 1929.

7. Colonel C.F. Stallard, a SAP member of parliament who was later to lead the breakaway Dominion Party. A pro-segregationist, his views had recently found expression in the Report of the Transvaal Local Government Commission (commonly known as the Stallard Commission) in 1922, which advocated restrictions on Africans living in towns.

8. C.W.M. Malan (1883-1933), one of the founders of the National Party in 1915, and a member of parliament for Humansdorp. In fact he was Minister for Railways and Harbours in Hertzog's cabinet, not Minister of Mines.

9. Dr Alex Roberts (1857-1938), born in Scotland, was a former teacher and principal of Lovedale, was nominated as a senator representing African interests from 1920 to 1930, and served as a member of the Native Affairs Commission for the same period.

10. A reference to the Native (Urban Areas) Act of 1923, which set out to systematise municipal policies towards Africans living in towns. Originally promulgated in 1918 (and referred to by Plaatje in *Legal Disabilities*, pp.255), the Act sought to restrict the rights of Africans to reside and acquire freehold tenure in towns. At the same time it provided for the establishment of local advisory boards in which Africans were to play a role.

11. The results of these investigations were published in the *Report of the Native Churches Commission* of 1925, but no immediate legislation followed from this.

12. Plaatje's letter on the subject of 'Native Taxation' was reproduced in the Johannesburg *Star* on 11 March, and in *Imvo Zabantsundu* on 1 April. Its central point was the contention that Africans payed far more in taxes than ever appeared in official figures and returns.

13. The issue of the franchise for white women was linked to the question of the 'Native vote', and legislation was delayed as a result of the delays with the 'Hertzog bills'. The Women's Franchise Act, extending the vote to all white

women, was eventually passed in 1930. The effect was to nearly double the number of white voters.

14. Tielman Roos (1879-1935), former lawyer, a prominent early supporter of General Hertzog, deputy Prime Minister and Minister of Justice in General Hertzog's government formed in 1924.

15. Tuskegee University (Alabama), Hollis Burke Frissell Library, Moton Papers, GC 109/810. Robert Russa Moton (1867-1940) was Principal of the Tuskegee Institute from 1915 to 1935. Prior to this appointment, in succession to Booker T. Washington, Moton had been at the Hampton Institute, Virginia, the leading centre for 'Negro education', in a senior administrative capacity. He acted as unofficial adviser to the federal government on racial affairs, and was President of the Negro Business League for more than twenty years. For further information on Moton, see W.H. Hughes and D. Patterson (eds), *Robert Russa Moton of Hampton and Tuskegee* (Chapel Hill: 1950).

16. Early in 1923 a new Negro Veterans' hospital was opened near the Tuskegee Institute. A dispute arose, however, over the decision to staff the hospital entirely with Afro-American personnel. The white Ku Klux Klan was particularly virulent in its opposition, and on one occasion threatened Moton with violence and the destruction of the Tuskegee Institute. By August 1923, after considerable publicity and the involvement of the United States President the opposition was overcome. White staff were recruited temporarily, but replaced as soon as qualified Afro-American personnel were available (Holsey, 'A Man of Courage', in Hughes and Patterson [eds], *Robert Russa Moton of Hampton and Tuskegee*). I am indebted to Bob Edgar for this reference.

17. Dr James E. Kwegyir Aggrey (1876-1927), Gold Coast educator and clergyman, and a member of the Phelps-Stokes Commission on Africa which visited South Africa in 1921. A second commission visited South Africa in 1924. For further information on Aggrey, see E.W. Smith, *Aggrey of Africa* (London, 1939).

18. Dr Thomas Jesse Jones (b. 1873), Welsh-born educator who became a leading figure in the advancement of Negro education in the USA, and a friend and supporter of Dr Aggrey. He was Education Director of the Phelps Stokes Fund in New York, leader of the Phelps Stokes Education Commission to Africa, and the author of several books on black education in the USA and Africa.

19. Prepared under the auspices of the Brotherhood movement, Plaatje had been seeking funds to publish this for five years – but never succeeded.

20. Dr F.R. Bridgeman, senior missionary of the American Board Mission on the Witwatersrand, and founder of the Bantu Men's Social Centre in Johannesburg in 1924.

21. Rev. Herbert Payne was an American Baptist missionary who travelled to South Africa in 1917 on the same ship as Plaatje. Refused entry on their arrival in Cape Town, Plaatje appealed to several South African politicians, including General Botha, and succeeded in getting the ruling reversed (see *Biography*, pp.251-33).

22. University of the Witwatersrand archives, Records of the Joint Council of Europeans and Africans (AD 1433, Ac.3.3.13), typescript of address by S.T. Plaatje.

23. The judgment was in one of the 'treason trial' cases during the Anglo-Boer War – *R. vs Rinke, Burke, Bruwer, Van Rooyen and Moolman* at the Special Treason Court sitting in Mafeking in November 1901.

24. H.J. De Villiers (1842-1914), Chief Justice of the Cape Colony from 1873 to 1910, and then of the Union of South Africa. The Mpondo chief Sigcau was arrested by government proclamation in 1894, but was released on appeal to the Cape courts, Lord De Villiers ruling in his favour in 1895.

25. William Pittman (1878-1964), first Dean of the Faculty of Law at the University of Pretoria, who had recently been appointed a King's Counsel.

26. Nicholas Jacobus de Wet (1873-1960), lawyer and politician, was Minister of Justice from 1913 to 1923, serving under both Botha and Smuts. The petition Plaatje drafted was sent by telegram (by Isiah Bud-M'belle, then General Secretary of the SANNC) to the Governor-General on 13 June 1919, and the strikers were released from prison two weeks later. For further information on this episode and the broader context in which this strike took place, see Bonner, 'The Transvaal Native Congress, 1917-1920', esp. pp.292-95.

27. Probably Rev. Abner Mtimkulu (*c.* 1875-1954), a prominent Cape Town Methodist clergyman, involved in the affairs of the Cape Town branch of the SANNC.

28. Central Archives Depot, Pretoria, Smuts papers, Vol 33, no. 43.

29. George Pilkington (1879-1958), until recently a senior civil servant and private secretary to Henry Burton, a member of General Smuts's cabinet in 1924 until the SAP's defeat in the general election that year. Pilkington then left the civil service, began cotton farming, then briefly entered politics before becoming a full-time artist, and went on to build a reputation as a seascape painter. He married into the well known Solomon family.

30. A reference to proposals, instigated by the Labour part of the Pact government, to protect white workers by extending the colour bar in industry, most notably in the Mines and Works Amendment bill, which was to become law in 1926 (see 'The colour bar', pp.343-46).

31. F.S. Malan (1871-1941), the former Minister of Native Affairs and Acting Prime Minister under the Smuts government.

32. Morris Alexander (1877-1946), a lawyer and member of Parliament with a reputation for defending African and coloured interests.

33. Frederick Beyers (1867-1938), lawyer, former Attorney-General of the Transvaal, Minister of Mines and Industries in General Hertzog's cabinet.

34. *Umteteli wa Bantu* (*Mouthpiece of the People*) was a weekly newspaper published by the Native Recruiting Corporation (of the Chamber of Mines), and the first issue

had appeared in May 1920. Plaatje had in fact been involved (whilst in England in 1920) in discussions with the proprietors, who had wanted him to be the editor, but he declined the offer (see *Biography*, pp.251-53).

35. A reference to a series of articles in *Umteteli* by 'Resurgam', a pseudonym of A.K. Soga, the one-time editor of *Izwi Labantu*.(see n.90, p.430).

36. For further information about the predicament of the Griqua at this time, see Robert Edgar and Christopher Saunders, 'A.A.S. Le Fleur and the Griqua trek of 1917: Segregation, Self-help and Ethnic Identity', *International Journal of African Historical Studies*, 15, 2 (1982):201-20.

37. Chief Samuel Moroka was banished from the Orange Free State in 1884 as a result of a succession dispute, settling in 1898 in the Tati district of Bechuanaland. In 1916 several thousand Barolong, primarily from the Thaba Nchu district, joined the Chief, but many died from the effects of disease. For further information on this episode, see Murray, *Black Mountain*.

38. Library of Parliament, Cape Town, manuscript annexures to the Report of the Select Committee on the Native Administration Bill, 1927.

39. As in Plaatje's letter – in fact the correct title was the Native Administration Act.

40. Named after Jan Hendrik Hofmeyr (1845-1909), statesman, newspaper editor, member of the Cape Parliament and one-time leader of the Afrikaner Bond. The 'Hofmeyr Act' of 1887 exempted Africans in the Cape with appropriate educational and income qualifications, as well as the possession of the franchise, from pass laws and various other regulations which applied to the mass of the African population.

41. *Cape Times*, 23 May 1927. In the interview, the Cape Administrator, Mr A. P. J. Fourie, announced that the white nurses' strike at Mafeking had been temporarily settled, but that the Provincial Council would soon be considering some proposals he planned to put forward to address the question of nurses receiving orders from 'native doctors, and attending native patients'. For further information on the politics of nursing and health care during this period, see Shula Marks, *Divided Sisterhood: Race, Class and Gender in the South African Nursing Profession* (Johannesburg: 1995).

42. Dr Modiri Molema (1891-1965) was a son of Silas Molema (see pp.359-61), and a close friend of Plaatje's. He had studied medicine at Glasgow University, and set up what proved to be a very successful medical practice in Mafeking in 1921. He was also the author of a number of books, including *The Bantu Past and Present* (Edinburgh, 1920).

43. Tuskagee University Library, Moton papers, GC 128/965.

44. The Imperial Conference was held in London in November 1926, and led to the Balfour Declaration, on which Hertzog's arguments had considerable influence. The Declaration stated that Great Britain and the Dominions were 'autonomous

communities within the British Empire, equal in status, in no way subordinate to
one another in any aspect of their domestic, or external affairs, though united by a
common allegiance to the Crown and freely associated as members of the British
Commmonwealth of Nations'.

45. J.W. Mushet (1881-1954) was a wealthy Cape Town merchant and philanthropist
(married to a niece of T.L. Schreiner). He was a South African Party member of
parliament between 1920 and 1922, and later became Minister of Posts and
Telegraphs. In the early 1930s he was to provide financial support for *Our
Heritage*, a journal of the Independent Order of True Templars, which Plaatje
edited during its brief life in 1931.

46. Blantyre was the largest town, and administrative centre, of the colony of
Nyasaland. The term 'Blantyre' was used more widely, however, to encompass the
region around Blantyre.

47. The four 'Hertzog bills' were interdependent components of his overall policy of
segregation: the Coloured Persons Rights Bill, which proposed to remove Africans
from the Cape common roll; the Representation of Natives in Parliament Bill,
which proposed that seven white MPs should represent Africans in Parliament; the
Union Native Council Bill, designed to formalise the existing Government Native
Conferences; and the Native Land (Amendment) Bill, which proposed to provide
more land for Africans as a quid pro quo for the loss of the franchise. Encountering
opposition from both the South African Party and African organisations and
opinion, the bills were eventually passed, in modified form, in 1936. For further
information on the tortuous passage of the Hertzog bills, see Tatz, *Shadow and
Substance in South Africa*, and Walshe, *Rise of African Nationalism*.

48. University of the Witwatersrand archives, Records of the SAIRR Part 2, Kb
32.2.5. For further information on Tswana language and literature, see Tore
Janson and Joseph Tsonope, *Birth of a National Language: The History of Setswana*
(Gaborone: 1991), and M.A. Peters and M.M. Tabane, *Bibliography of the Tswana
Language* (Pretoria: 1982). For further information on Plaatje's contribution, see
Biography, pp.324-48.

49. Plaatje attended the meeting of the Sotho-Tswana-Pedi language group, a sub-
committee of the Central Orthography Committee, in Pretoria in February 1929.
The 'radical changes' recommended (which Plaatje opposed) were in favour of
diacritic marks over letters of the Roman alphabet in order to indicate stress and
pronunciation. (See Plaatje's article, 'Suggested new Bantu orthography', pp.397-
403.)

50. Plaatje was fully occupied during these months in seeking to register African
voters for the forthcoming general election, and may have been supported in this
by the South African Party.

51. This manuscript has not survived, but it is probable that the praise poems to
Montsioa (part of 'Chief Montsioa, pp.413-19) were included in this.

52. In fact the completed typescript of the revised edition of Plaatje's *Sechuana Proverbs* (now in the Plaatje Papers, School of Oriental and African Studies, University of London) contains an additional 400 proverbs.

53. J.T. Brown, *Secwana Dictionary* (Third edition, London Missionary Society, Tigerkloof, 1928), first edition published in 1876.

54. David Ramoshoana, then a teacher at the Lyndhurst Road Native School in Kimberley, and a close friend and collaborator with Plaatje in his Tswana language work.

55. A copy of Brown's *Secwana Dictionary*, annotated by Plaatje, and containing many critical remarks, has survived, but the more substantial work which appears to have been carried out by Plaatje and Ramoshoana has not.

56. Oswald Pirow (1890-1959), lawyer, elected to Parliament in 1924 and appointed Minister of Justice in 1929.

57. Colonel Frederick Cresswell (1866-1947), founding member of the South African Labour Party in 1910, Minister of Defence and Labour in General Hertzog's Pact government from 1925, and leader of the Labour Party.

58. The Carnegie Commission of 1929-1932 eventually produced a five-volume report on poverty amongst whites, and the social, educational and health problems which accompanied this – the definitive investigation into the so-called 'poor white problem'.

59. De Beers archives, General Secretary's correspondence.

60. During the 1920s the provincial education authorities sought to promote the greater use and study of vernacular languages at both primary and secondary levels. In 1929 the Cape Departmental Junior Certificate course was revised to make the study of two languages compulsory, one of them being one of the two official languages (English and Afrikaans), the other an African language (generally Xhosa, Sesotho or Setswana). A total of 100 African candidates took the revised examination in 1929 (Cape of Good Hope, *Report of the Superintendent of Education for 1929*, CP3-1930). In his report for 1927 and 1928 the Chief Inspector for Native Education, W.G. Bennie, had noted that 'in the Native language, readers have been improved and better standardised . . . in Chwana, however, there is a need for a good series for Standards II to VI (Cape of Good Hope, *Report of Superintendent-General of Education for 1927 and 1928*, CP 2 '29, p.87).

61. Mr R. L. Meadows (d.1958) was principal (from 1924 to 1933) of the Perseverance Teacher Training School in Kimberley, which taught both African and coloured student teachers.

62. Plaatje's translation of *The Comedy of Errors*, *Diphosho-phosho* (literally, 'Mistake upon mistake'), was printed at Morija and published in July 1930; *Julius Caesar* (*Dintshontsho tsa bo Juliuse Kesara*) was published by the Witwatersrand University Press in 1937, after Plaatje's death, having been edited by Professor G.K. Lestrade; Plaatje's translation of *Much Ado about Nothing* (*Matsapa-tsapa a lefala*) was never

published, and the manuscript has not survived. For further information about Plaatje's Shakespeare translations, and reactions to them, see *Biography*, pp.327-33.

63. Sydney Bunting (1873-1936), one of the founders of the Communist Party of South Africa in 1921, and one of its leading figures thereafter. He stood unsuccessfully as a candidate in the Transkei in the 1929 general election, and had visited Kimberley in an attempt to raise support for a new League of African Rights. For further information on Bunting, see Edward Roux, *S.P. Bunting: A Political Biography* (Cape Town: 1944).

64. University of the Witwatersrand archives, Records of the SAIRR Part 2, Kb 32.2.1.5.

65. In 1923 Maletisa Lechaba appeared on a platform at the celebrations of the centenary of the work of the Wesleyan Methodist Missionary Society in the Orange Free State: he was described as being 'just on a hundred years old'.

66. A reference to the Basutoland Council of Chiefs, set up by the British colonial administration in 1903 to provide a forum for discussion and debate. The Council had 100 members.

67. Literally, 'Sesotho of old', or the Sesotho of ancient times. The first books from the Paris Evangelical Mission dated from the 1840s and 1850s, when there was no clear distinction between what subsequently became Sesotho and Setswana. This process of separation, encouraged by the Sotho king Moshoeshoe, then proceeded apace during the second half of the nineteenth century, and a standard Sesotho orthography was established in 1906.

68. The Mokotla mission festival was one of the major events in the calendar for the Protestant Church of Basutoland. It combined a celebration of Reformation Sunday with a large collection (*mokotla*) which was used to finance the salaries of all Basotho ministers in the church, and attracted many delegates and visitors from outside Morija itself.

69. *Leselinyana la Lesotho (The Little Light of Lesotho)* founded in 1863 and published under the auspices of the Paris Evangelical Missionary Society. The newspaper was now formally under the supervision of Rev. C. Christeller, but in practice was edited by Z.D. Mangoaela, by then a well-known public figure, writer and probably the foremost Sesotho scholar of his day. *Leselinyana* reported Plaatje's visit to Basutoland in its issue of 8 November 1929. I am indebted to Stephen Gill, Curator of the Morija Museum, for the information he has provided for notes 67-69.

70. Plaatje was not appointed a member of the Tswana sub-committee (to which he refers) set up at the meeting of the Sotho-Pedi-Tswana sub-committee of the Central Orthography Committee in February. Rev. P. J. Motiyane, who was at both meetings, questioned why Plaatje had not been invited, but the minutes of the meeting simply record that 'Mr Plaatje had not been reappointed by the Central Orthography Committee' (University of Cape Town, Lestrade Papers, BC255 A1.11, 'Minutes of meeting of Tswana sub-committee, 1 and 2 October 1929'). For further information, see *Biography*, pp.340-48.

71. The object of this article, Jones wrote, was to draw attention to the use of tones in Bantu languages 'by setting forth all the tonal forms of Sechuana nouns I have been able to discover in the course of an investigation of the pronunciation of that language'. The book drew upon the work Jones had previously done with Plaatje in London.

72. Dr Clement M. Doke (1893-1980) was at this time Senior Lecturer (later Professor and Head of Department), Department of Bantu Studies, University of the Witwatersrand, and a leading academic authority on Bantu languages, Zulu in particular. He took a keen interest in Plaatje's Tswana language work, and was instrumental in providing financial support for him (via the Bantu Research Committee, based at the University of the Witwatersrand). For further information on Doke, see G. Fortune's biographical and bibliographic sketch in *Catalogue of the C.M. Doke Collection on African Languages in the Library of the University of Rhodesia* (Boston: 1972), and obituary by D.T. Cole, 'In memoriam C.M. Doke 1893-1980', in *African Studies*, 1980.

73. Plaatje's list of disbursements included the cost of a subscription to *South African Outlook*, and a fountain pen for David Ramoshoana (£1.15/-). Both items were questioned by Dr Rheinallt Jones, who did not feel these would be acceptable to the committee. In fact the committee was satisfied with Plaatje's subsequent explanation that the items concerned were presented in lieu of payments for informants, which they considered acceptable.

74. I am very grateful to Mr B. O. Segopolo, University of Botswana, and Mr Peter Seboni for their translation of this passage.

75. Mrs W. Allan King was the widow of the late Allan King, Native Affairs Commissioner for Pretoria, who was killed in the Boer rebellion in 1914. Plaatje once described him as 'the best white friend in South Africa I ever had', and had evidently maintained contact with his widow since then.

76. M. Sammy was a wealthy Indian trader and businessman in Kimberley, prominent in the affairs of the local Indian community.

77. A north London suburb. Georgiana Solomon died three years later at the age of 89 (see n.67, p.442).

78. Transvaal Archives Depot, NA 62/276 (1), Native Economic Commission 1930-32, Minutes of Evidence (typescript).

79. Charles Loram (1879-1940) was a leading educationalist, a member of the first and second Phelps Stokes Commission on African Education, and was at this time Superintendent of Education in Natal He had strong American connections, and in 1931 left South Africa to become Professor of Education at Yale University in the United States. For further information on his views, see Richard Heyman, 'C.T. Loram: A South African Liberal in Race Relations', *International Journal of African Historical Studies*, 5, 1 (1972):41-50.

80. Michael van Reenen (1900-1986) lived opposite Plaatje in Angel Street,

Kimberley, and was able to assist in the correction of proofs because he was confined to his bed, having injured his foot.

81. Tuskagee University Library, Moton papers, GC 160/1304.

82. Botswana National Archives (BNA), Bamangwato Tribal Administration R-B1.

83. For *Our Heritage*, the organ of the Independent Order of True Templars, edited by Plaatje. In fact Plaatje did travel to Bechuanaland at the same time as the High Commissioner, Sir Herbert Sloley, and an extended report of his visit – in Setswana – appeared in *Our Heritage* in November 1931.

84. A reference to the Central Orthography Committee's attempt, strongly opposed by Plaatje, to secure agreement on a common orthography for Tswana and Sotho: the formal recommendation to this effect had been published in July 1930. For further information, see G.P. Lestrade, 'A Practical Orthography for Tswana', *Bantu Studies*, 11 (1937):137-48, as well as Plaatje's article, 'Suggested new Bantu orthography' (pp.00-00).

85. Henry Dumbrell (1885-1973), not in fact a professor, was Inspector of Education for both Swaziland and the Bechuanaland Protectorate, and later became first Director of Education of the Bechuanaland Protectorate. The extract from his letter to which Plaatje refers has not survived, but it seems likely that the *Dumbrell follies* were readers for schools in Setswana, which included some extracts from Plaatje's work (on which Dumbrell evidently awaited a reply from Plaatje). In fact these were never published. Plaatje considered them to be 'follies' on account of the orthography Dumbrell proposed to use for them.

86. T.D. Mweli Skota (ed.), *The African Yearly Register: Being an Illustrated National Biographical Dictionary (Who's Who) of Black Folks in Africa* (Johannesburg: 1932), pp.60-64. For an analysis of the contents of the book and its social significance, see Ch. 1 of Couzens, *The New African*.

87. Plaatje's account of the massacre of Plaatberg does not appear in any of his published writings, and I have been unable to trace it elsewhere.

88. *African Yearly Register*, pp.53-57.

89. The report is from the *Star* (Johannesburg), 1 March 1932, entitled 'Standardizing a Bantu language: Conference on Chuana, 50 years' controversy ended'. The conference took place at Kroondal, close to Rustenburg, was attended by missionaries and representatives of the education departments of the Cape, Orange Free State, Transvaal and Bechuanaland Protectorate, and followed an earlier meeting held in Bloemfontein in November 1931; its purpose was to agree on a standardised version of Tswana in order to make possible the publication of a new translation of the Bible. Ba-hurustse was to be taken as the 'primary basis', so it was reported, 'because they are the parent stock from which the other Chuana tribes have sprung'. This was not the end by any means of the '50 years' controversy', and this attempt at linguistic standardisation proved no more successful than its predecessors.

List of Documents and Extracts by Category

Articles and Editorials

99. Article, 'Suggested new Bantu orthography', *South African Outlook*, 1 May 1931. 397
104. Article, 'A white man's Native language', *Umteteli wa bantu*, 2 April 1932.   419

Letters

3. Letter from Barolong chief and headmen to Mafeking Civil Commissioner and Resident Magistrate [January 1900].   40
4. Letter to Lord Edward Cecil, 26 January 1900.   42
5. Letter to C.G.H. Bell, 30 January 1900.   43
7. Letter to unknown recipient [mid-January 1900].   45
8. Letter to CC and RM, 6 June 1900.   47
9. Letter to CC and RM, 18 July 1901.   49
19. Letter from Silas Molema to Sir H.J. Goold-Adams, Lieutenant-Governor of the Orange River Colony, 11 April 1903.   73
28. Letter to Attorney-General, Transvaal, 13 May 1904.   87
38. Letter to Henry Burton, Minister for Native Affairs, 8 November 1910.   133
39. Letter to W.P. Schreiner, 17 December 1910.   134
43. Letter to Henry Burton, Minister for Native Affairs, 3 May 1912.   147
46. Letter to the General Manager, De Beers, 17 July 1913.   154
56. 'Publication of the *Mendi* casualty list', letter to the editor, *Friend*, 10 March 1917.   222
57. Letter to Mrs Cobden Unwin, 18 May 1917.   224
58. Letter to Mrs Cobden Unwin, 10 July 1917.   225
59. 'Native bill: A leader's reply', letter to the editor, *Imvo*, 12 February 1918.   228
60. Letter to the General Manager, De Beers, 22 March 1918.   232
61. Letter to W. Pickering, General Secretary, De Beers, 13 May 1918.   235
62. Letter to the General Secretary, De Beers, 3 August 1918.   236
63. Letter to the President, Kimberley Chamber of Commerce, 19 November 1918.   237
64. Letter to W.Z. Fenyang, 2 August 1919.   239
66. Letter to Travers Buxton, Organising Secretary, Anti-Slavery and Aborigines' Protection Society, 29 October 1919.   247
71. 'Mr Sol T. Plaatje explains his mission', letter to the editor, *Negro World*, 18 June 1921.   283
72. Letter to Mrs Sophie Colenso, 31 March 1922.   287
77. Letter to R.R. Moton, Principal of Tuskegee Institute, Alabama, 22 September 1924.   329
79. Letter to General J.C. Smuts, 19 January 1925.   340
83. Letter to the Clerk of the House of Assembly, Cape Town, on the Native Administration Bill, 6 May 1927.   350
85. Letter to R.R.Moton, 29 June 1927.   357

Extracts from Books

Manuscripts

Pamphlets

Transcripts of Interviews

Bibliography

1. Archives

Botswana National Archives, Gaborone
    Bamangwato Tribal Administration files
Cape Archives Depot, Cape Town
    Attorney-General (AG) series
Central Archives Depot, Pretoria
    Native Affairs Department (NAD) series
    Smuts papers
Cory Library, Rhodes University
    C.G.H. Bell papers (MS7348)
De Beers Archives, Kimberley
    General Secretary's files
    Lyndhurst Road Native Institute file
Kimberley Public Library
    Kimberley Chamber of Commerce minutes
Library of Parliament, Cape Town
    Manuscript annexures
Natal Archives Depot, Pietermaritzburg
    Colenso Collection
Orange Free State Archives Depot, Bloemfontein
    Colonial Office files
Public Record Office, London
    Colonial Office (CO) series
Rhodes House Library, Oxford
    Anti-Slavery and Aborigines' Protection Society papers
School of Oriental and African Studies, University of London
    Plaatje papers (MS375)
South African Library, Cape Town
    W.P. Schreiner collection (MSC 27)
Transvaal Archives Depot, Johannesburg
    Attorney-General (AG) series
Tuskegee University Library, Tuskegee, Alabama
    R.R. Moton papers
University of Bristol Library
    Cobden Unwin papers

University of Cape Town Library
    Molteno/Murray Brown collection
University of Massachusetts Library, Amherst
    W.E.B. Du Bois papers
University of the Witwatersrand Library, Johannesburg (Historical and Literary papers)
    Molema/Plaatje papers (A979)
    South African Institute of Race Relations collection

2. Newspapers and Periodicals

African World (London)
Bechuana Gazette (Koranta ea Becoana)
Cape Argus
Cape Times
Christian Express
Diamond Fields Advertiser
Evening Star (Kimberley)
The Friend (Bloemfontein)
Friend of the Bechuana (Tsala ea Becoana)
Friend of the People (Tsala ea Batho)
Imvo Zabantsundu
Leselinyana la Lesotho (The Little Light of Lesotho)
Mafeking Mail Special Siege Slip
Negro World
Our Heritage
Pretoria News
South African Outlook
Transvaal Chronicle
Transvaal Leader
Umteteli wa Bantu

3. Government publications

Cape of Good Hope, *Report of Superintendent-General of Education for 1929.* CP3-1930
Hansard, *House of Commons Debates,* July 1919
Official Gazette Extraordinary of the High Commissioner for South Africa. 1906
Orange River Colony, *Government Gazette,* December 1903
Report of Native Economic Commission, 1930-1932. UG22-32
South Africa, *Report of the South African Native Affairs Commission, 1903-1904.* Cd. 2399
Union of South Africa, *South Africa Act, 1909*

4. Select Secondary Sources

Ashforth, Adam, *The Politics of Official Discourse in Twentieth-Century South Africa* (Oxford: Clarendon Press, 1990).

Bonner, Philip, 'The Transvaal Native Congress, 1917-1920: The Radicalisation of the Black Petty-bourgeoisie on the Rand', in Shula Marks and Richard Rathbone (eds), *Industrialisation and Social Change in South Africa* (London: Longman, 1982).

Bradford, Helen, *A Taste of Freedom: The ICU in Rural South Africa, 1924-1930* (Johannesburg: Ravan Press, 1987).

Branford, J., *A Dictionary of South African English*. New enlarged edn (Cape Town: Oxford University Press, 1980).

Bronstein, A.J., Raphael, L.J., and Stephen, C.J. (eds), *A Biographical Dictionary of the Phonetic Sciences* (New York: Press of Lehman College, 1977).

Brown, J.T., *Secwana Dictionary* 3 edn. (Tigerkloof: London Missionary Society, 1928).

Catalogue of the C.M. Doke Collection on African languages in the Library of the University of Rhodesia (Boston: G.K. Hall, 1972).

Chirenje, J.M., *Ethiopianism and Afro-Americans in Southern Africa 1883-1916* (Baton Rouge: Louisiana State University Press, 1987).

———— 'Sekgoma Letsholathebe II: Twentieth-century African nationalist.' *Botswana Notes and Records*, 3 (1972).

Clothier, Norman, *Black Valour: The South African Native Labour Contingent, 1916-1918, and the Sinking of the* Mendi (Pietermaritzburg: University of Natal Press, 1987).

Cole, D.T., 'In memoriam: C.M. Doke 1893-1980'. *African Studies*, 39, 1 (1980):99-102.

Couzens, T.J., *The New African: A Study of the Life and Works of H.I.E. Dhlomo* (Johannesburg: Ravan Press, 1985).

———— 'Pseudonyms in black South African writing'. *Research in African Literatures*, 6, 2 (Fall 1975):187-203.

Davenport, T.R.H., *South Africa: A Modern History* 4 edn. (London and Basingstoke: Macmillan, 1991).

Dictionary of South African Biography, Vols I-V (Pretoria: Human Sciences Research Council, 1969-1987).

Edgar, R.R. (ed.), *An African American in South Africa: The Travel Notes of Ralph J. Bunche* (Athens: Ohio University Press and Johannesburg: Witwatersrand University Press, 1992).

Edgar, Robert and Saunders, Christopher, 'A.A.S. LeFleur and the Griqua trek of 1917: Segregation, self-help and ethnic identity'. *International Journal of African Historical Studies*, 15, 2 (1982):201-220.

Elsworth, Ronald, '"The simplicity of the native mind": Black Passengers on the South African Railways in the Early Twentieth Century', in T. Lodge (ed.), *Resistance and Ideology in Settler Societies. Southern African Studies*, 4 (Johannesburg: Ravan Press, 1986).

Erlmann, Veit, *African Stars* (Chicago: Chicago University Press, 1991).

Feinberg, Harvey, 'The 1913 Land Act in South Africa: Race and segregation in the early twentieth century'. *International Journal of African Historical Studies*, 26, 1 (1993):65-110.

Geiss, Immanuel, *The Pan-African Movement* (London: Methuen, 1974).

Gerhart, G.M. and Karis, T., *From Protest to Challenge: A Documentary History of African Politics in South Africa, 1882-1954*. Volume 4: *Political Profiles 1882-1964* (Stanford, California: Hoover Institution Press, 1977).

Gollancz, I. (ed.), *A Book of Homage to Shakespeare* (London: Oxford University Press, 1916).

Grundlingh, Albert, *Fighting Their Own War: South African Blacks and the First World War* (Johannesburg: Ravan Press, 1987).

Heyman, Richard, 'C.T. Loram: A South African Liberal in Race Relations'. *International Journal of African Historical Studies*, 5, 1 (1972):41-50.

Holsey, A., 'A Man of Courage', in W.H. Hughes and D. Patterson (eds), *Robert Russa Moton of Hampton and Tuskegee* (Chapel Hill: University of North Carolina Press, 1956).

Hughes, W.H. and Patterson, D. (eds), *Robert Russa Moton of Hampton and Tuskegee* (Chapel Hill: University of North Carolina Press, 1956).

Jabavu, D.D.T., *The Life of J.T. Jabavu, Editor of* Imvo Zabantsundu, *1885-1921* (Lovedale: Lovedale Press, n.d. [1921]).

Jacobson, Marcelle (comp.), *The Silas T. Molema and Solomon T. Plaatje Papers*. University of the Witwatersrand Library, Historical and Literary Papers: Inventories of Collections. (Johannesburg: University of the Witwatersrand, 1978).

Janson, Toré and Tsonope, Joseph, *Birth of a National Language: The History of Setswana* (Gaborone: Heinemann Botswana, 1991).

Jeal, Tim, *Baden Powell* (London: Hutchinson, 1989).

Jones, D., *The Tones of Sechuana Nouns*. Memorandum VI. (London: International Institute of African Languages and Cultures, 1928).

Jones, D. and Plaatje, S.T., *A Sechuana Reader in International Phonetic Orthography (with English translations)* (London: University of London Press, 1916; repub. Farnborough, Hants: Gregg International Publishers, 1970).

Karis, T. and Carter, G.M. (eds), *From Protest to Challenge: A Documentary History of African Politics in South Africa 1882-1943*. Volume I: Sheridan Johns III, *Protest and Hope 1882-1934* (Stanford, California: Hoover Institution Press, 1972).

Keegan, Tim, *Rural Transformations in Industrializing South Africa: The Southern Highveld to 1914* (London: Macmillan, 1987).

Lacey, M., *Working for Boroko: The Origins of a Coercive Labour System in South Africa* (Johannesburg: Ravan Press, 1981).

Lestrade, G.P., 'A practical orthography for Tswana'. *Bantu Studies* 11 (1937):137-48.

Lewsen, Phyllis, *John X. Merriman: Paradoxical South African Statesman* (New Haven and London: Yale University Press, 1982).

Machobane, L.B.B.J., *Government and Change in Lesotho 1800-1966* (Basingstoke: Macmillan, 1990).

Marks, Shula, 'The ambiguities of dependence: John L. Dube of Natal' *Journal of Southern African Studies*, 1, 2 (April 1975).

———— *The Ambiguities of Dependence in South Africa: Class, Nationalism and the State in Twentieth-Century South Africa* (Johannesburg: Ravan Press, 1986).

———— *Divided Sisterhood: Race, Class and Gender in the South African Nursing Profession* (Johannesburg: Witwatersrand University Press, 1995).

———— *Reluctant Rebellion: The 1906-1908 Disturbances in Natal* (London: Oxford University Press, 1970).

Minutes of the First Non-European Conference held in the City Hall, Kimberley, 23rd, 24th and 25th June 1927.

Molema, S.M., *Montshiwa: Barolong Chief and Patriot* (Cape Town, 1966).

Morton, F., Murray, M. and Ramsay, J. (eds), *Historical Dictionary of Botswana,* New edn. (New York and London: Scarecrow Press, 1989).

Moss, Alfred A. (jr.), *The American Negro Academy: Voice of the Talented Tenth* (Baton Rouge: Louisiana State University Press, 1981).

Murray, Colin, *Black Mountain: Land, Power and Class in the Eastern Orange Free State, 1880s to 1980s* (Edinburgh: Edinburgh University Press, 1991).

Nelson's Royal Reader III (London: Nelson, 1872).

Odendaal, André, *Vukani Bantu! The Beginnings of Black Protest Politics in South Africa to 1912.* (Cape Town: David Philip, 1984).

Pakenham, Thomas, *The Boer War* (London: Weidenfeld, 1979).

Parsons N. and Crowder, M., *Monarch of all I Survey: Bechuanaland Diaries 1929-37 by Sir Charles Rey* (Gaborone: The Botswana Society; London: James Currey; New York: Lilian Barber, 1988).

Peters, M.A. and Tabane, M.M., *Bibliography of the Tswana Language* (Pretoria: State Library, 1982).

Phillips, Ray E., *The Bantu are Coming: Phases of South Africa's Race Problem* (London: Student Christian Movement Press, 1930).

———— *The Bantu in the City: A Study of Cultural Adjustment on the Witwatersrand* (Lovedale: Lovedale Press, 1938).

Plaatje, S.T., *The Boer War Diary of Sol T. Plaatje* (Cape Town: Macmillan South Africa, 1973).

———— [trans.], *Dintshontsho tsa bo-Juliuse Kesara (Julius Caesar)* (Johannesburg: Witwatersrand University Press, 1937).

———— [trans.], *Diphosho-phosho (The Comedy of Errors]* (Morija: Morija Printing Works, 1930).

———— *Mafeking Diary: A Black Man's View of a White Man's War.* Ed. John Comaroff, with Brian Willan and Andrew Reed (Johannesburg: Southern Books; London: James Currey in association with Meridor Books, Cambridge; and Athens, Ohio: Ohio University Press, 1990).

—— *Mhudi: An Epic of Native Life a Hundred Years Ago* (Lovedale: Lovedale Press, 1930; new edn, with an Introduction by T.J. Couzens, London: Heinemann Educational Books, 1978; new edn, with an Introduction by Tony Voss, Johannesburg: Ad. Donker, 1989).

—— *Native Life in South Africa* (London, P.S. King and Co., 1916; new edn, Johannesburg: Ravan Press, 1995).

—— *Sechuana Proverbs with Literal Translations and their European Equivalents* (London: Kegan Paul, Trench and Trubner, 1916).

—— *Some of the Legal Disabilities Suffered by the Native Population of the Union of South Africa and Imperial Responsibility* (London, The Author, 1919).

Roberts, B., *Kimberley: Turbulent City* (Cape Town: David Philip, 1976).

Roux, Edward, *S.P. Bunting: A Political Biography* (Cape Town: African Bookman, 1944).

Sanders, A.J.G.M., *Bechuanaland and the Law in Politicians' Hands* (Gaborone: Botswana Society, 1992).

Saunders, Christopher, 'F.Z.S. Peregrino and the *South African Spectator*'. *Quarterly Review of the South African Public Library*, 32, 3 (March 1978).

Skota, T.D. Mweli (ed.), *The African Yearly Register: Being an Illustrated National Biographical Dictionary (Who's Who) of Black Folks in Africa* (Johannesburg: R.L. Esson, 1931).

Smith, E.W., *Aggrey of Africa* (London, 1939).

Smuts, J.C., *Jan Christian Smuts: A Biography of his Father* (London: Cassell, 1952),.

Solomon, Richard A., *The Solomons: The Genealogical Tree and Short History of the Solomon Family in South Africa* (Cape Town: The Author, 1989).

Solomon, W.E.G., *Saul Solomon: The Member for Cape Town* (Cape Town: Oxford University Press, 1948).

Switzer, L. (ed.), *Fire With Your Pen! South Africa's Alternative Press in Protest and Resistance* (Cambridge: Cambridge University Press, 1995).

Switzer, L. and Switzer, D., *The Black Press in South Africa and Lesotho: A Descriptive Bibliographic Guide to African, Coloured and Indian Newspapers, Newsletters and Magazines 1836-1976* (Boston, Mass.: G.K. Hall, 1979).

Tatz, C.M., *Shadow and Substance in South Africa.* (Pietermaritzburg: University of Natal Press, 1962).

Tlou, Thomas, *A History of Ngamiland, 1750-1906* (Gaborone: Macmillan Botswana, 1985).

Walker, D., *The Oxford Companion to Law* (Oxford: Oxford University Press, 1980).

Walker, Eric, *W.P. Schreiner: A South African* (London, 1937).

Walshe, A.P., *The Rise of African Nationalism in South Africa: The African National Congress, 1912-1952* (Berkeley, California: University of California Press, 1971).

Wickens, Peter, *The Industrial and Commercial Workers Union of South Africa* (Cape Town: Oxford University Press, 1978).

Willan, B. P., 'The Anti-Slavery and Aborigines' Protection Society and the South African Natives' Land Act of 1913', *Journal of African History*, 20, 1 (1979):83-102.

────── *Sol Plaatje: A Biography* (Johannesburg: Ravan Press, 1984); also as *Sol Plaatje: South African Nationalist, 1876-1932* (London: Heinemann Educational Books, 1984 and Berkeley, California: University of California Press, 1984).

Williams, R., *How I Became Governor* (London: Murray, 1913).

Wilson, Sarah, *South African Memories* (London: Edward Arnold, 1909).

Woodward, C. Vann, *The Strange Career of Jim Crow* [New York: Oxford University Press, 1957].

Index

DATE DUE

MAY - 9 1997	